THE ABINGDON
PREACHING
ANNUAL
1996

THE ABINGDON PREACHING ANNUAL 1996

COMPILED AND EDITED BY

Michael Duduit

ABINGDON PRESS
Nashville

THE ABINGDON PREACHING ANNUAL 1996

Copyright © 1995 by Abingdon Press

This book is printed on recycled, acid-free paper.

ISBN 0-687-00121-8
ISSN 1075-2250

Unless otherwise noted, Scripture quotations are from the New Revised Standard Version Bible, Copyright © 1989 by the Division of Christian Education of the National Council of the Churches of Christ in the USA. Used by permission.

Those noted KJV are from the King James Version of the Bible.

Those noted NIV® are from the HOLY BIBLE, NEW INTERNATIONAL VERSION®. Copyright © 1973, 1978, 1984 International Bible Society. Used by permission of Zondervan Publishing House. All rights reserved.

Those noted NKJV are from The New King James Version. Copyright © 1979, 1980, 1982, Thomas Nelson Inc., Publishers.

The chapter "Benedictions," is reprinted by permission from *Litanies and Other Prayers for the Common Lectionary, Year A,* by Everett Tilson and Phyllis Cole. Copyright © 1989 by Abingdon Press.

95 96 97 98 99 00 01 02 03 04 — 10 9 8 7 6 5 4 3 2 1

MANUFACTURED IN THE UNITED STATES OF AMERICA

*To my parents,
who have been models of
Christian commitment
and encouragement.*

CONTENTS

ॐ

CONTENTS

FEBRUARY

CONTENTS

CONTENTS

JUNE

CONTENTS

JULY

CONTENTS

CONTENTS

NOVEMBER

DECEMBER

CONTENTS

INTRODUCTION

❧

Henry Ward Beecher observed, "A sermon is good that has power on the heart, and is good for nothing, no matter how good, that has no moral power on man."

Sermons are meant to do something. Preaching is meant to change minds, shape lives, and transform culture. Rooted in Scripture and empowered by God's Spirit, preaching is one of the most powerful forces on earth.

That it seems to lack power in so many instances is less an indictment of preaching than of its practitioners. In an age marked by jammed schedules and overflowing calendars, we too often move every other responsibility of ministry ahead of preaching—after all, it is easier to say no to the study than to church members seeking counsel or committees planning yet another meeting. Time is a tyrant, and our preaching often pays the price.

The *Abingdon Preaching Annual* will not miraculously add two hours a day to your schedule or eliminate those other pressing demands of ministry. What it will do is provide a practical, helpful tool that will give you a jumpstart and a useful resource in sermon preparation. It may not add hours to your day, but it can help you use some of those hours more efficiently.

The *Annual* offers several resources to assist in worship and sermon preparation. Using the Revised Common Lectionary as a basis, you will find a sermon brief for each of the three lectionary texts for a given Sunday. A sermon brief is a condensed version of the full sermon; it offers a suggested introduction, homiletical treatment, and one or more illustrations but doesn't provide the full development. It provides a good model for approaching each text.

In addition to the sermon briefs, the *Annual* includes a worship theme for each Sunday (based on one of the sermons for that day), a call to worship (based on the psalm for that day), and a suggested pastoral prayer (which often interprets the worship theme).

15

A special feature of this year's *Annual* is a series of devotional guides for the preacher, written by Calvin Miller. A best-selling author who now teaches at the Southwestern Baptist Theological Seminary in Fort Worth, Texas, Miller brings more than a quarter century of pastoral insights to the writing task. He understands the danger—both in preaching and in the personal walk with God—when preaching ministers neglect the spiritual disciplines in their own lives.

The *1996 Abingdon Preaching Annual* represents the work of dozens of people, including contributors, editors, and many more. Special thanks are due to Paul Franklyn and Cynthia Gadsden of Abingdon Press, who guide this project and hound the editor unmercifully! (Time is a brutal adversary to editors, too!) Thanks also to my wonderful wife, Laura, who puts up with late hours and stacks of paper scattered about her house, where they were not intended to reside.

May this book be a useful tool as you minister in Christ's name. God bless you as you proclaim the Word in the coming year.

Michael Duduit
Editor

SERMONS FOR
SPECIAL DAYS

MARTIN LUTHER KING, JR., CELEBRATION

The Legacy

❧

ACTS 13:44-48

It is amazing to me how God works to spread the message of salvation. Paul had been a persecutor of the followers of Jesus, but he had come to know Jesus to be the Light. At the point of this text, he has recognized his own calling to be a light to the Gentiles. He realizes that salvation is to all who believe.

In the book *365 More Meditations for Women,* I wrote the meditations for January and used "letting the Light shine" as my theme. As I addressed the birthday of Martin Luther King, Jr., it came to me that he, like Paul, was a light. He was a light to the United States and to the world, and he had seen the Light, the glory of the coming of the Lord. Consider part of that meditation:

> If Dr. King were alive today, he would ask us to give an account of our dreams, not his. He would ask us, "What have you done in my absence? Did I die for nothing? Have you moved toward freedom and justice for all? Are you finally at peace or are you still fighting pointless wars?
>
> In every generation there is a Light bearer, a prophet, a drum major for justice. Where is ours? Can we see the Light?

The comparisons between Paul and Martin do not end with their being bearers of the Light; there is a legacy associated with each. Our challenge is to discover our own legacies. To assist in your discovery, consider these three short statements:

> 1. Be something.
> 2. Do something.
> 3. Leave something.

Let's look at Paul and Martin as we consider the first statement: *be something.* Many believe Paul was the greatest apostle to the

Gentiles. He described himself as a servant of Christ Jesus, called to be an apostle and set apart for the gospel of God. That is what he was, and he made it clear that he was called not by people but by God. How many of us could and would describe ourselves as servants, set apart for the gospel of God? Martin did. He has been described as an apostle of Jesus Christ, a preacher of the gospel, a servant of his Lord.

Paul was also a strict Pharisee, an interpreter of the Jewish Law, and a Roman citizen. He was highly educated and had studied in Jerusalem under the great rabbi Gamaliel. He conscientiously observed the Law but believed that legalism could not bring about right relationship with God. Because of that, he recognized the threat that belief in Jesus posed to Judaism.

He was an approving onlooker at Stephen's stoning, and he was converted while traveling to Damascus in search of suspected Christians. His conversion convinced him that people are saved by what God has done through Jesus Christ, not by keeping the Law. This split the Jewish faith. Nothing in Christian history parallels Paul's conversion, for it removed Christianity's most violent enemy and gave it its most ardent evangelist and brilliant leader. Paul was somebody. We can say that he fulfilled the first part of the legacy to be something.

What of Martin? He was an ardent evangelist and a brilliant civil rights leader. He was highly educated, having earned his undergraduate degree at Morehouse College in Atlanta and his Ph.D. at Boston University. He was the 1963 *Time* "Man of the Year." At the age of thirty-five, he was the youngest ever Nobel Peace Prize winner. Martin was somebody. He fulfilled the first part of the legacy to be something.

Now what about you? What are you? How can we describe you? Some of you claim to be preachers of the gospel. What do those who listen to you have to say about that? Some of you claim to be teachers, social workers, postal workers, bankers, parents, students, and many other titles. But are you? If we were to document the requirements for the position, would you qualify? Are you guilty of being what you say you are?

Do we even know what it takes to be what we say we are? And are you a Christian? Can you even claim that in good faith? What have you done to let the Light shine? To whom have you brought the message of salvation? When have you studied and taught the gospel? Have you fulfilled the first part of the legacy to be something?

Let's move on to the second statement: *do something.* It is not enough to be something. We must also do something. How many times have we gone to a doctor only to discover that that person was a doctor in name only? He or she did not seem skilled in medicine. How many times have we gone to church and later wondered why the gospel had not been proclaimed with power and authority? How many times have you attended a seminar and felt that you had wasted your time and your money? Well, in each instance the leader had succeeded in being something in name only; that is, the person had completed the requirements for the title and had failed to do anything about fulfilling the role.

Consider Paul. He became the greatest missionary of the Christian faith. In fact, followers were not called Christians until he made his missionary journey to Antioch. He is responsible for the spread of Christianity. Remember that Jesus was not known outside the Roman Empire. Paul did something. He endured hardships, encountered danger, was jailed, beaten, stoned, and left for dead. But still he did something. He believed in what he was, an apostle of Jesus Christ. Against the advice of his associates, he insisted on going in person to Jerusalem with a special offering collected for the poor. His arrest and imprisonment were arranged, and he served two years without a trial. He was eventually acquitted before the Roman emperor but was rearrested and finally beheaded. He preached; he wrote; he traveled. He did something.

And what of Martin? He led the Montgomery bus boycott, which ended segregation on city buses. He implemented the use of nonviolence in the manner of Gandhi; he organized the Southern Christian Leadership Conference; he staged demonstrations, faced dogs, bombs, knives, and guns. He led the march on Washington and gave his "Dream" speech, which led to the passage of the Civil Rights Acts of 1964; he led voter registration drives and sought to combat segregation in the North. He taught black Americans to have a new estimate of their own worth. He preached; he wrote; he traveled. He did something.

What about you? What can we say that you have done? Have you helped anybody as you've passed along? Have you let your light shine?

21

Now for the third part of our legacy: *leave something.* Don't use up everything you find here. Leave something in this world that was not here when you came. Paul did. He wrote fourteen of the twenty-seven books of the New Testament. He wrote the letter on behalf of Onesimus from jail. He pleaded with Philemon for acceptance of Onesimus as a brother for love's sake. He also wrote Ephesians, Colossians, Philippians, 1 and 2 Timothy, and Titus from jail. He left something.

Martin Luther King, Jr., left something, too. He left a movement that believed "we shall overcome." He left his book of sermons, *Strength to Love,* and three of those sermons, "Love in Action," "Loving Your Enemies," and "Shattered Dreams," were written in jail. He left his history of the Montgomery bus boycott in his book *Stride Toward Freedom.* He left his letters from jail, his book *Why We Can't Wait,* and his many inspirational speeches. He left the Southern Christian Leadership Conference, and he left dignity and hope for a people who had no hope. He left something.

What about you? Are you just a user, using up everything and leaving nothing? What can you leave?

The legacy from Paul and Martin is to be something, do something, and leave something. Their lights are still brightly shining. You also have a light. Start now to let it shine. (Marjorie L. Kimbrough)

MOTHER'S DAY/FATHER'S DAY
*Why We Shouldn't Celebrate Mother's Day
and Father's Day*

ॐ

EXODUS 20:12

When I taught preaching, I required my students to prepare a preaching calendar for the year complete with titles and texts. Here are some of my favorites: *Enoch, Enoch, Who's There? God!, The Lord Is My Shepherd That I Don't Want, How to Avoid Becoming Lion Food, When Jesus Speaks, Some People Listen,* and *How to Prepare an Inexpensive Meal for 5,000.* But there were two titles that really caught my attention: *Every Man Wants to Marry a Rich Lady* and *To Find a Wife Is a Good Thing.* Those two titles were listed for Mother's Day! I used to tell my students that sermon titles should generate curiosity and be something like the bait used to hook 'em. We used to talk about hooking 'em for Jesus. They got the message.

The sermon title for this special day falls into that category. When one of our members saw the title, he said, "That's a joke! Father's Day isn't really celebrated anyway. Who cares about Father's Day? Nobody even goes to church on Father's Day." He may have a point. (Of course, I'm beginning to wonder if anyone goes to church between Memorial Day and Labor Day!) I remember asking my favorite florists if they got many orders for Father's Day. How do you think they responded?

But at least Hallmark has them both on the calendar. So even if one day gets a lot more attention than the other—I think Father's Day is just behind New York Rangers' Day in attracting the attention of most western Pennsylvanians—at least Hallmark pretends they have equal billing. I'm reminded of Ross Perot's response to a reporter who asked if he felt qualified to become president. Perot replied, "Compared to whom?" Father's Day isn't much when compared to Mother's Day. As a father, I can say that. I know from experience. I'd never say Mother's Day isn't much when compared to Father's Day. Aside from the fact I'm a father and not a mother, I wouldn't get out of here alive if I did.

23

Then why does today's sermon title suggest we shouldn't celebrate Mother's Day and Father's Day? The answer is simple. It's as simple as reminding folks that keeping the Sabbath includes the Sundays between Memorial Day and Labor Day. Fathers and mothers deserve more attention, affection, and allegiance than can be provided by the one day Hallmark keeps setting aside for them. That's what our Lord's fifth commandment is all about: "Honor your father and your mother." According to our Lord, every day is Mother's Day and Father's Day.

It isn't too tough to figure out what our Lord had in mind here. "This, then, is the sum," wrote John Calvin, "that we should look up to those whom God has placed over us, and should treat them with honor, obedience, and gratefulness." This commandment is about *always prizing our parents* and *usually obeying them.*

Our Lord's fifth commandment is about always prizing our parents. Back in 1981 as I was finishing the course work for my doctorate at Drew University, an older doctoral candidate said this as we strolled across campus: "Bob, you're very fortunate. You still have your parents. They are the only ones who really care about you in this life. They are the only ones who are really happy when you're happy and really sad when you're sad. And no matter whether you're happy or sad, in the good times or bad times, they never abandon you." Though many of us feel compelled to expand that list, my friend was telling me to prize my parents because their love is so special.

That conversation was a turning point in my relationship with my parents. I have shared it as often as I can with children of all ages who don't seem to prize their parents or who have a fractured relationship with them. I want them to understand, as Mike and the Mechanics sing, "It's too late when we die to admit we don't see eye to eye." I don't want children of any age to sit beside the caskets of their parents and hear Carole King's haunting refrain, "But it's too late, baby. Now it's too late." When it finally dawned on me that my parents will most likely go home before me, I decided to share and show the attention, affection, and allegiance that have always been in my heart, mind, and soul for them. That's when this commandment started to make sense to me. It made sense to honor or prize the parents who saw me through the womb, diapers, good times, bad times, awful times, worse times, better times, best times, and any times. I prize my parents because they are my parents.

And maybe there is a selfish part to the prizing of parents. Maybe it's something like the song in *Pippin* that goes, "God's wisdom teaches me that when I help others, I'm really helping myself." Maybe our Lord uses this commandment to spare us from the pain of not having prized our parents before he calls them home. God knows almost twenty years of ministry have introduced me to children of all ages who wished they had prized their parents before our Lord called them home. And while God knows all of our relationships will be reconciled in heaven, it can be a hell of a life to live with unreconciled relationships until then. That's why our Lord counseled through Paul, "So far as it depends on you, live peaceably with all" (Rom. 12:18).

We can't be responsible for the irreconcilable, mean, and nasty people in our lives—even the ones related to us—but we are completely responsible for how we react to them. In a world of dragons—even when those dragons are members of the family—our Lord has not given us permission to breathe fire. It's not a part of our agape ethic to get even or get over or get ahead at somebody else's expense, but it's always in our best emotional, intellectual, spiritual, and physical interests to pray and work to love the unlovable people in our lives. Our Lord has told us that the only guiltless, conscience-freeing, and profoundly peaceful way to live in this world is to love. And to love with the special agape love of Christianity is to pray and work for the best for others regardless of who, what, where, or when without the expectation of being loved back. It may not seem fair, but at least we can look in the mirror and into the face of our Father with a clear conscience.

Prizing our parents, just as prizing any other person in this world, doesn't mean our relationship with them is everything we would want it to be, but it does mean we've done our part. That's all our Lord expects from us. That's what it means to keep this commandment.

Our Lord's fifth commandment is about usually obeying our parents. Most children, especially during those years before becoming legal when they've got to obey their parents, think parents are a pain. It's a part of growing up. Parents are a pain because they prohibit children from doing certain things that would hurt them and because they insist children do certain things that will help them. That's why Solomon said, "Train children in the right way" (Prov.

25

22:6). That's why we are told to train or teach our children "diligently."

A few years ago in Washington, D.C., I heard James Dobson explain parental responsibility in a way I shall never forget. He said children walk through life something like walking down the hallways of school. And as they walk down the hallways of life, there are many doors. Some say music and sports and academics and clubs and church and love and friendship. Others say drugs and promiscuity and alcohol and gangs and the occult. Parents, said Dobson, have the responsibility to lock some of those doors. Parents have the responsibility to keep some of those doors shut. Parents are called by God to be a holy and righteous pain in the aspirations of children inclined to make bad choices.

One of the greatest theologians of our time, Alfred E. Newman of *Mad* magazine, once said, "Everyone knows the difference between 'right' and 'wrong.' . . . It's just that some people can't make a decision." Most children don't know the difference *until* they are taught the difference by their parents. And, at first, because of their natural rebelliousness, children think their parents are a pain by being the arbiters of the yesses and nos in their lives. But sooner or later, most children realize their parents were just doing their jobs. And most children eventually prize them as God's instruments of care and love in this world.

The big assumption is that parents are "in the Lord." Parents are told by our Lord through Paul to "bring them up in the discipline and instruction of the Lord" (Eph. 6:4). And when he told us to respect the authority of parents or the state or anyone "as you obey Christ" (Eph. 6:5), Paul was assuming the authorities are "in Christ" or working and praying to say the things Jesus would say and do the things Jesus would do. The point is, an authority in our lives—government, church, or even parent—must be "in the Lord" to be in charge. Parents must never forget who is really the head of the house: God in Jesus! That's why we must say our Lord's fifth commandment is about usually obeying our parents.

I remember hearing about the time a woman asked Karl Menninger when she should begin teaching her child about values. Menninger asked the age of the child. When the woman replied that the child was three years old, Menninger said. "Hurry home as fast as you can! You're already three years late!" It's like the parent who says, "I don't force my child to go to church. I want my child to decide."

But parents are called and commanded by our Lord to force children to do what is right. Parents are called and commanded to force their children to eat, wear clothes, go to school, go to the doctor and dentist, and all of the rest. What's more important than being related to our Lord through his church? What's more healthy than getting close to God?

I asked my wife to listen to an article I wrote not too long ago. After I finished, she made a few less-than-enthusiastic remarks. "Well," she said, "you told me to be honest." "No," I replied, "I told you to listen." But if we are to be honest today, we must admit that some parents feel guilty about their failures as parents and some children can't forgive their parents for those failures.

I cannot begin to tell you about all of the people who have come to me over the years to say they stay away from church on Mother's Day and Father's Day because of such burdens from the past. Certainly, only long hours of prayer and counseling can heal such memories and relationships. But for now, we can say parents who feel guilty need to remember a horse that is led to water doesn't always drink. All our Lord requires is that we pray and work and try to do our best. And if we failed to pray and work and try to do our best in the past, we can start right now. We are forgiven for the past if we pray and work and try *now*. That's the gospel. There's no death sentence in Christianity.

For children who feel they have not prized their parents in the past, the same is true. Forget the past and start now! And for children who are holding grudges against their parents, I have heard a few lines just for you: "The day the child realizes that all adults are imperfect, he becomes an adolescent. The day he forgives them, he becomes an adult. The day he forgives himself, he becomes wise." That's why Jesus came. He came to say we can be born again. We can be born again in all of our relationships—with him, with our parents, with our children, and with those around us. We don't have to live with the failures of the past. We can be born again. And that rebirth can last forever. Or as Paul wrote about the woman or man in Jesus, "Forgetting what lies behind and straining forward to what lies ahead, I press on toward the goal for the prize of the heavenly call of God in Christ Jesus" (Phil. 3:13-14).

A professor of Christian education once asked this question, "What would happen if a visitor from Mars came to your house and asked your children, 'Take me to your leader'?" Think about it. To whom would our children lead them? To father? Mother? Teacher? Baby-sitter? Bart? Madonna? Michael Jordan? They would take them to the one or ones who taught them most persuasively and persistently and patiently and passionately. It could be you and me. It should be you and me.

John Wesley said, "I learned more about Christianity from my mother than from all the theologians in England." I guess whoever said it all begins at home was right. Who said it? Our Lord said it through the fifth commandment. We shouldn't celebrate Mother's Day and Father's Day unless we're ready to keep this commandment every day. (Robert R. Kopp)

THE FOURTH OF JULY
Freedom Isn't Cheap

๏

LUKE 10:25-27

In July 1975, the *Nashville Banner* ran an article about David Burroughs. David Burroughs was an art collector who just happened to stop by a garage sale. When he saw what he saw, he could not believe his eyes. There was an individual who was selling all of her possessions to join a commune. One of the possessions she was selling was a black-and-white lithograph that he purchased for five dollars. He thought he knew what it was, but when he got home, he found his appraisal to be authentic. It was, in fact, an original Picasso. For five dollars, the woman sold an artistic work that was worth thousands of dollars for the thrill, if you will, of joining a commune. I could not identify with the man because I have never come across that good a bargain!

Then I began to think about her. She sold a prized possession for a very small amount for such a low ambition. It made me wonder as U.S. citizens, as inheritors of the greatest heritage of any nation, could we be in danger of doing the same? What kind of nation are we leaving for our children and their children? Have we forgotten the true price of freedom? Have our children forgotten? Will they remember because we have *taught* them to remember? Have we sold something very valuable for a very low price?

It is a great privilege to be a U.S. citizen. Yet I am disturbed that in our nation I find some very wrong attitudes. One of the attitudes might be characterized by this slogan: "America, love it or leave it!" This attitude says the United States is right, no matter what. This attitude equates God and nation, with no separation between the two. That was the attitude of the Sadducees of Jesus' day, who said, "The Romans are in power. We will do what we have to do to get along." This attitude asserts that the United States will forever be the land of white hat heroes and can never, never be wrong.

A good friend was called upon to deliver the invocation at a football game. His prayer went something like this: "Oh, Father, we

29

thank you for this day and for this contest of athletic prowess. I pray that you bless each and every person who participates on these two teams." His parting line was, "Lord, we hope you don't mind if we ask you to bless one team just a little bit more than the other!" After he said the "Amen," the crowd exploded in laughter, and everyone took it as good clean fun.

This somewhat relays the kind of attitude I am talking about. We cannot disillusion ourselves and say that just because we are Americans—just because we are red, white, and blue—we are always right; that just because we are Americans, God is on the sidelines rooting for us just a little bit more than he roots for everybody else. That is untrue to biblical truth as we know it. God is no respecter of persons. God looks at right and wrong more than at the color of our flag. This is a wrong attitude about our nation because it leads to exclusivism and pride.

Another wrong attitude is the opposite of the first. The other attitude says there is nothing right with our nation. These folks go back to the resignation of Nixon and beyond, and they are quick to inform us of all the things that are wrong about the United States. They are quick to point out our national debt and our trade deficit and our rising this and our lowering that. They play the game of "Ain't It Awful!" These were the Pharisees of Jesus' day. These were the people who lived in such a strict legalism that they could find nothing right about anything. Their religion was a list of "Thou shalt not's."

A third attitude is just as wrong and maybe even more so, and that is the attitude of apathy. We take for granted all these blessed privileges. We forget about the terrible price that was paid, the American blood that has been shed throughout the world for my freedom and yours. Some of our finest have given their lives that we might sit here in freedom to openly express our love of God without fear that someone would break in those doors and tell us that we cannot.

The greatest Americans have taken neither of these attitudes. The greatest Americans realized there were things wrong with our country, but they did not desert the ship—they stayed on board and worked to make it better. They worked within the process to make our nation great. This is the price that we can never forget.

I really believe that wrong attitudes can be replaced and corrected by right actions. You and I can take right actions to keep alive the American dream in our hearts and in the hearts of our children.

In 1968, a young man fought in the Olympic games. He defeated his Russian opponent and became the heavyweight boxing champion of the 1968 Olympics. When the decision was rendered, he took a small American flag and walked around the ring, waving the flag. He was asked afterward why he did so. He answered, "Well, you would have to know me to know why I did that. All of my life, I have been a loser. I have been in trouble with the law, I dropped out of school, but then I joined the Job Corps. All my life I have heard a lot of four-letter words, none of them good. For the first time in my life I heard a four-letter word that made sense, and that word was *work*. It was in the Job Corps that I learned about boxing, and I learned to give myself to a challenge that I had never had. I worked harder than I had ever worked. I grew more tired than I ever believed possible, but somebody gave me a chance and I took advantage of it." He went on to twice become the heavyweight champion of the world, George Foreman.

I want to talk to you about some four-letter words. The first I have already mentioned: *work*. Jesus said, "I must work the works of him that sent me. I am on a mission, and I am not at complete liberty to determine what I do. I have to live in respect of the wishes and desires of him who sent me and gave me the mission that I now have. The work I do I do for him." The same is true for us.

There is another four-letter word. It is the word *duty*. As you read the history of the beginnings of this nation, you find people like Thomas Jefferson who would rather have retired to his country estate to a life of well-deserved rest and relaxation, yet his country called. He felt a sense of duty, and to that sense of duty, he gave hard work. We owe many of our great historical documents to a sense of duty such as that.

Another American wanted to retire to the comfort of Mount Vernon, but his country called him to lead its young Revolutionary army. And it was to that sense of duty that George Washington responded. He realized that his country was built not so much on desire of what a man would want to do but on design of what a man *ought* to do. It was to a sense of duty that they gave themselves.

The word *free* is another four-letter word about which much of the world knows little. Many live under force. They don't live in the land of compassion; they live under a hand of coercion. Even the country of Greece in which the idea of democracy was born no longer enjoys that blessed idea. It reminds us that freedom is not free, and the minute we begin to take it for granted may be the day we begin to lose it.

Let's consider another four-letter word: *hope*. The psalmist said,

> O Israel, hope in the LORD!
> For with the LORD there is steadfast love,
> and with him is great power to redeem.
> It is he who will redeem [set free] Israel
> from all its iniquities. (Ps. 130:7-8)

That hope keeps us alive. It is a hope that the future may be brighter than the past: that our children will have the same opportunities that we have. Within our land, it *is* possible, but in so many others, it is not.

Hope keeps us from being idealistic optimists or despairing pessimists. It helps to keep us on an even keel. The United States isn't all right, but it isn't all wrong. It is a place where we can work, exercise our sense of duty, relish the freedom that we have, and invest the hope we cherish.

There is yet another four-letter word that brings together our thoughts. It is defined in God's Word:

> A lawyer stood up to test Jesus. "Teacher," he said, "what must I do to inherit eternal life?" [Jesus] said to him, "What is written in the law? What do you read there?" He answered, "You shall love the Lord your God with all your heart, and with all your soul, and with all your strength, and your neighbor as yourself." (Luke 10:25-27)

Love is the other four-letter word.

Within these verses we can see the division that God intends. We are not to love our God and our nation with the same kind of love. John Claypool, in a wonderful sermon entitled "Caesar, God, and the Christian's Responsibility," talks about the difference in this kind of love. With what is perfect, we should give perfect love and obedience. With what is imperfect, we should give nurture love to work within and make it better. There is only One perfect, and that is God. God alone deserves our worship love, our full obedient love. To our great but imperfect nation, we give nurture love. Nurture love is the realistic, intelligent love that looks at a situation with appreciation but also with the idea, What can I do to make it better? How can I go to work? How can I fulfill my sense of duty? How can I protect precious freedom? How can I be a part of making this great nation even better?

Claypool further illustrates with two men of the early 1800s, who began to attack one of the greatest blights on the history of our nation—slavery. The two men had the same objective in mind, but they went about it in completely different ways. One man was William Lloyd Garrison. In 1837, he characterized Americans as "land-stealing, blood-thirsty, man-slaying, in covenant with death and an agreement with hell." He condemned the Constitution and the Declaration of Independence. In 1854, he publicly burned the Constitution of the United States to show his disgust. Needless to say, by the time slavery was finally abolished, his word and his influence were almost nil.

The other man was Theodore Weld. He was converted under the preaching of Charles Finney, and he, too, had a burning desire to see slavery abolished from his beloved country. He "spoke home to the hearts of Americans" about slavery. His contention was that the Declaration of Independence and the Constitution already contained the idea of emancipation. He felt we should clarify these documents instead of burning them. He spoke the truth in love. For two decades, under all kinds of hardships, he went everywhere preaching his theme. As much as any other single individual, he helped to rid our country of slavery. When the Thirteenth, Fourteenth, and Fifteenth Amendments were finally adopted, they used the wording and language of Theodore Weld as a pattern.

I could pray a prayer for you and for myself. And it would be, first of all, a prayer of gratitude: "Thank you, God, for the privilege of being a Christian. Thank you, God for the privilege of being an American. These are two great gifts that I never earned. Lord, within my church and within my country, there are things I know that displease you, as there are things within me that displease you. But, God, help me not to stand on the outside and throw stones. Help me get within to work, to fulfill my sense of duty, to protect my precious freedom, to exert my hope. Lord, help me most of all to love that I might be part of the answer instead of part of the problem."

Freedom isn't cheap! May we never forget it. (Gary L. Carver)

JANUARY

ᝤ

Preparing to Serve

Encountering the Symbols of the Seasons

As a congregational leader, you may wish to precede each month's preaching themes with the three exercises suggested in the following paragraphs. The "Paraphrase Assignment" will consist of paraphrasing a single verse, or part of a verse, of Scripture that might serve as a banner inscription or worship motto tying the worship theme of the month together with the sermons to be preached. The second part of preparing to lead should be prayer. Month by month, a "Prayer Assignment" will suggest various intercessory issues that fit the particular season. Finally, the "Journal-in-Worship Assignment" will suggest that you interiorize your own spiritual pilgrimage using the various seasonal symbols we will be examining. The aim of this interiorization will be to incite the congregation to the special togetherness that occurs when a leader and the people arrive at that confessional inwardness described by Paul when he wrote, "It is that very Spirit bearing witness with our spirit that we are children of God" (Rom. 8:16). This interior work is the hard work. But only as pastors discipline themselves to know God in their personal worship can they really see God as the mortar of congregational communion.

Each month you may want to address the seasonal symbol with the intention of making it a matter of your personal spiritual journey and confession. In this case, I suggest that you be willing to write a confessional paragraph or two focusing on the symbol. Let me encourage you to use what you have written. You may want to use it in the worship folder of each Sunday of the season. You may also want to use it in a public worship service either in a presermon meditation time or in the sermon itself. Make every effort to be as confessional as you can be, both in your private writing of the paragraphs and in using the paragraphs to encourage members to be open in their own lives.

These suggestions for preparing yourself through the devotional contemplation of various Christian symbols fall rather naturally into three groupings. The baptism of Jesus through Pentecost comprises the first five of these worship leadership preparations. The post-Pentecost season includes six devotional studies built around the symbols that have to do with the Spirit's empowering of the church and its leadership. The Advent symbol of the star will complete the church-year cycle. It is the aim of these twelve studies, first of all, to prepare church leadership spiritually to serve during these seasons. But I have written them in such a way that the contemplative disciplines required of the pastor will also be directly usable in the church.

Now you are ready to begin the assignments for January.

The Symbol of Water

Paraphrase Assignment: John 3:5*b*: "No one can enter the kingdom of God without being born of water and Spirit."

Make a prayer list of persons who may have been born of the water but not of the Spirit. Please do this with no sense of judgment on the congregation. Rather begin, as always, with yourself. Which of the spiritual disciplines have been slipping in your life that you need to restore to acquaint your congregation fully with all that it means to be "born of water and Spirit"?

Journal-in-Worship Assignment:

In a study of the baptism of Christ, it is perfectly appropriate for me to encourage you to immerse yourself in the symbol of water. You were likely baptized as a child or an infant, but for the moment consider the significance of the symbol, not the age of your life. In each case consider the significance of the symbol in Scripture and link the event to a parallel. Make some simple notes telling how you felt at each level of encountering the symbol.

Genesis 1:1-2. In this passage, water appears as the glorious and waiting "soup" of creation. Even evolutionists who refuse to get God involved in creation agree that life evolved from such watery beginnings. As you consider this water of life possibility, write a paragraph on how God came to you in some chaotic state and commanded your disordered world to take shape.

Psalm 46:3. Water, in the form of seas and rivers, has at times been the barrier that separated continents and nations. Twice in the

Exodus—at the Red Sea and the Jordan—water appeared to be the barrier beyond which lay God's most complete will for Israel. But here in Psalm 46, the flood is pictured as a threat to security and safety. Write a paragraph or two celebrating some particular instance in your life when you were being engulfed by a flood of hurts and God appeared to divide the waters to make a way for you.

Romans 6:4-6. In examining the symbol of water, delve into all the commitments that surround baptism. How do you feel about those commitments and the new expectations that they introduce into living? Write a paragraph talking about the symbolism of new life that Paul discusses here. What would your life have been without these commitments? How can you challenge the church to celebrate commitment? After we make those commitments, what are the spiritual disciplines that need to be in place to carry out our commitments? Use these paragraphs to widen the congregation's view of baptism, from mere introduction to church membership to such utter commitments as baptism by fire (Matt. 3:11) and all that Jesus meant when he said to James and John they must be ready for costly baptisms of utter commitment (Mark 10:38). (Calvin Miller)

JANUARY 7, 1996

❧

Baptism of the Lord

Worship Theme: Baptism is an expression and symbol of God's blessing in our lives.

Readings: Isaiah 42:1-9; Acts 10:34-43; Matthew 3:13-17

Call to Worship (Psalm 29:1-2, 11):

Leader: Ascribe to the LORD, O heavenly beings,

People: **ascribe to the LORD glory and strength.**

Leader: Ascribe to the LORD the glory of his name;

People: **worship the LORD in holy splendor. . . .**

Leader: May the LORD give strength to his people!

People: **May the LORD bless his people with peace!**

Pastoral Prayer:

Lord, in these opening days of a new year—filled with challenge and hope, problems and potential—we come before you in gratitude for your provision and your presence. We thank you for the gift of a new year, with all the opportunities it represents—opportunities to love and be loved; opportunities to enjoy new discoveries and to be reminded of precious truths; opportunities to find our true and best selves even as we give ourselves in your service. We thank you most of all for your presence among us. Just as you demonstrated your blessing on Jesus at his baptism, so you have blessed us with the presence of your Spirit. May we live in faithfulness to that blessing and your presence each day during this new year, for we ask it in the name of the One who blesses us day by day, even our Lord Jesus Christ. Amen.

SERMON BRIEFS

BRINGING JUSTICE, AND GENTLY

ISAIAH 42:1-9

If you ask a child, "What do you want to be when you grow up?" it's unlikely you'll receive the answer, "I want to be a servant." "Servant" is not found on any of the lists of hot new careers for the rest of the nineties.

Yet servanthood is at the essence of our faith. Indeed, God chose the image of the servant to describe the One God would send to give his life on our behalf. What does Isaiah tell us about the role played by his servant—and about our own role as servants of Christ?

I. The Servant Belongs to God

Three things characterize the servant in this portion of Isaiah 42. First, the servant is firmly grounded in Yahweh's support. The servant's introduction is framed with ascriptions that link the servant closely with God: "Here is my servant, whom I uphold, / my chosen, in whom my soul delights" (v. 1). Further, "I have put my spirit upon him." The servant is clearly God's servant, someone whose very identity and purpose are derived from God who has chosen that one for service.

II. The Servant Is Committed to Justice

The servant's role is clearly defined: to bring justice to the nations and on earth. This focus is mentioned three separate times in three verses (vv. 1, 3-4).

III. The Servant Is Motivated by Grace

Finally, the servant will do the work of justice with care, gentleness, and perseverance. Justice will be brought about without the servant's voice having been raised, without a wick being snuffed out, and without the servant having been overcome by the size or difficulty of the mission. The images of restraint particularly (bruised reed unbroken, dimly lit wick unquenched) give new meaning to the word *grace*. If justice is the mission, it is not to be marched in by a lockstepping holy army, but cupped in hand, cradled in arms, shielded by the body.

In Frederick Buechner's fictional account of Jacob, *The Son of Laughter,* God is sometimes called "the Shield," meaning that God "is always shielding us like a guttering wick . . . because the fire he is trying to start with us is a fire that the whole world will live to warm its hands at. It is a fire in the dark that will light the whole world home."

This profile of identity and task leaves us with a picture of "the servant" that is both inspiring in its tenderness and exemplary for any life of faith. Not only does the image of such a strong yet gentle worker of justice give us pause, it also becomes a model for how we live our lives and pattern our Christian labors. (Paul L. Escamilla)

BREAKING DOWN BARRIERS

ACTS 10:34-43

A balloon vender was letting one balloon after another go up into the sky in order to entertain the children who had gathered to admire the balloons. Most of his balloons were gone when an African American child came up to him and said, "Mister, if you had a black balloon, would it go up into the sky like the others?"

The balloon vender, showing wisdom and perception that his occupation belied, understood what the child was really asking. He knelt down and said, "It's not the color of the balloon that matters; it's what's inside that makes it go up."

Regardless of our racial or cultural background, and regardless of what we have done wrong in the past, there is Someone who can always cause us to go up if he is inside us. His name is Jesus.

I. Christ Breaks Down Racial Barriers That Separate Us from One Another (vv. 34-37)

Jesus came to break down racial barriers. He gave his disciples the Great Commission to go to "all nations" (Matt. 28:19-20). He went to the Samaritan woman at the well (John 4).

It took a lot to convince Peter that Christ had broken the racial barrier. The words of Jesus, a trance, a vision, a miracle, and the conversion of Gentiles in Acts 10 were finally enough to cause him to make the bold declaration about the universality of the gospel in these verses.

However, even all that Peter experienced did not remove all the residue of racism in him. About eighteen years later in Antioch, he joined his Jewish brothers in snubbing the Gentile Christians and refusing to eat with them. The apostle Paul publicly challenged him, and he stood corrected. This public work of Christ all started with his baptism. It is *our* common baptism into Christ that makes us brothers and sisters in him and transcends all barriers between people, including race.

II. Christ Breaks Down Barriers of Sin That Separate Us from God (vv. 38-39, 43)

The prophet Isaiah wrote, "Your iniquities have been barriers/ between you and your God" (59:2). As Peter preached the story of Jesus, he included the indispensable element of the cross. It was on the cross that Jesus became the sacrifice for our sins so that the barrier erected by sin would be taken away. The veil of the Temple was rent, and now all those who call on the name of Jesus have full access to the presence of God because he died to secure our forgiveness.

As Peter stated, "Everyone who believes in him receives forgiveness of sins through his name" (v. 43). When someone receives him, immediately he takes away the penalty of sin, gradually he takes away the power of sin, and ultimately he will take away the presence of sin.

III. Christ Breaks Down the Barrier of Death That Separates Us from Eternal Life (vv. 40-42)

In his gospel sermon Peter also included the resurrection of Jesus. The apostolic preachers had little novel to say. They repeated the story of Jesus, and that was adequate to bring people to conviction of their need for him as their Savior.

How sad that people have heard the story of Jesus so many times that it has little effect on them. No matter how trained preachers are, or how well they can turn a phrase, Christian preachers must never get away from repeating the simple story that tells the good news of Jesus.

Part of the gospel story is the event of God raising Jesus from the dead. In fact, this truth is so important that Paul wrote, "If Christ has not been raised, then our proclamation has been in vain and your faith has been in vain" (1 Cor. 15:14). But the truth is that Christ *has* been raised, and through his resurrection, he secured eternal life for all those who follow him (Rom. 6:4-5). (N. Allen Moseley)

THE VOICE OF BLESSING

MATTHEW 3:13-17

Sometimes we preoccupy ourselves with important questions to the extent that we overlook equally important questions. For example, Matthew 3:13-17 often finds us asking the question, "Why did Jesus have to be baptized?" But let us not overlook the equally important question, "What did baptism mean to Jesus?"

Did it mean the time of the kingdom of God is now? Surely. Did it mean an identification with the Father? I think so. But it was also an experience of blessing for Jesus. God said, "You are on the right track. Continue with my blessing."

The voice of blessing is one that many people take for granted. Many people wander through life, like Esau, searching for a blessing that is never pronounced.

A single mother, upon leaving for a date, shuts the door on her teenage daughter who is staying home alone—again. "If only she didn't look so much like her father."

An adult male sits in church today dreading the Parent Dedication Service, asking, "Why did my parents abandon me?"

On the other hand, Bobby, who was as athletically gifted as a hoe handle, did not make his high school baseball team, to no one's surprise. But he did ask to be the manager—some said "batboy"—and he became a part of the team. He played the hand that he had been dealt.

What's an "unblessed child" to do? Feel inferior? Strike out in bitterness? Curse the dark silence of a voice never heard? The answer is found in the One who emerged from the Jordan hearing the voice of approval, "You are my Son. You are headed in the right direction. Continue all the way to the cross." All the way to the cross!

Blessing involves responsibility. Jesus lived in obedience after receiving the blessing. He took the hand he had been dealt and he played it. That's what we can do. That may be *all* we can do. We must be like Jesus and let nothing deter us. The crowds wanted to make him king. He resisted. His best friend wanted to talk him out of it. He refused. Judas tried to force another course. Jesus chose to play the hand God had dealt. We can do the same.

Parents and other significant adults will fail to bless us even under the best of circumstances. Other times we will not feel worthy of blessing. That is true—we're not worthy. As in Jesus' most famous story, the parent waits to bless whether or not we are worthy. God's presence depends not on our faithfulness but on God's. So we continue.

Keith Miller asked, "Who gives you your grade?" Who is the audience to whom we play out the drama of our lives? It can be an audience of the One who will never fail to be with us as we carry out God's will. John Claypool quotes a rabbi who once said, "When I stand before God, He will not ask me why were you not Abraham, Jacob or David?" He will ask, "Why were you not Bernie?"

In 1969, Bob Whelan, six two and two hundred pounds, departed for Vietnam. Within a year this fine athlete returned weighing eighty-seven pounds. A land mine had blown away both legs. A long recovery followed. Never did he bow to despair or see himself as unblessed. "Before," he said, "I had one hundred options. Now, only five, but I'll make the best of those five."

In 1990, Bob Whelan completed the Boston Marathon. He covered all twenty-six miles-plus running on his hands and arms—hopping much like a frog. When he crossed the finish line, few dry eyes were seen. He is a winner. He chose to look to God in gratitude for what he was, not what he was not. He played the hand he was dealt. So can we, for each of us already has the blessing. (Gary L. Carver)

JANUARY 14, 1996

❧

Second Sunday After Epiphany

Worship Theme: We are called to share with others what God has done in our lives.

Readings: Isaiah 49:1-7; 1 Corinthians 1:1-9; John 1:29-42

Call to Worship (Psalm 40:1, 3):

Leader: I waited patiently for the LORD;

People: he inclined to me and heard my cry. . . .

Leader: He put a new song in my mouth,

People: a song of praise to our God.

Leader: Many will see and fear,

People: and put their trust in the LORD.

Pastoral Prayer:

Father, we thank you for your awesome love, which was most vividly demonstrated on a rugged Roman cross outside Jerusalem. Though we do not understand how you could love us so much—we who fail you so often, who know what we ought to do and stubbornly persist in doing just the opposite—we thank you for the gift of your love. Yet having experienced that love, Lord, for some reason we seem determined to keep it a secret, we who proudly boast of a new car or a low golf score; we who loudly proclaim our latest bargain or our children's latest achievement. Having received the most remarkable gift in the world—the gift of divine grace—we fail to share the news with others. Forgive us, Lord, for the hypocrisy that allows us to receive your grace yet hide it in our hearts, when all around us are those who need what we have experienced. Thank you, Lord, that you are more generous with your grace than we are. Amen.

SERMON BRIEFS

THE CALL OF THE SERVANT

ISAIAH 49:1-7

In studying the four servant songs in Isaiah, we need to raise the question of the servant's identity. Is Isaiah referring to the nation Israel? Prophet? Messianic figure? In this, the second of the four servant songs (the last two are 50:4-9 and 52:13–53:12), the mystery is only heightened. Israel is identified with the servant at one point (v. 3), but then is placed over the servant further into the text (vv. 5-6; "Jacob" is a synonym for "Israel").

It is entirely possible that the enigma of the servant's identity is maintained by the prophet for a specific purpose, such as broadening the force of the message, allowing for identification with various figures or forces that act in the ways described, or leaving open the varying possibilities for God's "filling the shoes" of that figure, either individually or collectively (as with a nation or group).

The reality is that God used both the people of Israel collectively and Jesus specifically to fulfill divine purposes. And as followers of Christ, we are also called to the role of divine servants.

I. Divine Servants Are Called by God

On the order of Isaiah 42, this text tells us some very specific and important things about this mysterious servant, developing further the profile begun there. The servant was called "before I was born," named "while I was in my mother's womb," and formed to be God's servant "in the womb." These beautiful biological hyperboles express the sense of complete envelopment of this chosen one in God's care and providential direction.

In the sense that the servant is a type in which all of us may find our identity, the claim of being called from the very beginning is one of assurance, utter humility, and clear authorization for the given task. (See Ps. 139 and Jer. 1 for other examples of this in utero image.) Verses 2-3 are the natural extensions of that basic image.

II. Divine Servants Are Called to Be Reconcilers

The servant's role is cast again, this time slightly differently. If it was spoken of in terms of justice in the first song, here it could be

45

described as the work of bringing reconciliation and restoration to a broken, fallen people. Phrases such as "bring Jacob back," "gather Israel," and "raise up Jacob" fill out the meaning of the servant's justice mission.

For the servant, for Isaiah, and for Yahweh, justice is more than redistribution of goods and redress of wrongs, though these are certainly central to its meaning. Justice as fleshed out here includes mercy and tender reconciliation. It is finally about gathering in, not sending away, about restoration, not destruction.

III. Divine Servants Are Called to Reach Out

Finally, the servant will bring to its clearest expression what has been an undercurrent throughout the Hebrew scriptures: the spreading of Yahweh's saving work beyond the chosen people. In a beautiful turn of phrase, Yahweh speaks through the servant to say that "it is too light [or slight] a thing" to bring reconciliation only to Israel. The salvation of God is bigger than any subgroup within God's creation and so, through this servant figure, will "reach to the end of the earth." All nations, all generations, and all creation together are the beneficiaries of that extended scope.

Likewise, God calls us to reach out beyond the close and comfortable, to carry God's love and grace to those who have never known it. Just as Jesus became the suffering servant and gave himself for us, so God calls us to divine service to carry the good news of salvation to a lost world. (Paul R. Escamilla)

ARE YOU SURE YOU ARE
WRITING THE RIGHT CHURCH?

1 CORINTHIANS 1:1-9

Anthony Campolo speaks in many churches. On one Sunday morning he was running late to a particular church because he was driving through unfamiliar territory. When he finally arrived, the service had already begun, and he strode to the podium, trying to be as unobtrusive as possible. He was there a few minutes when one of the people on the podium, who was obviously a ministerial type, stepped next to him and asked him who he was. He had arrived at the wrong church! The only thing to do was to apologize and get directions to the right church.

The church in Corinth was having serious problems with schisms, immaturity, and immorality. Paul had heard about this distressful situation from a letter he had received from some of the Corinthian Christians. Paul returned their letter with one that could be regarded as damage control. Imagine trying to correct theological and moral mix-ups by yourself and through the mail!

Yet, amazingly, when Paul began his letter, he wrote of the Corinthian believers as "saints" and of his thanksgiving for the church. Sosthenes, who may have been Paul's secretary in this case, must have thought Paul was writing the wrong church. It wasn't that Paul glibly ignored all the bad news about the church; he took it very seriously and later addressed it directly. However, he was still able to give thanks.

In so doing Paul modeled behavior that is desperately needed in the modern church. He was able to look beyond the faults of fellow believers to see and affirm the good. Perhaps the paucity of this ability in today's church is the reason for the greener grass syndrome among ordained ministers. They transfer to First Church of Green Grass, often not stopping to think that the grass there was brown to the minister who just left it. This has not always been the case. In his research of eighteenth-century ministers, Donald Scott found that 71 percent of Yale's ministerial graduates between the years of 1745 and 1775 remained in the church to which they were first called until their deaths.

What may we be thankful for in today's church?

I. We May Be Thankful for Christ's Work of Sanctification

Paul called these Christians "saints," and he referred to them as "those who are sanctified in Christ Jesus" (v. 2). Certainly, they were not perfect, but sanctification is both a reality and a process. "Please be patient with me; God isn't finished with me yet" is more than a slogan; it is a request that deserves a positive response.

II. We May Be Thankful for Christ's Work of Salvation

Paul thanked God for his grace in their lives (vv. 4-5). They had much spiritual progress to make, but God's grace gave them the resources they needed to change into the likeness of Christ. They, like the Ephesian Christians, had been dead in their trespasses, "but God . . ." (Eph. 2:1-4).

God is the One who transfers us from the kingdom of darkness into the kingdom of light, and Paul knew that God was the One who was able to change the darkness in the Corinthians to light.

III. We May Be Thankful for Christ's Work of Glorification

Paul also looked ahead to the time when the saints would be "blameless" (v. 8) in the end time. Paul had hope. He saw the Christians as they were and also as they would be. God help us to do the same with one another. (N. Allen Moseley)

THE POWER OF A TESTIMONY

JOHN 1:29-42

Some pastors say that the use of personal testimony is their most effective vehicle for stewardship enlistment. Ron Proctor, in speaking about church growth, recently stated that personal testimony is the most significant way to communicate to baby busters. Elton Trueblood, in his book *The Company of the Committed,* said in 1961, "The method of evangelism is inevitably the method of testimony." There is something special about a personal testimony.

I. A Testimony Grows Out of Personal Experience

John the Baptist gave his testimony concerning Jesus: "This is the Son of God" (vv. 32-34). His testimony spoke out of personal experience and his own relationship with Jesus. He spoke of firsthand, personal knowledge pointing beyond himself to the Messiah. John, quite a popular figure himself, was willing to decrease in order that Jesus might increase, even to the point of "losing" some of his own disciples.

A severe malady has afflicted certain members of our society. Quiet, humble, nonassuming people are suddenly turned overnight into loud, boastful, obnoxious braggarts. These individuals are known as new grandparents. When we have something we want to say, almost all of us are willing to give testimony.

John's testimony about Jesus was so effective that two of his disciples chose to follow Jesus. One of the two was Andrew (v. 40).

Andrew, too, spoke out of personal experience, having spent the entire day with Jesus (v. 39). The Bible says that the first thing Andrew did was to go and find his brother Simon and tell him (v. 41). The Greek word here is *proton,* from which we get our word *pronto,* which means "immediately" or "straightway."

Although he was the first to win someone, it was the last time Andrew would be first. From then on he was always listed as "Simon Peter's brother, Andrew." Another glowing characteristic of Andrew's testimony, as with John, was that he was willing to be second. He just wanted to bring others to Jesus (John 6:8; 12:22). Of such is the kingdom of God, these quiet, unassuming, nonheadline-seeking persons.

II. A Testimony Can Be Shared Right Where We Are

Another characteristic of Andrew's testimony that we would do well to incorporate into our own was that he began where he was. He started at home. He went and found his brother. Often the greatest test of our spirituality is in the home among those who know us best.

As one of my professors used to say, "If you can be a Christian at home, you can be a Christian anywhere. But if you are not a Christian at home. . . ."

Think of the people Andrew has influenced through the life, witness, and writings of his famous brother, Simon Peter. There is a story of a German schoolmaster who bowed before his class every day before he began his lesson. Someone asked him why he did such a thing. "I bow before them each day," he replied, "because you never know what one of these students may become." One of those students was a young man by the name of Martin Luther. Only God and eternity can prove the worth of a testimony. (Gary L. Carver)

JANUARY 21, 1996

Third Sunday After Epiphany

Worship Theme: Our unity as believers is based on our shared salvation through the sacrifice of Christ.

Readings: Isaiah 9:1-4; 1 Corinthians 1:10-18; Matthew 4:12-23

Call to Worship (Psalm 27:1):

The LORD is my light and my salvation;
   whom shall I fear?
The LORD is the stronghold of my life;
   of whom shall I be afraid?

Pastoral Prayer:

Lord, we live in a world too often marked by strife and struggle. And too many times, the world looks inside the walls of the church and finds division every bit as bitter as the worst the world has to offer. Forgive us, Lord, for our foolish insistence on having our own way, even when it is not your way. Forgive us, Father, for our willingness to hurt others to achieve our own ends. Forgive us, Lord, for our propensity to choose up sides and fight instead of choosing brothers and sisters to serve. Remind us, Lord, that new life is found not in anything we can gain by our own efforts but only by what Jesus purchased for us on the cross, for we ask it in his name. Amen.

SERMON BRIEFS

FROM DARKNESS TO LIGHT

ISAIAH 9:1-4

One of the most pressing problems in our society is depression. Millions are affected by it; perhaps some in the congregation struggle with depression.

The prophet Isaiah ministered to a nation gripped by depression because of their circumstances. Although to many it seemed there was no hope, Isaiah proclaimed that even in the midst of despair, God is able to bring life and light.

I. The Darkness of Despair Feels Overwhelming

The reading of verse 1 is obscure but clear enough: gloom, anguish, and contempt are the daily bread of the people of Israel, who have borne the brunt of an Assyrian invasion of 733 B.C. Verse 2 fills out the image: "The people who walked in darkness. . . ."

It is not that darkness has come at nighttime, or that it has been created or arranged for some purpose in a closed-in room; darkness is what the people have lived with, day and night, week in and week out. To walk in darkness, to live "in a land of deep darkness," is to lose one's sense of reality, of bearings, of memory or hope.

What Isaiah describes is a kind of communal defeat and despair, an experience most of us have never known. We have all, however, witnessed such events, such tragedies, or read of their occurrence in history. Famine, genocide, plague, civil war, holocaust—all of these are instances where a crisis is so great it leaves the entire community or country in a chronic state of shock. We have to imagine such was the existence of these oppressed people during this time. They walked, but to where? They lived, but for what purpose? Any who have experienced acute depression know the weight of such darkness.

II. God Brings Hope in the Midst of Despair

Into the deep darkness comes a bold announcement: the coming of "a great light" (v. 2). A metaphor for God's saving acts toward the community of Israel, light can be imagined here as near to blinding as possible without actually being so. Weeks and months and years in complete darkness, all at once dissipated by great light, shining light, leave the eyes squinting, the hand shielding, the body crouching. But not for long. Soon eyes adjust, and from what we see and the way we savor what we see, it is as though we were given our sight for the very first time.

The result of such an experience of coming into light is expressed in verse 3 with one predominant word: *joy.* That word recurs in this one follow-up verse almost with a flutter: "You have increased its joy;/ they rejoice before you as with joy at the harvest." The image now is no longer of heaviness but its very opposite—lightness, levity, mirth.

The promise of Yahweh through the prophet Isaiah is that however heavy the darkness of national defeat, humiliation, and exile may be, the darkness is not the end. With the psalms, the prophet reminds his hearers that "weeping may tarry for the night, / but joy comes with the morning" (Ps. 30:5).

So it is with your life. Whatever the cause of your despair, God can bring new light and new joy to you if you will open your heart to God's love. (Paul R. Escamilla)

HOW TO MAINTAIN CHRISTIAN UNITY

1 CORINTHIANS 1:10-18

Louie Newton, a denominational leader among Baptists in a former generation, used to answer all his correspondence by hand-written letter. One night before retiring he wrote two letters. One was to a quarreling church in danger of splitting, and it contained extensive and specific instructions as to what to do about the division. The other letter was to the man who worked on his land and dealt with how to control an uncooperative bull; the message was simply, "Close the gate and keep the bull out of the pasture."

Unfortunately, Dr. Newton placed the letters in the wrong envelopes. When his worker received the letter to the church, he was confused, and when Dr. Newton's letter was opened and read in a tense church meeting, the people were infuriated that the simple statement was all the help they received.

Then someone in the crowd stood up and tried to interpret the letter in a positive light: "Maybe he's saying that the bull is the devil, and we have been letting him into our fellowship. Now it's high time we kept him out of this pasture so that this flock can be one in Christ again." It worked; the process of reconciliation began as they decided that Christ would rule their pasture and the devil would be kept out.

Paul also wrote a letter to a factious church, but the group received the right one. He supplied some clear principles as to how unity could be reestablished.

I. Unity Is Maintained
When the Church Decides to Work for It

Apparently, unity was not a priority among the believers in Corinth. The result was that Murphy's Law went into effect and unity began to unravel. One of Paul's evident intents in writing this letter was to motivate the Christians to make "the unity of the Spirit in the bond of peace" (Eph. 4:3) a priority. So he wrote, "I appeal to you . . . that all of you be in agreement" (v. 10). In other words, "Decide to work for unity!"

II. Unity Is Maintained When Christ Is Exalted

Paul appealed to them "by the name of our Lord Jesus Christ" (v. 10). Unity that is not by him, in him (Phil. 4:2), and for him is not worthy of the modifier "Christian."

Sometimes churches are unified merely because the people worked together on a building project. Sometimes the warm feelings generated by sharing potluck dinners are enough to hold churches together. Other Christian groups are bound together because they have a common foe.

Not one of these, however, is the distinctive unity of a New Testament church. Nor is it adequate to be bound together because of the influence of a charismatic leader. That was precisely the problem of the Corinthians. Different groups within the church claimed different "patron saints" (vv. 12-15). But Paul downplayed the significance of human instrumentality and called the people to affirm the only true source of their unity—Christ.

III. Unity Is Maintained
When Christians Have the Same Mind

Having the "same mind" (v. 10), of course, does not mean that churches have a cookie cutter mentality, expecting everyone to look, act, and be the same. In this same letter, Paul accentuated the different gifts of the different members in the Body of Christ (1 Cor. 12:1-25). However, Christians are to agree on their purpose—to exalt Christ, not self, in their lives and in their church. The "mind" that they are to have is none other than "the mind of Christ" (1 Cor. 2:16).

Is it possible for Christians to have the same mind? Paul apparently believed that it is possible; he referred to it several times in his Epistles (Rom. 12:16; Phil. 1:27; 2:2). May it be so in our churches. (N. Allen Moseley)

IT'S ABOUT TIME

MATTHEW 4:12-23

A professor quoted a newspaper ad that read, "For Sale: Hot tub, plumbing included. Will trade for pickup truck. Call, etc." It doesn't take a Ph.D. to determine that here is a life in major transition!

Often these major transitions of life are caused by crises. The disciples, in our text, are in the midst of major transition. Perhaps this transition is caused by the crisis of their decision to repent and follow Jesus (v. 17). Perhaps this transition is caused by the fact that John the Baptist has been put in prison (v. 12). Many of Jesus' disciples had followed John. It would have been easy for these disciples of John to succumb to disillusionment, retreat into fear, or just quit because they were tired. But in Jesus' voice, they heard a new call. It was *the* time to respond.

I. Jesus Calls Us to a Place

Why did they respond? Perhaps something was lacking in their lives. Sensing in John a glimmer of hope, they realized a new opportunity in the dynamic preacher from Nazareth. In Jesus, they found a place.

We all know that the church is people. The Greek word we translate as "church" means "called-out ones." But the church also is a *place*. Having a place is important.

When they sinned, Adam and Eve were tossed out of their place. Cain was doomed to wander without a place. Abraham and Sarah were called to journey looking for a place. The children of Israel were delivered from Egypt upon the promise of a place flowing with milk and honey. Having a place is important.

"Is this really ours, Mama?" the girl asks, eyes gleaming. "Yes, it really is," her mother says as she takes the keys from the Habitat for Humanity representative.

"Here it is, honey," he says. "Your very own first kitchen." With a tear in her eye and the arm of the man around her, the retiring pastor's wife walks into her very first and last home. A place. We all need a place. In Jesus, the disciples found a *place* where they could find mercy, purpose, stability, forgiveness, security, and a sameness that gave unity to their lives.

II. Jesus Calls Us to a Time

The Scriptures also report that they responded immediately, almost as if they left their father in the boat (v. 22)! "It is now time," Jesus says. "The kingdom is near" (v. 17).

Have you heard about the Procrastinators' Club? They boast five hundred thousand members. Actually, only thirty-five thousand members have joined. The others intend to but just keep putting it off! Jesus is saying, "Don't put it off."

The Bible uses at least two Greek words we translate as "time." One word is *chronos,* from which we get our word *chronology.* This is the linear, day-to-day living of our lives. Another word is *kairos.* This is crisis time. The moment is here. Opportunity awaits. Seize it. "The kingdom is near," Jesus said. Without delay, they followed him.

In the play *Becket,* the king selected his old hunting buddy and fellow carouser to be the archbishop, expecting to control his pal and the church. But in the role of archbishop, Becket changed.

"Something happened to me," he told the angry king. "When you put this burden upon me in the empty cathedral, it was the first time in my life that I had ever been entrusted with anything. I was literally a man without honor. Now, I am a man with honor, the honor of God." He had found his *place* because he recognized the time.

It's about time to respond to Jesus' call to live a life that honors God. (Gary L. Carver)

JANUARY 28, 1996

୧ଌ

Fourth Sunday After Epiphany

Worship Theme: We are called to faithful obedience in our walk with God.

Readings: Micah 6:1-8; 1 Corinthians 1:18-31; Matthew 5:1-12

Call to Worship (Psalm 15:1-4*a*):

Leader: O LORD, who may abide in your tent? Who may dwell on your holy hill?

People: Those who walk blamelessly, and do what is right, and speak the truth from their heart;

Leader: who do not slander with their tongue, and do no evil to their friends, nor take up a reproach against their neighbors;

People: in whose eyes the wicked are despised, but who honor those who fear the LORD.

Pastoral Prayer:

Almighty God, we eagerly seek your face. In a world of chaos and struggle, we are thankful for your reassuring presence and the confidence it brings. And we know, Lord, that you have called us to be instruments of peace in the midst of a turbulent world—to do justice, love kindness, and walk humbly with you. We do not always know what is just; teach us. We do not always act kindly; help us. We do not always walk humbly; chasten us. So often we walk away from you instead of with you; draw us to your presence even when we foolishly resist. Help us to walk faithfully with you, that others might see your glory reflected ever so slightly in our lives. We ask it in the name of the One who walked perfectly with you and even now intercedes on our behalf. Amen.

SERMON BRIEFS

PLAIN SPEAKING

MICAH 6:1-8

God has a complaint—what is sometimes called a covenant law-suit—with the people of Israel. Micah becomes the voice through which this charge is leveled. The specific nature of the wrongs committed is not verbalized here, except in an indirect way: God asks the people, through Micah, what God has done wrong. In other words, God is asking rhetorically, "What have I done to lead you to separate yourselves from me?"

God's question is answered with another question, this time the formulation of the prophet on the people's behalf: "With what shall I come before the LORD, / and bow myself before God on high?" (v. 6). Then follows a list of liturgical acts, ritual options that traditionally function either to please God in worship or to appease God for sin committed: burnt offerings, calves, rams, oil, and—more far-fetched—a firstborn child.

Here we are, then, with two questions—God's and ours. The dynamic sets up a distinct vacuum, begging for a declarative sentence, something to be spoken definitively rather than asked as a question. Verse 8 fills the void logically as well as in a literary sense: this is what you need to do. Then, in plain speech, what is good to do and be is elaborated: do justice, love kindness, and walk humbly with (or live in communion with) God.

I. Do Justice

The word *justice* is intended to mean more than merely "getting even" or "making others pay for what they did." Justice in Hebrew scripture has a far more comprehensive meaning: the restoration of balance, the righting of relationships, the application of fairness to all things.

Justice is not a deal struck but an atmosphere engendered within a community. In that sense, it is close kin to the richly laden Hebrew word *shalom*. What does the Lord require? That we do justice.

II. Love Kindness

Kindness (alternately, compassion or mercy) is as plain and pe-destrian a virtue as any. Not a day goes by that any of us would not have occasion to exercise kindness in some way—small or substantial. The kindness of a banker may spare a family about to be foreclosed profound heartache and misery; but the same kindness can bring a flower in a little child's hand across the street to the widow on the porch swing.

For Micah, the size of kindness is immaterial; what is essential is that it be there when called for. And one thing more, and this makes all the difference: that kindness be loved. Not merely the exercise of mercy, but the love of mercy. Not merely the doing of a kind act, but the appreciation of the deed. Not merely saying the helpful word, but meaning what we say.

III. Walk Humbly with Your God

The rare Hebrew verb for "to walk humbly with" is difficult to translate clearly. But something like "to live in communion with" gets the point across. To walk humbly with God must mean, then, among other things, to get our minds and hearts around the notion that the Other is also with us. God, who creates us, gives us breath, and receives us at our death, also walks with us through every step of life.

Humility, then, is not really about learning to keep our mouths shut at dinner parties; it is learning to recognize holy ground when we see it until eventually we come to understand it's the only kind there is. (Paul R. Escamilla)

SEND IN THE CLOWNS

1 CORINTHIANS 1:18-31

The Broadway play *A Little Night Music* was never considered much of a box office success. But one bright result of the play was a song that became a hit: "Send in the Clowns." Some have suggested that that song expresses what it's like for Christians to be sent into the world. We appear peculiar to a world that lives by a different set of values.

In a circus or a rodeo, clowns create a shift in theme; they change the subject. After the breathtaking danger of the flying trapeze, a lion tamer, or a bucking bronco, clowns enter to remind us of our purpose—to be entertained. Much like Shakespeare's Falstaff, they produce a break in the action just when we were caught up in the drama of the moment.

Just so, it is our nature and calling as Christians to remind people what we are here for: to know and glorify God. And like the clowns, our message changes the subject and often seems silly and out of place in a world that is caught up in another purpose: satisfying self.

Paul made the same point in 1 Corinthians. He wrote that on the world's wise-foolish continuum, Christians and non-Christians are on opposite ends. The world looks at that continuum from one side and sees Christians on the foolish end. But the scale on God's side is reversed, so that Christians are the wise and the world is foolish. From the perspective of the crowd, rodeo clowns look silly in comparison with the brave and strong cowboys, but from the perspective of those who work in the rodeo, clowns have the sanest job in the arena—to protect the lives of the cowboys who put themselves in danger.

What makes Christians so different from the world?

I. Christians Bear a Different Life Message

Paul wrote that it is the message of the Cross (v. 18)—through weakness we are made strong (2 Cor. 12:9-10). It is a message that is the inverted image of the world's philosophy. But the church looks at the cross and empty tomb of Jesus and knows that when we are crucified with him, we will be raised.

What looks like defeat today will be victory tomorrow. What is a photographic negative, on which black appears as white and white appears as black, will soon be a beautiful picture.

II. Christians Face Persecution in the World

Jesus promised such opposition (Matt. 10:22; John 15:18-20). The message of the Cross was a stumbling block and foolishness in Paul's generation (vv. 22-23), and it is the same today. It is a stumbling block because people, like the Jews of Paul's day, still want a king with worldly power to wipe out their enemies and grant then prosperity instead of a Savior to die for their sins. It is foolishness because people, like the Greeks, still prefer to find wisdom through their own ingenuity rather than let Christ forgive them of their utter failure and give them his wisdom (v. 30), with the result that they boast in the Lord and not in themselves (v. 31)

III. Christians Call Attention to Their Weakness That God May Be Glorified

Paul urged the Corinthian Christians to consider their humble background (vv. 26-27). Christians are to remember and even emphasize that they were saved not by their own goodness or intelligence but by God's grace (1 Cor. 15:10; Eph. 2:8-9). It is not that Christians cannot be very capable and brilliant people—the most intelligent thing someone can do is to come to Christ—but we have a spiritual humility that causes us to emphasize what God has done, not what we have done.

We know that we are also weak, but we have found that his grace is sufficient in our weakness (2 Cor. 12:9), and that is what we share with the world. (N. Allen Moseley)

HAPPINESS IS A CHOICE

MATTHEW 5:1-12

God wants you to be happy. A mentor of mine in the ministry was fond of saying, "Some people get enough religion to make them happy, while others only get enough to make them miserable." Jesus wants you to be happy.

"Blessed are you," Jesus says. "You are blessed with the choice of happiness because you are mine." This is "family talk." Jesus gathered his disciples to teach them while the crowd was allowed to "overhear."

I. Happiness Comes from a Christlike Life

This is where we preachers usually try to put words in Jesus' mouth and fill the air with admonitions of "ought" and "should." "You ought to be meek!" "You should be merciful!" That is not what Jesus is saying. Jesus is pronouncing a blessing. (Isn't it amazing how much light the Bible throws on the commentaries?) Jesus is saying, "You who have responded to my call with your faith are blessed. Because you are mine, you have the ability to choose a certain kind of life." When you make this choice, wonderful results can happen.

II. Happiness Comes from Our Inheritance

Here Jesus walks us around the inheritance we have as God's children: "Blessed is the one who acknowledges the personal need of God, for God shall reign in the heart. Be happy when you feel deep sorrow over wrong, for God's Spirit will be at your side. You will know joy as the relinquishment of your life to God's guidance and discipline molds you to receive what God has already promised. Blessed are you when the dissatisfaction in your life drives you to search after God's nature, for you will be satisfied. Oh, the blissful joy of the one who gives forgiving and healing love. You will receive what you have given. The joyful heart is yours because your single-ness of purpose conditions you to see God. God's children are those who stand in the gap between forces of opposition, making peace to be more than the absence of hostility, but the presence of love."

In his book *The Cost of Discipleship*, Dietrich Bonhoeffer asks, "Is there any place on earth for such a community? Clearly there is one place, and only one, and that is where the poorest, meekest and most sorely tried of all men is to be found—on the cross at Golgotha. The fellowship of the beatitudes is the fellowship of the crucified."

Even when you participate in the fellowship of the crucified, even when you are persecuted, even when you are a victim, you have the choice not to accept a victim mentality.

Jesus has reversed the world's values. He blesses the so-called unblessed of society. He blesses the poor, the brokenhearted, the captives, the prisoners, and the grieving (Isa. 61:1-3; Luke 4:18-19). As God's child, you have the choice to accept God's blessing and to bless others. You can take initiative, choose beforehand how to respond in any situation. As Fred Craddock says, "We are no longer victims; we are Kingdom people."

Said the wealthy woman to the disabled young man at the door, "Sure I'll buy your magazine to help you through college. Possibly by education you'll overcome your condition, although I'm sure it colors everything you do." "Yes, ma'am, it does," he replied, "but, thank God, I can choose the color." (Gary L. Carver)

FEBRUARY

❧

Preparing to Serve

The Symbol of Light

Paraphrase Assignment:
Isaiah 60:1: "Arise, shine; for your light has come, / and the glory of the LORD has risen upon you."

Prayer Assignment:
Make a prayer list of five new major scriptural insights you want to be sure that the members of your church understand. Then along with your prayer, begin to study those truths you want to make manifest within yourself.

Journal-in-Worship Assignment:
Consider the various uses of light in the following passages as you make the symbol usable to your congregation.

Genesis 1:3. *Fiat Lux!* What does this first command of God over all creation have to say about God's revealing himself in nature (see Rom. 1:18ff.)? Think about God's first miracle, light. Think about its necessity to reveal everything. Now write a paragraph describing a time when your own soul struggled through some "dark night." In what manner did the light come to you? In what way did God end your gloom with some glorious revelations that paved the way to a brighter future?

Consider a second paragraph or two describing how you feel about the God whose primal epiphany was a substance that traveled 186,000 miles per second and made vision possible. Think of a sunrise that dispelled some literal night with glory. Tie it in to your appreciation of God, whose glorious light fell on a darkened cosmos as he prepared the revealing of his own Son (John 1:3-9).

2 Peter 1:19-21. In 2 Peter 1:19-21 is the marvelous epiphany of Scripture. After reading this passage, write an account of a time when in your need light came from God's Word to show you the way. When you have described the coming of scriptural light to your life,

62

think also of some time when the church was bewildered about its ministry or future, and God used the Word to illumine both the necessity and the manner of the church's ministry. Begin praying as you write these paragraphs for the church to be illumined to the intensity of scriptural light through your commitment to making that light available to the congregation.

Galatians 5:19-24. Think through the celebration of Epiphany and the revealing of Christ as the Messiah. Think how this wonderful light came to your life. Maybe you have been forever nurtured in the church, but think through the darkness in which you might have lived had it not been for Christ. Write some paragraphs contrasting Galatians 5:19-21 with the verses that immediately follow, Galatians 5:22-24. The first passage tells us what we would have been without the Divine Light. The second tells us what his revealing light makes possible in our lives. Let your confession of how the light came to you waken the church ultimately to the celebration of the Christ light. (Calvin Miller)

FEBRUARY 4, 1996

❧

Fifth Sunday After Epiphany

Worship Theme: As we walk by faith, we present a positive witness to the world.

Readings: Isaiah 58:1-9*a* (9*b*-12); 1 Corinthians 2:1-12 (13-16); Matthew 5:13-20

Call to Worship (Psalm 112:1-2, 6-7):

Leader: Praise the LORD! Happy are those who fear the LORD, who greatly delight in his commandments.

People: Their descendants will be mighty in the land; the generation of the upright will be blessed. . . .

Leader: For the righteous will never be moved; they will be remembered forever.

People: They are not afraid of evil tidings; their hearts are firm, secure in the LORD.

Pastoral Prayer:

Father, you have given us eternal life and abundant living through faith in Jesus Christ. Although you never meant for us to keep Jesus only for ourselves, we confess the times we have not told family, friends, and neighbors about the love you have for them through Christ. Forgive us, O God, for keeping the gospel to ourselves when all about us are those who need the wholeness, happiness, and joy available through faith in Jesus. As led by your Holy Spirit, we recommit ourselves to the greatest mission of the church: introducing people to their Lord and Savior, Jesus Christ. Help us by creed and deed to point to Jesus as we pray in his name. Amen. (Robert R. Kopp)

64

SERMON BRIEFS

A NEW CALL TO WORSHIP

ISAIAH 58:1-9*a* (9*b*-12)

The setting for this prophetic oracle is probably postexilic Jerusalem or Judah. The community has been restored to home, and yet apparently has not learned from its experience of exile about the importance of just living, of sharing wealth with poor people, of making deeds of mercy the centerpiece of the service of God.

The fast, which is the only ritual act mentioned here, normally suggests sorrow or mourning. Perhaps the people were still pining for the restoration of their former, preexilic lives, for a lifestyle of harmony that had not yet become manifest since their return home. To that ritual petition for a restored way of life, God answers with very specific guidelines for bringing it about.

I. A Call to Worship

Verse 1 could come straight out of a Sunday bulletin. The trumpet, or ram's horn, was customarily used to call the community to worship. In this instance, the prophet may be setting up a poetic device in which two kinds of serving—ritual service and works of mercy—are juxtaposed.

If that is what is intended by this "call to worship," then the point is surely not to put down worship (see v. 13) but to lift up the other way in which God is served—through deeds of mercy and justice. The basic charge is laid out in plain view: the people are seeking to draw near to God without practicing holy living with one another.

II. A Call from Self-centeredness

The prophet gives us a glimpse here (vv. 3-4) of some of the specific behaviors manifested by the hearers. In four lines we find four charges against the people that cover a range from personal to corporate: (1) you serve your own interests, (2) you oppress your workers, (3) you quarrel and fight, and (4) you strike one another. We cannot say for certain how closely descriptive this is, but we clearly have the idea that people are worshiping one way and living another.

III. A Call to Righteousness

Then the people bring the word of Yahweh in the form of a question: "Is such the fast that I choose?" (v. 5). Hardly is the question completed before a literal flood of responses pours forth. From verse 6 to the end of the chapter, one after another of the behaviors called for by Yahweh is enumerated.

Initially, they are put in terms of the figurative "fast" that God chooses for the people to observe—that is, the fast is to end injustice, to share bread with the hungry, to clothe the naked, and so on. By verse 9b, the moral directives have become simply statements of action and consequence: "If you remove the yoke, offer your food, satisfy the afflicted, . . . then your light shall rise, God will guide you, your needs will be satisfied, your ancient ruins will be rebuilt. . . ."

By the chapter's end, no less than eighteen promises have been made to the people who will choose to fast in God's way—that is, by doing justice and showing mercy in every area of their lives and their community.

Fred Pratt Green's hymn, "When the Church of Jesus," warns of hearts lifted in worship "high above this hungry, suffering world of ours." His cautionary words echo those of Isaiah: going to God in prayer to work out what is wrong in the world is meaningless, even offensive, unless matched by intentional deeds that work toward making reconciliation happen. (Paul R. Escamilla)

THE MODUS OPERANDI OF EVANGELISM

1 CORINTHIANS 2:1-12 (13-16)

In a church's worship center a cross was prominently displayed behind the pulpit and choir loft. One Sunday when the pastor was on vacation a man, who was much taller than the pastor, preached the sermon. After the service a little boy who usually sat near the front with his family mentioned to his father that he liked their pastor a lot more than the visiting preacher. "Why?" his father asked. "Because he's small enough for me to see the cross."

The child said more than he knew. In order for Jesus to be visible in us, the self-life must be invisible. In order for him to increase, we must decrease (John 3:30). No one can impress people with fleshly, or natural, ability and at the same moment present Jesus as the mighty to save.

In the second chapter of his letter to the Christians in Corinth, Paul wrote of his practice of remaining small so that Christ would loom large.

I. We Proclaim Christ

Paul commented on the style, content, and purpose of his preaching. His style was intentionally devoid of "lofty words" (v. 1) and "plausible words of wisdom" (v. 4), but included the elements of "weakness," "fear," and "much trembling" (v. 3). Every person who has stood before a crowd to speak knows what Paul is talking about, but professors don't teach this style of delivery in seminary. Apparently, Paul did not mind appearing nervous; it probably accentuated the importance of his message ("this makes me so nervous that I wouldn't be doing it at all if it were not so important"). It was not the beauty of presentation that made his message so powerful; it was the depth of his conviction.

As to the content of his message, he preached the Cross (v. 2). Paul had come to Corinth from Athens where he had tried to meet the philosophers on their own ground. Perhaps his limited success there convinced him to keep his content simple and straightforward.

When a student athlete made four F's and one D on his report card, his advisor asked the coach what his problem was. The coach said, "Well, it looks as if he's been concentrating too much on one subject." The same accusation could have been made about Paul, and that one subject was Jesus. He exalted Jesus so that the faith of the people "might not rest on human wisdom but on the power of God" (v. 5).

II. We Demonstrate the Spirit's Power

Paul's life and ministry were living examples of what the Holy Spirit could do (v. 5) in and through the life of a human being. People need a demonstration of the Spirit even more than they need an explanation. They need to see the transformation that he has made and is continuing to make in us.

III. We Receive the Revelation of God

God's wisdom is a mystery to those who do not know God (vv. 6-9, 14). But to the saints, it is a mystery that has been revealed (vv. 10-16). Agnostics claim that God is beyond our ability to know or understand. Christians agree, but we add the important qualification that God has revealed himself. Paul argued that no one can know God except the Spirit of God, but it is God's Spirit that we have received! Since God's Spirit is in us, we "may understand the gifts bestowed on us by God" (v. 12). In fact, that is the beginning point of being a Christian.

Paul made his points in logical order, but they should be reversed to be in chronological order. First comes revelation, then demonstration, and last proclamation. (N. Allen Moseley)

BETTER THAN THE BEST

MATTHEW 5:13-20

Fred Craddock reminds us of the New York City bus driver who, after sixteen years of the same old route with the same people in the same old bus, on a certain day climbed into the bus and drove to Miami! Who hasn't felt that way? Who hasn't been there? Who hasn't wanted to say, "Let's throw out everything and start all over"?

There were those in the audience to whom Matthew's Gospel was written who wanted to do away with the old way: "The old rules don't work anymore. Let's throw them out and start all over with you, Jesus!" Even Jesus had been accused of laxity in keeping the Sabbath and dietary and fasting laws.

Here Jesus corrects that mistaken notion: "Do not think that I have come to abolish the law or the prophets; I have come not to abolish but to fulfill. For truly I tell you, until heaven and earth pass away, not one letter, not one stroke of a letter, will pass from the law until all is accomplished" (vv. 17-18).

I. Faith Builds on the Past

Jesus is saying that we are the children of Abraham, Isaac, Jacob, Rachel, Ruth, and John the Baptist. We must carry on in the biblical tradition of the continuing story of God's revelation. Where God's story connects and intersects with our story, there God speaks.

We must build on the past. Of course, every generation must construct new structures and forms for ministry and worship. But these new structures must be built with the old stones, as did Nehemiah. In seeking to address a new generation, we cannot throw out the baby with the bath water. In seeking to answer this claim that the old rules don't make it, Jesus—the new Moses—gives us a basic key to the understanding of Matthew's Gospel. Jesus is concerned about preserving the best of the past. And as we shall see, he is concerned about living in the present with moral and ethical integrity.

II. Faith Demands Obedience

When there are those who say that the old rules don't work anymore, there are those who will say that there are no rules. To this, Jesus says, "Unless your righteousness exceeds that of the scribes and Pharisees, you will never enter the kingdom of heaven" (v. 20). The Pharisees were the best of their day in trying to keep the Law. Jesus says that his children must be better than the best of this world.

There were those then and there are those today who say it doesn't matter what you do. Go ahead and cut the deal even if it hurts or destroys someone. To get ahead, you have to look out for number one. Allan Bloom, in his book *The Closing of the American Mind*, states that most college freshmen believe that values are relative and that there is no absolute truth. When there are no rules, selfishness reigns.

Jesus says it does matter what you do, because it determines what you are. It is not enough to compare yourself to the worst as if God graded on the curve. As one of God's children, you must be better than the best. That is why it is not enough to refrain from murder, adultery, and lying and to love only your friends. You must refrain from the underlying causes of these destructive actions and replace them with the positive actions of love.

III. Faith Provides a Witness to the World

We are salt and light (vv. 13-15). We are to be God's preserving, penetrating, purifying, and illuminating force in society. We will be so only as we are better than the best of this world. We must follow the example of the One who walked in the way of the Father (5:48). (Gary L. Carver)

FEBRUARY 11, 1996

❧

Sixth Sunday After Epiphany

Worship Theme: Christ calls us to accountability for our words and actions.

Readings: Deuteronomy 30:15-20; 1 Corinthians 3:1-9; Matthew 5:21-37

Call to Worship (Psalm 119:1-2):

Leader: Happy are those whose way is blameless,

People: who walk in the law of the LORD.

Leader: Happy are those who keep his decrees,

People: who seek him with their whole heart.

Pastoral Prayer:

Father, we are in the midst of a season of love. Hearts are everywhere as we send and receive valentines. We pledge our love to spouses and sweethearts, to parents and children, to teachers and classmates. We distribute candy and flowers and balloons as tokens of our affection. We are set adrift in a sea of sentimentality, talking of love as if we invented the idea. Remind us, O Lord, as we celebrate this secular season of love, that authentic love is ultimately expressed not through sentiment but through sacrifice. Remind us, O God, that by our words and deeds the world around us will truly judge the love that is in our hearts. Help us to share the truth that true love is found not in a card store but on a cross. For we pray in the name of the One who loved us more than we deserve. Amen.

SERMON BRIEFS

CHOOSE LIFE

DEUTERONOMY 30:15-20

A dedicated, beautiful, popular young woman made a poor choice in her mate for life. Until the day she died at the age of seventy, she felt the negative impact of that decision.

Israel had the God-given opportunity to make good choices instead of bad ones. Israel was given the option of either keeping the covenant with the Lord or rejecting the terms of that agreement. God made clear to Israel through Moses that obedience to the covenant would bring blessings and that disobedience would bring curses. Moses' last address to Israel was an admonition to choose wisely.

Christians have a covenant with God, also. It is the new testament in the blood of Jesus Christ. Our covenant has parallels to Israel's in regard to the choices involved and their repercussions. God's Word admonishes us to choose wisely.

I. We Can Choose to Disobey God in All of Life

Disobeying God involves turning our hearts away from God. This is the opposite of repentance. It means that our ultimate concerns in life oppose all that God is and all that he desires for us. Also, disobedience, according to our text, consists of turning deaf ears to God's Word, being obstinate and unyielding in regard to the divine will, and opting to worship and serve other gods. Such behavior, Moses cautioned Israel, will result in insecurity and death.

When people turn their backs on the gospel of Jesus Christ, they bring upon themselves eternal punishment (John 3:36; Rev. 20:11-15). When Christians become rebellious toward Christ as Lord, we bring upon ourselves destructive consequences spiritually, mentally, emotionally, and sometimes physically. I have observed again and again Christians who decide to become unfaithful to the local church. Eventually, they lose touch with God and plunge into lifestyles that cause pain and distress to them and to those who love them.

71

Stay yielded to the Lord. Daily deny yourselves, take up your crosses, and follow Jesus. If you do, you will avoid the heartache that follows disobedience.

II. We Can Choose to Obey God in All of Life

Obeying God in all of life consists of loving him, walking in his ways, and obeying his commandments. Since we enjoy the company of those we love, obeying God and walking in his ways give us joy.

When we choose to obey the Lord in all of life, we may expect the Lord's blessings. Though not identical always to those promised and delivered to Israel, they do parallel Israel's and are more desirable. Instead of a home on earth, we are assured of a heavenly home (John 14:2). Rather than a large progeny, we receive numerous spiritual fathers, mothers, brothers, sisters, and children through our involvement in the family of God. In place of a long life on earth, we are given everlasting life in Christ. Better than security in this world, we are told that no one can pluck us out of the Father's hand.

I do not suggest that those who obey God in all of life receive no blessings in this life. We certainly do! For example, a married couple were on the verge of divorce until they decided to rededicate their lives to God and attempt to rebuild their marriage according to God's Word. Now, nearly twenty years and two children later, they continue to discover the bliss of a beautiful life together.

The choice of obedience or disobedience to God's overtures to us is ours to make. Also, the consequences are ours to either enjoy or suffer. The choice is yours—choose life! (Jerry E. Oswalt)

ACCOUNTABLE CHRISTIANITY

1 CORINTHIANS 3:1-9

Accountability is not a very popular word in a world defined by convenience. Christian growth involves accountability as a necessary tool that seeks to enable us to be honest about who we are in our relationship with God in Christ. This truth is the tool Paul uses in this passage to confront the Corinthians in response to their frustration at Paul's simple teaching of the gospel.

Paul aggressively encourages the Corinthians to face up to their immature faith. Their criticism of Paul's preaching so simple a gospel becomes the springboard for this great preacher to honestly identify the immaturity of the Corinthians' expression of faith.

I. Immature Faith Majors on Minor Issues

The Corinthian believers were splitting into factions centered on loyalty to various human leaders. The church consisted of "preacher parties."

Paul confronts them with the truth that congregations who seek to center their growth and life on personalities are infants in faith who need to grow up. Only God causes growth.

Paul holds this young congregation accountable for their growth in the Christian faith as he addresses a nonissue and turns it into a clear example of their Christian immaturity. Paul would never allow such a hollow, immature nonissue to intimidate the vision of God he has been called to share.

II. Immature Faith Must Be Confronted
by Visionary Leaders

Paul dares to respond to the issue by defending the simplistic content of his preaching because it fit the audience to which he preached. The images used here are rich and powerful ones: infants in faith need receive the gospel only on the level they can handle it, as an infant can handle only milk. Paul's boldness with these Corinthians makes preachers' hair stand on the backs of their necks as they imagine such a dialogue in their own congregations over issues that so often are nonissues. How many churches have never been led with God's vision because leaders did not have the courage, with God's leading and grace, to confront the nonissues for what they are?

Paul has no time for such foolishness. Not only does he call their bluff, but he uses their issue as a platform from which to proclaim that they need to grow beyond such spiritual immaturity, led by the God who gives the growth.

Walt Kallestad, pastor of the Community Church of Joy, shares in his seminar "How to Grow a Church" that the primary role of the pastor is that of the visionary leader. Stephen Covey, in his breakthrough book *Seven Habits of Highly Effective People,* talks about the need for the visionary leader in any business or institution.

In the church we understand such vision to come from God. God grows persons from infancy to maturity in faith. Pastors, as the visionary leaders of their churches, share and proclaim God's vision.

III. Immature Faith Must Be Called to Accountability

God's vision demands accountability. The accountability Paul offers is honest. It is an accountability that offers so much more than just judgment; it offers the opportunity for growth and a more mature understanding of the God who enables and empowers such growth. In love and grace, Jesus himself never sacrificed the vision of God for people who needed accountability with the immature faith they sought to share. The vision of growth in faith demands accountability. Those who fail to be held accountable—as well as those who can bring accountability but don't—will discover little, if any, growth in their faith.

The vision of new life in the birth of a baby involves growing up. To remain an infant is to miss the whole point of life. Without effective and honest accountability, growth will be strangled. (Travis Franklin)

DANGER OF HELL'S FIRE

MATTHEW 5:21-37

Jesus says to the crowd around him that anyone who calls a sister or brother a fool stands in danger of hell's fire. To judge by the language and attitudes presented on TV, there aren't many people who still believe that, however.

Who could blame them? If you have been listening to the message from pulpits across this country, there has been a constant focus on the grace of God but little attention to the significance of our deeds. We have been promoting a form of Christian salvation that denies any significance of our human initiatives in the drama of life. We have been offering a form of redemption that actually seems to make our human conduct and words insignificant.

A friend commented that the most distressing thing he observed as he grew older was that it became more and more difficult to sin. Walker Percy writes about the desire of a doctor to find one clear and obvious evil. We have been working to eliminate sin. Nobody cares enough to hold us accountable. No one seems to expect anything from anyone anymore, so there can be no betrayal of commitment.

We have been so anxious to declare to everyone that God's unconditional love will accept us as we are, that what we have done in the past doesn't matter, God will receive us just where we are. The constant proclamation of God's unconditional love soon becomes the declaration that we as human beings do not matter because nothing we do has any affect on God or on God's love or even can affect our eternal salvation.

Douglas John Hall, in his recent book *Professing the Faith,* suggested that Helmut Thielicke's description of covert nihilism is the basic attitude of most of North America. It has a basic indifference about life. Covert nihilism practices detachment, noninvolvement, "value free" investigations. It affirms the possibility of objective research. It shuns commitment. It translates into apathy and "psychic numbing." Nothing that we do seems to matter.

The individual approach is to take a personal survival tactic with little conviction about the direction of the future. Covert nihilists are masters of repression. They will not even examine their spiritual emptiness. They are living with a massive loss of meaning for life and for eternity.

The gospel of unconditional love confirms this hidden and massive feeling that what I do and how I live have no meaning. The more the Christian faith tells people that forgiveness is simply God's unmerited free acceptance of our sins, the more suspicious people become about the real price of this kind of grace, which is the surrender and sacrifice of the dignity and meaning of our human existence.

God's forgiveness is not just to tell us the past did not matter; the real and powerful purpose of God's forgiveness is to say that we have such an important work to do as God's agents of stewardship of creation that God cannot afford to lose one good worker and so we are given back our future and told to get to work. Jesus Christ never expected those who entered the Kingdom to be pure and perfect when they entered, but he did expect them to strive to become perfect while they stayed.

Perhaps this word from Jesus—about the calling of a brother or sister a fool getting us eternal damnation—ought to remind us that God does expect much from us. God will not deal kindly with people who have seen divine love in Christ, accepted divine grace in Jesus, and done nothing with the power of the Holy Spirit.

It is a terrible thing for one to stand in danger of the fires of hell, it is an awesome thing to fall into the hands of a righteous God, but there is only one thing worse: to declare a grace that removes forever the possibility of standing in danger of the fires of hell. For the fires of hell and the glories of heaven give some eternal depth and height and glory to our human lives. (Rick Brand)

FEBRUARY 18, 1996

❧

Transfiguration Sunday

Worship Theme: Our lives are transformed by God's presence.

Readings: Exodus 24:12-18; 2 Peter 1:16-21; Matthew 17:1-9

Call to Worship (Psalm 99:1-3, 9):

Leader: The LORD is king; let the peoples tremble!

People: He sits enthroned upon the cherubim; let the earth quake!

Leader: The LORD is great in Zion; he is exalted over all the peoples.

People: Let them praise your great and awesome name. Holy is he! . . .

Leader: Extol the LORD our God, and worship at his holy mountain;

All: For the LORD our God is holy.

Pastoral Prayer:

On this day of worship and praise, O Lord, we come before you celebrating your love and grace. We are thankful that, in the midst of a world filled with bitterness and alienation, you are about the work of transforming a people and creating a community characterized by joy and unity. Help us, day by day, be transformed more and more into the likeness of your Son and our Redeemer. As his disciples looked on him that first day of transfiguration long ago, so let us gaze on him this day and recognize that he is worthy of our praise and our obedience. May this be a day of transformation in our lives, in our families, and in our church. For we ask it in the name of the One who gave himself for us. Amen.

SERMON BRIEFS

AN APPOINTMENT WITH GOD

EXODUS 24:12-18

A man told the story of going to the mountain retreat of a renowned evangelist for an interview. "Upon reaching the end of the meandering road at the top of the mountain, I found the retreat deserted except for the evangelist and God," the man facetiously explained.

Indeed the preacher did spend considerable time alone with God at his mountain refuge, preparing sermons and receiving divine guidance for his ministry. No doubt, he also was given strength for living the Christian life through his visits with God in that holy place.

Moses spent an extended time with God on the mountain, during which God gave him words of truth for Israel to live by. In the process, Moses also was strengthened for the enormous task of leading Israel to the Promised Land.

Anyone who seeks to live a life shaped and directed by God needs time alone with God.

I. We Meet God Upon God's Invitation

Moses distinctly heard God calling him to a meeting on the mountain. Only then did he consider the possibility of such an encounter. This trek up a mountain to meet God was as unpremeditated as the previous one when God spoke to him out of the burning bush. People are not inclined by nature to spend extended time alone with God. Whenever that motivation comes to us, we must consider it to be the voice of God inviting us to come to him for guidance, comfort, and strength.

Our Heavenly Father desires for us to spend time alone with him because he loves us and knows that such experiences will cause us to prosper spiritually. The Scriptures frequently state God's invitations to us to come to him. One of my favorites is the merciful call from Jesus: "Come to me, all you that are weary and are carrying heavy burdens, and I will give you rest" (Matt. 11:28).

A man determined that he would go into the mountains and pray all night if need be in order to become full of God's power. All he got was a sore back, for he did not go at God's invitation; he went out of his own selfish desire to get more of God's power to use for personal gain. We can move into God's presence and we should, but only in response to a compulsion to do so that comes from hearing God's invitation.

II. We Meet God Through Obedience to God's Call

Moses readily obeyed God. He climbed up the mountain and saw the cloud representing the glory of God covering the peak. He knew the Lord waited for him. Then, after receiving the word from God to advance to the summit, Moses proceeded and disappeared into the cloud of God's glory. There he remained in close communication with the Lord for forty days and nights. Through his obedience to God's initiative, Moses received blessings he surely would have missed had he stayed below when God beckoned him to the top.

We should readily respond to God's call to us to spend time with him in close, uninterrupted fellowship. We live such busy lives that we sometimes fail to obey that call. Through our neglect of such opportunities, we miss out on the beautiful blessings God desires to give us. (Jerry E. Oswalt)

WHO HAS THE AUTHORITATIVE WORD?

2 PETER 1:16-21

We live in a world filled with conflicting mesages. We are bombarded by efforts to persuade us to buy something, vote for someone, believe in something. How do we sort through these various "witnesses" that confront us?

In this text, Peter notes that the Christian witness is not simply another equal and competing claim on us. Rather, it is rooted in both personal experience and divine presence.

I. The Witness of Faith Is Based on Personal Experience

Today as we make the transition in the church's story from Epiphany to Lent, the focus shifts to transformation. The passage and season speak to the difference Christ's appearing makes in the lives of those who experience it. Such manifestation seeks to lead to transformation. Lent helps us examine such transformation and the difference it is or isn't making in our lives.

The emphasis in this passage is the personal experience from which the witness of faith finds expression.

II. The Witness of Faith Is Authenticated by Divine Presence

Peter notes that the witness of prophecy in and through persons is initiated by the working of the Holy Spirit. This text reminds us of a major concern of the early church as to the real source of its authority. In this passage, the Transfiguration is secondary to the real issue of apostolic witness and authority.

According to 2 Peter, authority in witness involves personal experience and the movement of the Holy Spirit. Such authentic testimony and prophecy are thus as a lamp shining in a dark place, as the dawning of the day, or as the morning star rising.

For Peter, there is an indisputable link between authenticating authority and its effect on those who receive such witness. Christian witness fails the test of authenticity if it is not inspired by the presence of the Holy Spirit.

In a day and age of convenience, in a time when religion has become prime time, the divine source of our authority must be recalled. For Peter, the Holy Spirit gives to the church authority to proclaim and witness to the experience of God's presence.

In her book *Windows to Heaven,* Diane Comp talks about her work with terminally ill children. Dr. Comp, in the beginning of her work, was an agnostic. She had grown up in the church and in her upbringing believed in God. However, as she went through college and on to graduate work, God became an outdated idea. In her decision to be an agnostic she believed that the only way she would come to believe in God again would be through the testimony of a credible witness. The book is the story of those credible witnesses who were her terminally ill children and how they became, for her, "windows to heaven."

Peter reminds us that the credibility and authenticity of the Christian witness to faith are to be discovered in the Holy Spirit. The church of today needs desperately to hold up that experience as to where the final and authoritative word must be found and shared if it is to be a credible witness to the God who is for us and who is among us. Only God through the manifestation of the Holy Spirit has the authoritative word. (Travis Franklin)

ONE MOMENT IN TIME

MATTHEW 17:1-9

The great Lutheran preacher Paul Scherer reminds us, "One is often amazed at the assumption that everything Jesus said is easy to understand. But what item is there in the record of scripture more insistent than this: that Jesus was being constantly misunderstood?" There is forever this simplified version of the Christian faith that keeps saying all we have to do is to listen to Jesus and do what he says, and yet nothing is so obvious in the Scriptures as the fact that even his disciples keep missing his point.

If the sayings of Jesus are challenging, how much more of a mystery to us and to the church are these stories in Scripture like the Transfiguration? What are we to do with this story of the Transfiguration?

All the Gospel writers include it in their Gospels. What do they want us to see? Does the church tell this story faithfully to show us something about Jesus? To make some claim on Jesus' behalf that he is the One through whom the glory of God is made visible to the world? Or does the church share this story as an example of the power of Jesus to bring us face-to-face with the indwelling grace of God to sustain us when the way is dark?

There was a time, not long ago, when preachers were embarrassed by such stories. This story of the Transfiguration does not fit into the modern scientific view of the universe to which our faith has been most anxious to conform and accommodate.

Yet a growing number of the brightest and best of our young people on college campuses and around the world are hungry for stories like this. They have mastered the logic of calculus, they know the advances of biology, and they are smart enough to realize that if there is not the possibility of mystery and power greater than what they already know, we are of all humankind the most to be pitied.

I. The Transfiguration Helps Us Better Understand Jesus

In this story of the Transfiguration, Christian people declare that something in Jesus is beyond our reason. Jesus is not just one of the shining saints honored through the years in every land. He has in him a mystery that is from beyond himself. The disciples report that they saw in Jesus a mystery that transformed history.

81

And the Christian faith has been struggling to put that mystery into words ever since. This Transfiguration story is the model for all our Christian theology. In Jesus Christ, we beheld the glory of God. In all of these stories, Christmas, Easter, Pentecost, there is the story of the mystery of God working in human history, God working and acting upon human life. But what makes this story of Jesus different from the story of the way God acted in Moses?

II. The Transfiguration Helps Us Better Understand God

The story of the Transfiguration is the story of the divinity of God being manifested in and through the humanity of Jesus. God is seen in Jesus Christ working to reconcile the world to himself. There on that mountain is the event that represents the Christian story: God is revealing himself in the person and work of Jesus Christ, not just in the things that happen to Jesus but in what Jesus says and does. The mystery of the universe is at work in the heart of Jesus the Christ.

This story carries our claim that Jesus was the personality of God. Jesus is the human life in which the power, mercy, and grace of God are made visible to us. Jesus is the power of God's love that captures the citadels of our hearts that force could not take.

III. The Transfiguration Helps Us Better Understand Our World

The Transfiguration story forces the Christian faith to keep God's spirit tied to humanity. God made visible in the flesh and blood of Jesus Christ affirms that our earthly lives are touched by the eternal.

There is a fundamental connection between creation and God. My moments of profound discovery of the power and grace of God will be encountered in historical places. The power of God will become most visible to us in ministry with others.

The Transfiguration makes a claim about Jesus, about the nature of God, and about our world. And the only hope there is for a future better than our past is in the middle of that story. (Rick Brand)

FEBRUARY 25, 1996

❧

First Sunday in Lent

Worship Theme: God provides the strength we need to overcome the temptations that confront us.

Readings: Genesis 2:15-17; 3:1-7; Romans 5:12-19; Matthew 4:1-11

Call to Worship (Psalm 32:1-2, 11):

Leader: Happy are those whose transgression is forgiven,

People: whose sin is covered.

Leader: Happy are those to whom the LORD imputes no iniquity,

People: and in whose spirit there is no deceit. . . .

Leader: Be glad in the LORD and rejoice, O righteous,

All: and shout for joy, all you upright in heart.

Pastoral Prayer:

Our Father and our God, as we enter this season of self-examination and preparation, we recognize anew our sinfulness and inadequacy. We have all sinned and fallen short of your glory, O Lord; we have taken your good creation and tainted it with our selfishness and thoughtlessness; we have abused our brothers and sisters, thinking only of our wishes and desires. Forgive us, O God. In this age in which we exalt self-esteem, remind us that in truth we have nothing in and of ourselves to esteem; on our own, we are unworthy to come before a holy and righteous God. Yet in your remarkable love and grace, you reach out to us through Christ and bring us into your very presence. And even beyond forgiveness, you endow us with your presence and provide the strength we need to overcome the temptations that confront us day by day. Thank you for love that we do not deserve but that we gratefully accept, as we ask it in the name of the One through whom you demonstrated your love on a cross. Amen.

SERMON BRIEFS

THE NATURE OF SIN

GENESIS 2:15-17; 3:1-7

The word *sin* isn't in the text, but sin is its theme nonetheless. In fact, this passage contains the familiar story of the origin of sin.

Eve and Adam learned the hard way that sin delivers destruction into the lives of those who commit it. They had been warned by God that serious consequences would follow from their disobedience, but they paid no attention. Sometimes we may become careless in our attitude toward the consequences of sin. When that happens, we should beware. Look at the cycle of sin as described in the text.

I. We Become Aware of God's Gracious Will for Our Lives

Adam and Eve knew beyond doubt that the Lord was gracious to them. He provided them with every essential gift for fulfillment in life. He kept from them only one thing—the fruit of the tree of the knowledge of good and evil. He even explained to them the reason for that single prohibition: they would experience evil, and evil would issue in death. In that case death encompassed both spiritual death, which is separation from God, and physical death, resulting from their loss of access to the tree of life.

The couple also clearly understood God's will for them. Eve confessed such an awareness in her response to the serpent. His initial effort to mislead her was not successful because she detected his lie. Sin becomes a possibility for anyone who has insight into the nature and purpose of God.

II. We Are Tempted to Rebel Against God's Gracious Will

The serpent persisted in the temptation of Eve, and his strategy was successful. He first forthrightly accused God of lying. Then he himself told another lie. By that time Eve had already entered into the mentality that made her vulnerable. She doubted God's word.

She doubted enough to consider the forbidden fruit, then she succumbed to its enticement and ate. Adam readily followed her lead.

Satan has the uncanny ability to make evil inviting. From the urge to get more of this world's goods, to the drive to lust, to the inclination to cling to bitterness, we know that the devil has power to persuade us to sin.

However, we have an advantage Adam and Eve didn't have. We have revealed to us in this text and in other places in the Bible Satan's strategy and methodology. Understanding his tactics assists us in resisting temptation, and when we do, the devil will flee from us.

III. We Experience Conviction and Shame Following Our Sin

Normally, conviction of sin will hit the transgressor immediately after the act. Eve and Adam knew immediately that they had sinned. They felt guilty before God and shame before each other. A dedicated Christian confessed the guilt and shame she sensed following a verbal expression of hatred for a person who had hurt her. A young man told of the time he was so burdened with conviction of sin that he fell before God in a catharsis of repentance and confession. All of us have experienced similar feelings when we've failed the Lord.

The cycle of sin begins with an awareness of God's gracious will for us. Once we know how good God is and what God desires for us, Satan will entice us to reject God's purpose for our lives. When we fall to that temptation, we sin, resulting in a sense of shame before God. The cycle can be broken before it leads to sin.

It may be broken when we are tempted to reject God's will. Our Lord taught us how by example. When he was tempted in the wilderness, he resisted Satan by refusal to disobey God. As a result, Satan eventually left him alone for a season. As James wrote, "Submit yourselves therefore to God. Resist the devil, and he will flee from you" (James 4:7). (Jerry E. Oswalt)

BEING AN AUTHENTIC PERSON

ROMANS 5:12-19

The bold ideas of facing up to our sinfulness and placing our complete trust in the free gift of God's grace as given are not all that easy in a culture obsessed with ownership and earning. Paul, however, wants to make it clear that because we are human we sin, and that the only way out of our sinfulness is the acceptance of the gift of God's grace as shared in Christ. This passage can be a most helpful one in the season of Lent to broaden our understanding of self-examination and the difference God's grace seeks to make in and through such an experience.

I. Self-examination Helps Us See Our Need for God's Grace

The temptation with the idea of self-examination is to understand it as something we do for ourselves, out of a sense of duty and obligation to God, so that we can better serve God. Such a discipline, done in such a way, misses the point of Paul's understanding of the free gift of God's grace. Self-examination does not begin with us; rather, it begins as we see ourselves in the light of God's grace. Such grace given freely in the moments we live exposes the shadows of who we are.

In Paul's way of thinking, we can only be the humans God created us to be. Being human means we are sinners. If we are to truly be involved in a self-examination that will be honest, such an experience must begin with grace. With the emphasis in our culture on self-help, this becomes a most ambitious understanding to relate.

II. Self-examination Is Valueless without God's Grace

Paul clearly identifies where such thinking leads. Left to the self, we will be left with judgment, condemnation, and death. Any Lenten self-examination not rooted in the experience of God's free gift of grace will end up leading to a try-harder mentality so as to win the approval of God. To do so is to miss the whole point of grace and what graces does in us and through us. The Lenten experience must include feelings of sorrow and resolve, and it must also seek, to express with joy and thanksgiving the difference God's grace makes in our lives.

The underlying reason for the Lenten experience both begins and ends in grace. To focus on self to the point that we are going to do better, outside grace, is to miss the whole point of the Lenten experience. For Paul, the human experience must be lived from only one perspective: grace.

Katherine Ann Power lived a life of hiding. As a college student in the early seventies, she was involved in a bank robbery that led to the murder of a police officer. Just recently, she left the life she had created that included a husband, a son, friends, and a job to turn herself in to authorities after two decades as a fugitive. Emerging from the shadows into the light, she stated she did so "in order to live with full authenticity in the present . . . with openness and truth, rather than hiddenness and shame."

That is what this passage and Lent are. It is a time whereby with the goodness and love of God's grace in Christ persons seek to live with full authenticity in the present . . . with openness and truth, rather than hiddenness and shame. For Paul, the human experience must begin and end in God's grace. Anything less than that experience has somehow failed to find God's vision for each life. All God has ever wanted for us is to be the authentic human beings we are. Only God's grace will help make that so. (Travis Franklin)

IN THE WILDERNESS

MATTHEW 4:1-11

Lou Holtz, who coaches football at Notre Dame, was interviewed after a Cotton Bowl game. People and the press were going on and on about the great impact of the game, and Lou said, "Wait a minute. The game isn't all that important. There must be three billion people in China who don't even care what happened."

Sooner or later we must leave behind all our mountaintop experiences, and we must return to the valley below—down where the dangerous days are for life and for faith. The peril to faith and trust comes in the ordinary days when monotony and the commonplace stretch out, like forty days in the wilderness. The same Holy Spirit who brought Jesus the announcement of God's approval at baptism now leads him out into the days of temptation and letdown.

I. Temptation Often Comes in the Wake of Commitment

It is always true that once we have accepted a high challenge and made a great commitment, there comes the temptation to forsake the cause. There is always the temptation to give up the commitment to the best and settle for something less. Once we have made a commitment to be God's persons, there comes the temptation to compromise and to settle for something less than God's best. The long, difficult journey always brings the temptation to give up the painful pilgrimage to paradise.

II. Temptation Often Comes in the Days of Ordinary Service

If we are to be disciples of Jesus Christ, we have to recognize that such obedience is going to take us through long periods of wilderness, frustration, work, and the ordinary. We need to be prepared for that.

That is why so much of the message of our consumerist economy is demonic. It is all part of the barefaced lie to convince us that we can escape the drab ordinary days of our lives by resorting to alcohol, new cars, trips to other places, new clothing, or sexual excitement. The devil tempts Jesus each time with the suggestion that he do something a little spectacular to escape the boredom of the day. Don't settle for soup and sandwiches—turn the stones into a real holiday buffet!

Jesus will not betray his commitment to God and humanity by escaping from our human limitations. Jesus knew that human life has its ordinary side. Jimmy Buffett sends his sweepstakes winner "Somewhere Over China" because it is his one chance in a million to "brighten up a boring day." But all of our human lives have drudgery and boredom.

III. God Gives Us the Grace to Defeat Temptation

Jesus was prepared for his long journey by his knowledge of Scripture. Everywhere along the way, Jesus' response to temptation was a response from Scripture. So it is with us. That is why the Christian community tries to spend so much time in making disciples by the normal means of grace—Scripture, prayer, worship, service, and giving—to develop the habits of faith to keep us faithful in the weary times.

It is not a matter of great feelings and passions. One suspects that Jesus did not glow with the great joy of being the Anointed of God out there in the wilderness being tempted. He was not being sustained by the warm spiritual glow or the power of positive thinking. It didn't matter whether he liked what he was doing or not. He continued in obedience and faith by his reliance on the promises of God in Scripture.

The story gives us the promise that God will sustain us and minister to us along the way. After the forty days, angels came and ministered to Jesus. Somewhere along the painful pilgrimage to paradise as you stay faithful, suddenly and unexpectedly an angel of mercy, some act of kindness, some word of hope, some gesture of inspiration, will be given to you to minister to you and to encourage you in the midst of the ordinary days of temptation. Such is the promise of God's Spirit to those who are God's disciples. (Rick Brand)

MARCH

ᘔ

Preparing to Serve

The Symbol of the Lamb

Paraphrase Assignment:

Revelation 13:8: "And all the inhabitants of the earth will worship it, everyone whose name has not been written from the foundation of the world in the book of life of the Lamb that was slaughtered."

Prayer Assignment:

Begin to pray for ways that you can teach the place of the Cross in the indulgent lives that we all lead. Seek, as usual, to make the Cross real in your own life, and then ask God for ways to make the Cross a living-and-yet-dying symbol in the life of the congregation.

Journal-in-Worship Assignment:

During Lent, the church should celebrate the glory of sacrifice. After each of the following passages, write a paragraph telling what that scripture means to you and how you used that scripture to encourage elements of surrender in your life.

Genesis 22:8. God will provide himself a lamb. In the near sacrifice of Isaac, God acquires the name of Jehovah-Jireh (the Lord will provide). After some period of self-sacrifice—the giving up of something you thought you could not live without—how did you find that God really did meet all your needs? Write this in celebration of your own relationship, but also write it to encourage the members of your church toward the voluntary sacrifice of something in their lives that will awaken them to the grand providence of the Jehovah-Jireh God.

John 1:29. Behold the Lamb of God who takes away the sin of the world. As Jesus' sacrifice paved the way for our relationship with his Father, what sacrifice have you made that made possible the deepening of relationships? Have you surrendered a selfish attitude or given up an indulgent habit that has brought your family or circle of friends closer together? If Jesus' sacrifice took away all sin, in what way have your sacrifices taken away the sin of overindulgence? Write

90

some paragraphs describing what self-denial has taught you about the overcoming life. Read Luke 9:23. Dietrich Bonhoeffer's famous paraphrase of this verse was "come with me and die." How closely have you identified your commitment with the cause of Christ? Can you confess a time in your past affairs with Christ that can be described only as utter yielding of "I surrender all"? Write it out as it happened. Let its confession encourage your congregation to seek some such moment of Christ-identity in their lives.

Revelation 5:12. Worthy is the Lamb that was slain! Encounter this powerful passage in the context of worship. Write two different accounts that you can somehow share with the people of your church. First, consider how the sacrifice of Christ first found its way into your private worship and adoration. When did you first decide that the Lamb was worthy of your worship and adoration? Second, when was public worship so overwhelming in your life that you praised the sacrifice of Christ? Did it motivate you to worship and praise of your own? Does exaltation always follow self-denial? Consider Matthew 4:1-11. After Jesus' three affirmations of surrender and self-sacrifice, the devil left him and angels came and ministered to him. Is this always the pattern? Talk about the symbol in Revelation of the Lamb slain and the Lamb exalted. Write of this as a theme for all Christians. Again, remember that what begins in your personal study and examination should be allowed to fuel the church for a confessional season of celebrating sacrifice. (Calvin Miller)

MARCH 3, 1996

❧

Second Sunday in Lent

Worship Theme: God's love gives us meaning and hope.

Readings: Genesis 12:1-4*a*; Romans 4:1-5, 13-17; John 3:1-17

Call to Worship (Psalm 121:1-2, 7-8):

Leader: I lift up my eyes to the hills—from where will my help come?

People: My help comes from the LORD, who made heaven and earth. . . .

Leader: The LORD will keep you from all evil; he will keep your life.

People: The LORD will keep your going out and your coming in from this time on and forevermore.

Pastoral Prayer:

O Lord, whose love created us and sustains us day by day, we marvel at your great love, expressed in such a powerful way through the Incarnation as divinity and humanity met in the person of Jesus Christ. As we view his remarkable life—how he reached out to persons others rejected, he touched the untouchable, he gave himself as a ransom on our behalf—we are awestruck in the face of such overpowering and sacrificial love. And to know that such love has been given to us—despite our sin and unworthiness—is the greatest wonder of all. As you have loved us, so help us be instruments of your love to those around us. Help us demonstrate your love to those who aren't easy to love, just as while we were yet sinners, Christ died for us. Amen.

SERMON BRIEFS

YOU ARE A PROMISE

GENESIS 12:1-4*a*

Children sing a song with the line: "I am a promise to be anything God wants me to be." What a wonderful thought for children to have instilled into their minds and hearts! It impresses upon them more than one important attitude toward life. Not only does it basically teach them to believe in God-given possibilities for their lives; in addition, it enables them to believe that with God's help and blessings, they can become blessings to the world.

God's covenant with Abram, which became the basis for future covenants with Israel and with Christians, was essentially a promise to bless Abram so that Abram and his descendants might bless the world. All future covenants between the Lord and his chosen people carried this purpose. God blesses a people in order to make them a blessing. Notice the blessings given in the covenant with Abram, and compare the parallel blessings given to Christians.

I. God Gives His People a Dwelling Place

From the beginning, a land was promised to Abram and his descendants. Abram never possessed the land. He was always a sojourner there, but he was a man always looking for a city, "whose architect and builder is God" (Heb. 11:10). The actual possession of the land came hundreds of years later when Joshua led Israel into Canaan.

Christians have the promise of a home, whose architect and builder is the Lord Jesus Christ (John 14:1-6). Our homes on earth are given by God and cherished deeply, but our ultimate home, the home of promise, is heaven.

II. God Gives His People a Great Name

Abram's (or Abraham's) name became and remains great because of an enormous progeny both physically and spiritually. He became the father of descendants as numerous as the stars and also became the source of three great world religions (Judaism, Christianity, and Islam).

93

The name of Christian becomes great through our "new name" (Rev. 2:17). The new person in Jesus Christ is represented by the "new name." Also, there is a parallel in our covenant promise to the great nation promised Abram. The 144,000 people of Revelation 14:1 represent an awesome complete number of folks who have the names of the Lamb and his Father written on their foreheads.

III. God Gives His People Security

God protected Abraham, Isaac, and Jacob from their foes again and again. Later God delivered Israel from slavery in Egypt, protected and provided for them in the wilderness, and eventually led them to conquest of as much of Canaan as they were willing to take. Throughout the period of the judges and the reigns of Saul, David, and Solomon, God protected his people when they remained loyal to the covenant.

Christians are given the security of eternal life in Jesus Christ. Jesus has promised to keep us in his hand (John 10:27-28). Furthermore, we have the promise expressed in regard to the church's triumph over evil. Jesus declared that "the gates of Hades will not prevail against it" (Matt. 16:18*b*).

God blesses his people according to his promises. God always has and he always will. May we be loyal to our promises to God so that his blessings in our lives will in turn make us blessings to others. (Jerry E. Oswalt)

IN WHOM DO WE TRUST?

ROMANS 4:1-5, 13-17

In our culture much attention is being given to the understanding of paradigms. In best-selling business books, Joel Barker and Stephen Covey identify the power of the paradigm as a tool to understanding the great truths concerning life and leadership. A paradigm is a kind of worldview—a way of seeing and understanding the world. A paradigm is the particular set of lenses through which you view the world.

Paul seeks to make the life of Abraham a paradigm to the early church as he identifies and interprets God's action in Christ and its meaning to the life of the world. This paradigm of Abraham is key because it links an Old Testament figure of faith to a New Testament interpretation of God's saving activity in the person of Jesus Christ.

I. Salvation Comes Through Faith, Not Our Actions

It was a paradigm shift—the transition from the Jewish under-standing of favor with God being a result and reward from works of the Law to the new paradigm whereby God seeks restored relation-ship by justifying the people by grace through faith in Christ. And it was a most delicate issue, especially among Jewish Christians. It was a paradigm shift in the way in which God sought to reconcile his children.

II. Salvation Is Possible Because of
What Christ Did, Not What We Do

The issue for Paul is one of trusting through faith what God has done and is doing in Christ. The work of redemption is at God's initiative as God's love in Christ finds its fullest expression in the Cross. That was also the burning issue for Luther, Calvin, Wesley, and all the great church reformers. Paul understands that the indis-pensable link between God and humans is our willingness to trust the salvation God has made possible in and through Jesus Christ.

Parents love their child. However, for that love to produce a meaningful relationship, the child must receive it. Abraham stands as the person in Hebrew faith who models this concept so powerfully. Abraham trusted God, and that trust was lived out long before the promises of God were realized. As such the realization from the paradigm is that the old idea of God's favor being given as a result of the works of the Law is dead.

The words of Martin Luther King, Jr., on the eve of his death illustrate the proper relationship of trust in faith as he said, "[God has] allowed me to go up to the mountain. And I've looked over, and I've seen the promised land." The famous sermon goes on to share his trust in what God will do on behalf of his children. Martin Luther King, Jr., simply and yet profoundly placed his trust in the love of God as revealed in Christ. This is the central issue of Paul's concern in this passage. It is an issue with which the church continues to labor. In a post-Christian United States these words need powerful expres-sion. So many persons get sidetracked in believing that God will

95

reward them because of who they are and what they have done. Paul's words remind us that such salvation is hollow and mocks the work of God's grace in Christ on the cross.

In Hebrews 11, we find the roll call of the faithful. As the names are shared, they are prefaced by the phrase "by faith." The authentic Christian witness to faith in Paul's eyes must be expressed from one place and one place only: by faith! (Travis Franklin)

FOR GOD SO LOVED THE WORLD

JOHN 3:1-17

"For God so loved the world . . . "—it stands there like a rock upon which the heresies of history have smashed and sunk. Over and over again we have tried to separate or combine the two. God—absent or transcendent, high above creation, indifferent to creation, just watching history. Or God—immanent, at one with creation, every tree and every brook pulsing with the creative power of life.

I. God's Love Is Unlimited

"For God so loved the world . . ." stands there against all our attempts to narrow and make specific God's love. Even the author of the Gospel faces the temptation to say that God doesn't love all humanity and history, God just loves his own: those whom Jesus has called out of the world. The disciples are spoken of as loving Jesus and are commanded to love one another, but they are never told to love the world. Even John seems a bit tempted to restrict the scope of Christian love to Christ and the church, and yet John can't get past this fact that love is the most adequate description of God's attitude toward all creation.

"For God so loved the world . . . ," the whole world, all creation. We have compartmentalized life so that most of us think that God loves us and we need to serve him. But we aren't very good at thinking what it would mean if God loves political power and corporate structures and natural energies and vast space. Our failure to understand the whole meaning of "for God so loved the world" has meant we have not cared very well for the whole world, which we were made to be God's stewards of.

II. God's Love Is Unconditional

"For God so loved the world . . . " is the beginning of a declarative statement. It is a given. God's love is for all creation. So often that word is spoken as if it were conditional, as if God will love us only if we meet some condition. If you are righteous, God will love you. If you are educated and literate, God will love you.

This phrase is our defense against thinking that God's love is some abstract and metaphysical emotion. God is not distant and unconnected from creation. God loves this creation in time and history. God loves and acts and is involved with this combination of time and space, energy and matter, people and power. It is this cosmos that God is concerned to bring to fulfillment of his intentions in creation.

God still loves this world and is still creating and working. Creation is still God's work. Creation continues to be sustained because God continues to love creation and sustain it.

III. God's Love Is Redemptive

"For God so loved the world . . ."—that love is the reason for God's continued actions to redeem and restore creation. God in Jesus Christ comes to save and to redeem. God gave himself in Jesus Christ with the desire and intention to redeem us.

"For God so loved the world . . . " that he acted in Jesus Christ. Those of us who have felt that love and know that grace are motivated to the same kind of compassion, hope, and love for all creation. As we are linked in Jesus Christ to God, so we begin to share his love for creation and bring into the service of that love all of our gifts and talents and desires.

For God so loved the world. (Rick Brand)

MARCH 10, 1996

છે.

Third Sunday in Lent

Worship Theme: Through Christ, God offers us a new life.

Readings: Exodus 17:1-7; Romans 5:1-11; John 4:5-42

Call to Worship (Psalm 95:1-3, 6):

Leader: O come, let us sing to the LORD;

People: for the LORD is a great God.

Leader: Let us make a joyful noise to the rock of our salvation!

People: For the LORD is a great God.

Leader: Let us come into his presence with thanksgiving;

People: for the LORD is a great God.

Leader: Let us make a joyful noise to him with songs of praise!

People: For the LORD is a great God.

Leader: O come, let us worship and bow down,

People: for the LORD is a great God.

Leader: Let us kneel before the LORD, our Maker!

All: **For the LORD is a great God.**

Pastoral Prayer:

Into the clutter of our everyday lives, O God, you come with your heavenly order; into the weakness you come with your strength; into the sin you come with your holiness. Give us the grace now to receive you, to open the doors of our beings and invite you in—not just over the threshold but into the inmost parts, the upper rooms and lower rooms, the nooks and crannies and closets. Dwell in us, O God, that we may glow with your light and pulsate with your presence. Let the peace that has stilled the hearts of saints in all ages still our hearts as well. Let the courage that has animated them animate us. Let the imagination that has possessed them possess us so that we may transcend what we have known of ourselves and devote ourselves truly to glorifying your name in all the earth. Amen. (John Killinger)

SERMON BRIEFS

TESTING GOD'S PATIENCE

EXODUS 17:1-7

Some people think that it is okay to ventilate their contentions with God. They believe that when they are exasperated with life as it is, they have a right to complain to God about the poor job God is doing.

Our text challenges that line of thought. The people of Israel grumbled to Moses about his and God's failure to provide them with an adequate supply of water. To Moses, they whined, "Why did you bring us out here to die of thirst?" They questioned God's faithfulness: "Are you among us or not?" The text refers to the complaint about water as a quarrel or an aggravation to Moses, but as a testing of patience to God.

Indeed, the Lord is forbearing toward people when they complain. Despite Israel's childish whimpering, God gave them water. The point of the text is that they pushed him and in so doing tested his patience. That wasn't a smart thing to do, and Israel learned that lesson through bitter tastes of God's wrath along the way, even though they escaped on this particular occasion.

We can avoid complaining to God by adjusting our theology so that we quit blaming the Lord for our problems. No matter how we may decide to integrate the reality of suffering with our concept of God, we will not profit from blaming God. Such an exercise is detrimental to both our faith and our witness for Christ. It also destroys initiative to help ourselves.

The worst scenario would be to push God beyond the limits of his patience, as Israel did on other occasions. Then God may let us discover how much more miserable life can be than it already is.

One of the most discouraging people I've ever known was a man who became embittered toward God because his wife died young. He resisted all efforts by Christians to win him to Christ. As the root of bitterness sank deeper and deeper into his soul, he became increasingly a miserable human being, driving everyone away from him, including his family. He went to his grave blaming God for his miserable life.

On the other hand, one of the most inspiring people I've ever known was a woman whose faith was caught by her five children, resulting in her daughters becoming missionaries and her sons deacons. Her husband lost a leg in a terrible accident. After that he never regained good health and became disabled. Then he died fairly young. She lived in poverty, refusing most efforts of her children to assist her. One of her sons died in a boating accident while still a young man. She lost her sight. Yet not one person, so far as I know, ever heard her complain about her circumstances. Her love for the Lord was too large to tolerate any consideration of blaming him for her circumstances. She probably never tested God's patience. Have you? (Jerry E. Oswalt)

HOPE-FILLED PEOPLE FOR A HOPELESS AGE

ROMANS 5:1-11

Richard Halverson, chaplain of the U.S. Senate, says, "Mastered by God, I become the master of myself and of my circumstances. Mastered by anything less than God, I become the victim of myself and of my circumstances." In this passage, Paul shows that in Christ, God is offering us a new life that, once received, masters us and gives us an abiding hope that will overcome any and all circumstances.

I. Christ Offers Us a New Foundation

Paul is describing in these words the difference a life mastered by God's love in Christ will make. Life is to be lived from the foundational experience and knowledge that "God proves his love for us in that while we still were sinners Christ died for us" (v. 8).

Our response to the circumstances of life, lived from this foundational truth, provides reason for hope, peace, and rejoicing. In Paul's way of thinking and living, this is why God's people become "more than conquerors through him who loved us" (Rom. 8:37). The foundation of God's love in Christ provides any person a strong place to stand against whatever the circumstances may be. In a culture where circumstances seem to overcome more often than not, these are words we all need to hear, heed, and accept as true.

We are now in the season of Lent. What better time than in this season of self-examination and confession to proclaim the hope, peace, and rejoicing that must be our response to the reality of God's redemptive love in our lives—even while we are still sinners!

II. Christ Offers Us a New Future

God's redemptive act in Christ leads people to become a new creation. According to Paul, this new creation is rooted and grounded in the realization that God's redeeming love is not only *from* something but *to* something. Paul wants us to realize that hope, peace, and rejoicing are the things to which redemption leads.

So many persons today are concerned only with half of what the love of God has done in Christ. The church has so many times clearly proclaimed the something from which we have been saved but has failed to say our salvation is also to something. The movement of the salvation experience is from redemption to creation. To have one without the other is to fail to realize the whole story of what God has done and is doing in Christ. We are never fully mastered by God until we have experienced and been claimed by both.

The hope, peace, and rejoicing we seek to offer a hopeless age are necessary expressions of the redemption experience in our lives. If there are no hope, peace, and rejoicing in our lives, then the redemptive experience is not complete.

A United Press release in a midwestern city told of a hospital where officials discovered that the firefighting equipment had never been connected. For thirty-five years it had been relied upon for the safety of the patients in case of emergency. But it had never been attached to the city's water main. The pipe that led from the building extended four feet underground—and there it stopped! The medical staff and patients felt complete confidence in the system. They thought that if a blaze broke out, they could depend on a nearby hose to extinguish it. But theirs was a false hope. Although the costly equipment with its polished valves and well-placed outlets was adequate for the building, it lacked the most important thing: water!

Our hope must be rooted in the redemptive experience of God's love in Christ. Without redemption we cannot have the new creation. Rooted deeply in God's love as shared in Christ, may we discover the power to witness with hope, peace, and rejoicing the difference God seeks to make in a hopeless age. (Travis Franklin)

GIVE ME A DRINK

JOHN 4:5-42

"How is it that you, a Jew, ask a drink of me, a woman of Samaria?" (v. 9). How is it that you, a resident of the suburb, ask a drink of me, a resident of the inner city? How is it that you, a northern factory worker, ask a drink of me, a southern tobacco farmer? How is it that you, who have been lumping all of us together into some invisible group, now suddenly ask something of one of us?

Forces of darkness and evil are constantly working to destroy life, to diminish the good, to make us into groups and treat us as statistics and thus destroy the edges, the individual gifts, the uniqueness of all creation. And the power of God's grace is constantly working to put us individually on stage, in public, and allow us to use our special talents and abilities for the benefit of all.

I. God Already Knows Who We Are

So Jesus and the woman are at the well. She is an invisible person. She is invisible to the Jews because she is a Samaritan. They don't see her. They see labels and symbols and history, but they don't look at her. She has secrets that most people do not want to hear about. That is why she comes to the well at midday.

Many of us try to be invisible—to keep a low profile—because we think there is something about us that would make other people reject us, dislike us, oppose us, or exclude us if the secret was out. Maybe we worked in a retail store, and we used to come home with unpaid-for merchandise. Maybe we did not get the college diploma we said we did. We do not want to be put forward; we don't want to be noticed because we are afraid the attention will expose our sins and we will be condemned.

But Jesus makes this woman visible because he has a need, a thirst, and the well is deep and he has no bucket. She becomes visible when

Jesus asks for help and talks with her as though she matters, talks to her as a human being, with respect and dignity, as if her being there at noon is nothing out of the ordinary.

II. God Knows Our Secrets—and God Still Wants Us

As the story unfolds, we discover the amazing thing is that Jesus already knows the secret. Jesus does not treat her with respect because he does not know. Jesus treats her as a human being even knowing the story. God already knows the secrets we are hiding. God is seeking us, calling us. God has work for us to do, and God already knows the secrets we are using as the reason for holding back.

Too many of God's people are holding back, trying to stay invisible, because we think we have secrets that will disqualify us from the work of God's kingdom. We let the secrets keep us from the challenges of being a part of the mighty work of the kingdom of God. Well, rejoice! God knows the secrets with which we live. God has forgiveness and grace available to bring those secrets to light. And in that light of his love and mercy the secrets lose power over us, and we are free to exert ourselves in the great joy and mission of God's people.

The secrets are known, and yet God still has a place and a job for us. It is not that what we did does not matter; it is just that what we might do as part of God's future is so much more important that God invites us to come out to the center stage of history and join this work of being the people of God. The past can't hurt the future of God's kingdom. (Rick Brand)

MARCH 17, 1996

ᔥ

Fourth Sunday in Lent

Worship Theme: Jesus Christ makes a transforming difference in our lives.

Readings: 1 Samuel 16:1-13; Ephesians 5:8-14; John 9:1-41

Call to Worship (Psalm 23):

Leader: The LORD is my shepherd, I shall not want.

People: He makes me lie down in green pastures;

Leader: he leads me beside still waters; he restores my soul.

People: He leads me in right paths for his name's sake.

Leader: Even though I walk through the darkest valley, I fear no evil; for you are with me;

People: your rod and your staff—they comfort me.

Leader: You prepare a table before me in the presence of my enemies;

People: you anoint my head with oil; my cup overflows.

Leader: Surely goodness and mercy shall follow me all the days of my life,

People: and I shall dwell in the house of the LORD my whole life long.

Pastoral Prayer:

O God, in whom are met all the issues of life and death, and who knows us and our frailties better than we know ourselves, we cast ourselves upon your mercy and ask for your continued grace in our lives. We praise you for the little things that make our days so rich and meaningful: the touch of a friend, the sight of a child sleeping, the memory of a good time, the sound of a particular voice, the appearance of a flower where yesterday there was none. Forgive us for days spent in not seeing, not hearing, not being open to the miracles that abound at our elbows and fingertips. Teach us to be sensitive: to know when a star falls, when a friend hurts, when the wind stirs, when someone needs something we have in our possession. Show us, in our faith, how to be transparent: so to live and move and think and care that others, looking upon us, see you and know that all creation is one in your love. Amen. (John Killinger)

SERMON BRIEFS

A KID AFTER GOD'S OWN HEART

1 SAMUEL 16:1-13

Question: What do the following stories have in common? Noah building an ark. Abraham setting out to sacrifice Isaac. Rahab harboring the spies.

It's true they're all Old Testament stories about early heroes, but that's not the answer. They're all stories about God, first and foremost. Bible stories aren't so much about the characters as they are about the God who works divine purposes through them and sometimes in spite of them.

I. God Selects His Servants

The story before us isn't so much about David as it is about God. *God* tells Samuel to anoint a new king. *God* warns against trusting outward appearances. *God* chooses David. God is the leading actor in this story.

II. God Doesn't Select as We Would

Samuel is to anoint a new king from among Jesse's sons. Eliab, the eldest, is striking, but he is not God's choice. Neither are the others. Samuel asks, "You don't have any other sons?"

"Well, *just* a shepherd boy."

"Go get him."

David enters, and Samuel announces, "You're the one." Young David is anointed Israel's next king.

What a selection—not just that God selects an insignificant shepherd, but David was the last of eight sons.

Psychologists note that a person's birth order impacts personality; for example, firstborns might be passive and those born second might be aggressive, and so forth. David was the eighth of eight boys. In psychological terms, he had to fight for even one chicken leg at dinner, and he could forget about using the telephone.

David was twelve, maybe thirteen. At an age when most kids think about making the team, David was selected king. An adolescent king? Do you remember Mark Twain's line? "When kids become teenagers, parents should put them in a barrel and feed them through the knot hole. When they become sixteen, plug the knot hole."

David was a teenager. Remember? A time of changing voices and bodies, pimples, and girls towering over boys. It was in this stage of life that God named David as Israel's king.

Of course, God has done this kind of thing more than once. God called Jeremiah before he began shaving. God chose the teenager Mary to carry the Messiah. And when Jesus was twelve, his parents found him in the Temple discussing theology.

It's not just in biblical times. In 1947, two shepherd boys were grazing their flocks in the Middle East. One of the animals strayed off, so Muhammed el-Dib went searching, hoping to find his sheep. He found something else—the Dead Sea Scrolls, the greatest archaeological find ever.

III. God Selects Servants Based on What's Inside

So, God picked an adolescent for king. Why?

Do you remember Cinderella's story? She lives with her cruel stepmother and stepsisters. Cinderella does all the work. Then the invitation comes for the royal ball. Cinderella dreams of going but can't. Later, her fairy godmother grants her wish. The prince falls in love with her, but she flees at midnight and he's left with her glass slipper. He searches for her everywhere. The stepsisters and the stepmother try the slipper on, but with no luck. The prince asks if others live there. "No one else, *just* Cinderella."

"Bring her here at once."

"But why? She's a nobody."

"Bring her here."

Remember? The prince slides it on her foot, looks into her eyes, and says, "You're the one."

What was it God saw in David? A heart. David was a kid after God's own heart. Of course, that can happen at any age and to anyone.

A crown that fit. A slipper that fit. God looks into your eyes and says, "You're the one." (Mike Graves)

LIFE IN THE LIGHT

EPHESIANS 5:8-14

First-century Christian gatherings had different nuances from our contemporary worship traditions. This text may give us insight into the worship and faith of the first-century churches. The exhortations in verses 8-12 rest on the principles of verses 13-14. The principle is, everything exposed by light becomes visible as a result of the light.

This is a truth taken from the natural world. This is also true in the spiritual realm because Christ is the light. Verse 14 may very well be a baptismal hymn used in first-century worship. The hymn exhorts the new believers as they emerge in baptism, symbolizing their movement from death into life: "Rise from the death of your dark sins, and Christ our light will shine upon you!" If this is the understanding of the initial steps in faith, then Paul's exhortations in verses 8-12 take on great significance.

I. We Share a Dark Past

Paul tells his readers that at one time they were darkness. Before conversion, believers abode in the dark chaos to which blindness is the best analogy. Before faith in Christ, improper judgment without discernment was the guiding force. This darkness is that of disobedience, and Paul states to even mention the specific deeds of people in darkness would be shameful (v. 12). The spiritual blindness of disobedience is magnified in that those abiding in the spiritual darkness do not have a desire to know their faults or shortcomings.

We must be careful at this point, lest we look too harshly at persons disobedient in Paul's day or in ours. Though sinful deeds make us blush with shame for them, we cannot be judgmental because Paul began by noting "once you were darkness." The point is for us to marvel at the grace of God in our lives, to "awake" us from our spiritual death and heal us from our spiritual blindness to see the light of the world, Jesus Christ.

II. We Are Called to Life in the Light

Life in the darkness is fruitless and is to be avoided by children of God (v. 11). As "children of light," we are to bear fruit in contrast to the barrenness of our former disobedience. Three commands outline how our lives should bear fruit of being children of light.

First, Paul says we are to "live as children of light" (v. 8). Children bear a resemblance to their parents: facial features, character flaws, attitudes, life views, and so on. As children of light, we must bear in us the likeness or image of the source of life, Jesus Christ. As children grow in the image of their parents, so we are to grow spiritually, being shaped into the image and likeness of Christ. With John the Baptist we must decidedly declare, "I must decrease that he might increase." Elsewhere Paul viewed this as a daily death to self, but a rebirth in the nature of Christ.

The fruit of light that we are to bear is all goodness, righteousness, and truth. These three general aspects of Christ's nature should be growing in our lives. Those who are willing to die to self, as symbolized in baptism, can be resurrected in Christ's life, bearing the fruit of goodness, righteousness, and truth.

Second, Paul makes clear that children of light should "find out" what pleases the Lord (v. 10). Darkness is a good place to hide—no one can see our faltering. We are brought out of the dark to be obedient children of God who are willing to know what God desires in our lives. When in darkness, we had no desire to please God, but as children of light, we should be looking to find those things God desires.

Finally, Paul exhorts us to avoid those deeds of darkness that once plagued our lives (v. 11). New Testament conversion always anticipated a change in character. A clear and radical change in nature, character, and deeds was assumed to be normative. Paul now encourages believers to avoid those deeds associated with the past.

Although it is not popular today, the New Testament is as clear about personal holiness as salvation. Our nature, character, and deeds are to be transformed by the Holy Spirit who moves us from our death of sin into the enlightened resurrected life of faith. We are to heed the Spirit's work, "Wake up, O sleeper." (Joseph Byrd)

A BLIND MAN AS A WITNESSING GUIDE

JOHN 9:1-41

Let's get the basic picture of this fascinating story. Jesus is teaching in the Temple when the Jews take up stones to kill him. He manages to escape them, melting into the crowd and making his way out of the Temple precincts. But in passing out of the Temple area he sees a man who has been born blind—the only case in all the Gospels of one who was so disabled and healed. Jesus stops. It is instructive that Jesus stops and notices the man under the circumstances, fleeing from his enemies who would kill him. And what happens after that is a marvelous lesson in witnessing.

Let this blind man be our witnessing guide. But you say, "Wait a minute! That's not fair. My conversion is not at all like his conversion experience. His was dramatic; mine was prosaic." Remember that whether your conversion was a slow turning to Christ as a child in the bosom of the church or a dramatic shattering of an old life, in both cases the same Christ has brought salvation. Remember that we are alike in that we all have a need that we bring to Christ. This man's need was not only physical blindness but also spiritual—he needed acceptance; he needed to know somebody cared. He needed to know that God cared. And Jesus filled his need. Jesus fills that need in all of our lives. When Jesus met that need for this blind man, it made a difference in his life. Look with me at the differences.

I. A Genuine Conversion Raises Questions About You

Look at verses 8-9. His neighbors, those who formerly knew the man, that he was blind, said, "This is not the blind man, is it?" And some people said, "Oh, yes, this is he." Others said, "No, this is not the blind man—it just looks like him." The man himself insisted, "Wait a minute. It is I!"

The tragedy is that we overlook people, and that's why they didn't really know whether he was the blind man or not. The physical change was very small. His eyes were shut, and now they were open. Why did they suddenly not know a man because his eyes were open?

Because they didn't notice him when his eyes were shut! But there was a definite change in the man who had been blind, not a big one physically, but very real—something definitely happened. He was running around, he was seeing, he was talking to people—he was different. And they were asking questions about it.

A genuine conversion experience ought to make changes. When you and I become Christians, there ought to be an obvious dimension of difference in our lives, an attractive difference, a good difference. I read of a little fellow who got converted and then went a week or so later to a camp. It was not a church camp but one sponsored by a community or civic club. Afterward he was unpacking and said to his mother, "Mom, we were there a whole week, and not one of them found out I was a Christian." I'm afraid that's all too true.

They asked questions not just about the man himself but also about Jesus: "Where is the man who did this? Tell us about him." It's good to see a crowd of people wanting to see Jesus without rocks in their hands. They were going to build their idea about the man who healed the blindness on the basis of what the healed man said and how he acted. That's worth noticing. It's really all the world has to go on.

II. A Genuine Conversion Leaves Room to Grow

Questions were left in the mind of the man who had been blind, too. They said to him, "Where is he?" (v. 12). And he said, "I don't know." The Pharisees criticized Jesus. "This man is a sinner," they said. "Give credit to God" (v. 24). The man's response was that he didn't know whether Jesus was a sinner or not. The fellow didn't have all the answers.

In witnessing there are two heresies. The first is to say you know it all—that is neither biblical nor true, and it damages your witness to say such. The other heresy is to say that since you became a Christian, all problems are gone, and all is sweetness, peace, and light. That's not true. The man still didn't know why he was born blind. Think about that. Jesus only told him what he was going to do with the blindness—glorify God. The man did not find out why Jesus picked him of all the people there on that particular Sunday afternoon who needed healing. You do not have to know everything to be a good witness.

III. A Genuine Conversion Brings Varying Responses

We also find that his sharing of what happened to him brought forth varying responses from the people around him. When the man was brought to the Pharisees and questioned, they were divided. Some said, "This man Jesus can't be from God. He healed on the Sabbath." Others said, "What do you mean? A man cannot do these things *unless* he's from God!" The Pharisees came back to the once blind man and said, "Well, what do you say? He healed you, you say. What do you think about it?" "He's a prophet." Then they laughed in his face, and it was clear they really didn't believe he had ever been blind.

There was also the response of withdrawal as his parents backed off in fear of the authorities. People are that way, even about their religion. And some folks get downright angry. The man was summoned again by the Pharisees who said, "Well, fellow, you might as well admit that this man's a sinner." That was when he got angry and suggested that they were supposed to know the answers: "You don't even know where he is from, and he healed me!" Their reply was to kick him out of the synagogue!

IV. A Genuine Conversion Gives a Natural Testimony

People say, "I don't know how to share what God has done for me. I don't know how to talk about it." Just share it as this man did. It was very natural—he just told what had happened to him. He told them, to the best of his ability, who did it. He didn't embellish it. He just told what happened.

People are interested in your story and my story; they want to know what happened to us when we met Jesus. The man witnessed naturally because he had been genuinely converted.

V. A Genuine Conversion Gives an Unshakable Assurance

Finally, here is a man who, because he was genuinely converted, had an unshakable assurance. He said, "Whether this man is a sinner or not, I don't know." He had a beautiful disregard for theological hairsplitting. Sinner or not, I don't know, but one thing I do know! Unshakable assurance. I was blind and now I see. One thing I do know—my life is not what it was or what it would have been without him.

So often you and I think that because we weren't saved from the very gutter, from the gates of hell itself, we are not different from what we would have been, but we are. I am not a child of the devil; I am a child of God. I am going to heaven. Change has been made, and because we love God, and because we pray, and because we study God's Word, and because we want to have fellowship with others who trust him—we have the assurance, as John says in his letters, that we have been born again. (Earl E. Davis)

MARCH 24, 1996

❧

Fifth Sunday in Lent

Worship Theme: Jesus Christ promises us victory over death.

Readings: Ezekiel 37:1-14; Romans 8:6-11; John 11:1-45

Call to Worship (Psalm 130:1-2a, 5):

Leader: Out of the depths I cry to you, O LORD.

People: Lord, hear my voice! . . .

Leader: I wait for the LORD, my soul waits,

People: and in his word I hope.

Pastoral Prayer:

We lift our hearts to you, O God, with thanksgiving for the beauty and glory of life; for the flowers of springtime that burst forth like radiant mysteries all around us; for the ever-restless sea that washes the shore of a burdened, littered land; for great stretches of wilderness that teem with life never seen by human eye; for children, who have not yet learned to dissemble or subdue their instincts, but speak truly to their elders; for courtship and marriage that refresh the race in every age; for qualities such as loyalty and fidelity that enrich our relationships on every hand; for the dear souls who worship here, bringing together their smiles, embraces, and warmth of spirit; and for the gospel of Christ that has shown us the Kingdom behind and beyond all else that matters, so that everything that matters, matters even more. Teach us to live each day as a special gift so that we may see the beauty of small things, hear the songs in the trees, and feel the energy that courses through all living beings. Help us especially to perceive the goodness in one another and live in peace and cooperation and the fullness of shared spirits. Comfort the mind bereaved, give wholeness to those who are ill, instruct the heart that seeks, and embrace the lost and lonely, for you are the God of all our

113

adoration and the object of all heavenly praise. Give ear to our prayers, and let your will be done in our lives, through Jesus Christ. Amen. (John Killinger)

SERMON BRIEFS

TO DREAM THE IMPOSSIBLE DREAM

EZEKIEL 37:1-14

Psychologists tell us that everyone dreams at least two or three dreams each night; we just don't always remember them. But a dream like Ezekiel's stays with you!

Ezekiel is standing around the coffee and doughnuts with the other prophets one morning. It's still ten until eight, so he says, "You're not going to believe this dream I had." Another prophet wipes the powdered sugar from his mouth and says, "Tell us about it."

He tells how the Lord set him among a parched pile of bones. The Hebrew meaning implies he crawled among them. Insects had long since eaten the flesh away. They had become brittle. Then God spoke, "Can these bones live?" Ezekiel responded, "O Lord GOD, you know." The old prophet knew that anything is possible with God.

Then God commanded Ezekiel to preach to those bones. Picture an old country church with a cemetery beside it, only with bones scattered everywhere, bones outside and *inside* the church. Then God asks you to preach a sermon. Ezekiel's sermon went like this: God is going to breathe new life into you. Life-giving breath.

That's Ezekiel's dream. Israel's bones had dried up. What happened was the Babylonian exile.

As U.S. citizens, we got a taste of exile when a group bombed the World Trade Center. Exile is realizing we are vulnerable, not as individuals but as a group. Imagine a *church* full of dry bones.

Ezekiel preached, and there was a rattling noise. The bones began to move, only they weren't breathing.

So God told Ezekiel to call forth the breath of God from the four winds of the earth. We miss it in English, but there's a wordplay in Hebrew. The word *ruah* is used ten times. The term can be translated as "breath," "wind," or "spirit." All three are used here. Ezekiel is led by the *ruah* (Spirit) of the Lord, who sends his *ruah* (breath), which comes from the *ruah* (winds) of the earth.

This passage conjures up images from Genesis 2, God breathing life into the creation. God's breath gives us life and sustains us every moment.

What a dream!

A church where bones come back to life. A God who makes impossible dreams come true. Who'd have dreamt it? (Mike Graves)

LIVING IN THE SPIRIT OF LIFE

ROMANS 8:6-11

The miracle of salvation is beyond human comprehension when viewed from the perspective of redeeming fallen human nature. While the act of faith is so simple in terms of believing in Christ, regeneration by the Holy Spirit is nothing less than a bona fide miracle. In this text, Paul describes the unfolding of spiritual maturity after an individual steps into the life-giving experience of salvation by grace.

I. We All Share a Sinful Nature

Paul describes our fallen human nature in these verses. This nature needs redemption, which is accomplished in the death and resurrection of Jesus Christ. The "mind" or thinking of human sinful nature is "death" (v. 6). Death was introduced in God's creation through the disobedience of humanity's progenitors, Adam and Eve (Rom. 5:12-21). Since that corporate act of disobedience, fallen human nature has been moving uncontrollably toward ultimate death.

Paul continues to define the character of sinful nature beyond its obsession to be driven toward death. The sinful mind is hostile to God (v. 7). Literally, there is an opposition in the mind-set of our sinful nature to God's nature and ways. The unregenerate mind does not submit to the righteous requirements of God. In fact, Paul notes that it does not even have the capacity to do so. Finally, Paul says that those living under the control of the sinful nature cannot please God (v. 8).

This description of fallen human nature as disobedient, unpleasing, and hostile toward God (the giver of life) highlights its ultimate goal of death. Around us each day are news stories giving graphic details of extreme examples of the fallenness of humanity. Those realistic accounts and Paul's theological description bring a dark prospect for the future of humanity. This pessimistic view, however, only directs our attention to a necessity to transform and redeem this fallen nature. In contrast to this dark picture, Paul exhorts us, "You are not in the flesh; you are in the Spirit" (v. 9).

There is more to the story than our sinful nature.

II. Christians Also Bear the Nature of God

For persons who have the Spirit of God in them—that is, those regenerated by grace through faith (an act of the Holy Spirit)—the picture of sinful nature is different. For believers, there is an ongoing process in which this old nature is being destroyed. Paul declares that the power of sin in our bodies is dead, but we are spiritually alive because of righteousness (v. 10)—Jesus Christ is believers' righteousness.

This redemption of our nature, this transformation of our spiritual character, signifies not only the presence of the Holy Spirit in our lives (v. 9) but also our identity with Christ. We are the possession of Christ, bought with his atoning sacrifice. The purpose of redemption was to return humanity to its rightful place in relationship with its Creator. The sense of alienation and isolation has been with humans since the Fall, and it is part of our society today. Redeemed nature abolishes that alienation to make us joint heirs with Jesus Christ.

III. Christians Also Enjoy a Promise of Eternal Life

The last verse of the text raises a final issue in regard to the Holy Spirit's miracle of redemption: resurrection. The same Spirit that raised Christ from the dead lives within each believer. The presence of the Holy Spirit not only seals redemption for believers but also promises an eternal quality of life given to the mortal bodies. The Holy Spirit not only regenerates but resurrects. The promise of that miracle in the life of a Christian is as sure as Christ's resurrection. (Joseph Byrd)

THE PROMISE THAT TRANSFORMS DEATH

JOHN 11:1-45

Several years ago a highlight of a pilgrimage to Israel was a visit to the traditional tomb of Lazarus. In Bethany, some two miles from Jerusalem, we saw the beautiful present church and explored the ruins of churches built on that site to mark the tomb of Lazarus since the fourth century. Taking a candle, I went down the twenty-three steps into the tomb of Lazarus. Just a small, dark room, but a room tied to one of the most beautiful stories in the New Testament, and a shadow of Easter.

We realize from the various references in the Gospels of Luke and John that Jesus was especially close to Mary, Martha, and Lazarus, a family in the little village of Bethany. Their home was a haven from the hate of his enemies, an island of calm amidst the turmoil of his ministry. But tragedy strikes even in the midst of this peaceful scene. Death, the most common experience of life, lays its icy hand on Lazarus, Jesus' friend. And we note that people haven't changed in the two thousand years since that time—like us, they send word of Lazarus' deepening illness to the One they want near them in this crisis. But Lazarus dies before Jesus returns, and friends gather from Jerusalem and the surrounding countryside.

There are confusion and anguish and even anger toward Jesus on the part of Mary and Martha. When Martha first goes to meet Jesus on his return, Mary stays at home to be with the friends. When Mary quietly leaves to see Jesus, the friends follow her, thinking she has gone to the cemetery to weep there. When Jesus stands crying at the tomb, the bystanders murmur softly, "See how he loved him." People haven't changed.

I. Miracles Remind Us of God's Glory

One of the great lessons of this story is found in the hesitation of Jesus when he gets word that Lazarus is sick. Jesus waits two days before starting for Bethany. The reason is twofold. First, this sickness is not for death, but for the glory of God. Can it be true that our sickness and trouble can also be said to be for the glory of God? Can God be glorified in whatever befalls his children? Jesus lingers because his waiting, until Lazarus is dead and buried, is part of this event being used to glorify God. Second, Jesus lingers because he is, no doubt, struggling to find the response to this illness that will both help his friends and be true to the will of God.

When Jesus reaches Bethany, he faces three problems. First, Lazarus has been dead four days. The Jews thought the spirit lingered about the body for three days, but then as the body began to show signs of deterioration, the spirit left and all hope was abandoned. Lazarus had been buried for four days. Second, many Jerusalem Jews were gathered in the home. Naturally, they would not do him harm in such circumstances, but word would get to the authorities. Here we see the gospel prefigured. Coming to bring life to his friend jeopardized Jesus' life. And, third, the sisters are confused and even angry with Jesus. Martha's frustration (v. 21) gives way to hope as she says that she knows whatever Jesus asks of God, he will receive. Perhaps she remembered the claim of Jesus recorded in John 5:21: "Just as the Father raises the dead and gives them life, so also the Son gives life to whomever he wishes."

When Mary sees Jesus, she also expresses her disappointment that Jesus was not there in time—the sisters had plenty of time to talk about that. We should notice that with Mary, Jesus cannot talk about it; he is filled with emotion at her tears and the weeping of those with Mary. "Where have you put him?" "Lord, come and see!" What a turnaround! We remember Jesus inviting the first disciples to "come and see" where he, the Light and Life, was staying—here a brokenhearted woman bids the Lord "come and see" where death rules!

Jesus wept. It is a softer Greek word than the wailing of Mary and the crowd, but surely as deep. They stand before the tomb. At the command of Jesus the stone is removed from the grave, while the grieving sisters look on in fear.

II. Miracles Point Us to God's Presence

"Lazarus, come out!" shouted Jesus. And he did, still bound in the grave-wrappings. What a moment! "Loose him, and let him go!" Perhaps the most amazing thing about this story is not that Jesus raised a man who had been dead for four days, but that some people who saw it apparently didn't believe it! (See vv. 45-46.)

III. What's the Point of the Miracle?

When we look carefully at this miracle, we see that it is meant to convince people not that Lazarus came back from the grave—although he did—but that Jesus had come from God. Look at the prayer of Jesus just before he called Lazarus out (vv. 41-42). The raising of Lazarus is a sign pointing to the resurrection of Jesus.

Jesus' resurrection is all that Lazarus's raising was not. Notice several points. First, Lazarus could come out only after men rolled away the stone—not so with Jesus' resurrection. Second, Lazarus came forth bound in the grave-wrappings, symbolic of the fact that he would need them again—not so Jesus, whose grave-wrappings were left in the grave because he would need neither wrappings nor grave again. Third, Lazarus returned to his daily round of sin and struggle—Jesus returned to heaven. Lazarus was merely a shadow, a sign pointing to the reality of Jesus' resurrection.

IV. Believest Thou This?

Now let us go back to the conversation of Martha with Jesus as she met him at the edge of Bethany (v. 23). Jesus tells Martha that her brother will rise again. Martha believes in the resurrection at the last day, the Judgment Day. We will all—both good and bad—be resurrected. That's not a special Christian doctrine; the simple hope of the resurrection of the body is not at the heart of Easter. Don't pin your hopes of victory over death on the resurrection of the Judgment Day. Many people are going to be resurrected, only to be sent away forever from the presence of God.

Jesus wants Martha to go beyond the teaching of the resurrection of the body: "I am the resurrection and the life." Apart from Jesus, that resurrection we will all experience is just a replay, at the end of the world, of the raising of Lazarus—no new life. Jesus is Lord of death, Lord of life, Lord of the resurrection. To believers, death is not important: those who have trusted Jesus are not dead but have made the transition to a more beautiful, eternal life with Jesus. Those who are alive and believe in Jesus will never really die—we will fall asleep and wake up at home in the Father's house.

Martha earlier said she knew as fact that her brother would rise again on the last day. Now she says, in faith, that she believes, trusts

Jesus as the Messiah, the Son of God, the One who is to come into the world.

I ask you the same question: Do you believe Jesus is the Christ? The true meaning of Easter is found not by belief in the fact of a resurrection, but by commitment to a person, Jesus. For only that trust will avail to apply the blood for cleansing of sins, for the defeat of death. (Earl C. Davis)

MARCH 31, 1996

❧

Palm/Passion Sunday (Sixth Sunday in Lent)

Worship Theme: Through Christ's death, we receive eternal life.

Readings: Isaiah 50:4-9*a*; Philippians 2:5-11; Matthew 27:33-42

Call to Worship (Psalm 118:1, 19, 22-24):

Leader: O give thanks to the LORD, for he is good;

***People:* his steadfast love endures forever! . . .**

Leader: Open to me the gates of righteousness, that I may enter through them

***People:* and give thanks to the LORD.**

Leader: The stone that the builders rejected has become the chief cornerstone.

***People:* This is the LORD's doing; it is marvelous in our eyes.**

Leader: This is the day that the LORD has made;

***All:* let us rejoice and be glad in it.**

Pastoral Prayer:

O God of earthquake, fire, and storm, yet God of the still, small voice that speaks within the human heart, teach us how to listen to you each day of our lives; how to hear your whispers of love and mercy, inviting us to find fullness of life by seeking your face; how to read the signs of your direction for living in the world, not with grasping or holding but with celebration and sharing. Teach us how to respond to your shouts of disapproval that many of your children are being left to starve or sleep in the cold or work in an unhealthy environment. It is so easy for us to live thoughtlessly and selfishly, and even to line the roads for Jesus, the way those people did on the first Palm Sunday, without understanding what it means to be

121

committed to him and the truth for which he died. We rise, we eat, we work, we eat again, and at the end of the day we sleep, in an endless succession of days. And if we do not think of you or listen to you or praise your name, how much better are we than the animals in the field or the pagans who live as the animals do? Show us a better way, O God, and draw us into it. Let our days become testaments of consciousness and of love, linking to one another as parts of a journey of growth and devotion, bringing us at last to the foot of your heavenly throne, where we shall fall down in worship and adoration, filled with a sense of your worth and glory forever. Help us to walk with Christ through this holy, somber week, remembering his suffering, savoring his love, and preparing our hearts for the Day of Resurrection when we will sing and dance and praise your name as though forever! Amen. (John Killinger)

SERMON BRIEFS

SERVING THE SUFFERING

ISAIAH 50:4-9a

In the movie *The Doctor*, William Hurt plays Jack McKee, an accomplished surgeon who jokes around, dances to music, and flirts with the nurses during surgery. On rounds with his interns he warns against involvement with patients: "I'd rather you cut straight and care less." He favorite saying is, "I know about pain. I'm a doctor."

But he learns that knowing about pain and experiencing pain are different. He is diagnosed with a malignant tumor. As he begins radiation therapy, he is outraged at how he is treated. He doesn't think he should have to wait like other patients, fill out forms, or share a room. And he is particularly upset about the callousness of his physician.

Everyone knows a doctor who is insensitive. Everyone knows a minister who doesn't seem to care. According to Isaiah, however, the servant should be caring and also personally acquainted with pain.

This text comprises the third of Isaiah's four servant songs. Everyone is familiar with the last one, "a man of suffering and acquainted with infirmity" (Isa. 53:3). That fourth song is the climax, but this is the first of the servant songs to speak of suffering. This is the song of preparation.

Isaiah declares that God has given him "the tongue of a teacher," that he might know how "to sustain the weary with a word" (v. 4). But God has also given him the ear of a disciple. Verse 5 literally reads, "The Lord GOD dug out my ear." In addition to the pain of being struck, having his beard plucked out, and being spat upon, he knew the pain of having his ear opened up.

From a New Testament perspective on this Passion Sunday, we acknowledge that these verses extend beyond the prophetic ministry of Isaiah to the messianic ministry of Jesus. Jesus was not only a suffering servant but also a servant to the suffering. He could look out over a crowded synagogue and sense the pain of a disabled and isolated woman in a man's world (Luke 13:10-17). He could look out over a group of people and cry for them who were like sheep without a shepherd (Matt 9:35-38). He could look out over a city and want to gather up the people like a mother hen protecting her chicks (Luke 13:34-35).

Jesus comforts us with the tongue of one who has learned about suffering and of one who has heard it and experienced it. Jesus knows your pain. He hears it. He has felt it. He will speak to it.

In the movie McKee learns what it means to care. In fact, he sees to it that his interns check into the hospital to eat hospital food, sleep in hospital beds, and undergo all of the appropriate tests for a variety of diagnoses. But the most significant evidence of his compassion is the relationship he forms with June, a young woman dying from a brain tumor. He learns from her what it means to care, and he sits with her on her deathbed, holding her hand.

After her death, he reads a letter she had written that includes a story: "There once was a farmer who owned much land and who used to keep the animals from his fields with traps. But the farmer was very lonely. So he stood in his fields with his arms outstretched calling the animals to himself, but none came. They were afraid of what looked to them like a new scarecrow."

June then writes, "Jack, let down your arms and people will come to you."

Of course, you and I know that people came to Jesus because he held his arms out, there on the cross. (Mike Graves)

HYMN OF HUMILITY

PHILIPPIANS 2:5-11

Our text contains a hymn that captures the nature of Christ. He calls and empowers believers to take on this nature. As we allow the Holy Spirit to carve us into Christ's image, we cannot dismiss Paul's charge that our attitude should be the same as Jesus Christ's (v. 5).

Redeemed nature includes a "new mind" or manner of thinking. What is our view of life, others, and ourselves in relation to them? Discipleship demands that we place even the area of our attitude under the lordship of Christ. How we think is part of our spirituality.

I. We Are Called to a Christlike Attitude

In verses 6-8, Paul describes the attitude of Christ. This attitude serves as our model. The first characteristic of the attitude of Christ is that of being nonpresumptuous. While Jesus bore the full nature of God, he did not selfishly assert it by reaching to grasp it (v. 6). As we see in verses 9-11, he waited for the exaltation of the Father. Human nature whines with arrogance, struggling to establish who we are and our value. It is not fashionable to wait for honors to be bestowed; we quickly point out how we were "overlooked" or "robbed" of our "earnings." As believers, however, our human nature is to be mortified, and we are to take on the nature of Christ to be nonpresumptuous, awaiting God's timing to bring deserved honor.

The second element of Christ's attitude is the nature of servanthood (v. 7). We might have exclaimed, "As the Son of God, I have the right to be worshiped and to be served, not to serve!" Sadly, even in the body of Christ, some speak more about rights than about New Testament responsibilities. But our attitude is to be willing to serve, not demand service.

Finally, Paul describes the attitude of Christ as humble obedience (v. 8). Christ was obedient unto death—death that he has conquered—even the shameful death of the cross. Obedience to God's Word and reverence for authority are parts of the Christian attitude. This attitude can be viewed as weak, but Jesus described kingdom members as "meek" (that is, self-controlled). A willingness to submit in obedience is an act of free will demanded of persons of faith.

II. God Honors Those with a Christlike Attitude

Because of Jesus' humble attitude, God exalted him to the highest place (v. 9). Christ's refusal to grasp the honor or exaltation results in the action of the Father of bestowing the honor due him as the Son of God. Verses 10-11 note that every knee would bow in worship and every tongue utter to confess Jesus as Lord.

Fallen human nature is tainted by the impact of Satan's vices. Lucifer, once the angelic worship leader, fell in arrogance grasping what was not his (the glory of God). Human beings, tainted with sinful nature, struggle for their recognition. But Christ came not grasping what was rightly his but awaiting the Father's bestowal. The Father was faithful to exalt Christ who receives the worship due him.

What are we willing to wait for? Do we trust God enough to allow God to be faithful in our lives? Do we view the intensity of a circumstance and desire to take it into our own hands since our pride is at stake? The fallen nature says, "Defend yourself and grasp what is yours." The redeemed nature reflects Christ's attitude of trusting the faithfulness of the Father. He will make all things beautiful and complete in his time. (Joseph Byrd)

HOW TO BUILD A CROSS

MATTHEW 27:33-42

Shall we build a cross? Crosses were commonplace two thousand years ago. Seventy years before Christ, after the smashing of the revolt of Spartacus, roads to Rome were lined with 6,000 crosses and 6,000 men dying on them. At the death of Herod the Great a revolt broke out, and the Romans crucified 2,000 people in Jerusalem. In A.D. 70 at the siege of Jerusalem, the Roman troops crucified as many as 500 Jews daily for several months.

In 1968, during excavations in Jerusalem following the Six-Day War, the remains of a man clearly put to death by crucifixion were found in a hidden tomb. His name was Jehohanan; in his late twenties, he was obviously from a well-to-do family. Jehohanan was fastened to the cross by nails, there being no standard way to put a cross together or to put a person on it. The victim could be fastened to the crossbar by either ropes or nails. Without some other support a person would die within two or three hours on the cross from muscular spasms and asphyxia, so the Romans devised ways to prolong the agony: a pointed peglike affair as a seat, and a footrest. With these aids, a person might linger for days. A long nail was driven through Jehohanan's heels; the nail went on into the upright beam and bent when it hit a knot in the hard olivewood. When his family attempted to get him off the cross after death, they had to cut off his feet, then bury a small section of the cross with his feet still attached to it, and the archaeologists found that.

How you build a cross depends on its use. If it is to be worn as a trinket around your neck, that's one thing. Arthur Blessit, on the other hand, puts wheels on the crosses he pulls across the country. In Passion plays the crosses are made of light wood. The rows of white crosses in cemeteries are often made of stone.

If you are going to save a sinful world by means of it, defeat all the powers of evil with it, crucify the Son of God on it, then making a cross requires more than fine craftsmanship, more than a vertical stake and a crossbar. Look with me at the kind of cross we need to build on which to crucify Jesus.

I. Endure God's Curse

Deuteronomy 21:22-23 tells us how shameful this death on the cross was, and we've lost that reality. Someone from the first century walking our streets today would be utterly appalled to see the cross on our churches and around our necks. It would be similar to you coming back to earth five hundred years from now and seeing little electric chairs on churches and on chains around folks' necks. Paul says the preaching of the Cross is foolishness to the Greeks and a stumbling block to the Jews. Yet he does not hide the shame of the cross. He embraces it, saying in Galatians 3:13 that Christ became a curse for us. The One who died on that center cross that day died as a man accursed by people and by God; a criminal soon to be dead, buried, and forgotten.

A drama pictures the mother of Jesus years after his crucifixion. Another son, Joses, and his wife have a new baby boy. They ask Mary what they should name him, and Mary stands gazing out the window for a time, then turns with tears in her eyes and, fumbling with her apron, says, "I would have you name the child Jesus. . . . I would not have him forgotten." Crucified, cursed, but forgotten? Never. But as we build our cross let us remember it must:

II. Hold a God

The irony is that the cursed One being nailed up is no ordinary thirty-year-old in the vigor of manhood; he is also God: "In Christ God was reconciling the world to himself " (2 Cor. 5:19). So what we have on the cross is divinity wrapped in human flesh; God willing to dwell among us and suffer with us and for us, for a higher purpose than anyone gathered around that cross that day could grasp. But let us keep working on this cross. It must be strong enough to:

III. Hold the Sins of the World

On the cross Jesus becomes the very embodiment of sin. Isaiah 53 vividly points out twelve ways that all the sins of the world—your sins and mine—were heaped on the God-man Jesus on the cross that day: "The LORD has laid on him the iniquity of us all" (v. 6). Peter, who may have stood at the edge of the crowd with head bowed in grief and shame, tells us that Jesus "bore our sins in his body on the cross" (1 Pet. 2:24). What a paradox! All the sin of this world gathered to the cross on which is dying the only sinless person ever to set foot on this earth. But let us keep building, for the cross must also hold the:

IV. Loneliest Man Who Ever Lived

There has never been a darkness like what spread over that hill at noon that day and covered the cross of the man Jesus. For when the sins of every human being gathered at the cross, he suffered the depths of all that sin means, and it is seen in the bitterest cry ever wrung from human heart: "My God, my God, why have you forsaken me?" (Mark 15:34). We know that just as the essence of heaven is the presence of God, so also the essence of hell is eternal separation from God, and that this cry is the agony of hell itself. Consider further the cross we are building for Jesus. It must be:

V. A Tall Cross

This cross of Jesus towers not just over the crosses of the condemned men on either side of him, but over all the ages, to draw people to it through the years. Jesus told Nicodemus that just as Moses lifted up the pole with the bronze serpent on it for the healing of the Israelites, even so must Jesus be lifted up on his cross, above all the nations, all the tyrants, all human achievements, for his lifting up is the only way men and women, boys and girls, can see the terrible power of their sin and the sacrifice of Jesus that sets us free.

VI. Rooted in the Heart of God

Christ took upon himself our sins by the will and appointment of God. He came as the old hymn says, from the heart of God, and that is also why the darkness and the agony of the cross were so deep. John 3:16 leaves us no doubt that Jesus came because God so loved the world. There is no division between the Father and the Son in their love and purpose—the Son of God came gladly, joyfully, to walk the road of the cross in obedience to the Father's will, and to offer himself up as the greatest act of love ever to grace this universe. I mention only one other aspect of the cross of Jesus; it must be strong enough to:

VII. Hold Two Persons

Remember what Paul said in Galatians 2:19: "I have been crucified with Christ." The New Testament says that the Christian "suffers with Christ," is "crucified with Christ," "dead with him," "baptized into his death," and "buried with him." We who believe are to be identified with Christ in his life, his ministry, his death. Yet in the deepest sense there is no way we can go with him all the way, nor could we have been actually crucified with him on the same cross. We cannot face the darkness he faced, endure the punishment, bear the sins, or die under that ridicule with a prayer upon our lips because we are not the perfect Son of God, the sacrifice without blemish for the sins of the world.

But we can kneel at the foot of that cross we have built. Built with our hands? No, built with our sins. We can kneel there and confess that when we survey the cross on which the Prince of Glory died, our richest gain we count but loss, and pour contempt on all our pride. We can kneel there and determine that love so amazing, so divine, demands our souls, our lives, our all. We can kneel at his cross in repentance and contrition, and accept forgiveness, healing, and peace. (Earl C. Davis)

APRIL

ॐ

Preparing to Serve

The Symbol of the Cup

Paraphrase Assignment:
First Corinthians 11:25*b*: "This cup is the new covenant in my blood."

Prayer Assignment:
In the symbol of the cup is suggested willingness to do all the will of God. List some unconquered areas in your life where you still (perhaps after many years) need to say, "Not my will but thine be done." Then begin to reckon with how to lead the people into a more submissive spirit concerning the will of God for their lives.

Journal-in-Worship Assignment:
Let us contrast for Holy Week three cups: the cup of abundance, the cup of refreshment, and the cup of requirement. Write a few paragraphs as your celebration, but write them so carefully that they might awaken the whole church to celebration. In your writing, discuss how the three relate. How does the cup of abundance, for instance, point out the cup of refreshment? In fact, isn't it the cup of refreshment that prefaces the cup of abundance? Can you point out some ways that in the last week of Jesus' life all three cups were present? How closely have abundance and requirement come together in your own life? Isn't it equally true that through the cup of requirement, God offers the cups of refreshment and abundance?

Psalm 23:5. The cup of abundance is the topic. Write of some time when life was especially full of rich evidences of the blessings of God. In what way did your cup run over? Was your testimony of God as lavish and abundant as God's blessings?

Matthew 10:42. The cup of refreshment is the topic. Reach back into your remembrance, and draw out a time when you were so spiritually arid that you were dying inside. How did Jesus come to you with the cup that slaked your thirst? Remember the savagery of your personal pain. Think through the sweetness of the water of life. Can you understand what Jesus meant when he promised the Samaritan woman in John 4:10 water so thoroughly satisfying that she would never thirst again? Write a paragraph or two confessing your need and his adequacy.

Mark 14:36. The cup of requirement is the topic. God gives us a cup that requires everything. Only those who are unreservedly committed can drink it. Contrast Jesus' cup with one you have had to drink in your life. Did you seek to turn from its heavy demands? In your devotional walk write about the cost of discipleship. What strong stands must the church of today take? What is required of you? Confess your feelings of inadequacy before the cup of God's requirement. How can your church members be encouraged to yield to the will of God as they drink of it? (Calvin Miller)

APRIL 5, 1996

৯৯

Good Friday

Worship Theme: Christ's death calls us to a response.

Readings: Isaiah 52:13–53:12; Hebrews 10:16-25; John 18:1–19:42

Call to Worship (Psalm 22:1-5, 27-28):

Leader: My God, my God, why have you forsaken me? Why are you so far from helping me, from the words of my groaning?

***People:* O my God, I cry by day, but you do not answer; and by night, but find no rest.**

Leader: Yet you are holy, enthroned on the praises of Israel.

***People:* In you our ancestors trusted; they trusted, and you delivered them..**

Leader: To you they cried, and were saved;

***People:* In you they trusted, and were not put to shame.**

Leader: All the ends of the earth shall remember and turn to the Lord;

***People:* and all the families of the nations shall worship before him.**

Leader: For dominion belongs to the Lord,

***All:* And he rules over the nations.**

Pastoral Prayer:

Why do we call this Good Friday? O Lord, as we consider the events of this day so many years ago, they seem anything but good. We consider in horror as Pilate passes judgment; horror, because we stood next to Pilate and confirmed the decree. We look on in pain as we see the soldiers whip and mock him; pain, for we stood there also, handing them the tools of punishment. We tremble in agony as we view Jesus hanging on that cross; agony, for we helped strike each blow on each nail. Truly, O Lord, there was nothing good about that day, and we stand before you guilty of sending Jesus to death on a cross; guilty because it was our sin, our rebellion, our self-centeredness he came to overcome, to forgive.

And yet, Father, we know that this day is good; not good because of anything we have done, but good because of your grace and power. You took this awesome, awful event and transformed it into an act of redemption. Forever after, the cross that had been a symbol of brutality was transformed into a symbol of overpowering love, which will reach to any length to restore your lost ones. Though we were once lost, O Lord, today we are found because of what Jesus did on that cross. It has become for us and for all humanity a Good Friday. Allow this day to once again do its transforming work in our lives and our hearts, for we ask it in the name of the One who gave himself for us, and who even now intercedes for us. Amen.

SERMON BRIEF

MISTAKES THAT MAKE THE DIFFERENCE

JOHN 19:13-16

I once made a mistake in buying a car. I allowed myself to act without adequate study, preparation, and evaluation. I made an impulse buy, the kind retailers only dream of! Sure enough, I hadn't been driving the car more than a few weeks before I began finding all kinds of things I absolutely hated about the car; within six months, I was trading it for another one (and losing plenty of money in the process). I'm glad you never make mistakes like that!

Mistakes come in all sizes, don't they? Some are small and have little long-term impact; other mistakes have enormous implications. They are like a stone thrown into a tranquil pond; the ripples can be seen far from the point of impact.

They had arrested Jesus and brought him to Pilate, who wanted nothing to do with this itinerant preacher. Yet politics being what they were, Pilate found himself backed into a corner and felt compelled to act on the mob's demands.

Some terrible mistakes were made that day; misjudgments that would have far-reaching implications.

I. They made the mistake of thinking Pilate was the real judge.

As Pilate sat at the judge's bench preparing to announce his decision, he saw only the short-term. He thought he was the only judge on that stone platform that day, but he was tragically wrong. The One who will someday judge all humanity, including Pilate, stood next to the Roman that day. Pilate just couldn't see it.

It is easy to judge reality only on the basis of what we see around us. Pilate saw the Roman soldiers with their weapons, answerable to him, and thought he had the real power. He just didn't realize what authentic power was.

Will you make the same mistake, evaluating life by the wrong criteria, and miss the truth of God's presence?

II. They made the mistake of overlooking their real preparation.

It was the day of Preparation for Passover, John tells us, when they would celebrate God's deliverance of his people in Egypt. It was an important religious ceremony, a time to worship God. Yet they foolishly overlooked the very Son of God who was standing in their presence—the only one who could truly prepare them to encounter the holy and true God.

Sometimes we make such mistakes. We get caught up in the externals of religion and lose contact with the deeper realities of faith.

Will you make the same mistake, allowing your attention to be diverted by ceremony or other external factors, and miss entirely the reality of God's presence?

III. They made the mistake of ignoring their real king.

The world looked to Caesar as the ultimate political power. Pilate certainly did, for his power was delegated by the emperor. The Sanhedrin did, for they knew their own protected status depended on a conciliatory attitude with the Roman authorities. The mob did, for they declared, "We have no king but the emperor."

They simply didn't realize that the one who stood before them as the accused was the true king—King of kings and Lord of lords. This one they were about to crucify was actually the one who will reign over all creation. Pilate didn't realize how true his words were when he asked the mob, "Shall I crucify your King?" The tragedy was that they ignored their true king.

Will you make the same mistake, placing your loyalties and your allegiance with the wrong ruler, and miss the true King who seeks a place in your heart?

Mistakes are only permanent when we refuse to correct them. Don't make the mistake of failing to recognize Jesus for who he truly is, and failing to surrender your heart and life to the true King. (Michael Duduit)

APRIL 7, 1996

୫

Easter Day

Worship Theme: The resurrection of Jesus Christ offers us hope and new life.

Readings: Jeremiah 31:1-6; Colossians 3:1-4; John 20:1-18

Call to Worship (Psalm 118:14-17, 19-20):

Leader: The LORD is my strength and my might;

People: he has become my salvation.

Leader: There are glad songs of victory in the tents of the righteous: "The right hand of the LORD does valiantly; the right hand of the LORD is exalted. . . . " I shall not die, but I shall live,

People: and recount the deeds of the LORD.

Leader: Open to me the gates of righteousness, that I may enter through them

People: and give thanks to the LORD.

Leader: This is the gate of the LORD;

People: the righteous shall enter through it.

Pastoral Prayer:

We remember many things on this special morning, O Lord: the thrill of a new bonnet or a new pair of shoes; the colored eggs hidden in the grass; the scent of lilies in the air; the great music; the crowds of people in church, on the streets, in the restaurants; the feeling of newness in the world; the sense of something transcendent, reaching beyond this world and uniting it with the life beyond. We praise you for the transcendence, for the awareness of divine presence, for the knowledge that when all earth's stories are told, of war and famine and disease and suffering, there is something else, another story of a man who truly

135

lived and loved and gave himself, who died on a cross and was raised to new life out of the very grave itself! How different our lives are because of this story, Lord! How different the world is because of it!

We hold before you today the entire community of faith in every part of the world—brothers and sisters in Christ in Zimbabwe and Brazil, in Denmark and Russia, in Korea and Nicaragua, and wherever hands are lifted to you in prayer. Let us all remember the victory of Christ and live in the coming triumph of your Kingdom. Even where there are fighting and sickness and starvation, where people die and there is much sadness, grant that there may also be a mood of hope and expectancy, an inner certainty that you will not forsake those to whom you have revealed and promised so much in your Son Jesus. We know that night is often darkest before the dawn, and therefore we are bold to pray even now, when there are so much unrest and injustice in the world, that your redemption may quickly come; that little children may grow up in a world without drugs; that mothers and fathers may always love one another; that elderly people may walk on the streets without fear; that poor people will be fed from the tables of the rich, and homeless people sheltered in the houses of the wealthy; and that all people will resort daily to the altars and sanctuaries of the Most High, to give you thanks and to receive your blessing and to live peaceably and joyfully with all their neighbors. To that end, receive and bless our worship here this day, and let your name be praised in glory by all the saints and angels, both here and in eternity, forever and ever. Amen. (John Killinger)

SERMON BRIEFS

EASTER: A TIME OF HOPE

JEREMIAH 31:1-6

Easter is a time of hope. After the gray days of winter, spring comes and life returns. Flowers bloom, leaves appear on trees, and green grass begins to grow. In the Christian life, Easter is a reminder of the hope we have in Christ. No matter the circumstance or the situation in which we find ourselves, we are reminded of new life in Christ.

Jeremiah is writing to people in despair. He has told them that their cities will be destroyed, and they will be taken captive by the Babylonians. We come to chapter 31 and the prophet's message of hope to a broken people. He speaks at least three messages from God that provide words of hope to broken lives today.

I. I See Your Condition (vv. 1-2)

First, the prophet assures the people of God's awareness of their broken condition. They are going to be taken in chains to a strange place, will raise their children in a foreign land, and will be dispersed across the northern kingdom. However, God will be with them.

Sometimes life doesn't seem to make sense. The faithful of Israel will suffer alongside the wicked. Why doesn't God punish the wicked and spare the innocents of the world? Rabbi Harold Kushner asks the same question of many: "Why do bad things happen to good people?" Surely, Easter reminds us that God understands suffering.

On that Friday we call "good," God watched his only Son die on a cross. Charles Bugg, in *Learning to Dream Again,* says of that day: "This God is a God who knows what it is to lose a child." God sees the condition of his people.

II. I Will Always Be with You (v. 3)

The prophet next reminds his hearers of God's steadfast love. God's love has been faithful even when Israel turned its back on God. Jeremiah says that God has never left or forsaken the people. Rather, God has "loved you with an everlasting love."

God's love is faithful and true today. The often quoted poem "Footprints in the Sand" reminds us that in the lowest and saddest times of life, God carries us. It's more than poetry, isn't it? As we look back on painful experiences, we can see that God stood beside us, if only we would notice. As we recall shameful experiences of the past, when we wandered off into a wilderness of our own making, we know God was but a prayer away.

God overwhelms us with love. Jeremiah finds hope for the future only because of God's wondrous love. In the midst of a confusing world, God's love is the one point of stability providing hope that life will be better.

It is also this astonishing love of God that compels us to follow. James Leo Green says, "If the realization that he loves us with a limitless love that goes the limit for us will not 'draw' us—melt our hearts and wills into contrition and submission—nothing else will."

III. There Is Hope for the Future (vv. 4-6)

The final part of the passage tells of a great homecoming and a new relationship between God and his people. The people will return from exile, and there will once again be rejoicing in Jerusalem. Fields will be replanted, homes and lives will be rebuilt, and there will be music in the streets. Jeremiah reminds his hearers that this future is based not on the power of the people but on the will of God. Therefore, they will worship God in acknowledgment of this.

In the wintertimes of life, when darkness seems all around and hope is gone, we can know that the spring is coming, and in the spring, God will fill us with life again. (Greg Barr)

TRANSFORMED BY HIS RESURRECTION

COLOSSIANS 3:1-4

The New Testament's firm confirmation of the Resurrection is clear. However, demonstrating the relevance to human lives years after the event and among alien Gentile cultures was something of a task. Applying the Resurrection to contemporary lives is no less difficult or more necessary. This passage details the results of the Resurrection in our lives. Paul begins the passage by saying "so if" we have been raised with Christ, indicating that the following results should occur in our lives.

I. Our Desires Are Transformed

Paul begins in verse 1 to command us to seek things "above." It is so easy to fall into the trap of avoiding the New Testament command to "seek after God's righteousness and the material things will follow in due course." This passage indicates that our belief in the Resurrection (Christ's and ours) changes our desires and the things we value.

When we recognize the reality of the Resurrection, more real than finite life here, temporal things, problems, and wealth begin to pale. In light of eternity, the statement "you can't take it with you" has a deeper meaning. Children of faith have high values placed on those elements of eternal quality; that is our treasure.

II. Our Perspective Is Transformed

In verse 2, Paul calls us to set our "minds" on things above, not on earthly things. Our view of life and responses to our dealings in life are to be tempered by our perspective of the Resurrection.

When we examine *how* we think, we realize we are the ones who largely determine the quality of our lives. God "sends rain on the righteous and on the unrighteous" (Matt. 5:45). Those who have placed faith in Christ realize that a little rain is just a temporary hassle in the larger picture of an infinite future with Christ. We can continue in joy even when we face difficulty.

This perspective speaks of contentment in any circumstance and the fruit of joy and peace in the lives of believers.

III. Our Lives Are Transformed

Verses 3-4 touch on how believers' lives are transformed through the Resurrection. There are two dimensions of this transformation. The first is the present life before eternity. Christians have "died"— that is, through the Holy Spirit victory over sin becomes possible. Believers' lives are presently "hidden" in Christ, ultimately forgiven and ultimately changed to bear his nature and image. Such lives are those guided by his Spirit to proclaim Christ as Lord of creation and Lord of their lives.

The second dimension of our transformed lives lies in the future. When Christ appears, we are guaranteed that we will appear with him "in glory." We may experience moments of human exaltation— splashes of glory in this present life—but our future glory with Christ defies human description and can be grasped only by faith. Such splendor is the spectacular conclusion of our lives, which in comparison will seem like dull tales. But in God's plan, through the act of Christ's resurrection, our future glory is a reality awaiting the fullness of time. Our hearts and minds should be set on that reality. (Joseph Byrd)

THE QUESTIONS OF EASTER

JOHN 20:1-18

It is odd that we know so little about a woman whose testimony to the resurrection of the Lord Jesus is so central. I speak of Mary, called the Magdalene. Both Matthew and Mark mention her by name as coming to the tomb on Easter morning, and John's resurrection account is essentially her testimony. What do we really know of this woman? Since St. Augustine in the fifth century, the "sinner" woman of Luke 7 has been identified by many with this Mary. Is this "sinner" also the woman from whose life Jesus cast seven devils, and who joined that group of disciples following Jesus? Since the "sinner" woman—Mary Magdalene—and Lazarus's sister Mary both anointed Jesus' feet with perfume, are these women one and the same? Is Mary Magdalene the quiet, devoted Mary of the Mary and Martha stories?

She had the honor of being present at the death of Jesus; she stayed at the sepulchre when all the disciples went away; and Jesus appeared to her first and made her an apostle to the apostles. Nobody has a testimony like hers to the life, the love, the death, and the resurrection of Jesus—and of herself. But then, nobody has a testimony like yours or mine, either. Each Christian has a unique testimony of what Jesus' resurrection has meant to him or her. The tragedy is that we do not share more of the difference Jesus has made in our lives and our love for him. But look with me step by step at Mary Magdalene's testimony of Jesus' resurrection.

I. She Came to Easter with Questions

In John 20, we note that Mary Magdalene came to Easter with questions. She must have had dreams of a glorious new kingdom, of Jesus taking the throne of David and sending the Romans packing. What of those dreams now? Surely she must have had fears that, without the encouragement of Jesus, she would fall back into her old lifestyle of immorality.

I expect, on that bleak morning, that she was also harboring some disillusionment about the disciples. After all, the men who said they loved Jesus more than life itself had broken and run away. Only John dared stand at the cross with Mary Magdalene and the other women. All these feelings are summed up in a heavy, concrete way by a practical question Mary Magdalene and the women asked each other as they trudged along to the tomb: *Who will roll away for us the stone from the front of the tomb?*

Every honest person comes to Easter with questions. The unbeliever asks, "Could such a thing happen?" The Christian asks, "Why can't I, why don't I, live a purer, higher Christian life with the power of the Resurrection available to me?" And many folks come to Easter with disillusionment with modern disciples: "Why don't church people show more of the power and the presence of the risen Christ?" I suspect that the person who comes to Easter without questions is spiritually dead.

II. Easter Also Asks Us Questions

Matthew's account tells us there was a mighty earthquake, and an angel rolled back the heavy doorstone of the tomb and sat on it, while the soldiers fainted—so much for this world's power! Apparently, the women were nearby, for the angel gave them the facts succinctly: Jesus has risen; come and see; go and tell. The women went inside the tomb with their burden of spices and perfumes with which to anoint the body, and they stood there weeping, unclear and unconvinced by what the angel outside said. This does raise a question about angels, doesn't it? Someone said to me recently, "Wouldn't you think that if you saw an angel, you would believe what he—or she—or it—said?" Well, remember that angels don't always appear angelic, with wings, halo, and so on. In fact, these angels at the tomb are referred to in some of the Gospel accounts as simply young men.

The angelic messengers in the empty tomb asked questions of the women: *Why are you weeping? Who are you seeking? Why do you look for the living among the dead?* And Luke's Gospel tells us the angels reminded the women that Jesus had told them he must be crucified and rise on the third day. *Easter is a call to remember,* to remember the promises of Jesus that he would rise from the dead, and to remember the power of the Father, a power that not only raised Jesus from the dead but also abides in the life of the believer.

Apparently after seeing the empty tomb, Mary left the other women and ran to find Peter to tell him the body of Jesus was gone. It seems she missed the message of the angels in the tomb and left with only the message that the tomb was empty. Peter and the beloved disciple went to the tomb, and while they went in, Mary stood outside weeping.

She saw Jesus standing near the tomb and, not recognizing him, asked if he was the gardener; if he was responsible for having moved the body, and if so, where she may find it. She did not recognize the person of Jesus, but she immediately recognized his voice as he spoke to her, saying only one word, her name—Mary. She responded, "Master," and fell at his feet. Then Jesus cautioned her not to touch him, "I have not yet ascended to the Father."

Why didn't Mary recognize Jesus? Why did he not want her to touch him? Was he a ghost, a phantom, an intangible body her hands would go right through? Was his body of some otherworldly substance that her touch would contaminate? We simply do not know. It is clear that both her lack of recognition and his comment are tied to the fact that there is a definite change from the natural to the resurrected body, and that this is tied to his coming ascension. There is a mystery to the Easter story that comes under the verse: "What no eye has seen, nor ear heard, nor the human heart conceived, what God has prepared for those who love him" (1 Cor. 2:9). We won't understand all about the Resurrection until we wake up on the other side of this veil we call death.

One more question about Mary Magdalene's experience: *Why didn't the disciples believe the good news?* Luke's Gospel (24:9-11) tells us that the women went to the entire group of the apostles and told them all these things, but they received it as idle talk. It is because the resurrection of Jesus is unnatural. There is nothing natural about it. The Pharisees believed in a resurrection, but not just now! Jesus' resurrection violated all their beliefs about the resurrection of the just at the last day. We know that Jesus is the "firstfruits," the early harvest of all Christians who will be resurrected on the last day and who, from the moment of their trust in Jesus, are set free from the power of death and the devil. There is nothing natural about God in human flesh dying on a cross and being buried in a tomb, so there is nothing natural about his flinging open the gates of death! It was so unnatural for the Creator in human form to die that the sun hid itself at his death; and the earth shuddered in earthquake at his resurrection.

III. Faith Answers Our Questions

Resurrection is unnatural and unbelievable until you and I actually *experience the Resurrection in our own lives.* I know a woman who cries when we sing "Because He Lives," and one day she asked me, "Why doesn't everyone cry when singing those words?" The long-form answer is, folks are put together differently emotionally and so on. The short-form answer is, *we all would cry when we sing that hymn if we had her experience!* She met the risen Christ, experienced the reality of his resurrection and her own, as an adult. Like Mary Magdalene, she realized her need for an exchanged life. And in Jesus she received the power to exchange the old for the new, the dead for the living, the earthly for the heavenly.

Easter is where broken dreams and the power of Jesus' resurrection meet. Easter is where disappointments and angels clash. Easter is where the worst the devil could do is destroyed by the power and love of God.

Experience Mary's Christ. (Earl C. Davis)

APRIL 14, 1996

୬ଈ

Second Sunday of Easter

Worship Theme: We can receive the blessings of Easter through repentance and faith.

Readings: Acts 2:14*a*, 36-41; 1 Peter 1:3-9; John 20:19-31

Call to Worship (Psalm 16:7-11):

Leader: I bless the LORD who gives me counsel; in the night also my heart instructs me. I keep the LORD always before me;

People: **because he is at my right hand, I shall not be moved.**

Leader: Therefore my heart is glad, and my soul rejoices. . . . For you do not give me up to Sheol, or let your faithful one see the Pit. You show me the path of life.

People: **In your presence there is fullness of joy.**

Pastoral Prayer:

Guide our church, O Lord, into a new sense of what it means to be crucified for the world: to stop thinking about ourselves and think about our neighbors; to stop trying to be great through having and learn about being great through serving. Stir our imaginations to see the new world the prophets saw, and the new world Jesus saw, and let us recommit ourselves to that world in this present age: not a world of hurry and bustle and make do and get by, but a world of slowing down and listening and caring and sharing and celebrating the one true faith, revealed in a cross and an empty tomb. Embrace our visitors in your love. Lift the burdens of those whose hearts are heavy. Guide the lost back to the path. Touch with healing those who need it most. And help us to rejoice today in your Word, in your presence, and in the privilege of worship, for this is a special place and a special hour, and we hope for a special encounter, through Jesus Christ our Lord. Amen. (John Killinger)

SERMON BRIEFS

WHEN YOU'RE CUT TO THE HEART

ACTS 2:36-41

What do you do when you've been cut to the heart? In this passage, we find ourselves in Jerusalem on the day of Pentecost. Peter preached, and the people felt such guilt over their sin that they begged the apostles, saying, "Brothers, what should we do?"

The focus of the Lenten season is understanding the depth of our sin and separation from God. As Easter came closer, we began to understand more about Christ's sacrifice on the cross. Perhaps, like Peter's hearers, you have come to realize your role in the death of Christ. You see, Christ didn't die just for people who lived two thousand years ago. It was for our sins that the Savior suffered, bled, and died. When we are cut to the heart by this realization, what must we do? Peter gives us direction in this passage.

I. Repent

The first thing Peter told his audience to do is repent. Peter is not simply saying that his hearers should feel sorry for their sin; he is calling them to a new way of life. *Repent* is one of those "church words" we often throw around without explaining. Repentance is much like the military term *about-face*. To repent is not to look over our shoulders and say, "I'm sorry, God." To repent means that we stop going in our own direction, turn around, and choose to live in obedience to Christ.

II. Receive Forgiveness

Something amazing happens when we repent of sin and ask God for forgiveness. The Bible tells us that the past is washed away and all things become new. We are given a new heart, a new start, a second chance in life.

145

If you've ever wished that you could start all over again, free from the baggage of your past mistakes, God offers you that opportunity. Though physical or material consequences of your past may remain, in a spiritual sense, you are set free. There aren't many places in life where you get a second chance.

III. Be Baptized

Peter also called on his hearers to be baptized. While scholars seem to agree that Peter was not setting forth some ritual path to salvation, the rite of baptism was certainly emphasized in the early church. Baptism is an outward sign of an inward change in a person's life. The baptismal ceremony is symbolic of death and resurrection in Christ. The old person dies, and a new creature is born, emerging from the water to a new way of life.

IV. Receive the Holy Spirit

A person who is "born again" comes into a new realm of life. It is called "abundant life" in the Scripture. In addition to the Holy Spirit's role as a comforter, the Spirit provides direction and guidance in life. When the Holy Spirit takes up residence in a person's life, he or she begins to understand things from a different perspective.

The basic premise of Charles Sheldon's classic book *In His Steps* is that Christ has called us to do the things he would do if he were in our shoes and had our opportunities. As we learn to live the Spirit-filled life, we will find ourselves seeing, thinking, and acting differently from before.

What do you do when you are cut to the heart? Repent, ask for forgiveness, be baptized, and receive the Spirit. Peter's audience heard him gladly, and the Bible says that three thousand were added to the church that day. Throughout the centuries, others have responded to this same invitation. There is room for you to come today. (Greg Barr)

REJOICE IN DIFFICULTIES

1 PETER 1:3-9

Peter sets the theme of the entire Epistle in this passage. In writing to Christians who face trials, persecutions, and difficulties, he reminds them that they have been birthed into a "living hope."

So Christians live in circumstances identical to those of unbelievers (in the world), but Christians' life-view and perspective are qualitatively different because of this living hope—a hope not "of" the world. That difference is afforded to us by the Resurrection.

Christians rejoice in this life although we may have to suffer grief in all kinds of trials (v. 6). All humans live in a world impacted by sin. Life in all its fullness, as God meant it to be, is lost in the reality of our broken human estate. Bad things happen to good and bad people. Believers face even more opposition in that faith is challenged on every hand because of its radical claims and resistance to society's "worldly" values. But in light of these difficulties, Christians have three promises and three characteristics that give more intrinsic meaning to the trials.

People with faith in Christ can find a purpose in the trials and grow from them in the context of these promises and personal characteristics.

I. Three Promises Worthy of Our Rejoicing

The first promise is found in Peter's exclamation of praise in verse 3. Christians have been shown God's mercy by being birthed into a "living hope." Christian hope is more than a faint possible dream. It is a "living" or vibrant hope resting squarely on the fact of Christ's resurrection. If Christ was not raised from the dead, our faith would be futile and our hope emptied of value to the point we should be pitied among all humanity. But the power of the Resurrection makes Christian hope a living reality.

The second promise is no less real than the historical fact of Christ's resurrection, but it is grasped only through faith. This promise is an inheritance that can never spoil but is kept in heaven for the believer (v. 4). The New Testament is not shy about speaking of rewards or awaiting an ultimate resolution and justice. This may not bode well in a contemporary Western society bent on instant gratification. However, the hope of the Christian's inheritance to be received after passing from this life is beyond human comprehension and well worth any time of waiting.

The third promise is that of protection in this life until the consummation of the believer's salvation in the afterlife. The believer is "protected by the power of God" (v. 5). The New Testament notes the enemy of God is the enemy of God's children. This promise is one of protection from Satan. The result of this promise is the release from fear and anxiety. The Christian resides in the protective power of God.

II. Three Characteristics of Our Rejoicing

The purpose of trials is that our faith may be proven genuine. Our faith has greater value than gold (v. 7). Christian rejoicing in trials proves and strengthens our faith. Many of us rebel against the thought of continuing in difficulties with a purpose of strengthening our faith. But here Peter says the ultimate result is praise, glory, and honor as Christ is revealed through us. We too often lose sight of the fact that our attitude and demeanor tempered by faith during trials and difficulties reveal Christ to unbelievers and bring praise to God.

The second characteristic of our rejoicing in trials is the joy that flows from our faith (v. 8). We love and believe in Christ, though we have not seen him. The result of such faith is being filled with "indescribable and glorious joy." How joyful are we? The verse seems to indicate the level of our joy acts as a barometer for the level of our faith. The intensity and singleness of our faith are directly proportional to the ecstasy of our Christian joy. Can individuals discern a qualitative difference in us as Christians when viewing our level (or lack) of unspeakable joy?

The third characteristic of rejoicing is receiving the goal of faith: salvation (v. 9). The process of redemption is nothing short of miraculous or glorious. The fruit of that redemption should be obvious in our lives. It should be demonstrable in difficulties because of our joy and faith through the living hope. (Joseph Byrd)

THOMAS—THE DOUBTER?

JOHN 20:19-31

Thomas, called Didymus, is the only disciple whose name has become a household word. "Doubting Thomas," the disciple from Missouri. He may also be the most mysterious of the Twelve. He is paired with Matthew, is there any significance to that? We have the *Acts of Thomas* and the *Gospel of Thomas,* and they aren't anything like the canonical writings. Some legends say Thomas was a twin of Lydia of Philippi, and others that he was a twin brother of Jesus.

Some traditions say the Twelve divided up the world for evangelism, and Thomas got India. Tradition has it that Thomas was killed by a spear thrust while he prayed, and that a church was built on that spot. In the 1500s there was a group called Saint Thomas Christians in India.

What do we really know about Thomas? Aside from the lists of disciples in the New Testament, he appears in three passages of Scripture, all in the Gospel of John. In John 11:14-16, at the death of Lazarus, Thomas is willing to go with Jesus back to Judea, even if it means going to die with Jesus. That doesn't sound much like doubt, does it? In John 14:1-5, Thomas asks a question about the way to heaven, and it sounds more like confused ignorance of what Jesus is really saying than genuine doubt. Finally, in John 20:24-29, we read that when Thomas is told of the Easter evening appearance to the disciples at which he was not present, he responded by saying he would not believe Jesus had risen from the dead unless he, Thomas, could see the wounds of the Crucifixion and actually touch them. Now that sounds like doubt, doesn't it? Or shock at hearing what you desperately want to be true but cannot assimilate for joy?

I. Doubt Is Common to All

Have you ever doubted? Doubted God? Doubted your salvation? The typical response of an honest person is that "I often wonder about such things, but I try not to let myself." Every honest person has doubts. It is simply not given to human nature to have certainty in some areas of life.

There are two kinds of doubting people and two kinds of doubt. There is *dishonest doubt.* It is rooted in the proud, sinful mind. This kind of doubt says it must have verification, in its own way, on its own terms, in order to accept and believe. The person harboring this kind of doubt really does not wish to believe.

Then there is *honest doubt.* For instance, consider the healing of the child at the foot of the Mount of Transfiguration and the father's honest doubt: "I believe; help my unbelief" (Mark 9:24). And Jesus did not rebuke that man. Here we see the character of honest doubt; it is agony and yearns for light.

There is something strong, something good, in honest doubt. It is not negative or neutral; it is actively seeking faith. Remember the

149

words of Tennyson's *In Memoriam,* written upon the death of his friend, Arthur Hallam:

> Perplext in faith, but pure in deeds,
> At last he beat his music out.
> There lives more faith in honest doubt,
> Believe me, than in half the creeds.
>
> He found his doubts and gather'd strength,
> He would not make his judgment blind,
> He faced the specters of the mind
> And laid them; thus he came at length
>
> To find a stronger faith his own.

Those who pass through the valley of honest doubt emerge with stronger faith than those who never dared face their doubts. Few things are more worthy to be despised, or of less value as a witness, than a pale, inherited, convictionless, untested faith. God grant us all doubt rather than such a faith.

II. Doubt Isn't the Problem—Discouragement Is

But Thomas's problem is not doubt. We have tied that label on him for being late once to church. If only Thomas had been there. And we speculate on why he was absent. Overwhelming grief? Some business or family problem? Meeting with some group of followers of Jesus? Checking out the rumors of Emmaus Road? I think Thomas's rash demand to touch the wounds of Jesus was born of regret that he was absent from that first meeting with the risen Lord and maybe a mixture of feeling that one should not joke about such things, if the other disciples were joking. We are all aware that when the proof was offered—when Jesus offered to let Thomas actually touch the wounds—Thomas didn't take him up on it.

The problem is not doubt—we never should have labeled Thomas that way. We could equally well have labeled him "Thomas the loyal" in light of his willingness to go and die with Jesus. Or "Thomas the committed" as, on these weeks after Easter, Thomas fell on his knees without availing himself of the proof and declared, "My Lord and my God!"

No, Thomas has a problem shared by many other Christians; he is a melancholy, discouraged personality. He sometimes sounds like somebody who has been reading Ecclesiastes too much. His emotions were bigger than the rest of him. He illustrates a danger of the gloomy temperament, the hesitation to cast off for new and distant shores.

The cure for the gloomy spirit is the fellowship of the committed. Eight days after his absence he is back, surrounded by other personalities, and in the presence of the Lord. And all is well.

Here is what Jesus says to all those of Thomas's temperament and spirit. First, there is a higher form of faith than that based on sight (v. 29). Second, Thomas—and all who are his brothers and sisters in temperament—is important even if he is out of step. It is noteworthy that Jesus took seriously and followed through on Thomas's request, even if Thomas didn't! And, third, Thomas can move out of the shadows into the sunshine of a stronger, more robust faith. Surely, there is much truth in the traditions of his exciting ministry in India. And maybe the Lord is saying the same things to you. (Earl C. Davis)

COUNTING THE EVIDENCE

Acts 2:14a, 22-32

Do you enjoy those courtroom dramas on television or in the movies? The attorney skillfully accumulates the evidence and puts it on display in order to demonstrate the defendant's guilt or innocence.

No courtroom ever held the drama of that remarkable day portrayed in the second chapter of Acts. The Holy Spirit has just been poured out on that band of Christian believers gathered in Jerusalem. As a result, they launched into the streets proclaiming the gospel, with each person miraculously sharing the message in his or her own native language. As you might expect, the entire scene created both questions and criticism.

Peter used the opportunity to speak to the crowd and to announce the reason for these strange events—the result was the first evangelistic sermon! Peter marshalled his evidence and demonstrated that Jesus was, indeed, who he said he was: the Messiah, God's Anointed One, sent to save his people from their sins.

In our own day, living in a society more secular by the hour, people want to know if there is some message of hope. How can we know Jesus is actually who he said he was? Peter offers three different types of evidence.

I. There is the Evidence of His Life (v. 22*b*)

Peter's first level of evidence was the life Jesus led, particularly the "deeds of power, wonders, and signs that God did through him." Many in Peter's audience had seen Jesus in action for themselves; they provided vivid confirmation of the evidence provided by his activities in their midst.

One of the ways we can know Jesus is Savior is the evidence provided by his unique life: born of a virgin, sinless before men, compassionate and loving, one who can heal the blind and lame, even raise the dead, and can also "teach as no man taught before." It is a life unlike any other, because only Jesus Christ was the incarnate Son of God, Word become flesh.

II. There is the Evidence of His Death (vv. 23-24)

There is another form of evidence to confirm Jesus' identity: his death and resurrection. Unjustly accused and tried, Jesus was brutally executed on a cross, hanging among thieves. Yet on the third day, "God raised him up." Again, there were many in Peter's audience that could confirm such evidence, for they had also seen him following the resurrection.

What remarkable evidence of his divinity: even the grave could not hold him. As Peter said, "it was iimpossible for him to be held in its power." Every man and woman must ultimately face death—but Jesus is no mere man. He is fully man *and* fully God. His death and resurrection demonstrate it.

III. There is the Evidence of His Disciples (v. 32)

Do you remember Peter on the night before Jesus was crucified? Confused, shaken, angry—when on lookers recognized him as one who had been with Jesus, he denied it with curses. When Jesus went to the cross, Peter—"the Rock"—was not to be found.

Yet look at Peter now: bold, confident, willing to proclaim the gospel before all of Jerusalem. What happened? He had been transformed by the power of the resurrection and the presence of the Holy Spirit. Peter and his fellow disciples had seen the evidence for themselves, and made the difference in their lives. They would serve Christ with boldness and power throughout their lives. They would come when nearly all of them would lay down his life as a martyr for the cause of Christ. Only the most compelling evidence would justify such sacrifice.

The most compelling evidence of who Jesus is continues to be the difference he makes in the lives of those who have given their lives to him. If you have never experienced the transforming power of Christ in your own life, there is no better day than today. (Michael Duduit)

APRIL 21, 1996

❧

Third Sunday of Easter

Worship Theme: God calls us to a life of holiness.

Readings: Acts 2:14*a*, 36-41; 1 Peter 1:17-23; Luke 24:13-35

Call to Worship (Psalm 116:12-14, 19):

Leader: What shall I return to the LORD for all his bounty to me?

People: **I will lift up the cup of salvation and call on the name of the LORD,**

Leader: I will pay my vows to the LORD in the presence of all his people. . . . in the courts of the house of the LORD, in your midst, O Jerusalem.

People: **Praise the LORD!**

Pastoral Prayer:

O God of holiness and might, we stand before you in awe of your majesty. We, who find it so easy to fall prey to the most foolish temptations; we, who fall so short of the ideal you set for us; we simply cannot comprehend your holiness. We live in such an unholy world—full of selfishness, hatred, and deceit—that we find it difficult to even understand what it means to be holy. And yet, amazing though it seems, you call us to be holy! In terms of this world, your call to holiness sounds utterly impossible; and yet we know that nothing is impossible in your hands. So we draw near to you this hour; we listen for your voice, pause to feel your touch, and await the empowering of your Spirit. Make us holy, even as you make us wholly your children. Amen.

154

SERMON BRIEFS

WHAT SHOULD WE DO?

ACTS 2:14*a*, 36-41

The good news is that "the entire house of Israel [should] know with certainty that God has made [Jesus] both Lord and Messiah" (v. 36). The Messiah has come. Rejoice! Jesus is Lord. Alleluia! The long-awaited One has finally arrived. All that our forebears yearned for has now come to full fruition in our lifetimes. We are the fortunate ones, for we are alive now and we get to know and experience the Christ in the flesh. We are a blessed people.

How quickly good news can turn to bad news, for Peter quickly adds this zinger: "This Jesus whom you crucified." What a dramatic and abrupt turn of events! For ten verses, he details the glories of having the Messiah arrive and catches us all up in the excitement of the moment, and then he tells us that *we* crucified this Messiah.

I. We Are Involved

Make no mistake. It was not the Jews who killed Jesus—it was humankind. It was not a character flaw in one nationality that produced the Crucifixion—it was a character flaw in humankind that crucified our Lord. The character flaw is called sin. Karl Menninger titled his book, *Whatever Happened to Sin?* The answer is, it is where it has always been: at the center of our lives. Every chance we get we are going to bite the apple, turn to God, who told us not to, and say, "Who do you think you are? God or somebody? I will do what I want in order to please me." That's called sin, and that attitude needs to be altered (or should I say "altared"?).

II. We Have a Troubled Reaction

Peter's hearers were "cut to the heart." Other translators say they were "pricked in their heart" (KJV), "deeply troubled" (GNB), and "cut to the quick" (Phillips). Some events in life will do that to us. They return us to our beginnings and remind us why we are here on earth, or they make us question our reason for being. What is the purpose of all this? "Brothers, what should we do?" (v. 37).

The killing of a Savior is such an event. The award-winning movie *Schindler's List* reminded millions of people of the atrocities of the

Nazis, but what really frightened viewers was the unveiling of the Nazi within all of us. When we make that discovery, we are "cut to the heart" and cry out, "What should we do?"

III. We Are Called to Turn from Sin

The gospel's answer for "deeply troubled" people is to call for a change of direction. If you want to get out of trouble, then change your life. Confess your wrong attitude and open yourself to the gift of the Holy Spirit. God has promised that God's power is available through God's Spirit (Acts 1:4-5, 8; Luke 24:49). Claim it! "For the promise is for you" (v. 39). Claim this promise of Jesus Christ.

Donald Shriver pointed out how an eminent psychiatrist remarked in a speech, "The greatest secret of mental health comes down to us in the words, 'Whoever would save his life will lose it; and whoever loses his life . . . will save it.' I forget who said that, but it is a great truth." "Too bad!" said Shriver. "Who said it is as important as what was said" (*Christian Century,* February 2-9, 1994).

Sometimes names are important, but sometimes it doesn't make any difference who said it or what you call it. When Reuben Mattus, a Polish immigrant, died, few people recognized his name. Yet he was the multimillionaire who decided that New Yorkers would not buy his ice cream unless it sounded different. He came up with the name for his ice cream that we now all recognize, Haagen-Dazs. Haagen-Dazs means absolutely nothing in any language. It was a nonsensical name, but it caught people's attention because it sounded intriguing.

When Jesus says something, you know that Someone stands behind it. His name stands for something. It is not just intriguing. It is authoritative. It says something vitally important.

When you give your life to Jesus, you don't lose anything. You find eternal life. (C. Thomas Hilton)

TAKE TIME TO BE HOLY

1 PETER 1:17-23

Many Christians sing the old hymn "Take Time to Be Holy." That hymn warms a multitude of hearts, but it leaves others asking what holiness is all about. Simon Peter addressed that issue in the first chapter of his first letter.

Holiness is not a word that slides easily off modern tongues. But it never has been easy to live a holy life. Let's consider what it is and how we may make it part of our lives.

I. Holiness Is Necessary Because God Is Impartial

Few people would want to go to court if they knew the judge was prejudiced against them. We want an impartial judge. Simon Peter proclaims that Christians are the children of God, who judges impartially.

He is both Father and impartial judge. The two roles might seem contradictory. If God is my Heavenly Father, shouldn't God also be inclined to favor me? The good news of the gospel is that because God is not prejudiced against anyone, all are potentially God's children.

A holy life, a life marked by the love of God and others, brings us into a Father-child relationship with God.

II. Holiness Is Possible Because We Have a Different Value System

People who live in a holy relationship with God get a different value system from the rest of humanity. Peter calls us strangers who live above the level of "perishable things."

We value ideals and goals that people who do not know God do not value. On the other hand, we discard things that some people would kill for. People who live a life of holy dedication to God are transformed.

In a sense we are exiles all our lives, but we are on a pilgrimage to another place. That other place is eternal life with God. But how do we achieve that eternal life? Consider another vital fact.

III. Holiness Is Available Because We Have a Redeemer

Verses 19-23 shift the focus to what God has done for us through Jesus Christ. We are not called on to struggle alone or achieve holiness by superhuman accomplishments. Instead, Christ himself has given us what we need to enter this holy relationship with him.

Listen closely to the language Peter uses here. Christ has given his "precious blood," and he is a "lamb without . . . blemish." He was revealed in order to redeem humankind. He was raised from the

157

dead and glorified. Because of that, we have been "purified" and "born anew."

This language is pregnant with meaning. Anyone even slightly familiar with the Bible realizes that these terms signify that God has done for us what we cannot accomplish alone.

So take time to be holy. The trip is worth the price. (Don M. Aycock)

THE REALITY OF REMEMBERING

LUKE 24:13-35

It is a seven-mile walk from Jerusalem to Emmaus. Two men were walking home toward Emmaus. Somewhere along the way a third person joined them. The new arrival noted the downcast look and the hopelessness shrouding the two. The third person did not seem to know what everyone else knew. Although he had been in Jerusalem, he did not act as if he had heard—he had not heard the shout of a mob, the sound of the lash, the clang of a hammer against spikes.

I. Memories Can Bring Pain

On the trip, the two recounted their memories of the past week in Jerusalem. They told their traveling companion everything they could remember. They spoke of the crowds and the acclamations just the week before. They told of Jesus' teaching in the Temple. The conflict with the Pharisees. The trials, the beating, the Crucifixion, the burial—all were presented.

II. Memories Can Bring Insight

Then the traveler told them about other memories. He spoke of Abraham, Isaac, and Jacob. He related stories of Saul, David, and Solomon. He disclosed memories of Isaiah, Jeremiah, and Ezekiel. He spoke of achievement and disappointment, banishment and renewal, faith and unfaith. As the third traveler explained and remembered the two remembered what they had not forgotten.

As they neared the end of their walk, the two residents of Emmaus followed the example of their forefathers, offering their house as a refuge. It was too late to go on that day. They offered the hospitality commanded by God through Moses.

It was a simple meal. They handed the stranger the bread so he could break off a portion.

III. Memories Can Bring Transformation

Then, a miracle occurred. As the stranger broke the bread, they remembered who he was. He was the One who had ridden the donkey into the city. He was the One who had been lashed. He had been nailed to the cross. He was the hope of Israel, a hope that seemed crushed with his death. The Romans were still in power. The people of God were still a captive nation. In remembering, the travelers from Jerusalem to Emmaus discovered a new reality about the events of the past.

The text from Luke illustrates how God reveals himself when we remember. The walk to Emmaus of past centuries can be our walk of remembrance. The three travelers remembered the history of their people. They remembered how God had visited them. Their memories were more than memories. A new reality came to be; a new experience was born in them. "Were not our hearts burning within us," was their memory.

Those two travelers had never experienced such a reality before. Their past was transformed. Their present became their future, new and different. Remembering is more than a thought. Remembering is a new reality. Remembering creates something more than what we remembered from the past. Remembering is a reality that reveals the constant truths of life. Remembering sets us on a journey that does not end. Remembering does make our hearts feel warm.

We remember the words, "He is risen!" In the remembering, that revealing truth comes afresh and anew for us. We experience anew the power and presence of God. He has come to us! We are made fresh through his power. The power of God, which brought Jesus Christ out of the bonds of death, brings us to true life. The power of God in Jesus who walks beside us brings us to life, true and powerful life. (Harold C. Perdue)

APRIL 28, 1996

Fourth Sunday of Easter

Worship Theme: Jesus Christ provides for our needs like a good shepherd.

Readings: Acts 2:42-47; 1 Peter 2:19-25; John 10:1-10

Call to Worship (Psalm 23):

Leader: The LORD is my shepherd, I shall not want.

People: He makes me lie down in green pastures;

Leader: he leads me beside still waters; he restores my soul.

People: He leads me in right paths for his name's sake.

Leader: Even though I walk through the darkest valley, I fear no evil; for you are with me;

People: your rod and your staff—they comfort me.

Leader: You prepare a table before me in the presence of my enemies;

People: you anoint my head with oil; my cup overflows.

Leader: Surely goodness and mercy shall follow me all the days of my life,

People: and I shall dwell in the house of the LORD my whole life long.

Pastoral Prayer:

We are your sheep, O Lord, and you are our shepherd. Though we so often roam into the wrong paths, endangering ourselves and others, you continue to seek us out and lead us back into the right way. When the storms come, the wind blows, and the lightning strikes, we are thankful for your calm and loving presence. Even as the forces of evil come against us like a wild animal, we are thankful

160

for your strong protection. You are a shepherd who loves and cares for the flock; we praise you for your faithfulness and rest in your power. When we stray, bring us back; when we falter, lift us up; when we struggle, carry us on. Thank you for love that never ends, even at the foot of a cross. Amen.

SERMON BRIEFS

FEELINGS AND DOINGS

ACTS 2:42-47

Pentecost had come and gone. The gospel had been preached, and "three thousand persons were added" to the rolls of the Christian church. Excitement was in the air. All those new people. They must integrate new members into the life of the church as soon as possible. It was imperative that all the new faces be woven into the fabric of the church immediately. It was imperative that they realize they were saved for service. When so many join by the front door, we must make sure that we do not lose them out the back door.

Luke, in this passage, tells us two significant things about the early church—and our church. He tells us about feelings and doings.

I. Feelings Are Important

One's feelings about church are important. This passage tells us about the awe that was evident by everyone "because many wonders and signs were being done by the apostles" (v. 43). Today is an age of disbelief and debunking in the United States. Many are cynical of any kind of leadership, including church leadership. Note, however, the members of the early church were in awe of their leaders. They respected their leaders; they revered their leaders.

They were also a glad people. The presence of the Holy Spirit can be measured. It reveals itself by the degree of joy that is present. Happiness is shallow and can be changed with the ring of a telephone informing us that a loved one has been injured. Bad news can destroy our happiness but can never touch the joy of our salvation, which is always good news.

The early Christians were also generous and thankful people, for they had "generous hearts" (v. 46). When the church is at its best, the feelings around a church are these feelings. It is a group that has "the goodwill of all the people" (v. 47). Have you ever been in a group like that? Was it a church group?

II. Doings Are Even More Important

It is equally informative to discover the Pentecostal afterglow in the early church regarding their "doings." This passage tells us exactly what they were up to. They immediately "devoted themselves to . . . teaching and fellowship" (v. 42). New Christians, filled with enthusiasm (which means "in God"), need and want more teaching. They yearn for more knowledge. They reach out to fellow Christians for support and fellowship. The breaking of bread could have been an informal *agape* meal, a repetition of the Lord's Supper, or simply a social event with newfound friends.

One thing the disciples always asked from Jesus was "teach us how to pray." It is logical that they most often prayed when they gathered together.

This passage is an endorsement of the fact that everything we have comes from God for the purpose of meeting others' needs. Once our basic needs have been met, nothing demands that we should spend the rest on ourselves or save it for our offspring. God has blessed us so that we might be a blessing to others. The family includes the whole human family of God.

The final "doing" of the early Christians was "praising God" (v. 47). For them, it was their reason for being, as it is ours.

Nick Stevens was an Australian tourist in Los Angeles on January 17, 1994. He woke up that day planning to do what tourists do. He said, "We had been planning to go to the Universal Studios, where they have the earthquake ride." Before he got a chance to go, a large earthquake, 6.6 on the Richter scale, rocked the area where he was and demolished a good part of the city, including the highway system. Stevens commented after the quake, "Now we won't have to bother [going to Universal Studios]." Once you have experienced the real thing, there is no need to experience a contrived event.

Life in the early church was the real thing. Can we experience it today, or do we have to settle for a contrived event? (C. Thomas Hilton)

SUFFERING CHRISTIAN STYLE

1 PETER 2:19-25

Suffering is one of those subjects that we like to avoid. Think about it. Who really likes to sit around and discuss suffering? A medical student may love talking about it, but not many others. But the Bible is a book about suffering. It tells us through many stories that humankind is a suffering race.

We need not endure suffering silently. The New Testament calls us to suffering Christian style. Hear Simon Peter as he leads us on a journey through suffering.

I. All People Will Suffer

Theologians of previous generations pointed out that all creatures have pain, but only humans suffer. The difference between pain and suffering is the difference between mere physical discomfort and the consciousness of wondering why. A dog can have pain, but it does not wonder why and it does not have emotional struggles with the pain. But people do. Some of the worst suffering we endure is not physical pain at all but the emotional knowledge that something has gone very wrong in our lives. A marriage went sour. A loved one died. Our dreams are unfulfilled. These things bring suffering.

All people, regardless of religious convictions, will suffer. That is simply part of life on earth. But what we do with our suffering matters.

II. Suffering Can Teach Us Much About God

In today's text, Peter speaks to a group of people who are suffering not because of a natural cause but because someone else is persecuting them. To be in pain is one thing. To be in pain because someone else wants you to be in pain is something else. That is suffering.

All people will suffer, some because they deserve it by their behavior. Verse 20 asks about someone who endures a beating because he has done something wrong. Peter asks how that helps someone. But if a person endures suffering for doing good, that endurance is commendable before God.

C. S. Lewis used to say that suffering is God's megaphone. We can hear God's voice loudly and clearly. God can use our suffering to draw us close to him.

III. Christ Is Our Supreme Example in Suffering

Peter reached back into his heritage and quoted the prophet Isaiah and related the statement to Christ: "He committed no sin/and no deceit was found in his mouth" (v. 22). Christians naturally think of Jesus when they hear that sort of comment. Peter went on to describe the insult he suffered, but he did not retaliate. Jesus accepted the cross. In all of that he "entrusted himself to the one who judges justly" (v. 23).

In our suffering, as in all other areas of our lives, Christ is our example. He knows what it is to suffer unjustly, but he redeemed the suffering. Because of that, as Peter puts it, "you have returned to the shepherd" (v. 25).

Suffering can draw us close to God, or it can drive us away. It can make us better or bitter. The choices is ours. (Don M. Aycock)

THE GOOD SHEPHERD

JOHN 10:1-10

It's unlikely that many young people, if taking a personality inventory, would choose "shepherd" as a career path. In fact, it's unlikely most of us have even seen a shepherd, except perhaps in a picture or on television. It's not a common profession in our culture, but in Jesus' day the work of the shepherd was well known.

Jesus often compared spiritual principles to things found in the everyday life of his contemporaries. In this teaching, Jesus uses the imagery of a shepherd to help us better understand how he relates to his followers. The first image is that of a shepherd going and coming through a door to the sheepfold. The second is that of sheep coming and going through that door.

I. The Good Shepherd Cares for Us

Jesus' words remind us of a low stone fence surrounding a Palestinian home. The shepherd shelters his sheep in the fold near the house at night. Thieves and robbers will climb over the wall, causing the sheep to bleat and scurry about. The shepherd knows that entry by the door of the fold is calming to the sheep. The sheep recognize their shepherd and respond with relief.

I often visit with friends at their ranch. These ranchers have both cattle and sheep in their pastures. When a stranger appears at feeding time, cows are curious but not anxious. Sheep run to safety until they recognize someone familiar. The good shepherd is deliberate, careful, cautious, caring. Those who sneak over walls really don't care about the sheep.

We have a shepherd who cares about us. In the sight of Jesus Christ, we are more than a social security number. We are more than a picture on a driver's license. We are more than the unused balance on a credit card. We are more than a statistic on a computer printout. We are known by God and cared for by our Lord. We are the sheep he tends.

II. The Good Shepherd Protects Us

The second image of this text is the door as exit and entry for the sheep. We imagine sheep safe in the fold during the night when harm might come to them.

I often hear people say that they can be religious without the church. I have my doubts about that. The church is a sheepfold into which we enter and from which we exit. It is a place of security, a place of safety, a place of promise. Life is not easy. In the community of other sheep, going and coming together, we find support for living.

Alan Paton was a leader against apartheid in South Africa many years ago. He once wrote:

> This year a friend of mine wished me a happy Easter and I, because my wife was gravely ill, replied that I did not think it would be very happy. When my friend reached his home, he sat down and wrote me that no Christian should be unhappy at Easter, because what happened at Easter was of an eternal order, whereas our griefs and problems were only temporal. I replied to him that I did not expect to be unhappy at Easter. I was prepared to face the future and whatever it might bring. I added, "I like to see happiness and to see happy people, especially happy children. I hope they may grow up happy also, but if I had to choose, I would rather see them brave."

Life is not easy. Bravery and happiness are gifts from the Good Shepherd. (Harold C. Perdue)

MAY

❧

Preparing to Serve

The Symbol of Wind

Paraphrase Assignment:

John 3:8: "The wind blows where it chooses, and you hear the sound of it, but you do not know where it comes from or where it goes. So it is with everyone who is born of the Spirit."

Prayer Assignment:

As the season of Pentecost is born and continues, pray for a continuing sense of spiritual renewal in your life. Then form a prayer list of all the programs in the church. Ask God what to pray for to see the structures of the church's program renovated by freshness. Seek to make your prayer concerns available to the small group structures within the church so that others may join you in your concern to see the freshness of spiritual vitality born first within the people and then the programs of the church.

Journal-in-Worship Assignment:

Pentecost is a good time to examine our spiritual passion. So let us first investigate and then celebrate the Holy Spirit's symbol of the wind.

Exodus 14:21. The wind of redemption is discussed. The word *ruah* means either "wind" or "breath." God's very breath held the water in walls so that Israel might be saved. Is it any wonder that God's breath was God's existence? The very word *YHWH* is a breath word suggesting that God's existence moved like the force of a desert storm. Shouldn't this very image stir us to feel God and celebrate divine power? God has saved us. Recall the event when you first felt the power of God's reality in your life. Write the experience in a paragraph or two to be shared with the church.

John 3:8. The wind of mystery is discussed. Jesus illustrated the mysterious power of God by using the wind as a metaphor. How beautifully and invisibly it moves to exercise its unseen power! It can unfurl a banner. It can destroy whole cities, yet it has never been seen by anyone. Write of a time when you have felt as one feels the wind the reality of God. Let this testimony stand in place to encourage the church to be confessional about times of experiencing the power of Christ.

Acts 2:2. The wind of spiritual passion is discussed. How glorious is the wind of Pentecost! It makes people fervent. It excites them to speak boldly to their culture all that they believe about Christ. Write of two very special times when you have been alive with the passion that speaks boldly of when you have been alive with the passion that speaks boldly of Jesus. How did you feel then? In the book of Acts, they were so impassioned that they went into the streets telling all about Jesus. When the Holy Spirit came to quicken your life in Christ, did it cause you to tell others more joyfully and freely who Jesus was and what he had done for you? Let your account of those times quicken the people in your church with the spirit of Pentecost. (Calvin Miller)

MAY 5, 1996

ॐ

Fifth Sunday of Easter

Worship Theme: Christ's presence enables us to overcome any fear.

Readings: Acts 7:55-60; 1 Peter 2:2-10; John 14:1-14

Call to Worship (Psalm 31:3-5):

Leader: You are indeed my rock and my fortress;

***People:* for your name's sake lead me and guide me,**

Leader: take me out of the net that is hidden for me,

***People:* for you are my refuge.**

Leader: Into your hand I commit my spirit;

***People:* you have redeemed me, O LORD, faithful God.**

Pastoral Prayer:

We live in a fearful world, O Lord. Our communities are troubled by crime and violence; in many of our cities, people are afraid to step out of their homes after dark. Even within our homes, Lord, many find no peace because of disrupted families and the destructive influence of drugs, infidelity, and other forms of abuse. Fear surrounds us. And yet as we gather in your presence during this hour, Lord, we find the source of authentic peace that overcomes any fear, for we recognize that you are with us—your Spirit enfolds and empowers us. We rest in the promise that he who rose from the grave, overcoming sin and death, can overcome any enemy we face if we will yield our lives and our hearts to his love. And so we come before you with thanksgiving and with praise, and we ask these things in the name of the One who overcomes our fears. Amen.

SERMON BRIEFS

HOW TO LIVE AND DIE

ACTS 7:55-60

The astronauts' observations of the earth from outer space are always awe inspiring. They wax eloquent about the astounding beauty of our planet. The pictures they draw are breathtaking. Those of us who are frequent flyers can attest to the earth's beauty from an even less elevated height, but what I have discovered is that almost anything is beautiful if you can just get far enough away from it. From ten thousand feet, even the city dump doesn't look bad.

The stoning to death of the first Christian martyr, Stephen, was a barbaric and shocking event, full of blood, pain, and slow death. Only as we view it today from such a great distance would we dare to romanticize it. Compared to stoning, the electric chair is kind.

And yet, we can learn spiritual lessons on how to live and how to die from Stephen.

I. While They Were Stoning

Luke informs us that "while they were stoning Stephen, he prayed" (v. 59). Even as they killed him, he prayed. In one of his darkest moments on earth, he turned to God. As naturally as he prayed in pleasant times, he turned to God in an impossibly difficult time and communed. Wherever he was and in whatever circumstance he found himself, Stephen found it natural to pray to God. Every disciple knew that could be the outcome, for Luke heard Jesus say, "They will put some of you to death" (21:16). That was being fulfilled.

II. A Prayer of Trust

Stephen's prayer was, "Lord, Jesus, receive my spirit" (v. 59). It was not a prayer of panic or fear. It was not a prayer of desperation or bargain. It was a prayer of trust and affirmation. He was saying, "I have always trusted you in life, and now I trust you in death."

Following the model of the way his Lord had died, he quoted a familiar Jewish children's prayer found in Psalm 31:5: "Into your hand I commit my spirit." These are almost the exact words of Jesus from the cross: "Father, into your hands I commend my spirit" (Luke

23:46). He had learned that whether he lived or died, he was the Lord's.

III. A Prayer of Forgiveness

Again, following the model of his Master on the cross who said, "Father, forgive them; for they do not know what they are doing" (Luke 23:34), Stephen prayed, "Lord, do not hold this sin against them" (v. 60). Jesus influenced Stephen, who influenced the apostle Paul (Acts 7:58; 22:20), who in turn influenced millions of others.

The popular 1957 film *The Bridge on the River Kwai* documented many of the atrocities that the Japanese perpetrated on the Allies during the Second World War. On February 19, 1994, some survivors from both sides got together. Some of the Allies refused to acknowledge their former captors' presence. "What the Japanese did was unforgivable," said British leader Arthur Lane. Takashi Nagase responded by saying, "The former prisoners' feelings were only natural." That is true. It took a supernatural power to bring about forgiveness in Stephen's life, and so it does in ours. (C. Thomas Hilton)

WHAT AM I?

1 PETER 2:2-10

Children like to play guessing games, especially ones where they pretend to be something that others have to guess. Adults do that sometimes, too, only the game can become a habit with no real answers.

Today's text uses a succession of images that tell us who we are as followers of Christ.

What am I? Paul suggests three images that demonstrate the nature of the Christian life.

I. We Are Hungry Babies

This is a humorous image. Can't you just picture yourself right now in a diaper fumbling with a big bottle? Or think about your spouse. Or your grown children.

Peter used the term in a serious way, though. The way a baby hungrily slurps a bottle is the way hungry Christians are to ingest spiritual milk in order to grow. The spiritual nourishment is the living Word of God that is both the Bible and the Holy Spirit living within us. We are to dine deeply at Christ's table.

What am I?

II. We Are Living Stones

Peter again reached back into his heritage and used an image from Isaiah. This image is about a "living stone." Isaiah spoke of a stone that was rejected as being useless but became the cornerstone. We can easily see why people heard that analogy and immediately thought of Jesus. He was condemned by the Jewish leaders as being worthless and was crucified. But like a stone at first deemed useless that later became the cornerstone of the building, Christ is the living cornerstone.

Peter tells us that people who follow Jesus are likewise living stones. But these stones are being used to build up a spiritual house.

What am I?

III. We Are a Chosen People

Throughout this section, Peter used a series of visual images to identify people and give them a new identity in Christ. In verses 9-10, he tells us that Christians are a chosen people.

That is good biblical language to identify people who are selected by God for a purpose. That purpose is to serve God and tell others about God's ways. Other ideas are "chosen people," "royal priesthood," "holy nation," and the recipients of God's mercy. In verse 10, Peter tells us that we were once nobodies without mercy. But in Christ, we are now the people of God and people who receive grace.

What are we? We are individuals who have experienced the transforming touch of Jesus Christ, and who are called to a higher and deeper purpose than any we have known before. (Don M. Aycock)

TROUBLED LIVES AND CALMING FAITH

JOHN 14:1-14

"Do not let your hearts be troubled." Again and again at funerals we read this passage. John's recollection of Jesus' words spoke to the disciples and speaks to us, also. The experiences of that last week troubled the disciples of Jesus. Jesus' ministry was moving to a meaningful climax. The people were willing to proclaim Jesus to be their Messiah. They should have been days of triumph, but Jesus was speaking of death. He was talking about his own death rather than his triumph. He portrayed the end of his ministry rather than its beginning.

Jesus knew the troubled hearts of his disciples. He had experienced the same emotions. Jesus stood with the sisters at the tomb of his friend Lazarus and shuddered (John 11:33). Facing the death of a friend was a troubling experience for Jesus. Jesus experienced the same troubling when he considered his betrayal by Judas (John 13:21).

I. Troubled Hearts Are Common to All

We also have troubled hearts today. We see our children waste their talents as they wander from the way of living we taught them. Our hopes and dreams are shattered as we see them wasted like the prodigal. Our hearts may be troubled by difficulty at work. Our hearts may be troubled by our lack of faith or our failure to develop our faith in God. Death of a friend or family member or self may cause our hearts to be deeply troubled. Whatever the reason for our troubled hearts, it is so similar to that experience of the disciples— even of Jesus himself.

II. Faith Can Overcome Any Fear

"Do not let your hearts be troubled." That is no glib or easy answer. It is an answer of faith. John MacMurray described most of us when he described many persons riddled by fear because they think they are alone in a hostile world. Like the disciples of long ago, we do have plenty around us that can trouble us—and does trouble us.

False religion promises that the worst will not happen. Many seek God to escape troubling times. We think that if we can only be with him, obey him, love him, ask him, then God will make sure we do not have to endure the worst. Such a promise is impossible. We cannot escape the troubles of life.

A teenage son of friends was killed in an accident. The father and the mother have given their lives and their talent to serve God. If any family should have received a special favor from God, it would be them. No one escapes troubles in life.

Jesus promises that when the worst does happen, one does not have to live in fear and pain. Faith can overcome fear. Calm can come to anxious spirits. Comfort can come to those in deep anguish.

Mark tells the story of Jairus's daughter. Jairus was the leader of the synagogue. His daughter was ill. Jairus came to Jesus begging him to cure the girl. While they proceeded through the crowds, friends admonished Jairus not to bother Jesus any longer since the daughter died. Jesus heard them and said, "Do not fear, only believe" (Mark 5:36).

Matthew couples fear and faith in a story found in chapter 8. Jesus and the disciples were in a boat during a storm. The disciples awakened Jesus and pleaded for him to act to save their lives. Jesus objected that their faith was not strong enough to overcome their fear (Matt. 8:23-27).

"Do not let your hearts be troubled." Jesus' words are no simple answer or flippant advice. Jesus' words are a call to faith. Believe in him; believe in God. One can have faith in the power of the divine. One can trust in him, depend upon him. With such trust and faith, the troubles of life will not disappear. They can be overcome. "Do not let your hearts be troubled." (Harold C. Perdue)

MAY 12, 1996

❧

Sixth Sunday of Easter

Worship Theme: The Holy Spirit indwells and assists every believer.

Readings: Acts 17:22-31; 1 Peter 3:13-22; John 14:15-21

Call to Worship (Psalm 66:8-9):

Leader: Bless our God, O peoples,

People: let the sound of his praise be heard,

Leader: who has kept us among the living,

People: and has not let our feet slip.

Pastoral Prayer:

We thank you, God, for the gift of life and the joy we find in living it—its good times and bad times, its sunny days and dark, all of its ups and downs. We come today with our heavy load of uncertainty and confusion, sins and failures, concerns and troubles, to rest ourselves in your presence. Help us to relax and to leave our heavy loads with you, who are able to bear them all with so much more strength. Help us to turn from anxiety to thanksgiving, from insecurity to confidence, from helplessness to strength, from despair to hope, from inner turmoil to peace of mind, and from distress to joy. Forgive us for our lack of faith, which causes us so much misery and which maximizes all our difficulties. Let all our problems and doubts find their solution in the death of our Lord Jesus Christ upon Calvary, in his resurrection from the grave, and in the eternal joy of life in your kingdom, which shall endure forever and ever. Amen. (Gary C. Redding)

SERMON BRIEFS

FOCUSING YOUR FAITH

ACTS 17:22-31

Writing in his *Spiritual Biography,* William Barclay told how his twenty-one-year-old daughter and her fiancé were both drowned in a boating accident.

He also told of an anonymous letter that said, "I know now why God killed your daughter; it was to save her from corruption by your heresies." Barclay wrote, "If I had the writer's address, I would have written back . . . as John Wesley said, 'Your god is my devil.' "

This is what the apostle Paul told the Athenians as he preached in the middle of the Areopagus.

I. Religion Is a Good Thing

Paul said, "I see how extremely religious you are in every way" (v. 22). This is a wonderful attribute. I hope that others think I am religious in every way. I wouldn't want people to think that I am not religious in any way. I like being considered a religious person, especially since I am clergy. To be viewed as a nonreligious ordained minister would be an insult. I will never write the book, *How to Be a Minister Without Being Religious*. It is a nice compliment to be considered religious. The Athenians were religious.

II. Religion Must Have a Focus

Their only trouble was that they were worshiping everything and everyone, and hence, in reality, no one. They should be complimented for their religious yearning. They should be encouraged in their religious search, for that is what life is all about. We are on a journey of faith.

The chaplain at Duke University, William H. Willimon, summed up their difficulty and our modern difficulty in this way in his book *Acts:* "Pagans criticize the Christian faith as being 'simplistic,' 'prescientific,' 'superstitious' and then rush to the strange consolations of astrology, transcendental meditation, parapsychology, esoteric cults, or happy hearted humanism." Paul is telling us that a religious journey is by definition what life is all about, but every journey must also have a destination. Where will you be when you get where you're going? If life is only a search, only a journey, only an adventure with no "arrival," then God is, in fact, "unknown" (v. 23a).

III. True Religion Finds Its Fulfillment in Jesus Christ

Paul believes that the Christian faith is more focused than simply feeling good and smiling and being nice. It is more than having peace of mind, giving generously, worshiping regularly, and attending Sunday school. A Christian worships a God who is like Jesus Christ, and we learn about this Christ in the Holy Scripture. Paul said, what you call unknown, "I proclaim to you" (v. 23b). The way to learn about God is to know Jesus Christ.

To take a picture with an unfocused camera is to produce a picture that is so unacceptable that the main characters may appear unknown. It can be so out of focus that the picture loses all meaning. The same thing can happen to "extremely religious" people who have not focused their faith on the Christlike God. Your god may be my devil, depending on how Christlike your god is. (C. Thomas Hilton)

BE PREPARED

1 PETER 3:13-22

Every Boy Scout knows the motto: "Be prepared." That is good advice for scouting kinds of events. If you go camping, take dry matches, a sharp knife, and a leakproof tent.

We read these words from Scripture, too: be prepared. These words do not come as friendly advice, though. They come as part of our very life skills. Simon Peter tells the church to wake up, get ready, and be prepared. As Christians, for what do we need to be prepared?

I. Be Prepared to Live Without Fear

Verses 13-14 touch first on the theme of suffering. Peter reminds believers that we might end up suffering for the sake of Christ. Suffering might come about even if we are not doing anything wrong! We might balk at that kind of justice but do not stop yet.

In verse 14, Simon Peter quotes the prophet Isaiah and says, "Do not fear what they fear, and do not be intimidated." Who are "they" mentioned here, and what do they fear? They are people who live their lives with no reference to God. What they fear is losing the respect of other pagans. Anyone who colored outside the lines, who did things differently, was suspect.

Guess what? That is you and me. We are considered abnormal for believing in Christ and for orienting our lives toward him. The good news is that we need not fear the put-downs of others. Christ is alive and among us. Be prepared to live without fear. Nothing can harm us that God cannot handle.

II. Be Prepared to Recognize Christ as Lord

Peter implied that people who reject Christ have their hearts filled with fear. Their lives are guided by what others think and do. But people who accept Christ have their lives filled with new attitudes and actions.

We are to be prepared to recognize Christ as our Lord. We are to orient our whole lives to him and his work. The love of Christ flushes our hearts clean of fear and replaces it with peace and courage.

II. Be Prepared to Give the Reason for Faith

If we love Christ, we will be different from other people. As we have just seen, we will not fear what other people fear. Further, we will have a new frame of reference for all of our thinking. That frame of reference is Christ dwelling in our hearts as our Lord.

Since our lives will be different, other people will notice that difference. They will ask what makes us tick. When they do, Peter tells us to be prepared to give an answer to everyone who asks us to give the reason for our hope. We cannot brag on our financial expertise or the savvy we might have in business. When it comes right down to it, the reason for our hope is Christ in our lives as Lord.

Peter was concerned about the way we answer people. We are to reply to the questions of others with gentleness and respect. The goal is to win those who ask. The Scouts and the Bible are right. Be prepared. (Don M. Aycock)

BELIEVING IS SEEING

JOHN 14:15-21

The "Show Me State" it is called: Missouri. It has become a folk saying: "I'm from Missouri. Show me! If I see it, I will believe it." So we get the saying, "Seeing is believing." It's like the person who was asked if he believed in infant baptism. "Believe in it?" he responded. "I've seen it!"

But in this bit of monologue from Jesus' Farewell Discourse with his disciples we get just the opposite perspective. Jesus is talking about the promised presence of the Spirit with the disciples, and he is talking about his own presence with them. He keeps dropping hints that he will soon leave them, but he keeps reassuring them as well that he will not leave them alone, or "orphaned" as the New Revised Standard Version so correctly puts it.

And he makes an interesting contrast between what the disciples will see and what "the world" will see. The world will not know the Spirit, "because it neither sees him nor knows him." In the same manner, soon the world will not see Jesus. But it is altogether different with disciples. They will know the Spirit because the Spirit abides with them and in them. Likewise, the disciples will know the resurrected Lord because he is in them and they are in him.

Disciples do not believe in the Spirit and in the resurrected Lord because they see the Spirit and Jesus. It is the other way around: Disciples see, or know, the Spirit and the resurrected Lord because of their faith. The revelation is as much *to* faith as it is *through* faith.

William Barclay puts it in a fascinating way: "The point of Jesus' saying is: 'We can see only what we are fitted to see.' " An astronomer will perceive much more in the night sky than an untrained eye. Someone trained in art will see far more in a painting than another person who has never studied art. The trained musician will enjoy a symphony much more than someone who is unfamiliar with musical style or technique. What we are able to perceive in any situation depends on what we bring to the experience.

Likewise, someone who has given up on the very notion of God won't be listening for him. If we hope to receive the Holy Spirit in our own lives, it requires waiting and watching for him, in expectation of his arrival.

If you want to know the presence of the Spirit in your life, don't challenge God to "Show me!" Don't take the attitude that if God wants me to know his Spirit, then God will make it happen. Don't take the position "I'll believe it when I see it." Rather, if you want to know that presence, then expect it, wait for it, prepare for it, believe in its coming. You'll see it. After all, believing is seeing! (J. Lawrence McCleskey)

178

MAY 19, 1996

❧

Seventh Sunday of Easter

Worship Theme: The Holy Spirit empowers us to be witnesses for Christ.

Readings: Acts 1:6-14; 1 Peter 4:12-14, 5:6-11; John 17:1-11

Call to Worship (Psalm 68:3-4):

Leader: Let the righteous be joyful; let them exult before God;

***People:* let them be jubilant with joy.**

Leader: Sing to God, sing praises to his name; lift up a song to him who rides upon the clouds—

***People:* his name is the LORD—be exultant before him.**

Pastoral Prayer

O God, our creator and redeemer, we thank you for your blessings this day: for the provisions of life, for shelter, for friends and family. Even while we thank you for such blessings in our lives, we recognize that others do not share many of the blessings we enjoy: there are many with little to eat, others who have no homes, still more who are isolated and alone. We lift them up to you, knowing that you love and care for all. We also ask you to remind us of our responsibility to share with others a portion of that with which you have blessed us. Most of all, strengthen and move us to share the good news of your love and grace, allowing your Holy Spirit to work in us to accomplish your purpose. Make us your witnesses at home and to the ends of the earth. Amen.

SERMON BRIEFS

THE PURPOSE OF POWER

ACTS 1:6-14

The traditional seven last words from the cross are not Jesus' last words on this earth. These words are to be found in this passage, and they give the church some definitive guidance.

After the Resurrection, Luke tells us in the first few verses of Acts that Jesus spent forty days instructing his apostles "speaking about the kingdom of God" (v. 3).

Their question to Jesus is all the more startling, for they ask, "Is this the time when you will restore the kingdom to Israel?" (v. 6). When will the Kingdom come, and when will Israel be restored? The apostles simply didn't get it. In answer to the *when* question, Jesus said that that is God's business, not humankind's concern. As he prepared to leave them, Jesus offered them three things they would need: a promise, a purpose, and a preparation. We have those same things.

I. We Have a Promise: the Power of the Holy Spirit

"You will receive power when the Holy Spirit has come upon you" (v. 8). A disciple can expect to receive power when the promised Holy Spirit arrives. This Presence will bring comfort (Acts 9:31) to the believers but also power. Today, all across the land, disenfranchised people are clamoring for power. Jesus' last words to his followers are that they will get power. You can count on it.

II. We Have a Purpose: to Be Witnesses

When it comes, it will be power with a specific purpose. When the power of the Holy Spirit arrives, the church will have been given power to fulfill God's plans on the earth: "You will receive power when the Holy Spirit has come upon you . . . [to] be my witnesses in Jerusalem, in all Judea and Samaria, and to the ends of the earth" (v. 8).

Holy Spirit power is for the purpose of witnessing to others, not restoring the kingdom to Israel. Witnessing begins where you are now (Jerusalem), but from there it reaches out to Judea, Samaria, and the ends of the earth. The structure of this book can actually be found here: "in Jerusalem" (chaps. 1–7), "in all Judea and Samaria" (chaps. 8–12), "and to the ends of the earth" (chaps. 13–28). The promised Holy Spirit power is for a specific purpose—sharing the Christian faith with the whole world beginning where you are now.

As the disciples heard these last words from the lips of Jesus, he ascended into heaven. As they "were watching" and "were gazing up toward heaven," two angels appeared and said, "Don't just stand there. Do something." Actually, they said, "Why do you stand looking up toward heaven?" (v. 11). Too often the church has been told what to do, and the church has settled for watching and gazing, instead of trusting and obeying. These disciples, however, had to be told what to do only once. They knew what they should do next, and they did it, much to the surprise of many in our modern church.

III. We Have a Means of Preparation: Prayer

"All these were constantly devoting themselves to prayer" (v. 14). The Acts of the Apostles begins with prayer. When told not to just stand there, but to do something, the apostles obeyed. They prayed. The apostles' response to instruction, to the promise of the Holy Spirit, to reproof, and to exhortation was immediate: they talked to God in prayer.

Ellen T. Charry pointed out, "Today money, sex and power . . . set the standards for achievement and status . . . looking for guidance from God is looked upon as a sign of weakness, or simply as an eccentricity. . . . Our culture shapes [us] for a world shorn of God. Christians see power in the crucified Jesus; popular culture defines power as winning in athletic or commercial combat. A Christian learns about hope from the resurrection; our culture sees hope in a new-car showroom. The church is again called upon to rescue people out of paganism" (*Christian Century,* February 16, 1994). Could this be the purpose of Holy Spirit power? (C. Thomas Hilton)

WHAT TO DO WITH YOUR PAIN

1 PETER 4:12-14; 5:6-11

A doctor called one of his patients and said, "Joe, I have some bad news and some very bad news for you." Joe said, "Well, tell me the bad news." The doctor said, "I got your test results back. You have only twenty four hours to live." Joe said, "That is bad, but what's the very bad news?" The doctor said, "I should have called you yesterday."

Life often comes to us in the form of bad or very bad news. We might think if we turn to the Bible, we will automatically find relief. But the fact is, the New Testament is the most realistic of books. It offers hope and comfort, but it never whitewashes reality. It speaks of sin, pain, heartache, and finally death.

The good news, though, is that it does not stop there. It tells us what to do with our pain. Hear these instructions from today's text.

I. Realize That Everyone Experiences Pain

First Peter 4:12, taken by itself, sounds awfully depressing. It sounds as if Peter is telling Christians that they will have problems just like everyone else. Guess what? He is.

The "fiery ordeal" he mentions was probably some sort of persecution. But who among us cannot identify with them? Everyone experiences some amount of pain. Everyone! There are no exceptions or exemptions. One of the things to do with our pain is to realize it is part of life.

II. Remember That You Do Not Face Life's Pain Alone

We hear Peter saying again and again, "Christ is with you. You are not alone in your trials. Your suffering can even be used to glorify Christ."

When a child goes to a doctor, he wants his mother or father with him. Facing a terrifying experience can be better handled if a loving parent is there, too. We are not much different when we grow older. We still want someone with us when we face a terrifying situation.

The gospel tells us that we have Someone with us. His name is Jesus. We can turn to him for help and comfort. As Peter puts it, "Cast all your anxiety on him, because he cares for you" (5:7).

III. Remember That You Will Get Picked Up Again

Being knocked down is not so bad if you know you can get up again. That is one reason why Christians face death very differently from the way non-Christians do. Non-Christians see this life as all there is. They fight and fear death.

But Christians trust Christ who went to the grave before us and then rose again. Because he conquered eternal death, we know that whatever we might face in this life, we can trust God. Again and again we may get knocked down, and every time God will pick us up.

One day death will swing a mortal blow and think we are down for the count. But a mortal blow is not an eternal blow. As Peter states, God will "restore, support, strengthen, and establish you. To him be the power forever and ever. Amen" (vv. 10-11). This is the eternal perspective.

We will face pain all right. Everyone does. But we need not face it alone. We can call on him who loves us and who will restore us. (Don M. Aycock)

SO THAT THEY MAY BE ONE

JOHN 17:1-11

It has been called the *real* Lord's Prayer—the one from Matthew. I have heard it referred to as the Disciples' Prayer, the prayer Jesus taught to his disciples for their own praying. This prayer in the seventeenth chapter of John, however, is one that Jesus prayed on behalf of his disciples. It is the Lord's prayer for his companions.

It could also be called the first prayer for Christian unity. Four times in this seventeenth chapter (verses 11, 21, 22, and 23) Jesus prays that his disciples may be "one." But if we look seriously at the multitude of divisions in Christendom today, we are tempted to say of Jesus' prayer, "It didn't work." We Christians are not one. In fact, we might even wonder if we really want to be!

We live with divisions among and within denominations: theological differences, worship differences, differences in positions on social issues, differences in ways of expressing our faith, differences in celebrating and interpreting the sacraments. And the differences often seem far more divisive than the similarities seem unifying.

But this prayer is not content to leave us in our divisiveness. The late Archbishop of Canterbury, William Temple, said, "We meet in committees and construct our schemes of union; in face of the hideous fact of Christian divisions we are driven to this; but how paltry are our efforts compared with the call of God! The way to the union of Christendom does not lie through committee-rooms. . . . It lies through personal union with the Lord so deep and real as to be comparable with His union with the Father" (*Readings in St. John's Gospel,* Macmillan & Co., Ltd., London, 1963, p. 313).

The unity of Christians is not to be found in whether we agree with each other about every interpretation of scripture or doctrine or church government but in whether we love one another, and whether in our love for one another we reflect the love of God in Christ for the world.

The greatest threat to Christian unity is not that Christians disagree on certain issues. The greatest threat to Christian unity is that some Christians take the position that their viewpoint is the only correct and truly biblical viewpoint, and therefore they attempt to impose it unlovingly on others. Our unity is not to be found in agreement but in love. And one way to describe that love is in terms of listening to and trying to understand one another.

There are vast and serious differences that separate Christians around the world—even in our individual sanctuaries and on individual pews. But we can be part of the answer to this Lord's Prayer if we affirm and celebrate God's love for us all and our love for one another. There may be many ways in which we will not be "one." But in the ways of love, the ways of mutual respect and understanding and acceptance, we can be "one" and know that this Lord's Prayer is answered through us. (J. Lawrence McCleskey)

MAY 26, 1996

ॐ

Pentecost Sunday

Worship Theme: The filling of the Holy Spirit promises new power for every believer.

Readings: Numbers 11:24-30; Acts 2:1-21; John 20:19-23

Call to Worship (Psalm 104:31-34):

Leader: May the glory of the LORD endure forever;

People: **may the LORD rejoice in his works—**

Leader: who looks on the earth and it trembles,

People: **who touches the mountains and they smoke.**

Leader: I will sing to the LORD as long as I live;

People: **I will sing praise to my God while I have being.**

Leader: May my meditation be pleasing to him,

People: **for I rejoice in the LORD.**

Pastoral Prayer:

Our Father and our God, who came upon that tiny band of believers gathered in an upper room, consuming them with your Spirit, anointing them with your presence, and empowering them with boldness to proclaim your good news, how we wish for such power—we who are so timid in the face of a culture that values nothing and questions everything. You have given us what has all value and answers every question of life if only we are willing to share it. Forgive us our reluctance to offer your riches in the midst of poverty; forgive us for failing to declare your good news in a bad news world. Fill us with Pentecostal power as we yield our lives and our hearts to the presence of your Holy Spirit. Use us, that the days ahead might be days of power and promise for your church and your world. Amen.

SERMON BRIEFS

EMPOWERED LIVING

NUMBERS 11:24-30

It had been a normal, busy, more-than-I-could-get-done kind of week when I sat down at the computer to type a message. The telephone rang as I was formatting the document. "Pastor, do you still need an alarm clock for that student you mentioned last night at church? I will bring one to the office tomorrow." As I resumed my typing, the phone rang again. "Pastor, did you know that Mrs. Doe had five bypasses today? Don't worry. Her deacon and Sunday school teacher were there, and everything is fine."

It just so happened that I was preparing the message to challenge our church during a deacon ordination service the following Sunday evening! Whether the lines of my appointment book reflect the trivial or the traumatic, there had been more than I could do alone. Moses, too, felt, the enormous pressure of the critical needs of God's people. God directed Moses to initiate a new plan whereby those needs could be met. The plan involved a team of seventy men whom God would empower for leadership. Today, God empowers every believer to perform ministry in partnership with him.

I. Empowerment for Ministry Originates with a Divine Summons (vv. 24-25)

God called out seventy men to assist Moses. Those called were empowered by inspiration, for Moses delivered the "words of the LORD." They were further empowered by a sacred identity. Moses positioned them at the tabernacle. Their work was not within the tabernacle, but from within. Like these seventy, every Christian has been called according to his purpose (Rom. 8:28) and empowered by the very issuance of the summons.

II. Empowered Living Is Also Affirmed by the Presence of the Spirit of God (v. 25)

God enabled the seventy by engrafting them with the same spirit that had indwelt Moses. Their ability to lead was provided by the nondiminishing presence of God. Moses' spirit was not diminished by division among the seventy. Rather, like a fire that blazes with greater intensity through extension, the effectiveness of their work was multiplied through extension. The empowering presence of God's Spirit also provided a nontransitory purpose.

The distinctive was immediately noticeable: they began to prophesy, and they did not stop prophesying.

When Moses sought a man to continue leading the nation after his death, God told him to appoint Joshua, "in whom is the spirit" (Num. 27:18). One qualification for sacred ministry has always been identifiable evidence that a person has been endowed with the Spirit of God.

III. Empowerment for Ministry Also Inspires an Extensive Leadership Network (vv. 26-30)

An inquisitive lad, a bean counter type, noticed that something was wrong. He told Joshua that there were only sixty-eight men at the tabernacle. Two of the seventy, Eldad and Medad, had remained in the camp and were prophesying. Joshua was envious and offended. He suggested that Moses prohibit them from prophesying.

Moses' response was, I wish "that all the LORD's people were prophets, and that the LORD would put his spirit upon them!" (v. 29). Joshua was envious because the two men were not commissioned by Moses. Their empowerment, however, did not come from the word of Moses; it was a result of the word of God. God was, and is, independent of the limits of place and space.

The account closes with Moses taking Joshua and the elders to the camp where the two others were ministering. Today, the Holy Spirit has been given to every believer. And all Christians have been given the "ministry of reconciliation" (2 Cor. 5:18).

Evidence of empowered living is that a person has been summoned by God, filled with the Holy Spirit, and expresses the will of God in practical daily living. (Barry J. Beames)

POWER FOR PEOPLE WITH A PURPOSE

ACTS 2:1-21

Before our Lord's ascension, he promised explosive and expansive power *(dunamis)* for the church's life and ministry through his Holy Spirit (Acts 1:8). That power was delivered on Pentecost. The church was empowered for people with a purpose.

I. God Gives Power for People (vv. 1-13)

The Holy Spirit's power swept up people into the unity desired by the psalmist (Ps. 133) and expected by our Lord among people who claim him as saving Lord (John 17). Only God's Holy Spirit has the power to move people from what separates them (e.g., language, socioeconomics, race, parochialism) to who can bring them together (Jesus!).

I experienced the unifying power of Christianity while serving as an interim pastor of Grace Presbyterian Church in Toledo, Ohio. At the beginning of my first sermon, I said, "God doesn't like black churches. God doesn't like white churches. God doesn't like red or brown or yellow or any kind of church that prevents people from coming together through him. He didn't live and die and resurrect himself to keep us apart from each other. His purpose was to enable us to experience existential and eternal unity through him."

It wasn't long before that formerly African American congregation became rainbow-colored. When asked how black and white and rich and poor could come together in life and ministry, I'd reply, "It's easy for people to come together through Jesus. People who are attracted to Jesus alone and not some kind of cultural or parochial prejudice will be attracted to each other. Color doesn't matter when we see each other through the eyes of Jesus."

The Holy Spirit's power draws people together in the name of Jesus. It happened on Pentecost. It happened in Toledo. It can happen anywhere.

II. God Wants People with a Purpose (vv. 14-21)

During a race in the Special Olympics, all of the contestants stopped just before the finish line and waited for the fellow who would have finished last. When he caught up, they all crossed the finish line together. *Nobody wanted to win at the expense of others.*

The church was empowered on Pentecost for people with a purpose. That purpose remains to invite everybody to experience the good news through faith in Jesus. Our Lord doesn't want anybody left behind. That's why he came in Jesus and continues to come through his Holy Spirit. He wants us to cross the finish line together.

That purpose prompted Peter to preach, "Everyone who calls on the name of the Lord shall be saved" (v. 21).

Everyone is invited and included through faith. It doesn't matter who, what, where, or when. That's the church's good news. That's the purpose of the church. That's why our Lord gave power to his people. (Robert R. Kopp)

GETTING YOUR SECOND WIND

JOHN 20:19-23

Molly was upset with her teenage son, Jack. He'd done something that hurt her deeply—in fact, cut her to the core, stabbed her like a dagger in the heart. She wept and then she waited. Only God knew where he was then. She was not God. She could not appear before Jack to tell him of the peace that was coming back to her after their quarrel. As she prayed, her strength returned and grew, and she had a vision. She saw Jack's room filled with balloons that she would and did blow up. Balloons from floor to ceiling, spilling out around the sign across his door that said, "Welcome Home!"

She prepared that place out of the inspiration and the abundance of new life and hope the Spirit had poured into her. And when it was ready, Jack came. And from that place they began again. But so much stronger and wiser, so much forgiven and with the great generosity of spirit that comes from receiving such gifts.

Every mother knows you always get your "second wind." Mothers have to know that, or they would have stopped dead in their tracks centuries ago!

John the Baptist saw it coming to the disciples in a very special way. John had said, "I baptize you with water for repentance, but . . . [Jesus] will baptize you with the Holy Spirit and fire" (Matt. 3:11). So here is the baptism of the Holy Spirit, who will come soon—in the Acts story—by fire.

I. Sometimes Life Takes Your Breath Away

The disciples had found out what the world does to God. If God came and lived here, what would happen to God? That, for them, was no longer a hypothetical question. They saw. It was hideous. It took away all their courage, hope, and peace. Their heartrending experience of Jesus' humiliation and death had left them lifelessly limp in body, mind, and spirit. Their self-knowledge of their denial and abandonment of Jesus was enough to leave them drowning in awful awareness of their sin forever. How could they recover from all that?

The only thing to do after all that is to lock yourself in and throw away the key. Both the world out there and the one in you are far too dangerous to risk being at large again.

II. God Wants to Give Us a Second Wind

There he is! Suddenly, unaccountably, through those locked doors, he "came and stood among them" (v. 19). And he said, "Peace be with you." He said it twice. He showed them the still clearly visible signs of the terrible injury the world and they had done to him. But he came back to them, filled with peace and palpable new life.

He told them they were to go back out again, too. He'd been sent out in the first place by God, knowing what he was in for from the start. They should not be caught mummified in the webs of humiliation and despair. There were peace and empowerment that did not depend at all on what the world did. They could have both from him, just as he had both from God.

The God who originally "breathed into [that dust] the breath of life" (Gen. 2:7) could do it again, and did, and does. But that was their second wind. The new birth carried with it not just physical breathing, but the Holy Spirit, who sanctified the life by reviving it consciously and so lifting it to a higher level of awareness of the gift.

III. God's Second Wind Brings New Power for Living

To be forgiven in that way, by the God you have denied outside and inside yourself, who nevertheless came back to revive you again! Ah, that is the second wind that will blow up balloons forever. After the pain of all our usually inadvertent (not knowing what we're doing) attacks on God's goodness subsides a bit, God is back.

Standing in our midst, despite all obstacles, this God assures us that there will eventually be enough balloons to lift us all and that the blowing of second winds will definitely continue until there are. (Kathleen Peterson)

JUNE

ભ્ર

Preparing to Serve

The Symbol of Fire

Paraphrase Assignment:
   Hebrews 12:29: "Our God is a consuming fire."

Prayer Assignment:
   Let the same sort of prayer accompany this symbol as you let accompany the wind symbol in May. Both the wind and the fire speak of the vitality that the church should have. Let the fire symbol speak to three areas of your life: (1) the passion you should feel when speaking about the things of God; (2) the kind of leadership that might join you in a prayer-support group to move this same kind of excitement into other areas of key leadership; and (3) ways the passion of pastors and key leaders can be made to infiltrate every area of church programming.

Journal-in-Worship Assignment:
   The following scriptures speak to important areas of the Spirit's involvement in the church. As with the other symbols, apply them first to yourself. In these first few weeks following Pentecost, see this important symbol in terms of the Holy Spirit's continuing leadership in the church.

Exodus 13:22. This passage of fire speaks to the image by which God guided Israel in the wilderness. All of us can think of times when we longed for this intense, obvious "pillar of fire" leadership. Call to remembrance, in your life or the life of your church, two or three times when you saw clearly God's leadership. Celebrate those times with a written description of how you felt when that happened.

1 Kings 18:24. This passage describes Elijah's struggle with the prophets of Baal. The contest was critical in a culture that had forgotten God. Elijah's challenge was, "Let the God that answers by fire be God." The Holy Spirit is to supply enough passion in our ministry that people can see that the church is "on fire" and that the leadership is, too. What are the evidences that you are filled by this fire? What are some things you can do to prepare the way for the Holy Spirit's obvious empowering of your ministry?

Luke 3:16. Here in John the Baptist's testimony of Jesus, he says that Jesus will baptize with fire. Christ is the empowering Lord of his empowered church. How can you strengthen your own being to be the channel of his power? Are there barriers to Christ's flow-through that keeps his empowering at bay? What things must you stop doing to enable his coming? What things must you begin to do to be sure he has access to your life and the lives of all those in your congregation?

Acts 2:3-4. Finally, let the fiery image of the Holy Spirit's first empowering of the church cause you to remember that he is the "near end" of the Trinity. Unless he has a place in an open ministry in the church, spiritual vitality will be withheld from both the pastor and the people. (Calvin Miller)

JUNE 2, 1996

☙

Trinity Sunday

Worship Theme: We experience God as Father, Son, and Holy Spirit.

Readings: Genesis 1:1–2:4*a*; 2 Corinthians 13:11-13; Matthew 28:16-20

Call to Worship (Psalm 8:1, 3-4, 9):

Leader: O LORD, our Sovereign, how majestic is your name in all the earth!

People: You have set your glory above the heavens. . . .

Leader: When I look at your heavens, the work of your fingers,

People: the moon and the stars that you have established;

Leader: what are human beings that you are mindful of them, mortals that you care for them? . . .

People: O LORD, our Sovereign, how majestic is your name in all the earth!

Pastoral Prayer:

We live in a world of mystery, O Lord, a world that confronts us with paradox. Even your nature—Father, Son, and Holy Spirit, one God, yet three in one—is beyond our understanding. Yet even though our minds cannot fathom the mystery of your nature, we understand Trinity because we experience it in our walk with you. We have seen your work as Creator and felt your comforting hand as Father. We have received the benefit of your sacrifice as Son and Savior. We have experienced the power of your Holy Spirit as Comforter and Advocate. Day by day, we sense your presence as you bless us in so many ways. Even as you have blessed us—as Father, Son, and Spirit—so use us to bless others, making us instruments of your love and grace on behalf of a world that needs so desperately to know you. Amen.

SERMON BRIEFS

AN EYE FOR THE FUTURE

GENESIS 1:1–2:1

Creation set in motion God's divine vision for the future. Creation is believable and dependable and it is marked by paradox. The creation account begins and ends with paradox: "In the beginning. . . . It was finished."

Paradox is also realized when we consider the source of creation. In the beginning "God created." That simple statement distinguishes Christian faith from the world's religions, which promote the beginning of the world as the work of multiple gods. Yet the God of creation who is one is also three: Father, Son, and Holy Spirit. The paradoxes are intentional. They are meant not to confuse but to clarify God's dynamic purpose for the human drama.

On the one hand, creation is characterized by silence. Before creation had form, a dominant void of silence existed. On the other hand, "God said. . . ." The limitless capability of God's mind could have thought creation into being. But God chose to speak it into existence.

That Word depicts the very nature of the Creator: "In the beginning was the Word, and the Word was with God, and the Word was God" (John 1:1). God's Word brought the universe into existence and daily sustains that existence. That Word also indicates the relational aspect of creation. When we become distanced from the Word of God, we experience a void of his power and purpose. That silence is more unconstructive than it is constructive.

On the one hand, creation is predictable. God ordered the universe. Creation was accomplished by design: six creative days, six creative events; land, water; night, day. Creation also was predictably good. And at the end of the sixth day, God pronounced that creation was finished.

On the other hand, creation is marked by promise. Each creative moment was a new beginning. We are filled with anticipation as the account of the beginning of time is revealed. Our anticipation is heightened, and the promise of creation is attractive, because we know in reality that it has been disfigured and corrupted. Although creation was good, the created world is not good.

Creation offers the promise of new beginnings. Each day God creates and we begin again. The plant and animal worlds illustrate the renewable character of creation. The psalmist declared that the mercies of God are new every morning. Paul described the Christian experience as renewed, or re-created.

Indeed, creation is predictable and dependable. God is faithful to his covenant and people. We are renewed through prayer in which God faithfully interrupts and punctuates the past and initiates new beginnings. We are renewed through an obedient experience with the progressive will of God. Yes, creation is predictable. It is also filled with promise.

On the one hand, God created. All of existence is an expression of God's nature. God is more immense than creation itself. God is limitless and incomprehensible. On the other hand, God "created humankind in his image." The Creator who cannot be contained by his creation chooses to be expressed through, experienced by, and resident within human life. What a paradox!

However, possibly the greatest paradox of all is the refusal of some individuals to be imaged by the predictable, promise-filled, progressive, and renewable nature of God. Today's crises are many. But at the heart of every broken relationship, world crisis, or depletion of hope is a primary image problem. (Barry J. Beames)

RESPONDING AFTER REMEMBERING

2 CORINTHIANS 13:11-13

The church knows God as the sovereign Father-God who invites as well as demands respectful intimacy, the saving Son—Jesus Christ—who as the enfleshment of God is the most historically clear revelation of the divine offering holy and eternal communion with the divine through faith, and the Holy Spirit who is the continuing presence of God in the world.

The Father is over us. The Son was with us. The Holy Spirit remains among us. The Father created us. The Son saves us through faith. The Holy Spirit empowers us for life and ministry.

While the manifesting forms of God differ, the content remains consistent. One God has revealed himself in three different, though complementary, ways. God is three yet one (*una substantia et tres personae*). "We believe and teach," wrote Henrich Bullinger in the Second Helvetic Confession (1561), "that the same immense, one and indivisible God is in person inseparably and without confusion distinguished as Father, Son, and Holy Spirit. . . . Thus there are not three gods, but three persons, consubstantial, coeternal, and co-equal. . . . For according to the nature and essence they are so joined together that they are one God, and the divine nature is common to the Father, Son, and Holy Spirit."

Simply, Father, Son, and Holy Spirit are the same but different. Same substance: God. Different forms: Trinity.

I. We Honor God by Remembering

We're visual people. We see things and attach meaning to them. We like to say, "I'll believe it when I see it."

So the church has used symbols, icons, stained glass, steeples, crosses, vestments, and so on to remind us of who he is and what he has done for us. After remembering who he is, we respond faithfully through our lives and ministries (vv. 11-13). We are compelled to please him (responding) after remembering who he is and what he has done (Trinity).

I meet with pastors every year for prayer, study, and support. Not long after gathering a few years ago, a friend pulled out a cross from his pocket and showed it to me. He said whenever he feels it or looks at it, he is reminded of who Christ is, who he is, and what the relationship is all about.

II. We Honor God by Responding

A preacher was called to a new church. After his first sermon, he was asked, "How do you expect to please so many people?" He answered, "I don't. I only pray and work to please One. And if it's okay with him, that should be enough for all of us." Lloyd Ogilvie echoes this idea when he asks people he hasn't seen for a while, "Are you more in love with Jesus than the last time that I saw you?"

We respond to who we remember. If he is our Lord and Savior, we pray and work to please him. (Robert R. Kopp)

KNOWING BEFORE SHARING

MATTHEW 28:16-20

A professor had become famous because of his book and course on decision making. Offers to teach at other universities began coming to him. A student walking by his office late one night noticed this professor pacing back and forth inside, looking quite agitated. The student stopped and asked if he were upset about something. The professor said he was trying to decide whether to take a position at another school.

"Oh, well!" said the student. "That should be easy for you by just using that whole system for making decisions that you have all worked out. You wrote the book on that!"

"Are you crazy?" shouted the professor. "This is important!"

I. We Are Called to Share God's Love

The disciples had hard decisions to make after Jesus' death: where to go, what to do. At the close of Matthew's Gospel, we find them where Jesus had told them to go: home, back in Galilee, on a mountaintop—a good place to clear your head for many biblical great moments. From there, Jesus instructs them to go out, with full authority, into the whole world. There, Jesus gives them what we have called the Great Commission to go out and raise lots of money and fill the church rolls. Or maybe that's not exactly what he said. Maybe it would be interesting and even important to look at exactly what he *did* say. Those disciples were to be the leaven to enliven the whole world. But how? Who, indeed, wrote the book on that? Whose instructions have we really been following on how to do that?

How has it been going in regard to making disciples of all nations and transforming the world? Let's be honest. Not too well. Many fine people have been dedicated to this mission, and the church has had a major presence in history for many years. Yet most of the world is worse off than it has ever been. Deep down we know that if we could only do more, give more, sacrifice more, the Kingdom would come in. It's our fault. We know we should give up our jobs, sell our homes, give all away, follow Jesus.

We should. But we won't. But if we can just do more than we have done—go to more meetings, give more money—somehow, something will happen. This is incredibly misguided, filled with prideful audacity, and wrong. It's fine to do these things if we want to, but . . .

II. Before We Share God's Love, We Must Experience Loving God

What was it Jesus sent them out to do? What was the reason for their going out into the world? To teach "them to obey everything that I have commanded you" (v. 20). What was that everything? Jesus said it was all summed up in two commandments: " 'You shall love the Lord with all your heart, and with all your soul, and with all your mind.' This is the greatest and first commandment. And a second is like it: 'You shall love your neighbor as yourself' " (Matt. 22:37-39; see Deut. 6:5). How much time have you spent loving God? Do you think you know how to love God? What does it mean to love God? If your answers to these questions seem a bit hazy, it could mean you've missed something, which happens to be the most important thing.

In fact, we pretty much assumed we had that first commandment covered and/or we decided we couldn't really do that right anyway until perhaps when we're dead. So we got on with number two.

The command to love God wholly, with everything in us, and to do that first and always, is the big one we may have missed. Jesus commanded his disciples to do this, while saying it summarized all the Law and the Prophets (which must be fulfilled). All this makes the first commandment awesome, fearsome, and very important. It means that we must take this very seriously. We must do this. It takes priority over everything else.

It also means that we can do this. Out of the glory of following this first commandment, comes the self, wholly in love with God—that self then whose being is to interact with others to bring them into a baptism of that presence. That self pulls other lives into direct contact with the whole Godhead (Father, Son, and Spirit) because it is in contact with the Godhead.

III. We Can Begin Right Now to Love God

If we don't know how to love God with the whole mind, body, and soul, then we can contemplate the vision of what it might mean for us to love God, and that completely. We can be quiet, pray, and seek.

No one else can tell you what it means for you to love God because when you're doing it, it's new. You are at the heart of creation then, with the ever new, living God. Don't worry. You won't drift into nirvana or disappear into the ether. But you might begin to discover why the biblical record is filled with words of joy, celebration, thanksgiving, and ecstasy from those who have immersed themselves in what it means to love God with the whole being.

We are to bring to all the rest of our mission the self that has loved God. In our eagerness for the signs of good discipleship, have we tried to force the fruit of a vine not even planted in our hearts yet? If we miss step one—the one that summarizes what everything else is just a natural outgrowth of—to try to go anywhere and do anything without that would be crazy. Loving God comes first—after that, we can't help sharing that love with others. (Kathleen Peterson)

JUNE 9, 1996

≥◆

Second Sunday After Pentecost

Worship Theme: God's love is greater than all our sin.

Readings: Genesis 12:1-9; Romans 4:13-25; Matthew 9:9-13, 18-26

Call to Worship (Psalm 33:1-12):

Leader: Rejoice in the LORD, O you righteous. Praise befits the upright. Praise the LORD with the lyre; make melody to him with the harp of ten strings.

People: **Sing to him a new song;**

Leader: play skillfully on the strings with loud shouts. For the word of the LORD is upright,

People: **and all his work is done in faithfulness.**

Leader: He loves righteousness and justice; the earth is full of the steadfast love of the LORD.

People: **By the word of the LORD the heavens were made,**

Leader: and all their host by the breath of his mouth. He gathered the waters of the sea as in a bottle; he put the deeps in storehouses.

People: **Let all the earth fear the LORD;**

Leader: let all the inhabitants of the world stand in awe of him. For he spoke, and it came to be; he commanded, and it stood firm.

People: **The LORD brings the counsel of the nations to nothing;**

Leader: he frustrates the plans of the peoples. The counsel of the LORD stands forever, the thoughts of his heart to all generations.

People: **Happy is the nation whose God is the LORD, the people whom he has chosen as his heritage.**

201

Pastoral Prayer:

While we were yet enmeshed in sin, O Lord, you allowed your precious Son to act as a sacrifice on our behalf. While we were at our most unworthy, you reached out in love and grace to redeem us and restore us to relationship with you. How are we to understand such an awesome love, O Lord—we who are so fickle and faithless? Your love is beyond our comprehension, Lord; your grace surpasses our understanding. Even though we cannot yet grasp all that Christ's death and resurrection represent, we nevertheless rejoice in your presence and praise your name. We trust the promise of your Word that no matter the extent of our sin, your love is even greater. Help us, day by day, to live more worthy of your love, for we ask it in the name of the One who gave his life that we might live eternally. Amen.

SERMON BRIEFS

THE MAKING OF A LEGEND

GENESIS 12:1-9

Among the legendary names and acts of history, Abram is remembered as the one chosen by God to establish a sacred community in which humanity could experience the blessing of God. He is revered by Jews as the founder of the Jewish nation and by Christians as "the father of the faithful." He is honored by Arabians as their progenitor. God perpetuates that legacy by using the same strategy with those he calls today—like you and me.

I. God Calls Us to a New Lifestyle

God's summons of Abram was a call to a legendary lifestyle (vv. 1-3). Whether you understand Abram to have received two separate calls, or one call at Ur and a renewal of that call at Haran, he was commissioned to a task that was larger than life. Through Abram, God would make the world recipient of his own blessing. God perpetuates that legacy by commissioning every believer to be a vessel through whom God can bless the world.

II. God's Call Involves New Consequences

The Talmudic rabbis taught that God would bless Abram with a sevenfold promise. First, Abram was to become the father of a great nation. The Hebrew word *goy* described a political concept that implied a territorial base. Yet, at age seventy-five, Abram had no heir. God also promised to bless Abram in his lifetime. That blessing included God's protection from harm and Abram's enjoyment of God's favor. Third, God would make Abram become a world figure by giving him a great name. Further, Abram would become a blessing to others.

The privilege of God's call should inspire great responsibility. God also promised to bless those who received Abram and curse the one who did not. It is significant that "those who bless you" is plural and "the one who curses you" is singular. God's assurance that the number of his friends outnumbered his foes was inspiring. Finally, as a consequence of God's call, Abram would have a positive world-wide influence.

III. God's Call Requires a New Commitment

An absolute dedication of life to a task is the stuff legacies are made of. Abram's surrender to God was remarkable (vv. 4-5). He left his home with no forwarding address. He had a large household to move: servants, family members, personal possessions, and his massive livestock enterprise. Further, at the age of seventy-five, Abram was likely beyond being motivated by highly sensational adventures. Obediently, however, Abram moved forward.

Abram was naturally inclined to journey toward the land of Canaan, the land of promise and blessing. What is more significant, however, is the brief note in verse 5: "when they had come to the land of Canaan." History is never changed by things that should be done. Abram was determined to do the will of God.

The legacy that Abram entered was also filled with surprises (vv. 6-8). Upon his arrival, Abram was surprised to find the land inhabited by Canaanites. Another encounter he did not expect was the appearance of the Lord reaffirming the value of Abram's obedience.

Abram surprised the Canaanites, also. The phrase "and the souls that they had gotten in Haran" in verse 5 (KJV) may reference an early religious community. Abram infiltrated one religious community (pagan) with another (sacred). Between Shechem and the oak of Moreh, in the plain shadowed by what was possibly a Canaanite sanctuary, Abram built an altar. That solemn act of devotion was a public profession of his faith in Yahweh. Then Abram went to Bethel and built another altar. That legacy of worship and obedience was accompanied by a victorious lifestyle.

As wonderful as that experience was, it is verse 9 that inspires me: "And Abram journeyed, going on still toward the south" (KJV). The legacy continues as we obediently follow God's leadership to make the world the recipient of the blessing of God that has been entrusted to us. (Barry J. Beames)

LOVE THAT'S LARGER THAN LAW

ROMANS 4:13-25

God's love has always been larger than the divine law. Paul used Abraham's example to illustrate that no matter how good we are or become or pretend to be, we'll never be good enough to satisfy God's law (vv. 13-22). That's why we rely on God's love in Jesus to make up the difference (vv. 23-25).

It's not that our Lord tolerates behavior that contradicts biblical revelation. It's that God loves us *anyway* and gives us opportunity after opportunity to be healed. Ultimately knowing we'll never get it perfectly correct. God offers himself as the price of our shortcomings. God invites us to walk through him from our sinfulness to divine perfection (v. 25).

I. A Contemporary Example of Breaking the Law

Healthy heterosexuals in singularly long-term monogamous relationships generally don't have to worry about contracting AIDS. For drug addicts, promiscuous heterosexuals and homosexuals, and in cases of bad blood transfusions, AIDS has been a devastating disease.

Christians who believe the Bible "is the only rule to direct us how we may glorify and enjoy Him" (*The Shorter Catechism* of 1647, Question 2) have never been able to affirm or encourage homosexuality as an acceptable or alternative lifestyle regardless of how culturally insensitive or politically incorrect that may sound.

And yet what the church believes about homosexuality has very little to do with how it responds to people with AIDS. When it comes to people with AIDS, honest-to-God-faithful-to-the-Bible Christians aren't as obsessed about the ethics of homosexuality as the homophobes who continue to prorate sexual sins to the top of God's no-no list or the heterophobes who keep trying to rationalize their behavior apart from biblical revelation.

II. God's Loving Response to People Who Break the Law

Christians want to know how they, as Christians, are supposed to approach the disease and those who have it. And whenever Christians want to know what to say and do, they recall what Jesus said and did.

Christianity as exemplified in Jesus and explained in the Bible extends a helping and healing hand to everybody regardless of who, what, where, or when. *Jesus loved them all.* There is not one instance in which his love for people was overshadowed by his ethical inspection of them. Rather than assessing and cataloging the personal culpability for their circumstances, Jesus was primarily concerned with praying and working for their healing.

Certainly, Jesus never affirmed or encouraged behavior antithetical to biblical revelation. As certainly, he never stopped loving and seeking redemption for those who fell short of that standard. After all, that's why he came in the first place. He came to save us from the damning distance between our imperfections and his perfection.

Does anybody seriously question how Jesus would approach people with AIDS? He said, "Just as I have loved you, you also should love one another" (John 13:34). He said that while knowing all of our emotional, intellectual, spiritual, and physical diseases. He also said, "As you have cared for the least of these who are members of my family, you have cared for me." (See Matt. 25.)

Several years ago in Kansas City, a man showed up in my study at 7:00 A.M. He quickly confessed that he had been drinking very heavily the previous night and he woke up that morning in the sack with a woman other than his wife.

He felt awful. He said he knew he could never be forgiven for cheating on his wife. I said that was wrong. And I told him the good news of Jesus coming into the world to save people from the consequences of their sins. I told him that's why we call Jesus our Savior. I told him about Moses the murderer, David the adulterer, Peter the traitor, and countless numbers of other people who have experienced God's forgiveness through confession.

Before he left, I asked him to pray with me. I'll never forget his part of the prayer: "I want to thank you for forgiving my sins—my past sins, my sins last night, *and the sins that I will commit in the future.*"

It brought to mind the man who met Jesus and confessed, "I did it." Jesus pointed to the cross and said, "That's why I did it."

It's the gospel. It's why divine love is larger than divine law. (Robert R. Kopp)

ASKING FOR HELP

MATTHEW 9:9-13, 18-26

It is not easy to locate the "heart" in a passage that has three separate centers of gravity—Matthew's call to follow Jesus and two healing narratives that form a kind of scriptural sandwich. But if we push on this passage, it can reveal an important connection between Jesus' asking for help from Matthew—one of the sinners or the "sick"—and two other persons' asking in different ways for healing from Jesus.

I. Self-help as a Social Image

Our culture gives mixed signals about asking for help. Churches are full of recovery group meetings, and bookstores are crammed full of self-help books on virtually every topic from assertive communication to zero down payment real estate. American men have long been taught to show that they are in control and that they have immediate answers for business or interpersonal dilemmas (as in the phrase "No problem!").

Yet the violent results of men's in-control image have reached epidemic proportions. And women, more and more often facing work and family structures that ask for self-confidence and quick problem solving, find that they need to convey the image of being self-assured and self-sufficient, whatever their inner feelings.

II. The Truth of Our Need for Help

"Always being in charge" sounds great but doesn't work. It is not biblically, historically, or even psychologically accurate. These brief stories in Matthew shine a clear and ultimately positive light on that fact. Jesus seeks Matthew's help, knowing Matthew's limitations as a member of a compromised profession. Both the synagogue leader and the woman with a flow of blood seek Jesus' help in physical healing, knowing that they alone cannot produce the results they seek.

Jesus affirms their acts of faith, explicitly in the case of the frightened yet courageous woman, and implicitly in the case of the religious leader's daughter, who is "asleep" rather than dead in the eyes of all who believe in the Resurrection.

People know whether we have actually traveled the road into the presence of Jesus the healer. They see in our eyes and hear in our voices the truth of our search, whether Jesus has come upon us unexpectedly as he did Matthew, whether we have come face-to-face with him in confidence as did the synagogue leader, or whether we have lurked behind him in the fear of public judgment and stigma. The important thing is for the actual human need and the power of the Healer to meet again and again.

III. Asking for Help—a Powerful Act

Faith is not only intellectual assent but also the confidence to move toward the light and the future. Wherever we are placed, and whatever the source of pain, there is always another chance to move toward the One who loves us and makes us whole. He comes to call not the righteous, particularly not the self-righteous, but all of us who are sick or needy or ashamed or compromised in this world. As in the pattern of African American worship, the call invites a response. Worship—in fact all of life—is not complete until the call and the response come together. Hallelujah! (Barbara Bate)

JUNE 16, 1996

۶ﻼ

Third Sunday After Pentecost

Worship Theme: Faith in Jesus Christ inspires confident living.

Readings: Genesis 18:1-15 (21:1-7); Romans 5:1-8; Matthew 9:35–10:8 (9-23)

Call to Worship (Psalm 116:12-19):

Leader: What shall I return to the LORD for all his bounty to me?

People: I will lift up the cup of salvation and call on the name of the LORD,

Leader: I will pay my vows to the LORD in the presence of all his people.

People: Precious in the sight of the LORD is the death of his faithful ones.

Leader: O LORD, I am your servant; I am your servant, the child of your serving girl. You have loosed my bonds.

People: I will offer to you a thanksgiving sacrifice and call on the name of the LORD.

Leader: I will pay my vows to the LORD in the presence of all his people, in the courts of the house of the LORD, in your midst, O Jerusalem.

People: Praise the LORD!

Pastoral Prayer:

O Lord, who promised us life abundant and life eternal, we come before you in these moments as a people who know so little abundance. We know some things in abundance, of course. Many of us have been blessed with an abundance of material things, and we are abundant in our envy of those who have more. We have an abundance of petty jealousies and frustrations, and we are willing to express our anger in abundance. What a pity, Father, that we so often revel in the abundance of things that devastate and destroy, when you have made a way for us to know the richness and fullness of life as you intended it in all of its authentic abundance. Help us, Lord, to have an abundance of thankfulness and praise in our hearts; give us an abundance of love and concern for one another; help us, Lord, to have an abundance of compassion for those who struggle and hurt all around us; make us abundant in our witness of the good news of Jesus Christ. Thank you, Lord, for your abundant grace, which draws us to you even though we do not deserve to be in your presence. Amen.

SERMON BRIEFS

OPEN OR CLOSED?

GENESIS 18:1-15 (21:1-7)

Abraham had sought relief from the stifling midday desert heat by sitting in the shade provided by his tent. Realizing three men were standing nearby, Abraham extended to them the ordinary courtesy of a host. But it was not to be any ordinary day, for they were not ordinary guests and their mission was not an ordinary task.

Abraham recognized that one of the visitors was the Lord, who announced that Abraham and Sarah would have a son. That announcement was met with mixed reviews. Their reactions to the announcement illustrate both appropriate and inappropriate responses to the revealed will of God in our lives.

I. We Can Receive God with Open Minds and Hearts

Abraham's response demonstrated hospitality at its best (vv. 2-8). Guests were to be treated with great respect. That was why John's summary of Jesus' experience, "He came to what was his own, and his own people did not accept him" (John 1:11), was so stunning.

Custom dictated, and Abraham promised, to offer his guests a little water and a morsel of bread (vv. 4-5). What he delivered, however, far exceeded what was customary. Abraham supplied milk and a yogurt-type refreshment, instructed Sarah to bake bread from three measures of meal, and ordered a young tender calf be prepared for the celebration. Once the feast was prepared, Abraham stood and served his guests while they ate.

That the Lord ate at his table is without precedent in the Old Testament. God continues to perform unprecedented acts in our lives. An appropriate response to divine movement is to develop a spiritual sensitivity that recognizes the unique actions of God. Another appropriate response is to maintain a servant posture before the Lord. A final appropriate response is to respond to the Lord in such a manner that exceeds what is customary.

II. It Is Also Possible to Face God with Closed Minds and Hearts

Sarah's response, on the other hand, is unbelief at its worst (vv. 9-15). The Lord told Abraham that Sarah would have a son. Sarah's response was revealed to be inappropriate on three accounts.

Sarah demonstrated an incidental involvement in God's plan (v. 9). Sarah was to play a significant role in Abraham's becoming the father of a great nation. For whatever reason, Sarah was absent from the group. Her interest was only to eavesdrop by listening to the conversation through the wall of the tent. Many times we participate in the work of God at a distance when God has purposed for us to play a significant role in the accomplishment of the divine will.

Sarah also laughed at the notion that God could give her a child (v. 12). Her doubt is a striking contrast to Abraham's faith. Yet God knew her heart and responded, "Is anything too wonderful for the LORD?" For Sarah, the greater surprise was not that she would have a child but that the Lord knew her heart. The message, however, not the messenger, was the real issue. Anytime we doubt the message, the Word of God, our response is inappropriate.

If that was not enough, Sarah added insult to injury. Once the Lord confronted her disbelief, Sarah denied it (v. 15). The greater tragedy was not Sarah's unbelief, but her refusal to be honest about her thoughts. It is one thing to disbelieve God; it is another thing to deny that you disbelieve God. The man in Mark 9:24 needed a miracle and experienced a miracle when he begged Jesus, "Help my unbelief!"

There is a right way and a wrong way to respond to God. Abraham and Sarah demonstrate both responses. Your response to the unfolding purposes of God in your life will reveal hospitality at its best or unbelief at its worst. Either way, be assured, God always has the final word. (Barry J. Beames)

THE SAVING SCENARIO

ROMANS 5:1-8

The essential message of Christianity is simple: believing in Jesus inspires confident living as it insures eternal life. Or as Paul and Silas assured the Philippian jailer who asked how he could be saved, "Believe on the Lord Jesus, and you will be saved" (Acts 16:30-31).

To believe in Jesus is to acknowledge and applaud him to be who he said he is (John 14:6) and affirm with Peter. "There is salvation in no one else, for there is no other name under heaven given among mortals by which we must be saved" (Acts 4:12).

Considering our Lord's repeatedly inclusive invitations—*whoever* believes—to experience his good news (e.g., John 3:16; 11:25-26), Christianity's saving scenario is the ultimate theme of every book in *the* Book. "The arrival of Jesus," Eugene H. Peterson wrote in his introduction to *The Message* "signaled the beginning of a new era. God entered history in a personal way, and made it unmistakably clear that He is on our side, doing everything possible to save us."

Romans 5:1-8 highlights the saving scenario by Jesus (vv. 1-2), through suffering (vv. 3-5), and in spite of sin (vv. 6-8).

I. Saved by Jesus (vv. 1-2)

Believing in Jesus inspires confident living as it includes justification (just-as-if-we'd-never-sinned) and peace with God (harmonious relationship). Believing in Jesus insures eternal life because he is our access—our way—to eternal life. Paul emphasized justification and peace through faith in Jesus in recognition of Jesus as the mediator of God's grace (Col. 3:17).

Christianity has never embraced the notion that there are many paths to the top of the mountain. We have maintained there are many paths to the bottom of the mountain. We have taken Jesus at his word as being the one way to confident living and eternal life.

Remembering the inclusive invitations to experience the good news, Christianity cannot be considered exclusive. The only ones who aren't included are those who exclude themselves. C. S. Lewis explained, "If we insist on keeping Hell . . . we shall not see Heaven. . . . All that are in Hell, choose it. . . . No soul that seriously and constantly desires joy will ever miss it. Those who seek find. To those who knock it is opened" (*The Great Divorce*).

II. Saved Through Suffering (vv. 3-5)

Although believing in Jesus doesn't make us immune to suffering, our faith enables us to see beyond it. When Paul wrote Christians "boast in our sufferings," he didn't mean "because of " our sufferings. He was explaining how the eternal security of Christianity inspires confident living regardless of existential circumstances.

Corrie ten Boom and *The Hiding Place* quickly come to mind. It is the true story of a Dutch family who hid Jews from the Nazis. Shortly after the whole family was arrested, Corrie received word that her father died. She prayed, "Dear Jesus, how foolish of me to have called for human help when You are here. To think that Father sees You now, face to face! To think that he and Mama are together again." She wrote on her cell wall: "March 9, 1994. Father. Released." Not long after that, she cradled her dying sister in her arms. Betsie said to Corrie, "We must go everywhere. We must tell people that no pit is so deep that God is not deeper still. They will believe us, because we were here."

III. Saved in Spite of Sin (vv. 6-8)

Verse 8 sums up God's amazing grace in Jesus. We are loved not *because of* who we are and what we do but *in spite of* who we are and what we do. When God loved us to death in Jesus, God proved an unconditional love that is irrespective of our behavior.

One of my favorite stories is about the fellow who was greeted at the gates of heaven and asked, "What's the password?" After several failed attempts, he sighed, "Well, then, I give up." And the gates of heaven opened for him.

We need a Savior. We've got him in Jesus through faith. (Robert R. Kopp)

SCHOOLING DISCIPLES

MATTHEW 9:35–10:8 (9-23)

What does it take to build disciples? A seemingly miscellaneous passage from Matthew's Gospel gives us realistic answers to that question, answers that speak to churches and leaders trying to move into the future together.

Jesus models the three tasks of ministry—teaching, healing, proclaiming—and then guides the Twelve toward their own journeys as bringers of good news.

I. Realism About the Tasks of Ministry

Realism marks Jesus' instructions to the disciples. They are to begin with prayer to the Lord of the harvest for increase in their work. They are to start their ministry with the lost sheep of Israel, focusing their energies rather than trying to reach everyone everywhere.

Since this Gospel was written and circulated years after Paul's account of the ministry to the Gentiles, we can see this as an account of foundational training for the Twelve rather than a decision by Jesus never to move beyond the Jews. Remember the account of the Syro-Phoenician woman in Matthew 15 and the dialogue with the Samaritan woman in John 4.

II. Realism About Local Communities

The disciples are called to be realistic about possible opposition from the local communities they visit. Some will welcome them; some will not. The Teacher encourages them to travel simply—no extra clothes, food, or other encumbrances—and to keep their equilibrium (presumably with each other's help) if they are not welcomed and treated peacefully on their travels.

The wonderfully vivid image of shaking the dust from one's feet in verse 14 evokes a modern song lyric that advised a bereaved lover to "pick yourself up, dust yourself off, and start all over again." The parallel is appropriate, for discipleship is a love affair with the world God so loves.

III. Realism About Life and Death

In the extended version of this passage, Jesus makes clear to his adult students that opposition is quite likely to take on an apocalyptic quality; it is a matter of literal as well as spiritual life versus death. There is no assurance of public acceptance, only of the necessity to proclaim truthfully that "the kingdom of heaven has come near." (For these twelve partners it is a "kin-dom" as well.)

IV. Realism for Contemporary Trainees

Contemporary congregations have heard the word *discipleship* often enough that its repetition by itself does not necessarily grab our attention. But focus on the ways Jesus acts as a trainer for this particular cadre of civilized revolutionaries—a small motley crew of people with a holy gleam in their eyes. Those twelve named men, like the rest of us individual humans, didn't just wake up as disciples. They, like us, had to grow into that identity with the aid of visionary, yet realistic, leadership.

What does it take to build disciples today? Prayer, vision, information, realism about both positive and negative futures, and ongoing support from each other. The best candidates for Jesus' discipleship school were those who had as many needs as they had skills. Like us, they had to be teachable persons, not so convinced of their own perfection that they would preach a gospel of ego massage or self-righteous judgment of the rest of the world.

Any of us—pastors as well as laypersons—can use the instructions from this manual in Matthew to affirm that being disciples is both costly and uniquely enriching. Participating in the teaching, healing, and celebrating acts of God is better than any diploma yet earned on earth. (Barbara Bate)

JUNE 23, 1996

❧

Fourth Sunday After Pentecost

Worship Theme: Christ will provide the resources we need to walk faithfully with him day by day.

Readings: Genesis 21:8-21; Romans 6:1*b*-11; Matthew 10:24-39

Call to Worship (Psalm 86:1-5):

Leader: Incline your ear, O LORD, and answer me, for I am poor and needy.

People: For you, O God, are good and forgiving.

Leader: Preserve my life, for I am devoted to you; save your servant who trusts in you.

People: For you, O Lord, are good and forgiving.

Leader: You are my God; be gracious to me, O Lord, for to you do I cry all day long.

People: For you, O Lord, are good and forgiving.

Leader: Gladden the soul of your servant, for to you, O Lord, I lift up my soul.

People: For you, O Lord, are good and forgiving.

Pastoral Prayer:

In the midst of the challenges of daily life, O Lord, we are thankful for your gracious and comforting presence. When we face hostility, you provide love; when we feel weak, you provide love; when we are confused, you provide direction. Though time and again we have fallen short of your will for our lives, you are good and forgiving; you reach out to reconcile and restore us. What amazing love, O Lord! We are undeserving of it, yet we gratefully accept it as your gift. Yet we know, Lord, that most of those around us do not know that love in their own lives. We see them every day: in the office, at school, at the shop, in our own homes. Help us, Lord, to be faithful witnesses of your love; stir within us an urgency to share your good news with those who so desperately need to hear it. Even as you have loved us, make us instruments of your love to others. For we ask it in the name of the One who loved us, even to the point of a cross. Amen.

SERMON BRIEFS

FAMILY MATTERS

GENESIS 21:8-21

Strained relationships, jealousy, favoritism, and stress are a few of the normal struggles every family must manage. I was thirty-four years old when our youngest son was born. I cannot imagine how Abraham and Sarah dealt with the chronic fatigue and sleep deprivation that accompany being a preschooler's parent at the age of one hundred! Add to that the dynamics of a blended family and you have tension with a capital T!

I can understand why the parents would celebrate when he finally disposed of Isaac's last diaper (v. 8). I have also learned to be cautious because with many celebrations another crisis is waiting to crash the party. Like Abraham and Sarah, you and I are often crushed by the brutal reality of our family matters. This episode in their lives models for us three dynamic principles that greatly enhance our own family matters.

I. Impure Motives Damage Meaningful Relationships (vv. 9-11)

Life is in constant motion and that fluidity means change. Once Sarah was not able to have children. Because of a miracle of God, she and Abraham have a son. But now, Sarah is devastated that Isaac and the stepson Ishmael are not only playmates but joint heirs, even though Sarah had encouraged Abraham to make her handmaid, Hagar, the mother of his child.

This is not the first marital conflict of this family matter. Immediately after Ishmael was conceived, Sarah was angry, filled with guilt, and she began to assign the blame to others. For many years theirs had been a rocky relationship. Sarah's jealousy had infected her relationships—first with Abraham, then her servant, and now her son. But that jealousy resulted from a poor decision.

Even though Sarah's gift of Hagar to Abraham was culturally correct, socially acceptable, and religiously redeemable, the consequences were relationally devastating. The decision Sarah made prior to her experience with God was different from her after-God experience. Did Sarah lose hope and abandon her faith in God and take matters into her own hands to manipulate the will of God? Did Abraham's nagging wear down Sarah's faith defense mechanism? Or, as often happens, did Sarah's selfless passion for Abraham fade as her own personal identity emerged to prominence? Regardless, one thing is certain: Sarah's selfish jealousy infected her relationships and caused Abraham to grieve.

II. The Purposes of God Prevail in Spite of the Circumstances of Life (vv. 12-14)

It was an emotionally charged situation characterized as cruel, angry, and broken. God told Abraham to not grieve but to do as Sarah said. Abraham sent his firstborn away. You never know what it is to have a firstborn son until you have a secondborn son.

Again, because of his faithfulness, Abraham discovered that God's plans were bigger than he understood. God would make a nation from each son, both Isaac and from Ishmael. Grasp that principle: God's purposes for our lives will prevail, regardless of the circumstances in which we find ourselves! The most demanding family matters deserve to be understood against the backdrop of God's ultimate purposes for our lives.

III. God's Provision Is Always Adequate to Accomplish the Divine Will in Our Lives (vv. 15-21)

That is difficult to believe but it may be even more difficult to accept. God gave Hagar and Ishmael everything they needed as strokes in the mural of his redemptive history.

That is encouraging! First, God's provision for you will never be less than adequate and will never be late. Second, God's purpose for you is not merely for survival but a daily experience as the bride of Christ, an heir of the Creator.

Family matters do not have to be bitter or blistering. Abraham and Sarah's experience enables you with three winning family principles: jealousy always infects relationships, the purposes of God prevail in spite of our circumstances, and God's provision is always adequate to accomplish his exalted purpose for our lives. (Barry J. Beames)

LIVING LIKE JESUS ROSE FROM THE DEAD

ROMANS 6:1*b*-11

Some people live like Jesus never rose from the dead. They are moderately committed to him. They are moderately Christian. They remind me of the statement by Frank Layden, the former coach of the Utah Jazz, who said to a player, "Son, I don't understand it with you. Is it ignorance or apathy?" The player replied, "Coach, I don't know and I don't care."

Some people live like Jesus rose from the dead. They pray and work to be holy unto him (vv. 2-7). They live confidently in the assurance of eternal life through faith in Jesus (vv. 5, 8-10). They are "alive to God" (v. 11)

Living like Jesus rose from the dead is confirmed through confession (what we say), countenance (how we look), and conduct (what we do).

I. We Declare Our Faith Through Our Confession

Rising from the dead confirmed Jesus' identity as our Savior and Lord. We are assured of eternal life through faith in him as our Savior (vv. 5, 8-10). We are committed to honor him through our lives and ministries as our Lord (vv. 2-7, 11).

We are baptized into or *marked off for* him (vv. 3-4). That's why we confess with Paul, "I am not ashamed of the gospel; it is the power of God for salvation to everyone who has faith" (Rom. 1:16). Confidently and courageously, we confess his preeminent place in our lives as Savior and Lord.

Within our confessional context, we order our lives and ministries in response to three questions. First, do we honor the name of Jesus alone through what we say and do? Second, do our priorities, plans, and programs promote his kingdom on earth as it is in heaven? Third, what would Jesus say about our lives and ministries?

II. We Display Our Faith Through Our Countenance

One of the saddest indictments against the church comes from children. When asked what they think of church, they will invariably blurt out, "It's boring!"

The visitor to a rather staid congregation comes to mind. He became excited during the sermon and exclaimed, "Praise the Lord!" An usher rushed to him and said, "I'm sorry, sir, but we don't do that here." "But I've got religion," the man explained. "Well," huffed the usher, "you didn't get it here." It's like the fellow who said, "I would have become a preacher if they didn't look like undertakers."

Countenance confirms confession (v. 11). How we look is the enfleshment of what we believe. Or as we've heard, "The only gospel that some folks will ever hear or see is the gospel according to you and me."

When we know who he is, we look like we know him. We are "alive to God." Our confession is confirmed rather than concealed by our countenance. It's like the song, "If you're a Christian and you know it, then you really ought to show it."

III. We Demonstrate Our Faith Through Our Conduct

Behavior measures belief (vv. 2-7, 11). Conduct confirms confession and countenance. "Good works do not make a good man," wrote Martin Luther in *The Freedom of a Christian* (1520), "but a good man does good works." John Calvin concluded people who know Jesus as Savior and Lord show the signs of their salvation: "Briefly, the more earnestly any man measures his life by the standard of God's law, the surer are the signs of repentance that he shows" (*Institutes of the Christian Religion,* 1536).

Living like Jesus rose from the dead is as simple as the ending refrain of an old gospel favorite: "You ask me how I know he lives? He lives within my heart."

If he is alive to us, we are alive to Jesus through confession, countenance, and conduct. (Robert R. Kopp)

BREAD FOR THE JOURNEY

MATTHEW 10:24-39

Have you ever tried to condense many thoughts and feelings into a very short and memorable form? For example, can you imagine trying to explain a symphonic orchestra on a postcard or putting a lifetime of advice to a child into several short directives?

In a sense, that is what Jesus is doing in this text. He is giving instruction to the disciples to prepare them for the hostility and suffering they will encounter on their mission, and he is trying to help them maintain a hold on the vivid life they have experienced together.

If we look at his teaching in this manner, it does not seem so much a disjointed group of sayings but more like shorthand instructions around a unifying thread: bread for the journey, especially the kind you drop behind to help you find your way back.

I. On the Journey, We Will Encounter Opposition

He begins with an age-old warning: they will be called names, and as we all know, names do hurt us. Even being misunderstood is painful, to be seen as other than we believe ourselves to be. Jesus has been called the devil himself and so asks what his disciples can expect from their detractors.

Implicit in his statement that a disciple is not above the teacher is a call for each of his followers, then and now, to experience the fullness of life as he led it. We should not assume that we will not have to suffer since Jesus took care of everything. Jesus is telling us that our lives will not be easier than his, and he urges us to embrace the life of faith with all of its pain and glory.

II. On the Journey, We Will Encounter God's Love

Jesus then urges the disciples to have no fear of those who abuse them. In fact, he is insistent regarding fear, repeating three times that they need not be afraid. He encourages them to speak boldly the things they have previously discussed privately, without regard for the local authorities, and to remember that they are answerable only to God, who alone has power over both their bodies and their souls.

He takes time to tell them how infinitely precious they are to God, reminding them that the divine "eye is on the sparrow" and they are of much greater value. Then Jesus challenges them to hold fast to their faith, acknowledging him before others.

These words still challenge us today. Our cultural indifference to religious values leads many of us, even clergy, to not mention prayers answered, we don't tell of moments of spiritual insight or share the poignant moment in church, nor do we talk of the struggle in the life of faith; we simply let the moment pass. We don't do it because the surrounding cultural apathy feels like hostility, and yet Jesus warns of spiritual consequences if we deny our allegiance to him. He urges us to break out of fear.

III. On the Journey, We Will Encounter Decisions

Jesus continues his directions by challenging the disciples in their allegiances. He states the strain that their new life in the gospel will place on their strongest loyalties. He pits true discipleship against any bond of affection and familial fidelity that would stand between the disciple and the life of faith.

Finally, Jesus issues the ultimate challenge to those who would follow him: that of picking up our individual crosses and being willing to lose (and, paradoxically, find) our lives in the service of his greater life among us.

These words for the disciples are still relevant for disciples today. Jesus is calling us to a more open proclamation of what we value most, to move beyond fear and the tired emptiness that consumes our culture. If we listen and follow, we can find our way back (through these broken bread bits of guidance) into the freshness and fullness of his extravagant life. (Penelope Duckworth)

JUNE 30, 1996

Fifth Sunday After Pentecost

Worship Theme: Absolute obedience is essential to a deeper walk with God.

Readings: Genesis 22:1-14; Romans 6:12-23; Matthew 10:40-42

Call to Worship (Psalm 13:5-6):

Leader: I trusted in your steadfast love;

People: my heart shall rejoice in your salvation.

Leader: I will sing to the LORD,

People: because he has dealt bountifully with me.

Pastoral Prayer:

We are a people, O Lord, for whom obedience does not come easy. Like our fathers and mothers before us, our instinct is to stake a claim for our own will, rejecting all other claims. As we walk day by day in the midst of a self-absorbed society, obedient to nothing beyond its own desires, help us, Lord, to learn to trust you enough to obey your will, even when it is in conflict with our own will. Teach us, Father, to draw on your wisdom for direction because our own wisdom will lead us to destruction. We are thankful, Lord, that you were willing to sacrifice the life of your own Son that we might have life in you; help us to be willing to sacrifice so that others might also know your life and your love. Amen.

SERMON BRIEFS

A WILLINGNESS TO SACRIFICE

GENESIS 22:1-14

The possibility of a child to bless the home of Abraham and Sarah hinged on a promise given by Jehovah and seemed only a remote possibility. After all she was in her nineties, and he was about one hundred. Who would ever dream that it could happen? But nothing is impossible with God, and Sarah became pregnant with her "child of promise." Both she and Abraham rejoiced! She cried out for the entire world to hear, "God has brought me laughter, and everyone who hears about this will laugh with me" (Gen. 21:6 NIV).

Over the years, Isaac brought smiles to Abraham's face and laughter to his mother. He had been worth waiting for. But it seems that in the beginning verses of chapter 22 of Genesis, God was about to play a cruel joke on this old couple. Out of nowhere comes God's voice saying, "Take your son, your *only* son Isaac, whom you love, and go to the land of Moriah." So far so good, but then the sadistic joke—"Offer him there as a burnt offering" (v. 2).

Can you imagine Abraham's shock? God could not be asking that of him. Other people sacrificed their children, but they were heathen! What about the promise of a child? What about the promise of a great nation coming from Abraham's seed? Would it die on the mountainside? What about Sarah's feelings—her great love for this boy who had brought incredible joy into her life? And what about Abraham's happiness? No, it just couldn't be God speaking!

But it was God, and Abraham knew it. He had to respond as he had done all his life. A willingness to obey God pervaded Abraham's spirit and life.

As willingness dominated Abraham, so it must dominate us. Three thoughts stand out in the text.

I. The Willingness of Abraham's Availability (v. 1)

Abraham says, "Here I am." Great people of faith have always made availability their trademark. Moses (Exod. 3:4), Joshua (Josh. 1:16), Samuel (1 Sam. 3:10), David (1 Sam. 17), Isaiah (Isa. 6:8), and Jesus (Luke 22:42) are a few examples. Availability means a readiness to do what God wants and wills.

One of Robert Louis Stevenson's earliest memories concerned the old lamplighter who passed down the streets of Edinburgh as darkness would fall. One by one he would light the street oil lamps. Stevenson recalled years later, "What I remember best about the lamplighter was he always left a light behind him."

The availability of God's faithful people has left a light behind them for others to follow.

II. The Willingness to Sacrifice (vv. 2-5)

As Abraham and Isaac traveled together, the idea of sacrificing his son must have troubled Abraham. It certainly would trouble me! I have a son whom I love, who is in his mid-twenties, about the age that scholars believe Isaac was at this time in the story. I cannot imagine the idea of human sacrifice of my son. However, at an altar before God and people, when he was a baby in arms, my wife and I dedicated him to God. We stated that whatever came, he was God's for time and eternity. Whatever God wanted for Jeff's life, we were sacrificing our will for God's will. Those were not empty words.

God asks that our human desires for our children be sacrificed on the altar of life so that his desires and will might be accomplished. Will you do that?

III. The Willingness to Be the Sacrifice (v. 9)

Our human struggling must cease so that we can be sacrificed on the altar of God's purpose. Isaac's will was sacrificed.

Our question to God must include a commitment. Where, God, do you want me to go? Should I stay? How much time do I give? Is this enough to give? Take me, God—lock, stock, and barrel—to be yours.

Are you willing to climb on the altar of sacrifice today, to jump into the fire of God's Spirit and will? If you do, you will come out a different person! (Derl G. Keefer)

LIVING TRIUMPHANTLY

ROMANS 6:12-23

In Paul's letters, the word *therefore* serves as something of a hinge; it connects a theological principle with an application or implication of that principle. In verse 11, Paul has just noted that as believers, we are "dead to sin and alive to God in Christ Jesus." *Therefore*, there are some implications to being alive to God in Christ.

Paul wants us to understand that being alive to God in Christ produces a triumphant existence characterized by an entirely new kind of life. What does it mean to be alive to God in Christ Jesus?

I. Being Alive to God Means We Have a New Lifestyle (vv. 12-14)

The power of sin has been broken, and we are free to live for God rather than being bound to sin. Indeed, living godly lives is not an option of the Christian walk; it is a necessity.

Paul assumes that sin is still present and still a concern for believers. We have not been mystically transformed into a state in which we are no longer tempted; we are tempted, and we do fail at times. But the believer must not allow sin to reign or hold dominion in his or her life; Christ alone must be Lord.

You and I face the constant temptation to yield to sin; sometimes we even rationalize that it's just a "tiny sin" and won't do any permanent harm. Bill Tuck tells of a buzzard flying over the Niagara River on a bitterly freezing day, when the bird spotted an animal carcass floating in the river toward the great falls. The buzzard knew it could feed for a brief time before his "dinner" went over the falls, so the bird landed on the carcass. But moments later as the falls approached and the buzzard attempted to fly away, it discovered that its talons had frozen to the carcass, and it went over the falls to its destruction along with its prey.

Evil can be seductive, and it may seem harmless, but we have been made alive to God in Christ, and sin has no place in our lives. We have been called to a new lifestyle.

II. Being Alive to God Means We Have a New Priority (vv. 15-21)

Paul uses slavery as a metaphor for human existence. It is not a question that we are slaves; the only question is to what or to whom do we owe our allegiance? We were once slaves to sin, but Christ has purchased us. We owe our allegiance to God; we serve a new master.

Whereas sin once held dominant influence over our lives, we now have a new priority: to live for Christ. You cannot be a slave to two different masters, for slavery implies an absolute allegiance and obedience. We are to be just as wholehearted in our commitment to walk with Christ as we once were in our bondage to sin.

What is the ultimate priority in your life? If priorities are measured by our investment in them—in time, resources, enthusiasm—what would you identify as your most significant priority?

III. Being Alive to God Means We Have a New Future (vv. 22-23)

In our former life as slaves to sin, our future was mapped out: death. The inevitable consequence of sin is death. The word Paul uses, *wages*, was the term used to describe the payment given to Roman soldiers. His point is clear: If you serve sin and evil, you will receive the promised payment for such service, which is death.

By contrast, because we have been freed from sin and placed into a new relationship with God in Christ, we have a new future: eternal life. It is not something we could earn, like wages; it is a free gift, totally at God's discretion. It is a new kind of life, to be experienced both now and beyond this present life.

That is how we are able to live triumphantly: we have been freed by Christ from our bondage to sin, and we are assured of eternal life with God. What a great motivation to live true to the One who has freed us! (Michael Duduit)

HEAVENLY HOSPITALITY

MATTHEW 10:40-42

Have you ever been en route to a social engagement and felt suddenly ill? You will recall the sense of weariness and the hope that you can manage the hours ahead. If you are lucky, you will also have had the experience of hosts who somehow made you feel better over the course of the visit. Something happened in the encounter that was healing or restorative. I believe it is no accident that our word *hospitality* contains the word *hospital*, for in genuine hospitality, well-being reigns and healing is an honored guest.

I. To Render Hospitality Is a Divine Gift

In the Gospel text, we have a brief teaching of Jesus that was directed to the disciples as they embarked on a mission. Earlier in his directions Jesus had warned the disciples of hostility and danger, but here he speaks of those who will welcome them. He says that since they are on a mission for him, anyone who welcomes those coming in his name welcomes him and God who sent him.

The ancient Gaels of Ireland had a rune or incantation of hospitality. It goes like this:

I saw a stranger yestreen;
I put food in the eating place,
drink in the drinking place,
music in the listening place;
And he blessed myself and my house,
my cattle and my dear ones.
And the lark said in her song
often, often, often,
goes the Christ in the stranger's guise,
often, often, often,
goes the Christ in the stranger's guise.

Jesus spoke of the rewards of those who render hospitality. He said those who welcome a prophet in the name of a prophet will receive a prophet's reward. The prophets were not rewarded handsomely in Jerusalem, as Jesus later lamented. Similarly with the reward of those who welcome a righteous person in the name of a righteous person; they are to receive a righteous person's reward, and all we have to do is look at the story of Job to see what that might be. Clearly, those who give a drink of cool water to the disciples are placing themselves under the same threat of danger as their guests and the rewards mentioned make them equals.

II. To Receive Hospitality Is a Divine Gift

But this passage is not directed at those who practice hospitality. It is written for those on the receiving end. It is not a directive but a promise, and it is a promise that contemporary disciples still need to hear. In the midst of suffering there will be signs of God's favor, just as Simon of Cyrene came to carry Jesus' cross on the way to Calvary.

We may not be comfortable seeing ourselves as in need, but all of us are needy at one time or another. The dangers to discipleship differ from those in Jesus' time, but they are still here. We may not have the threat of a life-or-death struggle, but we face profound cultural indifference that can kill in another way. Yet, even within the tedium and discouragement that ordinary people encounter in living out their faith, Jesus promises gifts of grace.

Most likely you have experienced them. Perhaps you did not recognize them as such, but you had the experience: the concerned and encouraging word, the warm meal that fed body and soul, the unexpected letter that renewed your faith. Take them, our Lord says, you who are weary and disheartened; receive this gift, this hospitality. It is a sign of God's favor. It comes with healing in its wings. Rest and be welcome. Let yourself occasionally be the cherished guest, for Christ's sake and in his name. (Penelope Duckworth)

JULY

છ

Preparing to Serve

The Symbol of the Fish

Paraphrase Assignment:
Psalm 37:25: "I have been young, and now am old, / yet I have not seen the righteous forsaken / or their children begging bread."

Prayer Assignment:
Let your prayer times this month focus on the faithfulness of God. Remember as the church calendar moves from Pentecost that the Holy Spirit is the earnest that God provides for his pastor and his church, giving them all that they require and more. First of all, write a thank-you for all that God has done for you and all the material needs God has met in your life. Why not then gather your leaders together in an evening of retreat and celebrate the Holy Spirit and the providence of God?

Journal-in-Worship Assignment:
These paragraphs should gather themselves around the marvelous care of God as displayed in the following passages.

Luke 11:11-13. In Jesus' statement, the kindness of earthly fathers in providing for their children is contrasted by the kindness of our Heavenly Father in giving us the Holy Spirit. When did you first appropriate God's grace meaningfully in your life? Now write a paragraph about when you first felt the providence of God in giving you the Holy Spirit. Be sure to detail the full extent of this first remembrance of God manifesting his reality to you.

Matthew 17:27. In this passage, a timely financial miracle occurs so that the taxes can get paid. Can you think of a time when, if God hadn't come through for you, you would not have been able to make it? Describe the exact nature of God's providence in your life.

John 21:6. This passage demonstrates that God's providence often fills the need we all have to feel that we are producing something. To have fished all night and caught nothing is a metaphor of how much it hurts to feel that we have not accomplished anything. Remember an instance when God marvelously rescued you from meaninglessness by giving you a feeling of accomplishment. Write of your glorious feelings of celebration over the faithfulness of God. (Calvin Miller)

JULY 7, 1996

୬

Sixth Sunday After Pentecost

Worship Theme: The call of Christ is a call to commitment.

Readings: Genesis 24:34-38, 42-49, 58-67; Romans 7:15-25*a*; Matthew 11:16-19, 25-30

Call to Worship (Psalm 45:17):

Leader: I will cause your name to be celebrated in all generations;

People: therefore the peoples will praise you forever and ever.

Pastoral Prayer:

Unto you, O Lord, we lift our hearts in praise. We praise you as our Creator, who gave life and breath, and who even now sustains your creation with the power of your word. We praise you as our Redeemer, who freed us from the self-created bonds of our own destruction, and who even now provides the strength to withstand evil's seductive allure. We praise you as our Shepherd, who reached out to save us when we were without hope, and who even now provides direction and guidance along the way. Even as we praise you—you who are Creator, Redeemer, Shepherd—we renew our commitment to you as sovereign Lord, worthy of all praise and worthy of our full obedience. Teach us, day by day, what it means to be committed to you; show us what a difference such commitment will make in our lives, our thoughts, our attitudes. We offer this prayer in the name of the One who was committed to the uttermost, even to death on a cross. Amen.

SERMON BRIEFS

THE POWER OF COMMITMENT

GENESIS 24:34-38, 42-49, 58-67

Stuart Briscoe points out that in a society like ours, where "The Dating Game" and computer dating are considered normal, the whole notion of Abraham sending out his servant to find a wife for his son is remarkable. But it was perfectly normal behavior for a culture that understood that healthy marriages take more than romance and physical attraction to thrive. They realized that commitment was central.

The use of the word *commitment* has been so misused, abused, and overused that there is a hesitancy to discuss it. However, commitment should never become an overly used idea. The concept of commitment lies in the ability to trust someone.

I. Commitment Opens Our Lives to Friendship (vv. 34-38)

Friendships draw people together and bind human hearts through sharing and sacrifice. Scripture does not reveal the name of Abraham's servant, but it does indicate that he was the chief servant. He was one who had served Abraham the longest and was probably much more than a servant. He was a real friend, a man of integrity on whom Abraham could rely.

How often we need a person who will be our friend, to stand by and help, care and share when our world falls apart.

Richard Lee writes in his book *Windows of Hope* about two young German artists and friends in the 1400s who found themselves in a desperate situation. They couldn't eke out a living to keep food on the table or art supplies for painting.

One friend named Hans made a drastic decision. He concluded that he would drop out of school, and his friend, Albrecht, would continue and graduate. After Albrecht's graduation, he would then help Hans through art school. So the decision was made, and Hans laid aside his brushes and began manual labor.

Years passed and Albrecht began selling his paintings. He became extremely successful. His integrity intact, he kept his promise to his friend Hans and made arrangements for him to attend art classes.

However, the years of hard manual labor on behalf of his friend had gnarled and deformed Hans's fingers and hands. He would never be the artist he had hoped to be in life.

Albrecht thought about what he could do to repay his close friend for his years of sacrifice. He did the only thing he knew best—he painted a picture. He immortalized the calloused hands of his friend by painting them and entitled his piece *The Praying Hands*. It stands today as a tribute to the love and devotion of a friend.

Friendship is an incredible treasure in this life. Time and distance will not weaken the bonds that hold this kind of relationship. If you have that type of friendship with someone, thank God for it.

II. Commitment Opens Our Minds to God (vv. 42-49)

The servant asked God for direction. He waited for God's reply, and it came in the form of Rebekah.

Prayer is a relationship, a fellowship with God. We need to pray with a clean conscience, asking boldly and praying expectantly. That's how the servant of Abraham prayed, and God did not let him down. God will not let our prayers go unnoticed or unanswered!

III. Commitment Opens Our Hearts to Love (vv. 58-67)

Abraham's servant found the answer to his prayer. He discovered the woman God wanted for Isaac. There is the anticipation of her response regarding her decision to go back home with him or not. After her positive response, there was the thrill of the trip back and the wonder of Isaac's response.

At the end of the journey the result of the servant's commitment was rewarded by a fulfilled love for his master's son. He brings Rebekah to Isaac, and as verse 67 says, Rebekah became his wife, and "he loved her."

Commitment within marriage opens the heart to a loving relationship with the spouse. Without true commitment, marriage is simply a legal arrangement; with commitment, it is a divinely linked partnership rooted in love.

Likewise in our relationship with God, only as we commit ourselves to him do we experience God's love in its fullest, richest dimension—for only a committed life is open to experience God's presence. (Derl G. Keefer)

THE BATTLE WITHIN

ROMANS 7:15-25*a*

We live in an age in which self-fulfillment has become a virtual law of the land. A young woman described for her therapist a life of indulgence that was becoming self-destructive: parties, alcohol, sex, and drugs. It was a downward spiral. Then the therapist asked her a question: "Why don't you stop?" She appeared stunned by the question, then responded, "You mean I don't have to do what I want to do?" Like her, countless millions seem to be victims of their own desires.

Paul could well understand such a predicament, for he felt much the same. He sensed raging within himself a battle between good and evil, between God's will for his life and Paul's old human nature, pulling him away. Most of us can understand that battle as well, for we have felt its pull within us.

As We Survey the Battlefield, on One Side We See God's Law, Calling Us to Obedience.

God's law reflects God's character: pure, righteous, holy. As Paul indicates in verse 7, the law enables us to understand God's expectations for our lives; it is a teacher, a standard by which we can measure our lives.

Paul, who had experienced the transforming power of God in his life, was drawn to God's law; there was within him a desire to be obedient to God's will and purpose for his life day by day. But there was something else at work within Paul, just as it is present within us.

On the Opposite Side of the Battlefield, We See the Seductive Power of Sin, Calling Us to Destruction.

Oh, evil is not that honest. Satan never comes to us with the invitation to disobey God and devastate our lives. No, the invitation is usually to a moment of pleasure or profit that "won't hurt anyone" and "no one will ever know." But it does hurt, starting with us, and God knows.

Yet Paul knew, as we do, that evil can seem overpowering. Paul lamented, "I can will what is right, but I cannot do it" (v. 18).

Although many scholars argue that Paul is referring to a time before his conversion, I think it reflects the reality of Paul's life after he has come to Christ, desiring to do what is right yet constantly falling short. It is a struggle with which we can relate. We've been on the same battlefield—wanting to do right, but time and again succumbing to the temptation to cut corners, grab the gusto, surrender to what we know is less than God's best.

Yet There Is Hope Because of God's Presence and Power.

Thankfully there is hope. As Paul exclaimed, "Thanks be to God through Jesus Christ our Lord!" (v. 25a). Though the battle within seems to be set at a fever pitch, the reality is that for those who are in Christ, the outcome is already decided! Christ is already victorious over sin and death, and as we are able to claim His victory in our own lives day by day, we experience his growing power over sin, his growing presence in our hearts.

Jesus Christ alone frees us from the battle within. That freedom comes in part during this earthly existence as we receive his strength to withstand temptation; the freedom will come in full one day when we are allowed to stand in his glorious presence. (Michael Duduit)

THE CALL OF CHRIST

MATTHEW 11:16-19, 25-30

The people of Galilee were deciding how they would respond to the ministry of Jesus. In the midst of their ambivalence, Jesus spoke out to say clearly what he was about and what kind of response he was calling for: "Come to me, all you that are weary and are carrying heavy burdens, and I will give you rest" (v. 28). In those few words, he gave an address, an invitation, and a promise.

I. Jesus Addresses Our Needs

Jesus addressed himself to those who care deeply and who are trying hard to make life good for themselves and for others.

In his own day, Jesus addressed those who were struggling to make life good by following the demanding way of the Pharisees.

In our own day, those who are trying hard may be those who take seriously the requirements of the Christian faith and try hard to live up to them. They may also be those who work hard at making life good in other ways—young people who try to live a morally wholesome life in a world that seems to have stopped caring about that, young parents who struggle to provide for their children and to raise them up in a wholesome way, people who strive to excel in their careers, people who work at building a better world.

The grace of God is not for those who don't care or who are looking for an easy way. It is for those who care deeply and try hard. Is it for you?

II. Jesus Invites Us to Come to Him

Come to whom? To Jesus, a man who lived a long time ago? Yes, but more significantly, we are invited to come to the eternal God who made himself known through Jesus and is still alive and at work in our lives and in our world today.

Whether or not we realize it, all of those who care deeply and want to make life good are trying to put themselves into a right relationship with the greater reality that is God.

The invitation calls us to turn to Jesus rather than to the other ways in which we might try to make life good.

But more important, the invitation tells us that the One for whom we are yearning is ready to welcome us—because God loves us.

A young couple who had no money for luxuries or for recreation went for a walk in a village one evening for a date. They stopped for a while to watch a machine in the window of a baker's shop making doughnuts. They didn't realize how hungry they must have looked until the proprietor came out and gave them a bag of doughnuts.

III. Jesus Offers a Special Promise

The promise goes with the invitation: "I will give you rest." What can that mean? We do not see that the Christian faith gives us rest from the work of trying to make life good. No, but it does give us rest from guilt, self-recrimination, anxiety, and struggling.

A tourist in China commented to her guide on the grace with which a Chinese woman carried her baskets of produce hanging from two ends of a pole balanced across her shoulders. The guide said, "Yes, but it is very heavy." The yoke that Jesus offers will enable us to bear the really significant burdens of life with grace and dignity. (James L. Killen, Jr.)

JULY 14, 1996

Seventh Sunday After Pentecost

Worship Theme: Christ enables us to overcome conflict.

Readings: Genesis 25:19-34; Romans 8:1-11; Matthew 13:1-9, 18-23

Call to Worship (Psalm 119:105, 108, 111):

Leader: Your word is a lamp to my feet and a light to my path. . . .

People: Accept my offerings of praise, O LORD, and teach me your ordinances. . . .

Leader: Your decrees are my heritage forever;

People: they are the joy of my heart.

Pastoral Prayer:

Lord, though we claim to serve the Prince of Peace, so often we seem to be consumed by conflict. Our world is filled with conflict—sometimes fought with guns and planes, other times fought with money and influence. We live in a nation marked by conflict, as special interests vie with one another to gain the upper hand, and most of us turn to whichever hand seems to offer us the biggest share. Even in our personal lives, Lord, there seems to be so much conflict: family disagreements, neighborhood fights, office squabbles, even struggles within the church for power and control. Forgive us, Lord, for talking peace while we wage war; forgive us for confessing Christ as Lord with our mouths while we cultivate conflict. Help us to sense your presence in such a powerful and dynamic way that we have no choice but to become peacemakers because Jesus Christ has become so real in our lives. Use us to bring a forgiving touch, a healing hand, a compassionate word. Make us truly instruments of your peace. Amen.

SERMON BRIEFS

DEALING WITH CONFLICT

GENESIS 25:19-34

If a story ever revealed differences in a pair of brothers, it is this story about Jacob and Esau. Even within Rebekah's womb the boys were in conflict (v. 22). As they were born, a struggle developed (vv. 24-26). As they grew, their appearance and attitude displayed a definite difference between the two. The impetuousness of Esau versus the cunning patience of Jacob caused a deep rift for years (vv. 27-34). Later, deception of Isaac by Jacob would cause his brother to hate him more, even to the point of wanting to do great bodily harm to him.

The theme of this story is conflict. Conflict occurs today between husbands and wives, parents and children, employers and employees, pastors and laypeople. It results from a variety of reasons including ridicule, criticism, rejection, gossip, threat, misunderstanding, inattentiveness, and lack of acceptance. Conflict causes hurt, frustration, judgment, separation, divorce, abuse, feelings of dehumanization, and much more!

Jacob and Esau provide a classic case of conflict allowed to grow to an extreme. What causes such conflict—and what can be done to heal the breaches caused by conflict?

I. Sometimes Conflicts Start Small and Are Allowed to Grow

Jacob and Esau were competing from the womb. Rather than being dealt with while they were young, the conflict between the two brothers was obviously allowed to grow relatively unhindered. By adulthood, it had turned into open warfare!

If you are experiencing conflict, act to bring an end to it today. The longer it goes, the bigger it grows. What a shame Isaac and Rebekah couldn't have helped their sons develop a closer relationship while they were young. But that suggests another source of conflict.

II. Sometimes Third Parties Contribute to Conflict

Rather than bringing the twin boys together, the parents played favorites (v. 28), thus accelerating the rivalry.

Parents, spouses, friends, and coworkers can often take a small conflict and turn it into a big one. A thoughtless word, an unhealthy comparison, or a negative comment can add fuel to the flame and cause an eruption, where positive, loving concern might have otherwise eased the tension and produced healing. Are you a conflict encourager or healer?

III. Sometimes Conflict Is Worsened by a Selfish Act

The famous story of Esau selling his birthright is an example of taking advantage of a brother in a moment of weakness. (It's also an example of foolish choices, but that's another sermon!) God had already promised Jacob his place of leadership; it was not necessary for him to take matters into his own hands, particularly in such a manner. All Jacob managed to do was increase the level of rivalry and conflict with his brother.

Have you let your own wishes and desires create a wedge between you and another person—a member of your family, a neighbor, or a friend? Are you willing to swallow your pride and reach out in love?

How can the struggle and conflict be diffused? One key is attitude. When dealing with conflict, check your attitude toward the person and the reason for the feelings.

Another key is humility. The conflict might involve a power struggle. Who has more might than the other? Humility should be enlisted to diffuse the conflict. Philippians 2:3 states, "Do nothing out of selfish ambition or vain conceit, but in humility consider others better than yourselves" (NIV). Martin Luther wrote, "God created the world out of nothing, and so long as we are nothing, He can make something out of us."

A third key is positive encouragement. Unplanned moments of encouragement just happen, but there are also planned moments of encouragement. Writing a note or letter, saying the right words, sharing smiles, and offering pats on the back encourage so much.

Charles Allen wrote in his book *Road to Radiant Living* about a little girl who fell down on a sidewalk and bruised her knee. She said to her mom, "Wouldn't it be wonderful if all the world was cushioned?"

We can help cushion the blows of the world by dealing with conflicts. Esau and Jacob finally ended their feuding and conflict, but it took time, distance, and God. Don't allow personal conflict to engulf you. (Derl G. Keefer)

FREEDOM THAT LASTS

ROMANS 8:1-11

It was an old stereo, broken down, used up, and good for nothing, so Mary put it out with the rest of the trash. That's where Tommy found it—sitting atop a pile of junk, destined for the landfill. He asked Mary if he could take it and work with it; she didn't care if he wanted to waste his time with a piece of junk, so he claimed it and took it home. He opened it up, replaced some parts, cleaned it up, and discovered that it had within it the capacity to play wonderful, beautiful music. What was one day junk, destined for destruction, became a valued possession.

Paul wants us to understand that just as Tommy retrieved that stereo from the junk pile and reclaimed it for useful service, so also Jesus Christ has taken us from atop life's trash heap and freed us from the destruction toward which we are inevitably heading. Christ has freed us from the condemnation we deserve. But how is that possible?

I. Christ Frees Us from the Law of Sin and Death (vv. 2-4)

When the Holy Spirit enters our lives, it brings liberation from the bondage of evil and produces new power for holy, faithful living.

If you question whether our world is captive to the law of sin and death, just read the newspapers or watch the news on TV. Murder, rape, vicious assaults, the depravity of much of the drug culture—we live in a world in which sin seems to be king and death is his tax collector.

But sin and death do not have the last word. The last word belongs to Christ, because of what he did for us in his own sacrificial death and triumphant resurrection. The law alone could not produce such liberation; only Christ could overcome sin and death and free us from their destructive bonds.

Because of that freedom, as believers we are able to walk according to the Spirit—that is, the Holy Spirit now lives within us and empowers us to live the kind of overcoming, victorious life that honors Christ and demonstrates his love to others.

II. Christ Frees Us from Our Sinful Nature (vv. 5-8)

Most people do not walk according to the Spirit; they "live according to the flesh." By *flesh*, Paul means human nature in all of its willfulness and self-centeredness. The flesh is the attitude that rejects God's will and demands its own will; the flesh seeks self-gratification above all else.

Paul says those who are without Christ are preoccupied by things of the flesh; they are controlled by it. In fact, so dominant is this flesly preoccupation that they cannot see beyond it. It limits their perception. That's why so much spiritual truth that appears so obvious to the believer seems just as incredible to the nonbeliever; it is beyond their capacity to see it. And the result of this bondage to the flesh is death—the utter and complete absence of the authentic life God intends for us.

By contrast, when we enter the life of the Spirit through God's grace, we are freed from this bondage to the flesh. We are the recipients of God's gift of life and peace.

II. Christ Frees Us to Life in the Spirit (vv. 9-11)

The believer has been freed from sin and death, from his own sinful nature, and now enjoys an entirely new power made possible through the indwelling presence of the Holy Spirit. The Spirit *dwells* or lives within us; the Spirit is not a visitor but a permanent resident.

Because of this new life in the Spirit, we have the ultimate promise of resurrection and eternal life. Christ has given us new power in this present life, plus power to move beyond this life to spend eternity with God.

Such incredible love demands a response. How will you respond today to God's offer of freedom? (Michael Duduit)

PREPARING FOR NEW POSSIBILITIES

MATTHEW 13:1-9, 18-23

Have you ever watched a farmer preparing land for planting? Now farmers do that work with big tractors, but not long ago it was done with a handheld plow pulled by a mule and maybe finished with a hoe. The farmer knows that the soil must be carefully prepared so the seed will grow.

Today's parable makes that a symbol of the preparation necessary to receive the new possibility that the Bible calls "the kingdom of God." If we let God's love into our lives, it will grow and change us and give us new and more fruitful lives.

But we have to be ready to receive God's new possibility. The parable tells us how.

I. We Must Be Ready to Understand

We do not want the love we receive to be like the seed that fell on the hard-packed soil of the path. Understanding requires us to take a step beyond just hearing and knowing. To understand is to stand under—or within—a thing and not just to look at it from the outside.

Sometimes it is hard work to understand. Many people learn religious formulas like the creed, the catechism, and the plan of salvation so that they can recite them or base a claim on them. But these people never get inside them so that they can experience the dynamic interactions with God that they represent. Consequently, they never enter into God's new possibility.

II. We Must Also Be Willing to Let God's Love Get into the Deep Soil of Our Lives

That's how we can grow and make a difference. Too often it falls into our lives like seed into the shallow soil over rocky ground. Many people receive the Christian faith eagerly, especially in a time or a social context where it seems that being a Christian is the thing to do. But many make commitments with reservations. They say, "Okay, I'll be a Christian but don't ask me to give up my beer," or ". . . don't tell me what to do with my money or how to run my business," or ". . . don't talk to me about loving people of other races," or ". . . don't ask me to give up my bitterness." Sooner or later the conflict will become a crisis that will force us to choose, and we may forsake God's new possibility.

We must be willing to dig out the rocks—or at least to break them up so that the roots of God's love can get into them and eventually break them down into good soil.

III. We Must Be Willing to Clear Away the Preoccupations and Business That Can Choke Out God's New Possibility and Keep It from Growing

This must certainly be the biggest problem for really good people. We are so busy trying to provide a good living for our families, doing what our careers require—sometimes two or three careers to the family—doing the good things that need to be done in the community and, yes, in the church. You have to take charge of your life and give God's love a chance to work. If it really works in your life, it will make a place for every good thing that really needs to be part of your life.

But what must you do then to see that your life is "good soil"? Don't worry about that. God has already made your life good soil. Just give God's new possibility a chance to grow in your life and you will see. (James L. Killen, Jr.)

JULY 21, 1996

Eighth Sunday After Pentecost

Worship Theme: Great dreams begin with God.

Readings: Genesis 28:10-19*a*; Romans 8:12-25; Matthew 13:24-30, 36-43

Call to Worship (Psalm 139:23-24):

Leader: Search me, O God, and know my heart; test me and know my thoughts.

People: See if there is any wicked way in me, and lead me in the way everlasting.

Pastoral Prayer:

We thank you, our Father, that you are the source of all good things. We thank you for the warmth of summer sun, for the refreshing pleasure of a cool stream, for the joy of family and friends spending time together. We thank you for these long summer days, which remind us that you are the creator and sustainer of all good things. And yet, Lord, we know that you want to create in us more than a pleasant day; we know that you have placed within each of us a dream, a purpose that you are ready to unleash in us if we will but allow you to do so. Give us the courage to dream your dream; give us the boldness to claim your vision; give us the strength to carry out your purpose in our lives. Perhaps there are some who have not yet discovered that dream; work within them to help them find and nurture what you have already planted in their lives. Others know the dream but struggle with it; help them find that perfect surrender to your will that alone will give them freedom to soar. Help us to lift up your vision in our lives as we pray in the name of the One who was lifted up for us. Amen.

SERMON BRIEFS

DREAMING GOD'S DREAM

GENESIS 28:10-19*a*

Helen Keller was asked what would be worse than being born blind. She responded, "To have sight and no vision." One of the essential keys to success in life is a dream, a vision, something to drive us to greater things.

Jacob needed a dream! His possessive mother, Rebekah, had schemed with him to take his brother's birthright away, resulting in Esau's wrath beginning to pour out. Before Esau could kill him, Jacob ran away. He had no dream; he had only the moment. Many people today are attempting to escape from their Esaus. They have no dreams; they see only today. Like Jacob, they need a Bethel where they can dream God's dream.

I. Great Dreams Must Begin Somewhere (vv. 10-12)

It was a dream that would change Jacob's life. His dream began in a routine way. After running all day, he was exhausted. Using a rock for a pillow, he stretched out for a night of slumber, never expecting to experience such a dream.

Our dreams start right where we are, in the routine of life. John Maxwell, pastor of Skyline Wesleyan Church in California, says there is a natural sequence to beginning our dreams. A dream whizzes by. He calls it the "I thought it" stage. He says it progresses to the "I caught it" stage; the individual gets excited about the dream and talks about it. The natural progression then leads to the "I bought it" stage; an investment of time, talent, effort, or money is put on deposit. The "I sought it" stage allows the dream to possess the person until it finally becomes the "I got it" stage, where the dream belongs to the individual. He is satisfied that the price paid was not too high. But it all starts with the beginning of the dream.

II. Great Dreams Come from God (vv. 13-15)

Jacob saw God in his dream, and he heard the Lord's plan for his life. God has a big dream or plan for the entire human race. God's dream is that we be saved (2 Pet. 3:9). God's dream is that his people be holy (1 Thess. 4:3). God's dream is that his people share the good news of the gospel (Matt. 28:19-20).

But you want to know God's specific portrait for your life. There are some principles for discovering God's dream in your life. One is that God's dream will probably use the innate talents and gifts God has already given you. The exciting thought is that God often conveys his plans through natural talents.

Scripture is also important in finding God's dream. The Lord may provide insight from a specific verse, or the Bible may bear out the circumstances of your life at the moment.

Another principle involves your own attitude. Are you genuinely honest about wanting to know and follow God's will? Are you willing to be led by the Holy Spirit, whatever the result may be?

III. Great Dreams Demand Action (vv. 16-19a)

There is a time to dream, think, and plan, but there is also a time to act. An anonymous writer observed, "The vision to see, the faith to believe, and the will to do will take you anywhere you want to go." Are you willing to act on your dreams today? (Derl G. Keefer)

ALL IN THE FAMILY

ROMANS 8:12-25

As a small child, did you ever threaten to run away from home? I remember once that I became angry at my parents—I was all of six or seven years old—and told my mother that I would be running away. She offered to help me pack my bag, and I suspect that was what started my reconsideration of the entire process! If I had managed to get away, however, it wouldn't have been long before I would have missed my own bed, my place at the dinner table, my parents. I would have missed being part of my family.

In the verses just prior to our text, Paul has been talking about the wonderful freedom we receive through life in the Spirit, as we walk day by day with Christ. In this passage—particularly verses 12-17—he proceeds to demonstrate a further blessing that comes our way as believers: we become part of the family of God.

We are not naturally God's children, though we are God's creation. Membership in God's family is a gift of divine grace and becomes realized as we walk in the Spirit as Christian believers. Paul makes it clear that we have received a great gift as God welcomes us into his family. What does it mean to be in God's family?

I. We Receive the Gift of Life (vv. 12-13)

True life, authentic living, comes only through relationship with the Author and Creator of life. Apart from membership in God's family, we are destined for death.

Living according to the flesh leads to death, because the flesh binds; it destroys; it kills. The flesh demands self-gratification and self-glorification yet offers no ultimate satisfaction. By contrast, the Holy Spirit within the believer helps us recognize that only in walking according to God's will do we discover true satisfaction and true glory.

When Paul talks about putting to death "the deeds of the body," he uses a word for a continuing action. Overcoming the flesh is not a one-time event, but a continuing effort in the life of the believer. And the same Spirit that empowers us to holy living also empowers us to experience real life in Christ.

II. We Receive the Gift of Adoption (vv. 14-17)

What does it mean to be adopted into God's family? Paul uses an image from Greek and Roman society (adoption was not a Jewish practice), in which an adopted child is given full rights and privileges of sonship in a family in which he was not a natural member. The child had no natural or legal claim on membership in the family, but received a gift of family membership through adoption.

Likewise, we have no natural claim on God's family. Through our own sin, we have turned or rebelled against the God who created us. Yet in divine love and grace, God extends a hand to us and brings us into his family. As members of God's family, we receive all the rights and responsibilities of family membership.

As children, we are also heirs. Paul does not use this in a material sense; since God does not die, there is no material inheritance to receive. Rather, as heirs we are recognized as occupying a privileged position within the family. Though we have no dignity in and of ourselves, God has bestowed upon us a unique dignity that comes from being a member of his family.

III. We Receive the Gift of Future Glory (vv. 18-25)

Some historians in the early 1990s talked of the world having reached "the end of history," in the sense that we were achieving the culmination of human achievement through the spread of democracy around the world. Quite a few million people might question that judgment, as would those still affected by war, conflict, disease, famine, and other evidences of a corrupted world.

But a day is coming when all of history will reach its climax, as God redeems history and creation and ushers in a true new age. And as members of God's family, we have been provided a unique, unmerited opportunity to share in that future glory. What an amazing gift! (Michael Duduit)

REALITIES OF THE KINGDOM

MATTHEW 13:24-30, 36-43

David's wife plays the piano at one of the area churches, but he does not attend and has never accepted Christ. When the pastor visited him, David told the pastor that he lived as good a life as any of the church members and he saw no reason to change. He was right about living a good life. Many people who become Christians will need to change very little of what they do in their daily routines, but the focus of their lives and their eternal destiny have been totally changed.

Jesus deals with the issue in his own special way in the parable of the wheat and weeds. This passage is often understood to refer to the church, but Jesus said that the field in the parable refers to the world (v. 38a). Understanding the realities of Kingdom life should provide us help to focus on what is most crucial: being citizens in God's kingdom. What are the realities of Kingdom life?

I. Christians and Non-Christians Must Coexist in the World (v. 30a)

Jesus makes it clear in this passage that the people of the church and the people of the world are going to progress through this life together. Knowing this is instructive for both groups.

First, it is a warning for the church to avoid two extremes: the church must avoid compromise with worldly philosophies that are unacceptable to God; and the church must avoid seeking isolation from worldly people. The idea is to be in the world but not of the world, just as Jesus modeled with his own life.

Second, it is a wake-up call for the people of the world. There needs to be understanding that togetherness does not mean sameness. It is clear from the text that although coexistence is a reality, people of the world and the Kingdom are very different.

II. Christians and Non-Christians Often Look Alike (vv. 38-39)

Externally, the Christian and the non-Christian often look alike. They may work at the same office or factory. They may live on the same street and be involved in many of the same community activities. This is true because both groups are affected by the norms of their culture.

But internally, they are totally different. In verse 38, we see that in spite of their similarity in appearance, one has a Kingdom relationship, and the other has a relationship with the evil one. Therefore, external appearance can be very deceptive. We need to look into our own hearts to discover with whom we have a relationship.

III. Christians and Non-Christians Are Destined to an Eternal Difference (vv. 41-43)

It is clear from the apocalyptic text that Christians and non-Christians will not coexist and look alike forever. A separation is sure to come. The wicked will suffer eternal destruction while Christians will "shine like the sun." The final reality of Kingdom life helps one realize that what is most crucial is a new citizenship that comes through a relationship with the Lord Jesus Christ.

It seems to me that there are two urgent admonitions in this text. First, it is not enough to just look like a Christian; you must surrender your life to Jesus. Second, do all that you are able to share Christ with as many as you can. It is the greatest gift you can give to anyone! (Douglas Bunch)

JULY 28, 1996

ॐ

Ninth Sunday After Pentecost

Worship Theme: Life in God's kingdom is the greatest treasure we can possess.

Readings: Genesis 29:15-28; Romans 8:26-39; Matthew 13:31-33, 44-52

Call to Worship (Psalm 105:1-4):

Leader: O give thanks to the LORD, call on his name,

People: make known his deeds among the peoples.

Leader: Sing to him, sing praises to him;

People: tell of all his wonderful works.

Leader: Glory in his holy name; let the hearts of those who seek the LORD rejoice.

People: Seek the LORD and his strength; seek his presence continually.

Pastoral Prayer:

We celebrate the joy of this community, O Lord, and the lives of the countless men and women who have sacrificed to impart form and substance to its redemption. Give each of us a feeling for history and for the way your hand is at work within it, molding it finally toward the purposes of your new age and heavenly realm. Let Christ be in our midst today, steadying those who have lost their footholds in life, encouraging those who have forgotten their way, comforting those who have buried loved ones, and inspiring all of us to be kind and loving and generous. Gather up our spirits in your Holy Spirit, that we may experience oneness and unanimity of purpose, and that we may become a sweet offering to you upon the altar of the world, living and dying in behalf of the poor and outcast, for whom Christ himself gave his life upon the cross. Amen. (John Killinger)

SERMON BRIEFS

THE ROMANCING OF LOVE

GENESIS 29:15-28

I read about a minister who had reached that part of the wedding ceremony where he asked, "And do you take this woman for better or for worse, for richer or for poorer, through sickness and in health, in good times and in bad, in . . ."

The bride, almost in tears, whispered to the pastor, "Please, if you aren't careful, you're going to talk him out of it!"

Jacob would not be talked out of his love for Rachel.

Love is part of any marriage, especially a Christian one, for it involves purity, devotion, and a strong sense of fidelity to the individual. Jacob and Rachel's love shows us what really is involved in a loving relationship.

I. Love Involves Emotion (v. 17)

An emotion is a strong, surging feeling marked by an impulse for outward expression, or it is any strong feeling. A feeling is a sensation, either physical or psychological. God made us as emotional creatures. We have strong feelings or impulses to love. Those feelings usually come first in a relationship. Unfortunately, feelings or emotions are the first to leave when relationships turn sour in marriage. Here are some tips to keep emotions alive and positive:

Speak kindly to each other. Include affectionate terms in your life.
Keep a positive spirit. Nothing kills a relationship like negative undertones.
Be spontaneous—at least occasionally!
Keep fit. Experts have discovered that exercise actually causes your brain to release "happy" chemicals called endorphins, which boost sagging spirits.
Say no to alcohol and drugs. These cause mood swings and affect emotions. There will be a chemical boost after using drugs or alcohol,

but be prepared for a crash at the next turn. That boost is only temporary.

As H. Jackson Brown wrote in *P.S. I Love You,* "Sometimes the heart sees what is invisible to the eye."

II. Love Involves Work (v. 18)

Carl Jung said, "Seldom, or perhaps never, does a marriage develop into an individual relationship smoothly and without crisis; there is no coming to consciousness without pain." And André Maurois stated, "A successful marriage is an edifice that must be rebuilt every day." How does a couple make a marriage work? Some basic rules are helpful.

Commitment. Antoine DeSaint said, "Love does not consist in gazing at each other, but in looking outward together in the same direction."

Communication. At a golden anniversary party an elderly couple was being honored. The husband was moved by the occasion and wanted to tell his wife how he felt about her. She was very hard of hearing, however, and often misunderstood what he said to her. With many friends and relatives gathered around, he toasted her with these words: "My dear wife, after fifty years, I've found you tried and true." Everyone smiled approval for his endearing words, but she replied with an "eh?" He repeated his statement louder. His wife shot back, "Well, let me tell you something—after fifty years I'm tired of you, too!"

Christ as head of the marriage union. The miracle of Christian marriage occurs when two minds and two hearts seek the will of Christ.

Many years ago I read a paraphrase of Matthew 7:24-27. As I recall, it goes like this: "Therefore if a man and a woman who plan to become friends, husband and wife, and lovers hear my words and put them into practice, they are like the wise couple who built a house on the rock. The rains of life came down—mortgages, taxes, jobs, unemployment, lawsuits, kids, PTA, college bills, unexpected injuries, blown-up transmissions, church involvement, club memberships, grocery buying, live-in in-laws, disease—the streams rose, the winds blew and beat against the marital house; yet it did not fall, because its marital foundation was on the Rock.

"But the couple who hears my words and does not practice them is like a foolish couple who built a house on sand and when the rains of life came, and the streams rose, and the ill winds of adversity blew and beat against the marital house, they went to the divorce court with a great crashing and bashing of each other, or lived in absolute disdain of each other."

III. Love Involves Fulfillment (vv. 21-30)

Jacob's dream of Rachel in his arms and life finally came to reality. Love finds a way to be fulfilled. Love is not something to fall in and out of; rather, it is a choice of uniting together in a lifetime bonding process. That type of love stems from a God-given love fulfilled in each other. As Jesus said, "Therefore what God has joined together, let no one separate" (Matt. 19:6). (Derl G. Keefer)

THE AWESOME POWER OF GOD'S LOVE

ROMANS 8:26-39

Can there be a more overused term in the English language than *love?* It shows up in movies, popular songs, television, even commercials. It is used to describe how you feel about your spouse, your kids, your cat, your new car, and the way that new and improved detergent takes care of the soil around your shirt collar. Don't you just love it?

Tragically, the term *love* is so tossed about in our culture that many of us may have little real understanding of what it truly means. A wonderful starting point for such knowledge is this passage of scripture—particularly verses 31-39—in which Paul affirms the awesome, remarkable power of God's love for us, his children.

What does God's love mean for us? Paul suggests three remarkable promises that are ours because of God's awesome love.

I. God's Love Offers the Promise of His Provision (v. 32)

Have you seen the commercials in which the "Prize Patrol" visits people's homes to deliver the good news that they have won the $10 million sweepstakes? Or the ads for state lotteries, that imply that investing just $1 in a lottery ticket could provide everything you'll ever need? If only it was that easy!

The only real source of true provision is found in God's love. The Creator of the cosmos loves us so much that he willingly gave his own Son to die on our behalf. If God provides for us this ultimate provision, should we worry about his willingness to provide anything else we truly need?

Scripture is filled with examples of God's provision for his children, but one such example is found in the earlier portion of this text (vv. 26-27): God's provision of the Holy Spirit, who ministers on our behalf.

Whatever your need, our God will supply it "according to his riches in glory."

II. God's Love Offers the Promise of His Protection (vv. 33-34)

Christ is the guarantor of our protection; his death and resurrection are the basis of his intercession on our behalf. As Paul noted in verse 31, "If God is for us, who is against us?"

I remember a show in which a small boy in the neighborhod had grown tired of being constantly abused by the bigger boys, and the day came when he finally stood up to them. Unknown to the small boy, his big brother quietly came up and stood a few feet behind him, and when the neighborhood bullies saw the older brother they took off running!

In a sense, Jesus is like that older brother who protects us, keeps us safe and in his care. That doesn't mean we won't encounter problems or tough times, but it means that nothing can take us out of God's protective love and care.

III. God's Love Offers the Promise of His Presence (vv. 35-39)

Absolutely nothing can take the believer out of the loving presence of God. Paul goes through a list of potential hazards—both physical and spiritual—and assures us that God's awesome love is greater and more powerful than anything that might try to remove us from his presence.

Paul had certainly experienced opposition in his own life—critics, beatings, imprisonment—and eventually he would face execution. Yet he knew that God's love was greater than anything he would ever encounter, and that knowledge gave him confidence to serve Christ with boldness.

Have you experienced God's love in your own life? That remarkable journey can begin today. (Michael Duduit)

LIFE'S GREATEST TREASURE

MATTHEW 13:31-33, 44-52

What is the treasure of your life? In North America, our treasure is often material in nature. The passionate pursuit of these things as life's treasure is a futile and empty effort.

There is treasure, however, in relationships. My granddaughter, Emily, climbed onto my lap when she was less than three and, without provocation, said, "I love you, Popaw." On another occasion my wife sent me a card that said, "God must have sent you into my life so there would always be love in my heart." Those were treasured moments in my life that were very fulfilling. But even those warm moments are not life's greatest treasure. Life's greatest treasure is to be a part of God's kingdom through Jesus Christ, our Lord. Why?

I. The Value of the Kingdom Is Greater Than Anything Else (vv. 44-46)

The central point of these parables is that the Kingdom is more valuable than anything else. There is a twofold message here concerning the value of the Kingdom. First, it is worth more than anything or anyone else we can know. It is worth more than all the money or possessions that we can accrue. It is even worth more than our most treasured earthly relationships. Second, because it is worth more than all else, it requires that we be willing to surrender all to Jesus in order to possess the Kingdom, life's greatest treasure.

II. The Nature of the Kingdom Is to Persevere to the End (vv. 31-33)

We have two parables here that point to the persevering nature of the Kingdom. The mustard seed of Jesus' land was similar to that in the United States but grew much heartier in the fertile soil of the Jordan Valley than in most other places. Yeast, or leaven, is often used elsewhere as a metaphor for evil. But here it represents the Kingdom, which will inevitably reach the completion of its task.

Neither of the parables should be understood to suggest that things are going to get better in this world. Far too many passages teach that the opposite is true. Therefore, the message here is one of perseverance. That is to say, the Kingdom is life's greatest treasure not only because of its great value but also because it will endure until its planned culmination. All other things will fail, but the Kingdom will persevere to the end.

III. The Work of the Kingdom Is to Share This Treasure with Others (vv. 51-52)

After Jesus had completed this series of parables, he confirmed that his disciples understood. He then appointed them to be scribes who would be able to communicate the message of the Kingdom.

To be a scribe is to be honored. A scribe in Palestine was highly respected. Jesus thus bestows honor on his disciples by entrusting them with this ministry. Even more, to be a scribe is also to bear the responsibility of teaching others the truths of God. In other words, Kingdom disciples have an evangelistic responsibility.

IV. The Joy of the Kingdom Is Available to All (vv. 47-50)

The picture of the dragnet demonstrates the availability of the Kingdom to all. When a dragnet is used, the idea is to sweep up everything in its path. So it is with the Kingdom; the purpose is to touch every soul with the gospel of Jesus Christ.

The tragic reality, however, is that many will choose to reject the Kingdom. Becoming a part of God's kingdom through Jesus Christ is life's greatest treasure. What is the treasure of your life? (Douglas Bunch)

AUGUST

ᔢ

Preparing to Serve

The Symbol of the Dove

Paraphrase Assignment:
Romans 8:14: "For all who are led by the Spirit of God are children of God."

Prayer Assignment:
In the Matthew 3:16 and the John 1:33 passages, the Spirit descends in some very obvious ways to John the Baptist to point out that the One he has just baptized is the Son of God. It has now been several weeks since Pentecost, but ask God's Holy Spirit to begin designating these same truths in your life. Ask him, as he once manifested Jesus as the Son, to continue his designating ministry in your life, pointing out the significant presence of Jesus in Scripture and where he ought to be obvious in your life as well.

Journal-in-Worship Assignment:
Write three paragraphs describing the moments when the Holy Spirit pointed out these three great truths to you.

John 1:33. Consider how the Holy Spirit descending "like a dove" (v. 32) gave assurance to John that Jesus was the Christ. Now ask God to help you see Jesus in the various hospital and evangelism calls of your ministry.

Psalm 139:9-10. This entire psalm seems to point to the omnipresence of God. Think of a moment in a far distant place when God's Holy Spirit declared himself to you. Then make this testimony available to others you serve. Summon the church to believe that the Holy Spirit is able to relate to all the church in every part of the world at once. When Jesus said in John 16:7 that he had to go away in order for the Spirit to come, what did he really mean? This might be a good time to involve your own part of the Body of Christ in mission endeavors—

both local and international. What are some steps you might take to see this happen?

Acts 19:2. What does it mean for the church of Corinth to have to admit, "We have not even heard that there is a Holy Spirit"? Make a list of things about your church that would continue to happen even if there were no Holy Spirit. Bring this list to your church leaders and solicit their ideas on how the church might quicken every part of its programming by real Holy Spirit dependency. (Calvin Miller)

AUGUST 4, 1996

⅔

Tenth Sunday After Pentecost

Worship Theme: Christ calls us to demonstrate compassion toward people in need.

Readings: Genesis 32:22-31; Romans 9:1-5; Matthew 14:13-21

Call to Worship (Psalm 17:6-7):

Leader: I call upon you, for you will answer me, O God;

***People:* incline your ear to me, hear my words.**

Leader: Wondrously show your steadfast love,

***People:* O savior of those who seek refuge from their adversaries at your right hand.**

Pastoral Prayer:

Almighty and ever blessed God, with songs of praise upon our lips and eager expectations in our hearts, we turn our steps toward the place where your truth and honor dwell. We thank you today for open doors. For the open door of the sanctuary through which we may enter and learn the true meaning of life. For the open door of confession, where we may face up to our humanity and through which we can feel the reach of a hand that lifts us up. For the open door of ministry by which your Word is declared. You have taught us in our praying always to be mindful of others, so we lift before you the sick, the lonely, the disabled, the helpless and hopeless children of our generation. Lend your strong arm to those about to stumble, that they may have a closer walk with you. Help us to show compassion toward others, even as you had compassion on us. Amen. (John Bishop)

SERMON BRIEFS

WHAT'S IN A NAME?

GENESIS 32:22-31

In the local bookstore is a group of books listing hundreds of children's names. It is not unusual for expectant parents to pick a name because they "like its sound," or it is "unusual" or "unique." The people of biblical times would find choosing names for children this way baffling.

The ancients, and even more recent generations, viewed names very differently. Names had significance, even inherent power. The choice of a name was serious. Names chosen often conveyed a message or story. A name might reflect family tradition or lineage.

Jewish and Christian parents often gave biblical names. My name, Steven Robert, reflects such practices: a variant of the name of the first Christian martyr (Stephen) is followed by the name of my father.

When Jacob wrestles a stranger in Genesis 32:22-31, names are central to the action and reflect their symbolism and power.

I. Jacob's Name Reflected His Personality

Jacob's name certainly described his inner personality. *Jacob* means "heel grabber" (Gen. 25:26), or "supplanter" (Gen. 27:36). Named when it was observed he grasped his twin brother's heel at delivery, Jacob will later live up to (or, perhaps better, down) his name.

Fulfilling his name, Jacob tricks his brother Esau out of his birthright, then obtains their father's blessing (Gen. 27). Later, Jacob himself is tricked regarding his marriage (Gen. 29) before turning the tables in a way that brings great wealth (Gen. 30).

Jacob's name is a powerful and vivid connection with his past history and descriptive of his inner personality.

II. Jacob's Name Change Reflected a Change of Direction

Names often change at pivotal moments in the Bible. Abram becomes Abraham (Gen. 17:5), or Jesus renames Simon (Mark 3:16). Early Christians received a new "Christian" name at their baptism.

Genesis 32 tells of Jacob's name change. Jacob has sent his animals, goods, and family across the river to encourage reconciliation with his long-estranged brother Esau. As a result, Jacob is alone.

A figure appears in the darkness. A wrestling match ensues, clearly hinting of Jacob's inner struggle. The wrestling match is a draw, even after the stranger displaces Jacob's hip in an apparent low blow. His unknown adversary asks to be let go as daylight approaches, but Jacob asks first for a blessing. Such a blessing cannot be given without Jacob's name, replies the stranger.

The blessing given to Jacob is a bit of a surprise: he gets a whole new name (*Israel,* meaning "he who struggles with God")! This new name *is* a powerful blessing, suggesting freedom from his checkered past and portending future blessings.

This name change fulfills his dream (Gen. 29). It is a turning point for the nation Israel. The importance of this to both Jacob and the nation Israel is confirmed in Genesis 35:9ff.

Those who would understand the Bible accounts would do well to pay close attention to names and the part names play in the unfolding story of God's people. We would also be well advised to pay more attention to the names that are already ours and the names we give to others. There are clearly power and symbolism in names that we moderns often overlook!

Given this new name, Jacob (now Israel) can cross the river and begin a new life in peace with his brother and with the promised blessing of God assured to him. What's in a name? For Jacob, at least, the answer is clear: a new life. (Steven R. Fleming)

PEACE BETWEEN CHRISTIANS AND JEWS

ROMANS 9:1-5

Today some churches are recognizing a Day of Prayer for World Peace. It is appropriate for us to examine our relationship with and attitude toward other people. Only as attitudes are changed can peace be desired. We need to understand three truths about the relationship between Christians and Jews.

I. We Must Recognize the Church Has Been Guilty of Bigotry

From the early stories of the church in the book of Acts, we know Jews persecuted Christians. Paul, for example, was a Pharisee who pursued and jailed Christians for their perversion of the faith. After Paul was converted and called to be a missionary, other Jews persecuted him, often jailing him and beating him.

But as time passed, followers of Christ grew in numbers and acceptance. After Constantine became Christian and made Christianity the legal religion of the Roman Empire, Christians were strong enough to turn the tables and begin tormenting their persecutors.

From the time of the fifth century, Jews were blamed with the death of Christ. Texts such as Romans 11:28a, "As regards the gospel they are enemies of God for your sake," were misinterpreted to mean Christians were supposed to consider Jews enemies and suppress them.

Anti-Semitism has reared its ugly head in many areas of Christendom.

II. We Are to Love God's Chosen People

In Romans 9–11, Paul bares his heart concerning the people of Israel. Like Moses before him, he wishes he could offer himself a sacrifice in order to save all of his people. He reiterates they are still God's chosen people, still owners of God's Law, and still beloved of God. Paul's "heart's desire and prayer to God for them is that they may be saved" (Rom. 10:1).

Paul's love for the Jewish people is something every Christian should share. Rather than gloat over our election in their place, Paul reminds us that we can be taken out and God's first chosen people grafted back in very easily (11:17-24). There is no room in the Christian faith for any kind of racial arrogance, especially not toward Jews.

III. We Must Have Loving Respect and Faithful Outreach

Fortunately, very few Christians still refer to Jews as "Christ killers." Most of us have come to realize that if Christ died for us and for our sins, we actually killed him. Our sinfulness and our rebellion drove the nails. Only the person who had no sin and for whom Christ did not have to die can stand back and point a finger at anyone for killing Jesus.

Anti-Semitism is on the decline in the church, but it is not dead. *Schindler's List* was a painful reminder that the Holocaust took place in a "Christian country." Many Christians still belong to country clubs that exclude Jews. Many churches are involved in interfaith agencies that exclude Jews.

The call of our text today is for peace between Christians and Jews. We must add our prayers and our concerns to those of Paul. We must work as he did for the conversion of Jewish people, and we must do it in a way that recognizes their dignity and the fact that God's call to them is irrevocable (Rom. 11:29). Pray for Jews who feel alienated from God because of the Holocaust. Pray for peace in Israel and Palestine. Pray for us and our attitudes toward God's first chosen people. (Bill Groover)

ON BEING COMPASSIONATE

MATTHEW 14:13-21

There is no denying the fact that talking about compassion is a lot easier than being compassionate. We readily praise compassion as a virtue, but in practice compassion can be a real inconvenience and, quite literally, a downright pain. The word itself comes from two Latin words that together mean "to suffer with." To be compassionate is to share the suffering of another person. It is to participate in the other's pain.

Let's face it. That is hardly the kind of pastime that gets promoted in our culture. When we have a choice about it, we prefer to keep our distance from pain and avoid confronting suffering. We hate to grapple with things that may be depressing. This attitude was epitomized in the title of a self-help book published a few years ago. The book was entitled *F.L.Y.E.R.S.*, and acronym for *Fun Loving Youth En Route to Success*. The lengthy subtitle of the book was this: *How to remain oblivious to the arms race, the budget deficit, acid rain and other current events that could put a damper on your bright future.*

We are not malicious, but we live in a culture that fosters self-absorption. We don't like to be troubled by the thoughts of war and disaster victims, AIDS, world hunger, homelessness, and other tragic elements of human existence.

I. Where Some See Obstacles, Jesus Sees Opportunity

Of course, we are not unique. Even the apostles wanted to avoid the inconvenience and disturbance that compassion can bring into life. Large crowds gathered around Jesus, and many people with disabilities were brought to him for healing. Jesus was getting ready to move into another region, but in front of him was a mass of folks who didn't even have the good sense to bring food with them when they began their journey. Jesus wanted to dismiss them, but he feared for their well-being because of their hunger.

Jesus surveyed the crowd, and deep within himself he felt their need and said, "I am unwilling to send them away hungry." Jesus was moved by their plight. He didn't stand back and judge the people or blame them for the ache in their empty stomachs. He didn't try to evaluate whether they were truly needy or worthy of his help. He didn't excuse himself because he was too busy with his own important work to get involved with something else. No. He sensed the suffering of the people; he had compassion and did something to help the hungry. The apostles saw obstacles, but Jesus saw an opportunity to do good.

II. We Are Called to See as Jesus Did

As Christians, we have been called to follow Christ in ways of compassion. Because of this calling, we cannot endeavor to preserve a quiet and untroubled mind at all costs. If the compassion of the Lord is within us, we realize the pain of others as our own pain. This shapes the way we look on our own lives.

I recall a bit of dialogue in one of my favorite movies by the now politically incorrect and morally dubious Woody Allen, *Annie Hall*. In this picture, Woody Allen plays the part of Alvy. His girlfriend Annie says to him, "Alvy, you're incapable of enjoying life, you know that?" In response Alvy says, "I can't enjoy anything unless . . . everyone is . . . you know, if one guy is starving someplace . . . it puts a crimp in my evening." Alvy is certainly an extreme. Compassion and the capacity for enjoyment are not mutually exclusive. But compassion does put a bridle on self-indulgence and refuses to allow us to ignore needy persons.

Christian sociologist and author Anthony Campolo tells of a trip he made to Haiti. While there he went to a restaurant. The waiter seated him beside a large window. Not long after taking the order, the waiter returned with a fine-looking dinner that he placed in front of Campolo.

Campolo was about to eat a bite of steak when he happened to look to his left. There he saw eight hungry Haitian children with their noses pressed up against the glass, staring at his food. He immediately lost his appetite and laid down his fork. When the waiter saw what had happened, he quickly moved in and lowered the blinds. He said to Campolo, "Enjoy your meal. Don't let them bother you." But people of compassion cannot help being bothered.

Because there is more suffering in the world than we can possibly address, compassion can be frustrating. We may very well feel that our efforts to alleviate the problems of hunger, homelessness, disease, and other misfortunes count for nothing. But that is not so. Our acts of compassion are signs that God uses to show the world that life does not have to be pitiless and unjust.

We may not feed the population of the world, but every time a hungry mouth is fed, that is a sign of the kingdom of God. We may not be able to house all the homeless, but every time we work to provide shelter for one more family, that is a sign of the kingdom of God. We may not heal the AIDS epidemic, but every time we embrace and comfort a person with AIDS, we show a sign of the kingdom of God.

The magnitude of the problems in the world need not paralyze us. God can use even a cup of cool water given to a thirsty person to promote the divine work of compassion on earth. (Craig M. Watts)

AUGUST 11, 1996

୨ଈ

Eleventh Sunday After Pentecost

Worship Theme: Salvation is found only through faith in Jesus Christ as Lord.

Readings: Genesis 37:1-4, 12-28; Romans 10:5-15; Matthew 14:22-33

Call to Worship (Psalm 105:1-4):

Leader: O give thanks to the LORD, call on his name,

People: make known his deeds among the peoples.

Leader: Sing to him, sing praises to him;

People: tell of all his wonderful works.

Leader: Glory in his holy name; let the hearts of those who seek the LORD rejoice.

People: Seek the LORD and his strength; seek his presence continually.

Pastoral Prayer:

Unto you, our Creator and our God, we lift up our voices in praise and thanksgiving. In the midst of our rebellion and sin, you reached out to us with love and grace. While we were yet sinners, Christ died for us. We do not deserve such amazing love, O Lord, but we accept it and praise you for it. When we become complacent about our faith, remind us of the great price that was paid on our behalf. When we fail to share your love, remind us of the grace that came to us when we were least deserving. To all of those who have not yet heard, make us messengers of your love; to all of those who have yet to believe, make us faithful examples of your transforming grace. We ask it in the name of the One who gave himself for us. Amen.

SERMON BRIEFS

BEWARE THE DREAMER!

GENESIS 37:1-4, 12-28

The story of Jacob reads like the script for a television miniseries. Jacob (also called Israel) is the patriarch of a great, though troubled, family. In his younger days, Jacob cheated his brother out of his inheritance and their father's blessing; was later himself tricked in marriage (ultimately getting revenge on his father-in-law); fathered a number of children by several wives and their attendants; and wrestled with a stranger who gave him the new name Israel.

An interesting family, don't you think? There is more: Jacob has twelve sons, though one is clearly his favorite. Joseph, a child of Jacob's "old age" (v. 3), is heartily disliked by his older brothers and for good reason! First, Jacob gives Joseph a "richly ornamented robe" (v. 3 NIV). Although the meaning is unclear, it set Joseph apart from the rest of the brothers and was suggestive of kingly attire (see 2 Sam. 13:18).

Second, Joseph is a tattletale who willingly gives a "bad report of them" to their father. Joseph is on another of these missions (vv. 13-14) when captured by his brothers and sold into slavery.

The main reason Joseph is so disliked can be found in the comment "Here comes this dreamer" (v. 19). This refers to an earlier moment (37:5-11) when Joseph tells two of his dreams. Although dreams in themselves don't necessarily create problems, these two dreams implied Joseph would one day rule over his brothers and his parents. It is one thing to have a brother who is the favorite of aging parents, is given special gifts, or even spies on you. It is quite another thing to have to put up with a brother who dreams of the day when you and the rest of your family will bow down to him!

Dreamers are always getting in and out of trouble in families, schools, companies, society, and politics. Dreamers see things in a new way, often envisioning new possibilities and suggesting new relationships and power structures. In suggesting such new possibilities, dreamers often find themselves at the center of any plan for a new order. Needless to say, the world dislikes dreamers because they upset the status quo and challenge the established.

Clearly, Joseph does just that: he challenges the natural birth order in his family (which his father also did with Esau), and he dares to dream of a time when he will be politically as well as socially superior to his entire family. No wonder his brothers—despite the strong moral imperatives against fratricide—plot to kill him. A series of events follows that God uses to prevent Joseph's death and that ultimately lead to Israel's salvation. But that's another story.

Here is a clear message: "Beware the dreamers!" Dreaming is risky business. Our dreams, hopes, and aspirations may turn out to be quite troublesome to others and even put us in some sort of danger. The account of Joseph reveals that such dreamers—if they are faithful to God—can be used for purposes far beyond their understanding. (Steven R. Fleming)

TODAY'S ANSWER TO AN OLD QUESTION

ROMANS 10:5-15

A trip to a bookstore or video rental store will prove people are still asking the question: "What happens after death?" With advancements in every area of science, people wonder if there have been any breakthroughs in this area. When profits can be made, self-made prophets will speak.

I. People Still Seek a New Answer

That is not a modern development. Moses warned the people of Israel about such searches. In his farewell address he warned the people not to search for a new answer in the heavens or across the seas. The old answer, the truth, was already near them, even in their mouths.

Paul quoted Moses when he told the church in Rome his gospel was not a new answer to the old question. Paul said they needed no new answers from either heaven or the abyss. The old answer was still near them.

Today people are still looking. One of the best-selling books of 1994 was Betty Eadie's answer, *Embraced by the Light*. Eadie claims she died during the night following an operation. She went to heaven while she was dead. No one called her husband or told her. Five years later, her doctor admitted she had died during a shift change. A medical team had revived her when they noticed what had happened. But they did not mention it at the time. Hardest to believe, the hospital did not charge her a penny for the resuscitation! Millions bought the book. Why? People are seaching for a new answer.

Another example would be Jane Roberts. She claims the spirit of an ancient warrior, Seth, takes control of her body and mouth to share his ancient wisdom with people of today. An innocent game of Ouija board developed into a lucrative career. Several books of Seth's answers to old questions are available. Why do people buy these books? They are still looking for a new answer.

One author claims to have gone to heaven for her message. The other has heard from the abyss. New answers abound, but do they stand up?

II. The Old Answer Is Still True

The Bible says such quests are futile. The answer, "the word of faith," has been revealed to us by God, is near us, on our lips and in our hearts.

Twenty years ago I felt God touch my heart when I heard the old answer: "Everyone who calls upon the name of the Lord will be saved." I believed in my heart, and I confessed with my mouth. My heart and life were changed. I have seen many others experience the same thing. Can the old answer of the Bible be in your heart and in your mouth? Through faith and prayer, it most certainly can!

III. Those Who Know the Answer Must Share It

Many people say unchurched people do not want to hear anything religious. Then why do books such as *Embraced by the Light* and Raymond Moody's *Life After Life* hit the best-seller list? Theaters pack people in to see movies like *Ghost, Always,* and *Flatliners.* People are looking everywhere for an answer. They want to hear what we have to say.

They do not want a confrontational conversation. They want to discuss religion, not have it crammed down their throats. They want something in between shouting and silence. First, ask them what they believe. Listen. Earn your right to be heard. Then share your experience. If people will pay seventeen dollars a copy for Betty Eadie's experience, they will listen to yours for free.

Paul says they can never believe unless they hear. If we don't tell them, Betty Eadie and Jane Roberts will. Those who know the "old answer" must share it. (Bill Groover)

WHEN FAITH FAILS, GOD DOESN'T

MATTHEW 14:22-33

I remember several years ago when a milestone was passed in our household. Our four-year-old son, Jonathan, asked me to take the training wheels off his bike. Apparently, he saw one of the little boys down the street cruising around unencumbered by side supports. Seeing another fellow near his own age speeding along on two wheels challenged and inspired Jonathan.

As soon as I finished the job, he grabbed the bike, eager to embark on the new adventure of two-wheel travel. As it turned out, getting up and staying up on those two wheels proved to be more difficult than it looked. And after about a dozen false starts, Jonathan came trudging back, pushing his bike, saying, "Daddy how 'bout we put the training wheels back on."

I'm not so sure things are very different when we grow up. It is always difficult to make a change in life, to learn a new skill, to break an unhealthy habit, to move into another profession. But from time to time some person or event clamps on to us in just the right way and gives us a hand. We move forward with faith, excited by the possibilities before us. But then we collide into some sort of barrier or face a threat or inconvenience. Our faith starts sputtering. All of a sudden, the status quo begins to look a whole lot better than it did before. We want to put the training wheels back on.

The apostles seem to have picked a lousy time for a midnight cruise. After they got their boat some distance from land, the waves and wind began to pitch and toss them about. The situation was frightening, but it got worse. For through the spray, something eerie appeared. It looked like someone walking on the water, perhaps a ghost. No, it was Jesus. He called out to the apostles and identified himself.

Peter was not content to be a mere observer of the strange occurrence. He wanted to be a participant. So when Jesus invited Peter out for a stroll on the rolling sea, Peter stepped right out of the boat and began to walk on the water. Then, like a cartoon character that runs off the edge of a cliff and remains suspended in midair until he looks down into the abyss below, Peter looked around and realized the impossibility of his situation. And he began to sink. Peter had the faith to get out of the boat, but he lacked the faith to stay on his feet.

Our faith is reasonably sturdy stuff—so long as the dangers we face are minimal and the risks we face are modest. Beyond that, it is sort of touch and go. We don't want to end up like Peter and get in over our heads. Even the most daring and dedicated of us have limits. We have faith, but we don't want our faith to make fools of us. Consequently, we don't stray very far from the tried and true. I mean, what would happen if we quit that unfulfilling but financially rewarding job to move into something more meaningful?

Robert Fulghum tells a story of a young American woman he met in a Hong Kong airport. She was dressed in the traditional garb of the East. Beside her sat a well-worn backpack that showed the sign of hard travel. Clearly, the woman had been exploring the world. Now she was on the way home. Fulghum envied her.

But then he saw tears begin to run down her face and drip off her chin. Soon she was racked with sobs. It took a box of tissues to contain all the tears. You see, the young woman had traveled as far as her money would take her, and she had just enough to purchase the cheapest plane ticket back home. She had spent two days in the airport, waiting to fly standby, without enough to eat and with too much pride to beg.

Finally, the plane was about to go. But she had lost her ticket. She had spent the last three hours rummaging through her things again and again to find it, but with no luck.

Fulghum offered to take her to lunch and to help her talk to the airport authorities about her problem. She stood up and turned around to pick up her belongings. And then she let out a sudden scream. It was her ticket. For three hours she had been sitting on her own ticket!

Isn't that the way it is with us? We want to do something great, we want to go somewhere significant, but we manage to misplace our faith. In fact, we may be sitting on our own ticket. Sometimes to make any progress, we have to get up and get moving, even though we don't really know how we'll reach our destination.

God does not stop working for our good just because our faith is too small. The faith of the Israelites faltered when they saw the Egyptian army on their heels. Peter's faith faltered when he paid more attention to the wind and waves at his feet than he did to Jesus. But the limits of faith are not the limits of God's power. Even in the face of their uncertainty God reached out to save his people. And God still does. In fact, sometimes it is when our faith is the most severely tried that God works most powerfully. (Craig M. Watts)

AUGUST 18, 1996

Twelfth Sunday After Pentecost

Worship Theme: God can turn the difficulties of our lives into blessings.

Readings: Genesis 45:1-15; Romans 11:1-2*a*, 29-32; Matthew 15:(10-20) 21-28

Call to Worship (Psalm 133:1, 3):

Leader: How very good and pleasant it is

People: **when kindred live together in unity! . . .**

Leader: It is like the dew of Hermon, which falls on the mountains of Zion.

People: **For there the LORD ordained his blessing, life forevermore.**

Pastoral Prayer:

O God, who has called us aside this day from the toil and tumult of our world, free us also, we pray, from its cares and idle concerns. The world consumes our thoughts; our souls are oppressed by its anxiety, worried by its turmoil, frustrated by its priorities. How we long, O Lord, for the peace of your sanctuary, the comfort of your presence. Forgive our sins, cleanse our hearts, and strengthen us for struggles yet to come. Remind us that the worst the world can do to us is no match for what you are already producing in us. As we step back into the society in which we live, help us to be in the world but not of the world; free us from our bondage to the world's deceits, that we might be free to know your truth. Make our hearts your temple and our lives the place where your Holy Spirit works. Amen.

SERMON BRIEFS

TURNING ADVERSITY
INTO ACCOMPLISHMENT

GENESIS 45:1-15

Susan White-Bowden, one of the first female television newscasters in Baltimore, found her life shattered. First, her former husband committed suicide. Then, her teenage son, Jody, did the same. The tragedies nearly destroyed her personally and professionally. But Susan began to share her experiences with others. As she spoke to various groups about the tragedies, she helped others. She would write a book, *Everything to Live For,* and spearhead efforts to prevent similar tragedies. People listened because they knew her accomplishments were rooted in the pain of great personal adversity.

The story of Joseph's reunion with his brothers suggests a similar journey from great adversity to accomplishment. Our text suggests two key truths about life.

I. Life Is Characterized by Adversity

Modern North American culture assumes that things should or must "go right," that we are entitled to success, material well-being, and personal satisfaction.

In contrast, the Bible portrays life as difficult, challenging, and often troubled. That was true even for Joseph, who by this point in the biblical account has become a real success. Second only to Pharaoh in power, prestige, and influence, Joseph is responsible for seeing that Egypt and its neighbors are well prepared for a famine.

This achievement came only after a long and difficult personal journey of incredible adversity. Sold by his own brothers into slavery and taken to Egypt, Joseph rises to a position of prominence. But when he spurns the advances of his master's wife, Joseph is unjustly thrown into prison with virtually no hope of release.

While in prison, Joseph interprets other persons' dreams (Gen. 40) in a way that ultimately attracts the attention of Pharaoh. When Joseph interprets Pharaoh's dreams (Gen. 41), he is placed in charge of preparations for the coming famine predicted in those dreams. Talk about a life of struggle and adversity. Joseph lived such a life.

II. God Uses Adversity to Accomplish the Divine Will

Joseph's brothers come to him for assistance. When he identifies himself, his brothers are filled with terror and unable to answer. After all, they had betrayed him! How would Joseph now treat them? The calm, clear answer: "Do not be distressed . . . for God sent me before you to preserve life" (v. 5). Joseph has the perspective of one who realizes God wove his trials and tribulations into the larger scheme of things.

In a marvelous way—quite beyond the understanding of either Joseph or his brothers—God took what was meant for evil and instead used it for good. In their moment of mutual forgiveness and brotherly reunion, Joseph states, "God sent me before you to preserve for you a remnant on earth, and to keep alive for you many survivors" (v. 7).

How many of us, when facing our own moments of personal trial, tribulation, adversity, or even betrayal, need to look beyond the present moment trusting God is at work behind the scenes? Someone else who understood the way God uses adversity was the apostle Paul. He put it this way in Romans 8:28: "We know that all things work together for good for those who love God, who are called according to his purpose."

We see in this joyous reunion story of Joseph, his brothers, and ultimately his entire family an example of how God can transform our adversities into avenues of accomplishment. What adversities in your life and mine can God use to accomplish a greater purpose—if you and I are open to allow God to work in us? (Steven R. Fleming)

WHAT ABOUT THE JEWS?

ROMANS 11:1-2a, 29-32

A question that intrigues many Christians is: "Are Jewish people saved?" If most pastors polled their churches, they would get mixed responses. Our text from Romans comes from the conclusion of a lengthy discussion (chaps. 9–11) of God's relationship with his chosen people. Let's look at Paul's answer to this sticky question.

I. The Chosen People Are Still Chosen

Paul makes this point emphatically: "I ask, then, has God rejected his people? By no means!" (Rom. 11:1). Still this statement must be held together with Paul's introduction to the topic. In Romans 9:3, he says, "For I could wish that I myself were accursed and cut off from Christ for the sake of my own people, my kindred according to the flesh." He, like Moses, would sacrifice himself if he could know all his kinspeople would be saved.

The keys to understanding the question are scattered through the context of Romans 9, 10, and 11. In chapter 9, the covenant belongs to the Israelites (v. 4), but not all Jews (children of the flesh) are Israelites (children of the promise) (vv. 6-8). Within the nation there have always been some who rebelled and some who became a faithful remnant. For a Jew to receive the promised gift of righteousness, he or she must receive it by faith. Thus,

II. Even the Chosen Must Choose God by Faith

Too many Jews had tried to earn their righteousness by keeping the Law and had failed (9:31-32). Because of their failure, God chose more people, the Gentiles, to become his children. The Gentiles received their righteousness by faith (9:30).

Paul was concerned for his people not because God had rejected them but because the Jews had not accepted God on his terms. In Romans 10:1, he says, "Brothers and sisters, my heart's desire and prayer to God for them is that they may be saved." He then quotes Moses to prove his message is consistent with the Law and the Prophets. Not even the chosen people will be saved just by having been chosen; they must choose God: "For, 'Everyone who calls on the name of the Lord shall be saved' " (10:13).

The Jews, Paul says, were "broken off" from God because of unbelief. The offer of election, however, still stands, and they can be grafted in again (11:20-23) because "the gifts and the calling of God are irrevocable" (11:29).

Thus the answer to our question: Are all Jews saved? No. Are all Jews lost? No. Are all Baptists saved? No. Methodists? Catholics? The answer is the same for all: "The scripture says, 'No one who believes in him will be put to shame' " (10:11). Believers are saved, not Jews, not Catholics, and not Protestants. Those chosen by God by grace must also choose God by faith.

III. As Christians, We Are Called to Share the Gospel with the Chosen

As Gentile Christians, we must remember the Jews still have a special place in God's heart. They always have been, and always will be, God's chosen people. We must never think ourselves to be more favored of God. Paul says if the natural olive branch (the Jews) can be broken off from the vine (God) and the wild branch (Gentiles) grafted on, God will break off the wild branch and graft back the original (11:16-24). God wants to use the Gentiles to help win back the Jews, not drive them farther away as much Christian anti-Semitism has done. (Bill Groover)

THE BLESSING OF PERSISTENCE

MATTHEW 15:(10-20) 21-28

Very good people can have very serious flaws. We manage to continue calling these people very good because their flaws are not obvious in most situations. It takes a special turn of events to evoke the worst in them.

I remember a man who lived near me when I was in Nashville, Tennessee. He was a warm, friendly guy. He was always ready to help. For years he let me use his lawn mower when I was a poor student, unable to afford one of my own. He volunteered to climb the tree in my front yard and remove dead limbs. I was too chicken to do it myself; I was more concerned about preserving my own limbs. He offered to help me paint my house. He was a very likable guy.

But he did have a serious flaw. He was a raging racial bigot. He couldn't say enough bad about African American people. All the social ills of our country he laid at their doorstep. In most areas if we disagreed with each other, we could do so calmly and respectfully. But when it came to race relations, he was beyond all reason. The goodness that I had seen in this man would never be seen by a black person.

You may know people who are like that. There is so much about them that you appreciate, yet they occasionally surprise and appall you by some belief or behavior that seems out of character. Usually, you shake your head and say with a touch of sadness, "Well, no one's perfect."

In today's passage, Jesus surprises us. In today's text, the tender Christ seems missing. The One who healed the broken, who gave dignity to prostitutes, who ate with tax collectors and sinners and opened his arms to everyone with need, is not who we find. Instead, he draws a circle around the chosen people—his people—and he keeps the Canaanite woman and her child out.

Evidently, Jesus' reputation had reached outside Israel. A woman came out of her home when she heard Jesus was in the area. She started a ruckus, shouting, "Have mercy on me, Lord, Son of David" (v. 22). That was odd for her to call Jesus Son of David. That is a Jewish title, and she wasn't Jewish. The woman was in essence calling him Messiah. Even the apostles hadn't yet done that in the Gospel of Matthew. "My daughter is tormented by a demon," she said (v. 22). But Jesus pretended she wasn't even there.

Finally, he said, "I was sent only to the lost sheep of the house of Israel" (v. 24). He wasn't sent by God to travel to the far reaches of the world to teach and heal. The little nation of Israel, the nation through which God would reach out in love to the rest of the world, was his focus. But the woman's mind was not satisfied with Jesus' words. Her daughter was in torment and needed to be healed. That one thing mattered to the woman. Loving parents are that way, aren't they?

What happened next is startling to me. Jesus replied, "It is not fair to take the children's food and throw it to the dogs" (v. 26). Was Jesus calling the woman and her child dogs? That's the way it seems. That was not uncommon language for Jews to use to describe non-Jews in the first century. But without missing a beat the woman replied, "Yes, Lord, yet even the dogs eat the crumbs that fall from their masters' table" (v. 27).

The Canaanite woman wouldn't give up. Though the disciples wanted to send her away, though Jesus ignored her and then said his mission was to Israel alone, she continued to cry out for help. She was like Abraham who wouldn't complacently go along with the plan when God decided to destroy Sodom and Gomorrah. Abraham haggled with God. Years later Moses ended up bargaining with God when the Lord got fed up with the children of Israel in the wilderness and wanted to destroy them.

Centuries later, another haggler came along who couldn't take no for an answer. She wouldn't be ignored or put off. She pressed her case just like Abraham did, just like Moses did. And like God had done before, Jesus responded to the persistent pestering cries and helped the woman and her child.

Instead of explaining, excusing, or judging Jesus, perhaps we should follow the Canaanite woman's example and just trust him. Certainly, Jesus didn't make her any more comfortable than his response to her makes us. But she didn't give up. She pleaded and pressed her case because she believed he could give her what she wanted—health and wholeness for her child. Finally, Jesus said, "Great is your faith! Let it be done for you as you wish" (v. 28). And her daughter was healed. Jesus saw in the woman a faith that equaled the best Israel had to offer. He couldn't say no to a person with such faith.

Now the mission of Jesus is inclusive and world-embracing. It is the church's responsibility to fulfill this mission. Israel was God's pilot project. The episode of Jesus with the Canaanite woman gives no justification to anyone who wants to be narrow and stingy with love and acceptance. Instead, it gives us an example of faith.

Many of us know that our spiritual lives are not all they could be. Maybe the problem is that we have not been as persistent as the woman who made Christ bless her. As Jesus said in his Sermon on the Mount: "Keep on asking and it will be given to you; keep on searching and you will find; keep on knocking and the door of blessing will be opened to you" (Matt. 7:7, paraphrase). We need to keep on. If we do, who knows how Christ might bless us? (Craig M. Watts)

AUGUST 25, 1996

જી

Thirteenth Sunday After Pentecost

Worship Theme: Confessing Jesus as Lord produces a transformation in our lives.

Readings: Exodus 1:8–2:10; Romans 12:1-8; Matthew 16:13-20

Call to Worship (Psalm 124:8):

Leader: Our help is in the name of the LORD,

***People:* who made heaven and earth.**

Pastoral Prayer:

Eternal God, whose word spoke a universe into being and whose touch transformed our lives, we gather today to celebrate a living Lord, who has broken down death's gate and loosed the chains of sin that once held us powerless. And like our brother Peter so many centuries before us, we also confess that Jesus Christ is Messiah, the Son of God. We praise you, Lord, for the power of the Resurrection that has transformed our world and our lives utterly and completely. Even as we have been recipients of your grace, so make us instruments of your good news. Help us to bind up wounds of sorrow, to comfort broken hearts, to share your forgiveness with shattered lives. Help us, in our words and our actions, to confess you more richly and deeply with each passing day. Amen.

SERMON BRIEFS

MIDWIVES TO A NATION

EXODUS 1:8–2:10

The statistics are clear, their implications worrisome to many: in the United States, Canada, and many European countries, the birthrate of immigrants is significantly higher than among these countries' present populations. Such statistics are leading to increasing xenophobia and worldwide restrictions on immigration.

Fear and anxiety about immigrants are nothing new. Nazis sought to destroy Europe's Jewish population; the minority whites in South Africa feared the majority native blacks. Here in the United States, many persons once were concerned about Irish immigrants. Now many worry about growing numbers of Hispanics and Asians.

When a new king comes to power in Egypt, he also faces the reality of a growing immigrant population. This king fears that "the Israelite people are more numerous and more powerful than we" (1:9b). Attempts are made to control the rapidly growing immigrant population. The efforts ultimately fail as the more the Israelites are oppressed, the more the people multiply and spread (1:12). As a result, harsher methods are decreed: midwives are to kill all Israelite boys at birth.

But even this decree is thwarted when God raises up two midwives: Shiphrah and Puah. Because of their fearlessness and faithfulness, God blesses the people of Israel (and these two midwives) even more. Of the many truths in this text, the story of these midwives deserves our special attention.

I. God Uses Faithful Women to Accomplish His Purposes

It is fashionable for some to criticize the Bible as solely the story of men and male accomplishments, yet a closer reading shows this is hardly the case. Women play an extraordinary—and quite crucial—role in Judeo-Christian history in both Old and New Testaments.

Clearly, these two women are key players in the people's survival. Their courage and devotion to God challenge all of us. Might the Holocaust have been avoided if there had been more courageous people (like these midwives) refusing to go along with the Nazis?

Not only are they fearless, Shiphrah and Puah outsmart the Egyptians. When questioned by the king about the growing Israelite population in spite of his decrees, they have an explanation. The Hebrew women are much stronger than Egyptian women. In fact, the Israelite women have their babies so quickly that it's finished by the time the midwife gets there! No weak women, these Israelites!

II. God Uses Those Who Fear Him to Accomplish His Purposes

There is another timeless message to be found in the story of the two midwives. It is the way that those who fear God (1:17) can be used to defeat a powerful evil. The midwives hardly seem able to challenge a king. First, they are women. Second, they are immigrants. And finally, they have no families (or power bases) of their own although later God will reward them for their faithfulness (1:21).

It's a quite impossible situation except for one crucial fact: these women "feared God"—fear in the sense that Almighty God would punish them for killing the children, and fear in the sense of reverence, belief, and trust.

Because of their faith in God, two women challenge a powerful king. Doing so, they save a weak, defenseless people from hostile forces seeking their destruction.

One person, with God at her or his side, is a majority. Here, two midwives—with God at their side—assist in the birth of an entire nation. (Steven R. Fleming)

KNOWING GOD'S WILL

ROMANS 12:1-8

One of the most rewarding aspects of living the Christian life is knowing and doing God's will. The Bible gives us many examples of God's will in general (such as 12:9-21), but how do we know God's will for us in unique situations? The Bible won't give you a verse saying, "Take the job offer in Toledo," or "Marry Ted." How does a finite human know the mind of an infinite God at these times? In Romans 12:1-8, we find four keys for knowing God's will.

I. Commit Yourself to Doing God's Will

Christians use expressions like "giving our lives to Christ." Paul is calling us to such commitment on a daily basis when he says, "Present your bodies as a living sacrifice" (v. 1). Giving him our lives implies a commitment to doing his will, regardless of what it may be. I find God speaks most clearly when we ask his direction and not his suggestion. And we listen more intently to directions we know we will need than to directions we don't think we will use.

The Bible says, "Trust in the LORD . . . and he shall direct thy paths" (Prov. 3:5-6 KJV). Trusting precedes knowing.

II. Let God Reprogram Your Mind

"Do not be conformed to this world, but be transformed by the renewing of your minds" (v. 2). A contemporary way of expressing this idea is: "Don't let the world mold your thinking, but let Christ reprogram your mind." Statistics say a television set is on seven hours a day in the average U.S. home. What you watch will influence you or program you. Remember the old computer adage: "garbage in; garbage out"—in other words, you can't take out of a computer better information than you put into it.

Paul might say, "God's will in; God's will out!" Divine reprogramming is part of what *repentance* means. We turn from sin, but we also change our minds about what sin is. A nonfollower of Christ can say, "I don't see any harm in telling a lie, but God will punish me if I do. Thus, I had better not, though I sure would like to!" Repentance is: "I once thought it was okay to tell a lie, but God says it is wrong. Thus, I say it is wrong, and I no longer want to tell lies." Such a mind would be renewed.

III. Have Realistic Self-esteem

Verse 3 tells us we need a proper view of ourselves to know God's will. We must not think of ourselves more highly, or more lowly, than God does. We make a mistake when we think that we are too good to do something God wants us to do ("They asked me to be on a do-nothing committee; I should be chairman of the board!") or that we're not good enough. If we are to know God's will, we must have an accurate view of ourselves, our capabilities, and our limits, and who we are in Christ as well as who Christ is in us.

IV. Recognize the Diversity of God's People

God's will for you may be different from God's will for another: "For as in one body we have many members, and not all the members have the same function" (v. 4). Just as your will for your hand differs from your will for your foot, so does God's will differ among the parts of his Body, the members of the church.

Paul uses the analogy of differing body parts to describe Christian unity and diversity. It is not God's will for all Christians to be preachers. Preachers (and all Christians) need doctors, teachers, dry cleaners, entertainers, and so on. Thus, God calls people into each area where he needs people to serve. Whatever role God has called you to perform, do it to God's glory! (Bill Groover)

A TRANSFORMING CONFESSION

MATTHEW 16:13-20

Despite the multitude of religions that have appeared on the scene of the twentieth century, there is still something unique about Jesus Christ. Even among those who reject his claims to divinity, there is a profound respect—a recognition that he is unlike other men.

The Unitarian William Ellery Channing said, "I know of no sincere enduring good but the moral excellency which shines forth in Jesus Christ." George Bernard Shaw observed, "I am no more Christian than Pilate was . . . [yet] I am ready to admit that I see no way out of the world's misery but the way which would have been found by his will."

But is it enough to confess Jesus as a great teacher or a supreme religious example? As Jesus quizzed his disciples that day, they pointed out that the Nazarene preacher was being compared with John the Baptist, Elijah, and other prophets—high praise indeed. But it was Peter's confession alone that elicited Jesus' confirmation. As Peter and the other disciples would learn, to confess Jesus Christ as Lord makes a transforming difference in our lives because of what God does in us.

I. God Gives a New Perception (v. 17)

The very understanding that Peter had gained as to Jesus' identity was not his own doing; it was a revelation, a gift of God. The world didn't know it—the people were chasing military and economic solutions to every problem. Reason didn't uncover it—the very idea of a suffering Savior would seem ludicrous to those who lived by reason alone.

Only God could reveal this insight. If you have come to the realization that Jesus Christ is Messiah, Son of God, and Savior, you have received that new perception from God. And because you have been given this new mind—this new "filter" through which to perceive the world—every part of the world will now be seen with a different understanding.

II. God Gives a New Purpose (v. 18)

Peter would have lived and died a Galilean fisherman, but his faith in Jesus transformed his life's purpose. Henceforth, he and his fellow believers became foundation stones on which God would build the church.

It's a large foundation—in fact, it continues to be laid today. You and I are part of that same foundation if we have confessed Jesus Christ as Lord. We have a new purpose: to be part of the building of God's kingdom.

III. God Gives a New Power (v. 19)

Those who have become part of the Kingdom through confessing Jesus as Lord receive supernatural power because of the new relationship with God. Through our faithful witness to Christ—as the Holy Spirit works through our lives—others will be able to enter God's kingdom as well. It is an enormous power and responsibility: to be the gateway to the Kingdom for family, friends, coworkers, and others. Who will find his or her way to the Kingdom through your witness?

Our confession of Christ produces a remarkable new world to us—but only as we truly surrender ourselves to his authority. The story is told that during the Civil War, a small band of Confederate representatives met with President Lincoln in the cabin of a river steamer. Stressing the terrible human cost and suffering on both

285

sides in the war, they unrolled a map and pointed out several concessions of territory and frontier boundaries the Confederacy would make if the Union would agree to lift any claim to the remainderoftherebelstates. Attheconclusionoftheirpresentation, Lincoln placed his large hand onto the map and said, "Gentlemen, this government must have all."

God's kingdom makes the same claim on your life and mine. If we confess him as Lord, we give him our all. (Michael Duduit)

SEPTEMBER

૨ૡ

Preparing to Serve

The Symbol of the Bride

Paraphrase Assignment:

Matthew 22:2: "The kingdom of heaven may be compared to a king who gave a wedding banquet for his son."

Prayer Assignment:

If you have not already preached a series on the home, you may want to let Paul's emphasis in Ephesians 5:21-33 start you on some intensely relevant messages on relationships. Dealing now with the church as bride, evaluate how you can further enhance your marriage so that you catch a glimmer of how Christ loved his church. Begin praying that his love for all your church members will be yours. List church members who may be a trouble to you, others, God, or merely themselves.

Again get other members of the church involved in this period of trying to understand the bridegroom and bride imagery of Scripture.

Journal-in-Worship Assignment:

Ephesians 5:21-33. Consider the issue of your earthly relationships. Now call the members of the church to seek an understanding of how their own marriages are metaphors of love and service that parallel Christ's great love for his bride, the church. Write down the time when this passage became obvious within your family. Use this paragraph to make the idea of marital love and Christ's love for the church as inextricably mixed together as they are in this Ephesians passage.

Colossians 1:18. Although the days are gone when Christians are interested in talking about the submission of the wife, show how in this passage all Christians, regardless of gender, are to be in submission to Christ as Lord. Suggest ways in which you and your spouse found it possible to come together in spiritual submission, both

287

serving Christ. Now write out a church service in which you explore the mutuality of Christian service within the home.

Revelation 19:7, 9*b*. Write how you feel about that time when the church of all ages is gathered in before the throne. Describe how the church is to feel about when, as the bride of Christ, the church is gathered into his eternity for the endless song of the Redeemed. (Calvin Miller)

SEPTEMBER 1, 1996

❦

Fourteenth Sunday After Pentecost

Worship Theme: God often uses the unexpected to accomplish the divine will.

Readings: Exodus 3:1-15; Romans 12:9-21; Matthew 16:21-28

Call to Worship (Psalm 26:1-3):

Leader: Vindicate me, O LORD, for I have walked in my integrity, and I have trusted in the LORD without wavering.

People: Prove me, O LORD, and try me; test my heart and mind.

Leader: For your steadfast love is before my eyes,

People: and I walk in faithfulness to you.

Pastoral Prayer:

Almighty God, you are the same yesterday, today, and forever. We thank you and praise you for keeping your word and for honoring every promise that you make. We bring to you our many hurts, scars, and painful wounds that have been inflicted upon us by the broken and unfulfilled promises of family, friends, and countless others on whom we have depended. Heal our hurt and disappointment. Help us to forgive those who have failed to keep their promises to us, especially those unfulfilled commitments that continue to burden our daily existence. Forgive us for failing to always keep faith with our own promises: for the things we said that we would do, but never did; for the things we promised we would never do, but did anyway; for the things we denied doing, even when the responsibility was completely our own. Let truth, integrity, and peace rule our hearts and our homes, our places of work and worship, and all our relationships. In the name of Jesus, who has never made us a promise he is unable to keep, we pray. Amen. (Gary C. Redding)

SERMON BRIEFS

GOD'S RELUCTANT HERO

EXODUS 3:1-15

The greatest American hero of World War I was a farmer from the Tennessee hills named Alvin York. A God-fearing man, York was drafted into the army and initially requested conscientious objector status. But in the battle of the Argonne (October 8, 1918), Alvin York would win the Medal of Honor for bravery under fire for killing or capturing more than one hundred enemy soldiers. Asked why he had killed when philosophically opposed to it, York replied he acted to save the lives of other soldiers from the murderous machine-gun fire. Alvin York was—in fact—a quite reluctant hero who would later refuse lucrative business deals offered solely because of his war experience.

When Moses is called by God into service against the Egyptians— *drafted* is a better term—he, too, is quite a reluctant hero. Exodus 3 is a series of calls from God followed by Moses' turning God down. There is a quite real and human touch found here, best understood by those who have done something outstanding they were initially quite reluctant to undertake. Each one of us just might be God's reluctant heroine or hero if only we would be more attuned to how God works in calling Moses.

Our text contains several truths about how God may use you and me as his next reluctant heroes.

I. God Calls Us Out of the Midst of Everyday Life

God speaks to Moses—not in some religious setting, but in the midst of everyday work. Moses, tending the flocks, spots the burning bush (v. 2). God turns that grazing spot into "holy ground." While many Christians are waiting for God to speak to them at some religious service or site, in fact, God more likely speaks to us in the midst of our everyday lives. Most folks today simply don't look—or listen—for God in such "ordinary" places.

II. Any Place Can Be Holy Ground

Good Christian people often say they feel closer to God outdoors or at religious sites. Certainly, we may be more open to God's voice in such places. The reality is that God can transform our places of business, our kitchens, our schoolrooms, our assembly lines, and virtually any place where people of faith are to be found into "holy ground." The question is, are we open to allowing such a thing to happen? Or do we prefer to keep the "spiritual" neatly separated from where we spend most of our days?

III. God Provides the Means to Accomplish the Divine Will

As hard as Moses tries to beg off feeling inferior to the task, God promises to supply the means. Moses claims he is really a nobody (v. 11*a*). Moses then tries another way out: "They will not believe that I have spoken to you because I cannot give them your name as proof of this conversation." This is a clever strategy by Moses, since no one in those days spoke aloud the name of God! God proceeds to give Moses the divine name to be spoken: "I AM WHO I AM!" Again, God provides the means to move the people—if only our reluctant "hero" will get going!

Thousands of years later, we can still read this account of Moses' call and see a very real, very human, very reluctant person being called by God to extraordinary service.

How many of us, given similar circumstances, would respond just as Moses does? How many of us, to be honest, are God's reluctant heroines or heroes? (Steven R. Fleming)

ALL WE NEED TO KNOW

ROMANS 12:9-21

In *All I Really Need to Know I Learned in Kindergarten,* Robert Fulghum said the simple rules he learned as a child, if followed by adults, would make a better world. Paul, nineteen hundred years earlier, published a similar essay in Romans 12:9-21. These verses deal with our relationships, with other Christians as individuals, with the body as a whole, or with those who are being hard to love.

I. Our Relationships with Other Christians

Verses 9-10 give us Paul's expression of Jesus' commandment from John 13:34 (see also 1 John 1:23). Paul may have anticipated something I once said, "The Bible says we are to love each other, but it doesn't say we have to like each other." That must have sounded logical at the time, but it cannot be reconciled with, "Let love be genuine" (v. 9). Paul also gives a definition of *agape* love when he says, "Outdo one another in showing honor" (v. 10).

We are also told: "Rejoice with those who rejoice, weep with those who weep" (v. 15). Anyone who has been told, "Cheer up," at the funeral of a loved one knows how needed this encouragement to share appropriate feelings is.

Verse 16 calls us to unity: "Live in harmony with one another." If you and I disagree and we have trouble maintaining unity, a quick trip back to verses 9-10 may help.

II. Our Relationship with the Church

The terms in verses 11-13 describe how we are to function within an organization and how we are to serve. Don't you wish everyone in church did not "lag in zeal," was "ardent in spirit," and served the Lord (v. 11)? There wouldn't be much about which to complain.

Verse 12 describes the attitude with which we worship and serve: "Rejoice in hope, be patient in suffering, persevere in prayer." Acts 6 gives us an example of verse 13: "Contribute to the needs of the saints; extend hospitality." We are all responsible to make others feel welcome within the church, even those Christians who are hard to love.

III. Our Relationships with Those Who Are Being Hard to Love

Paul begins in verse 14 and continues in verses 17-21. Before I could sit down to write this sermon, I had to apologize to someone who had been rather difficult. I know it is easy for us to demand our rights, stand up for what we deserve, and make enemies respect us. But if we are going to live under the canopy of verses 9-10, we won't relate to others in these ways. Verse 14 is the natural partner of verse 9, and verses 17-21 can be seen as commentary on verse 10.

I once learned what the Bible means by the statement, "You will heap coals of fire on their heads" (Prov. 25:22). A deacon verbally attacked me in a meeting, telling the others they needed to fire me. All I said in my defense was, "I am sorry you feel that way." He knew how to fight a fighter; he did not know how to deal with grace. His hot head almost glowed with coals as he turned up the heat. When he did, he became vulgar. His best friend, seeing that attitude, opened the door and told the angry man to leave. The deacons told me they were sorry I had to endure such abuse.

Fulghum noted how nice this world would be if everyone, governments included, lived by rules we learned in kindergarten: share, don't hit; clean up your own mess. How good would our churches be if we could follow these practical verses. (Bill Groover)

BREAKING THE WILL:
NOT PRETTY, BUT BEAUTIFUL

MATTHEW 16:21-28

The wild horse enters the riding ring. With nostrils flared and back arched, the unbridled animal resists any form of limits. The rider knows, however, that the wild animal must be tamed. Hours pass while rider and animal fight for control. The horse rebels against the weight of saddle and bridle; the rider pulls the reins even more tightly. A battle for control rages in this scene of dust and sweat. Eventually, the rider wins. The dust settles and the noise softens. The wild horse, now tamed, and the rider, although tired, begin to work in parallel motion. The horse instinctively knows the direction of the rider, and the rider understands the mood of the horse. And they travel throughout the countryside in beautiful parallel motion, all the while forgetting the pain and agony of long training sessions.

For the modern mind—especially freedom-loving children of the sixties—this notion of breaking wills and constraining powers goes against the grain. It simply is not pretty. It is antithetical to our understanding that life should have no constraints, that life should be lived the way we understand it to be: free, happy, prosperous, without conflict.

I. Sometimes Beauty Is Hidden in the Ugly

Our Gospel lesson, likewise, is not a very pretty picture. Who wants to see Peter, the pillar of the church, rebuked in public? Who wants to hear Jesus tell about his coming suffering and death? Who wants to really realize that preconceived notions of the Kingdom could be far, far from the truth? It happens here in these verses.

Jesus has to tell the disciples three times that he will die (16:21; 17:22-23; 20:17-19). And three times no one believes him. It is not a pretty picture. Listen to Jesus' prediction as if you were one of the disciples. Your leader is saying that the end is near, that he is going to Jerusalem and will suffer because of the religious establishment (your own religious tradition), then be killed, and then raised on the third day.

Like Peter, we would probably respond, "That won't happen to you, no way!" We would probably say, "That wasn't in the plan. I don't recall reading that chapter in the manual. We only talked about what positions of authority we would have in the new kingdom, and now you are going to die on us. That is not the way we planned it, Jesus. Something is wrong here."

Jesus rebukes Peter for his inability to see the beauty hidden in the ugly. Peter's view of the future had been shaped by visions that belonged to this world—hope in the security of a Jewish political system untainted by Roman oppression, of an individual position of authority and control over others. To Peter, that was the beautiful picture of hope for tomorrow—certainly not images of suffering, blood, passive acquiescence to the opposition. That picture was beyond his dreaming, and he refused to even consider it.

II. Sometimes Life Is Found in Death

Jesus' lesson in verses 24-28 describes what beauty looks like in intimate detail. The words still sound strange to us, just as they must have to Peter. I mean, how can anyone lose life to find it? The reality of the paradox of faith is just as far-fetched as Jesus' death predictions were to the disciples.

It is in the giving that we live; it is in the suffering that we find life; it is in the breaking that we can be whole. No, it still isn't very pretty. Recall the garden in your backyard filled with weeds from weeks of neglect. Who wants to use the energy needed to tame the garden? The sweat, the hours of backbreaking labor, the dirt in your nails and your hair, the sacrifice of time—all of that is not very pretty. But wait; in a few days, when you have your morning coffee outside and watch the hummingbirds nestle in those fragrant blooms, you then realize that you have touched beauty.

Or see this picture. The Olympic athlete trains constantly. The hours on the track, running in the rain and snow, the sacrifice of time with family and friends—they are not very pretty pictures. But on that day when the mind and the body are working together and concentration is right where it should be and you make the run—exceeding all other times—and you win, then it is beautiful!

III. Sometimes Victory Is Hidden in Defeat

The Christian faith is not pretty, but it is beautiful. To follow Christ means that we will experience pain, at times even defeat. It means that we often will not look successful by contemporary standards. But the life of faith as described by Jesus in this passage offers a view of life that eyes have not seen nor have ears yet heard. And that is beautiful. (Linda McKinnish Bridges)

SEPTEMBER 8, 1996

❧

Fifteenth Sunday After Pentecost

Worship Theme: Christian discipleship involves reordering our priorities.

Readings: Exodus 12:1-14; Romans 13:8-14; Matthew 18:15-20

Call to Worship (Psalm 149:1-2):

Praise to the LORD!
Sing to the LORD a new song,
    his praise in the assembly of the faithful.
Let Israel be glad in its Maker;
    let the children of Zion rejoice in their King.

Pastoral Prayer:

Lord, we are so often consumed with acquiring the things of this world. Yet no matter how much we accumulate, it never seems to be enough—it always seems that we need just a little more to make us fully happy. We are slaves to our desires, bondslaves to our appetites. Help us to understand that happiness comes not from new possessions but from a new heart. Help us to recognize that so long as we remain slaves to things, we can never be fully alive to Christ. Create in us a new heart, O God, that we might understand more completely all that you can place in our hands when we release our grasp on the temporary treasures surrounding us. Amen.

SERMON BRIEFS

A MEAL TO REMEMBER

EXODUS 12:1-14

It is customary for a people being delivered to celebrate their freedom. The quirky nature of the Exodus story is that it is surrounded by two such celebrative meals: this one, the fast-food version of Passover, eaten hurriedly, was the forerunner of a more elaborate Passover ritual still celebrated today.

This first meal was to be eaten on the night of the last plague (that of the death of the firstborn). While eating the meal, the men were to hold their walking sticks in hand, and everyone at the table was to have shoes on, as though in preparation to leave. The bread that accompanied the meal was to be unleavened, emphasizing the urgency of what was about to happen. This first ritual meal was to celebrate the Lord's Passover.

As directed, the ritual meal was perpetuated, and the story of deliverance was woven into the fabric of this celebration. The Passover following the deliverance of Israel from the house of bondage is more elaborate. There is less urgency—the family members recline on cushions instead of sitting as if to make a run for it. Perhaps we recall times when table fellowship in our own families was important.

Do you recall the movie *Babette's Feast*? It is a beautiful film in which a poor French cook finds herself on a desolate peninsula. The townsfolk have been greatly influenced by their minister, who died some years before the arrival of Babette.

Babette has been buying lottery tickets with the little money she makes, and eventually, word gets back to her that she has won the lottery, some ten thousand francs! The anniversary of the minister's death is about to be celebrated, and his daughters plan the celebration, which would have been a drab affair. However, Babette steps in and asks if she can fix the food for the feast. Until then, she was forced to make the minister's prescribed menu for the community: hard, crusty brown bread and fish soup. Now, Babette is going to fix a culinary masterpiece. She sends off for ingredients: turtles, all manner of edible fowl, vegetables, and specialty items that the villagers have long ago forgotten or have never seen.

Babette goes to work, and many of the townsfolk think she must be some sort of witch, with all the pots and kettles going. They decide that they will not enjoy the food of the feast. But Babette's cooking transforms the villagers. Never before have they tasted anything like what they eat. Their entire lives are changed by the meal. They will remember it for the rest of their lives!

Imagine what Passover must have been like when Jesus took the bread and cup of this ritual feast and changed their meaning for all who follow him. The unleavened bread that reminded them of the manna in the wilderness was not the true food of eternal life. *Take. Eat. This is my body, which is for you. Do this in remembrance of me.*

Imagine the wondering eyes of the disciples as Jesus might well have taken up the cup of wine reserved for the prophet Elijah during the Passover celebration, changing its meaning as well: *Take. Drink. This cup is the new covenant in my blood, which is shed for you and others for the forgiveness of sins. Do this, as often as you drink it, in remembrance of me.*

Why is this meal different from all the others? Perhaps it is because in it we remember how Jesus really has passed over from death to life and how he has given us this life, too. (Eric Killinger)

WHO OWNS YOU?

ROMANS 13:8-14

Few among us have not experienced indebtedness. Even if all of our bills are paid, we owe a debt of gratitude to persons who have given freely of themselves to help us along the journey.

Another kind of debt is more familiar, and more burdensome, in our economic society: financial indebtedness. Financially, most of us owe something to someone, from the mortgage on our homes to the financing of our automobiles.

Today's text is a wake-up call regarding the burdens of life, financial and otherwise. It should sound an alarm within us regarding the debts and burdens that we allow to come between us and God.

I. The Sin Is Not the Debt

Owing on a mortgage or a car or a college loan is not, of itself, sinful. Sinfulness lies in our attitude and behavior. When we think and act like something (or someone) is more important than God, we have given ourselves over to idolatry. It is not a sin to be in debt, but it is a sin to be bound by something other than God.

When I was a young pastor, I decided I needed a new car. There was nothing wrong with the one I had; I was simply tired of it. I spent countless hours reading about, looking at, and test-driving new vehicles. Having a new car became so important to me that I lost my perspective. I did not need the car; I coveted having the car. When I finally selected, secured a loan for, and purchased the car I desired, I felt guilty for owning it. The car became a symbol of my avarice and selfishness.

II. We Are Free to Love When We Are Not Bound by Things

The Christian life is lived with the mind of Christ. Christians put mission before money, people before possessions, Christ before credit cards. When the apostle Paul says in verse 8, "Owe no one anything, except to love one another," he is calling us all to a higher order of living.

The command to "love your neighbor as yourself" (v. 9) is about a life of grace that values all human life as sacred. It is impossible to treat as objects those whom we see as persons of sacred worth. The homeless persons we pass on the streets, the impoverished children through whose neighborhood we drive, the victims of war whose faces we see on the news, are brothers and sisters to whom we owe our love and service. When we view life with the mind of Christ, consumers become stewards, possessions become opportunities, money becomes an instrument of service, and people become our priority.

III. To What Are We Truly Committed?

What owns our allegiance? What takes most of our time and energy? We may spend more than forty hours per week earning a living, but what is our true motivation? Is lifestyle, income, personal accomplishment, family, or God our driving force?

A church board was discussing the proposed budget for the ensuing year. The finance committee had recommended a 10 percent increase. The discussion was building into a crescendo of voices calling for cutbacks and budget reductions.

"We cannot afford this!" one board member exclaimed. "This is asking too much of our members," another cajoled.

One of the older saints of the church asked to speak. He slowly rose to his feet, and in a calm and quiet voice he said, "This church can afford what it chooses to afford. I drive through the neighborhoods where our members live and see new cars in the driveway and boats in the yard. I hear of European vacations and ocean cruises. It is not a matter of having enough; it is a matter of being a good steward with what we have."

For Christians, the love of Christ has called us to a life of grace. We respond to that call by reordering our lives. Our priorities change. Through prayer and self-discipline, we strive to move from our human desire to God's desire. We begin this process when we ask ourselves the vital question, "What owns you?" (Gary G. Kindley)

THE REMARKABLE IMPORTANCE
OF RELATIONSHIPS

MATTHEW 18:15-20

Relationships are important. Oh, we may minimize them and say, "It really doesn't matter how I relate to the person sitting next to me in the church pew or the one sitting at the desk next to mine at work." All that matters, we think, is that we do the job well, get home, feed the kids supper, help with homework, and then go to bed to start the day all over again tomorrow.

Low on the list of priorities is the bitter relationship that seems to never get mended at the office. Who has time to ponder the harsh words that were said between you and a fellow church member that resulted in a cold, awkward silence between you both? We have too much to do to stop and consider relationships—or do we?

I. Relationships Matter to Us

Relationships are so important to Matthew, the evangelist, and to the congregation centered in Matthew's Gospel that detailed instructions are given in the event a relationship turns sour. If someone sins against you or treats you unjustly, you are instructed to go and confront the person. If there can be a hearing, then you have gained a true friendship. If, however, the brother or sister who has offended you will not listen to you, then go again, taking one or two others as witnesses. And if the offender refuses to listen to them, then tell it to the church. And if the offender refuses to listen to the church, then let it rest. Let the offender be to you as "a Gentile or a tax collector" (two groups of people a good Jew would try to avoid).

II. Relationships Matter to God

What work! What energy! Why not just consider those who have wronged you as Gentiles and tax collectors from the beginning and bypass all of this running around? Why go to all this effort? Because Jesus says that relationships are very important—that how we live together in this life has eternal consequences. Now, that puts a new dimension on the office squabble or the recent church disagreement, doesn't it?

According to the teachings of Christ, we cannot leave them alone. The principles are clear: confront the person, over and over again until the air is clear, wounds are healed, and the relationship has opportunity to build again.

III. Relationships Matter Ultimately

And the mystery of all of this is that "whatever you bind on earth will be bound in heaven, and whatever you loose on earth will be loosed in heaven" (v. 18). I must confess that I do not know exactly what this verse means. Does it mean that the friend you have on earth will be the one you have in heaven, and likewise the earthly enemy will be your heavenly one? I don't think so.

Looking at the passage in context gives us interpretive help. In verses 23-35 of chapter 18, the parable of the unforgiving servant is told to give us a vivid illustration of binding and loosing. Forgiveness releases and results in freedom. Unforgiveness binds and results in prison.

Could it be that forgiving relationships have so much redemptive value that one's eternal destiny could be changed? Could the attention given to mending broken relationships actually result in someone, either an observer or the offender, being introduced to Kingdom life? Could the releasing of human hurt and pain incurred in earthly relationships actually prepare one to receive the heavenly forgiveness and redemption of God? I think so.

If so, then the opposite is also true. Lack of attention to those relationships can cause binding—a kind of imprisonment to self, to others, and to God. Little things have eternal consequences. Life is not really made by giving all our attention to the so-called big things, like job promotions, salary increases, and new houses. The good life, the life that matters, pays attention to the so-called little things—our relations with one another. For it is there that we can see the power of God and find redemption. (Linda McKinnish Bridges)

301

SEPTEMBER 15, 1996

❧

Sixteenth Sunday After Pentecost

Worship Theme: We are to forgive others even as God has forgiven us.

Readings: Exodus 14:19-31; Romans 14:1-12; Matthew 18:21-35

Call to Worship (Psalm 114)

Leader: When Israel went out from Egypt, the house of Jacob from a people of strange language,

People: Judah became God's sanctuary, Israel his dominion.

Leader: The sea looked and fled; Jordan turned back.

People: The mountains skipped like rams, the hills like lambs.

Leader: Why is it, O sea, that you flee? O Jordan, that you turn back?

People: O mountains, that you skip like rams? O hills, like lambs?

Leader: Tremble, O earth, at the presence of the LORD, at the presence of the God of Jacob,

People: who turns the rock into a pool of water, the flint into a spring of water.

Pastoral Prayer:

O Lord, you reach out to us in love, even when we are unlovely; you stretch out your hand to us, even when we stubbornly ignore you; you extend to us your marvelous grace, even when we remain obstinate and undeserving. Forgive us our foolish pride that rejoices in your forgiveness of our sin while refusing to forgive our brothers' and sisters' offenses against us. Help us to discover afresh the joy that comes from experiencing your forgiveness of our sin and the joy that comes from allowing ourselves to forgive others even as you have forgiven us. Amen.

SERMON BRIEFS

RIGHT OF PASSAGE

EXODUS 14:19-31

It's hard to forget the cartoons of *Mad* magazine that depicted Moses as a kid. There was one of Moses in the bathtub. The water formed walls on either side, and his little rubber duck sat on the dry patch in the middle of the tub. Out in the hall, his mother exclaimed that she couldn't understand why Moses never got clean. Another cartoon depicted Moses parting the broth of his chicken soup so he could eat the noodles first. Again, his mother chastised him, that time for playing with his food. In their way, the cartoons portrayed rites of passage in Moses' life. He was running what the later biblical writers would call a race, being chosen by God to share in an extraordinary life with God. And all of Israel was picked to share in this venture, the rite of passage.

I toyed with the idea of adding a subtitle to this sermon brief so it read, "Right of Passage: God Willing and the Creek Don't Rise," because several things were going on in the trip through the sea. It was by *right* that Israel was able to pass through on dry ground. God had chosen Israel to be his people. Nothing was able to get in the way of this choosing—not Pharaoh, not an assault on the rear flank, not even a natural obstacle.

This is not to say that a passage with God is a piece of cake. On the contrary, the Israelites had to prove themselves worthy of relationship with God as they would soon discover in the wilderness. Besides, this walk through the sea marked a transitional period in their lives, not always a simple and painless process. The Israelite army was caught in what Victor Turner would call a liminal state: a situation in which one stands between what is dead or no longer of any value and what is not yet born (or unknown). This is a fearful place to be.

Yet it was the will of God that the Israelites should be spared and given the chance to prove themselves true to relationship. God had heard their cries and sent Moses to bring them to the holy mountain. It was a great (and gracious!) work. The people were in awe of God's grace and believed in the Lord and his servant Moses. So grateful were they that Moses led them in singing a song to the Lord (Exod. 15:1).

The *right* of passage became a *rite* of passage, a celebration that accompanies a change in the life of an individual, a community or, as in the case of Israel, a nation. I read somewhere recently that when the great explorers began navigating their way through the great seas of our world, their mapmakers invariably drew dragons and other great seabeasts in the areas where ships failed to venture.

Some seafarers thought the strange creatures actually lurked in the deep to devour unsuspecting sailors if they entered the waters. Others, who refused to be put off, made history with their tremendous discoveries of new worlds. They, too, were caught between old ideas of no value and the unknown, which had yet to be born in their lives. Their *rights* of passage became *rites* of passage. Their rites have become ours, as well. We celebrate with Israel and with Columbus and Magellan; we rejoice at the accomplishments of Jonas Salk and Helen Keller and Albert Einstein—in fact, all explorers who stand at the threshold of new experiences of the grace of God, who gives us life in the unknown. (Eric Killinger)

JUDGED AND FOUND WANTING

ROMANS 14:1-12

The idea of judging another individual has such a heavy and powerful connotation to it. One of the most liberating things about the gospel is that it is based on grace and mercy, not judgment and condemnation. This is important to remember, despite the emphasis some preachers (and church members) place on the latter while ignoring the former.

Certainly, we must make prudent choices and decisions in life. We need good judgment in how we conduct our spiritual, personal, and business affairs. This is not the same as judging other human beings by viewing them with condemnation or rejection. Christ's love compels us to love others, even those who hold us in contempt.

I. When We Judge Others, We Limit God

Scripture clearly tells us that God is at work in our lives (Rom. 8:28; Phil. 2:13). God's Spirit and re-creating power are alive and at work in human life, redeeming, reconciling, and making new. We do not give God room to be at work in life when we judge others. Human beings were not meant to be categorized, boxed, or limited in any way since change is a constant of life.

Imposing our prejudice, or our own personal standards on others, is sinful and therefore impairs our relationship with them and with God. If each has sinned and fallen short of God's glory, then only human conceit would measure others' lives by our own standard.

II. Judgment Limits Our Ability to Love

Discipleship, following Christ's life and teachings, involves teaching others by example. Judgmental attitudes and a condemning spirit limit our ability to love our neighbors as ourselves. We limit our ability to teach others by closing ourselves to God's Spirit, which is at work in and through us.

A churchman was vehemently outspoken against persons who had contracted AIDS. His words taught hatred, revulsion, and prejudice. That changed when his adult son came home to die from AIDS. God's Spirit was at work in the heart of that father. His contempt turned to compassion. His words of rejection became words of reconciliation, calling other men and women in his church to see beyond illness and lifestyle to the humanity of the persons with the disease.

Paul says it eloquently, "We do not live to ourselves, and we do not die to ourselves . . . Whether we live or whether we die, we are the Lord's" (vv. 7-8b). Just as God has welcomed and claimed us, God welcomes and claims those whose opinions, appearance, and life-styles may be very different from our own. God's ways are not our ways, and God's love, grace, and mercy are beyond what we deserve. We need to remember that when we tend to judge and condemn others.

III. Surrendering to Christ Is a Sign of Christian Maturity

Christ is in control. We need not feel that we must control all of life. We cannot do it. Life's diversity, serendipity, and spontaneity are beyond our capacity to control. When we yield our desire to be in control to Christ, we experience a freedom that unfetters us from the chains of human sinfulness.

Paul reminds the church at Rome, and those of us who read their mail, that "each of us will be accountable to God" (v. 12). God demands our obedience and worship in response to God's marvelous grace. We dare not strive for anything less, or the day might come when we may be the ones judged and found wanting. (Gary G. Kindley)

THE FORGIVENESS PRINCIPLE

MATTHEW 18:21-35

"Seventy times seven" is a lot of forgiveness. Once is tough enough. Twice, almost unreasonable. Remember the adage: "Hurt me once, shame on you. Hurt me twice, shame on me." "Seventy times seven?" Mother Teresa would have trouble with that!

Yet that is precisely what Jesus advised in his dialogue with Simon Peter. Keep on forgiving, he counseled, even when forgiveness seems illogical. For often forgiveness is more of a gift we give ourselves than a favor we bestow on others.

I. Unforgiveness Carries a Heavy Cost

Jesus illustrated that principle with the story of a servant who owed the king a bundle. "Ten thousand talents," to be exact—several years wages. No way possible he could ever pay up! But his pleading for mercy touched a tender chord in the beneficent king, and the servant was forgiven. His account was marked "paid in full."

However, the servant soon met another man who owed him a mere handful of denarii—several days wages. The debtor pleaded for mercy but received a sentence to debtors' prison instead. The king, upon hearing of the first servant's refusal to forgive, rescinded his former offer, and the servant wound up on the locked side of a prison cell "until he would pay his entire debt" (v. 34). His refusal to forgive was his undoing.

So it usually goes. The most seriously depressed person I ever met was like that. He was trapped by grief over the loss of an older brother. The brother had swindled him in a land deal nineteen years earlier. Apologies and offers of restoration had been rejected, and at last the older brother died. After the funeral, reality set in on the remaining brother—reality that he had forsaken family in order to nurture a grudge. He had been inflexible too long, and it was too late. His depression resulted from his refusal to forgive.

Current medical research indicates that persons who are unforgiving are *more* susceptible to a variety of illnesses than are their more tolerant counterparts. *The New England Journal of Medicine* reports that type A personalities (long thought to be particularly prone to cardiovascular illness) are no more likely than anyone else to suffer heart attack or stroke. The culprit, researchers say now, is anger. Type A persons are in danger only if they carry around unresolved hostility. It is anger, not activity, that places a person at risk.

Forgive seventy times seven? Jesus knew it was for our own good. People who refuse to forgive rarely do significant damage to the other person but can seriously jeopardize their own well-being.

II. Our Forgiveness Is Linked to God's Forgiveness

There is, of course, a keenly spiritual dimension to the forgiveness principle. It is an awareness of God's love for all. A woman who disliked a singularly obnoxious neighbor was put in a bad mood every morning when, while standing at her sink fixing breakfast, she would see him driving off to work. Finally, one morning she watched him drive away, and as the familiar feelings of resentment began to rise, she whispered, "He is a person for whom Christ died." That morsel of theological insight was the antidote to her resentment. If Jesus loves others enough to die for them, perhaps our refusal to forgive them is spiritually inappropriate.

A final thought: God's willingness to forgive us is somehow linked to our willingness to forgive others. So said Jesus, "Forgive us our trespasses as we forgive . . ." That alone is all I need to know to "forgive not seven times, but seventy times seven." As Wilford Brimley says, "It's the right thing to do." (Michael B. Brown)

SEPTEMBER 22, 1996

❧

Seventeenth Sunday After Pentecost

Worship Theme: God can bring blessing to us even in the midst of suffering.

Readings: Exodus 16:2-15; Philippians 1:21-30; Matthew 20:1-16

Call to Worship (Psalm 105:1-3):

Leader: O give thanks to the LORD, call on his name,

People: make known his deeds among the peoples.

Leader: Sing to him, sing praises to him;

People: tell of all his wonderful works.

Leader: Glory in his holy name;

People: let the hearts of those who seek the LORD rejoice.

Pastoral Prayer:

Father of our Lord Jesus Christ, we come before you as people who know pain and struggle. You know our hurts—families in conflict, jobs and careers that sometimes seem to be going in the wrong direction, relationships with jagged edges. Some in this place come before you knowing physical pain or the threat of disease. Yet in the midst of our pain, we are reminded that you also know pain, for in Christ you accept abuse and suffering so that we might have life, abundant and eternal. For us, suffering is part of the human condition—the inevitable consequence of sin's corruption of your good creation. Yet you willingly took upon yourself our pain, the tragic consequence of our sin, and in the very process you transformed, a gruesome instrument of execution into a symbol of grace. Transform us, as well, into instruments of your peace. Amen.

SERMON BRIEFS

DON'T PASS OVER THE WILDERNESS

EXODUS 16:2-15

From the outset, I think we should take note that nearly all wilderness journeys are experiences of purification. We might not know it at the time, but such journeys prepare us for something special in life.

At the beginning of their wanderings, God could have directed Moses to lead the Israelites by the shortest and easiest route. Instead, they are taken the long way about because God doesn't want the people to turn to him too quickly. God reasons that should the people turn too soon, they will want to go back to Egypt and not be the people of God . . . a jealous God indeed.

We probably are familiar with all the complaining along the way. The Israelites were, more often than not, unhappy. After all, they lived up to their name: *Israel* meant "the one who contends or wrestles with God." I can hear them now, can't you? "Oh, my feet are killing me! These confounded sandals are rubbing blisters on my toes."

If my brother had been there when he was four or five years old, he would have asked, "Are we there almost-just-about?" at least a gajillion times.

"I'm hungry. Moses, Moses! What have you done? Did you bring us out here into this wilderness to starve to death?" Imagine if adman Sam Sedelmeyer had been making a movie of their wilderness trials instead of C. B. DeMille. Some elderly woman really might have yelled from deep within the throng, "Hey! Where's the beef?"

The crucial thing for us to see in their experiences of the wilderness years is that God wanted to purify them, get them ready to enter the Promised Land. There was something very special about it, for which their hearts and minds and souls (and perhaps even their imaginations) had to be prepared.

The same goes for Jesus, in that he was driven into the wilderness by the compelling guidance of the Holy Spirit to prepare himself for his ministry. As the humble, obedient servant of God, he went willingly. You see, in all the years between the Exodus and Jesus, there was a shift in people's thinking about the wilderness. In the later development of this stubborn and stiff-necked people whom

God more than once thought about writing off, Israel came to see that the wilderness was *the* place to go if anyone wished to discover the way of God.

The wilderness was a natural place for Jesus to go from his baptism. For him, it was just going with the flow, matching his actions to the rhythm of God and the wilderness. Jesus didn't mind being there because he put himself into the heart of God's will. The Israelites celebrated their deliverance from the wilderness with the Passover meal *before* they packed their bags to leave! They celebrated. Maybe that was why Jesus didn't seem concerned about being in the desert.

What about us? I hope we see the wilderness is not such a bad place to find God. There are scores of stories of men and women who have gone to the desert to find God. A ninety-year-old minister friend lives in the California desert. He once wrote a book about his experiences, why he likes living there and why, for him, he can always find God where he is. The wilderness isn't such a bad thing. It's a place where we can get down to the bare bones of being with God, experiencing God's love and care, God's reaching out to us and holding us close to the holy and wonderful. (Eric Killinger)

THE PRIVILEGE OF SUFFERING

PHILIPPIANS 1:21-30

One verse that leaps out at you when you read today's text is verse 29: "For [God] has graciously granted you the privilege not only of believing in Christ, but of suffering for him as well." Most of us would not consider suffering a "privilege."

The apostle Paul is lauding the Philippian church for their faith and perseverance even in the face of hardship and struggle. There is also a call here to readers outside the Philippian community, such as you and me. Paul is not calling us to be martyrs, but he does bring to our attention the dimension of suffering as a part of Christian discipleship.

I. Suffering Can Bring Us Closer to Christ

There are many forms of suffering. Typically, we think of physical suffering such as pain and chronic illness. We can also suffer emotionally and spiritually from broken relationships, divorce, and conflict with others. When we do experience suffering, the Christian response is to turn to God for hope and strength.

In doing so, we discover that God is not an abstract philosophy but a gracious, loving God who took on human form to reveal God's ways to humanity. God's grace is such that, crucified and in agony upon a cross, the Christ calls out, "Father, forgive them; for they do not know what they are doing" (Luke 23:34).

In Christ, we find our example of a life of perseverance and a life wholly yielded to God's desires. We can choose to use our suffering as an opportunity to explore Jesus' life, grow closer in our relationship with him, and emulate Christ's life through discipleship. In some way, we participate in Christ's suffering. Out of our own agony, we deepen our compassion for Christ's agony.

We are reminded of the words from 2 Timothy 2:3: "Share in suffering like a good soldier of Christ Jesus."

II. Suffering Can Be Redemptive

If the heart of the gospel is relationships (with God, Jesus, and others) and suffering can bring us closer in our relationship with Christ, then suffering is closely tied to redemption.

Lest this be misunderstood, it is *not* that God causes us to suffer for our redemption. This idea is incompatible with the God of grace whom Christ reveals. Rather, God's marvelous ways are such that God can be at work for good, even in the midst of suffering. God can bring hope out of tragedy, trust out of betrayal, strength out of weakness, and encouragement out of anguish. Such is the wondrous nature of this redemptive God we worship.

III. Suffering Can Put Life in Perspective

It is easy to allow life's daily busyness to preoccupy our thoughts so that we fail to see the bigger picture, the larger scheme of things. God has acted to redeem the whole world through Christ, but often we do not live or act like that is so.

When we personally experience suffering, our experience can remind us of what is truly important in life. The scripture tells us: "Trust in the LORD with all your heart, / and do not rely on your own insight" (Prov. 3:5).

God's ways are not our ways. The suffering that we experience along life's journey does not always resolve itself as we would like. Even so, God's ability to provide for our needs in the face of suffering is wondrous. God offers us the promise of the divine presence through the power of the Holy Spirit. We are not alone.

Rev. W. James White, in a sermon called "Life's Turning Points," puts it this way: "Crises like these become turning points leading us to new places—places into which we would never have gone, to people we would never had met, to strength we never knew was possible, to happiness we might never have found." (Gary G. Kindley)

WHO CARES ABOUT BEING FAIR?

MATTHEW 20:1-16

Thirty years . . . but I still remember quitting jayvee basketball. I had slaved four years hoping for a starting spot. It was my turn. I had earned it. Then came a walk-on, fresh from varsity football season. He wasn't a basketball junkie. He hadn't suffered through preseason conditioning drills and scrimmages. He just waltzed into practice midseason and suddenly was given a jersey and a place in the starting five. I was asked to come off the bench and give him a bit of rest from time to time.

It just didn't seem fair. So I quit. I regretted it later, but I'm not going to be anybody's doormat. Was the other fellow a better player than I? Was it the coach's right to play whoever he chose? Hey, don't bother me with facts! Fair is fair.

In the corporate world, the world of politics, and even the church, "fair" is not always the definitive policy. Sometimes seniority doesn't count for much. Nepotism counts. Or talent. Once in a while the boss is even motivated by grace.

The early birds in Christ's parable thought the pay scale was unfair. They worked from sunup but were paid no more than the lazy scoundrels who showed up an hour before quitting time. So they took their case to the labor relations board, which immediately filed a class action complaint against the corporate CEO. His response was honest and logical: "Friend, I am doing you no wrong; did you not agree with me for the usual daily wage?" (v. 13). In other words,

"Your contract has not been violated. I paid exactly what you asked for."

"But what of those other guys," they countered, "who worked only one hour? They're getting as much as we are. It's not fair!" The vineyard owner answered, "I choose to give to this last as I give to you" (v. 14). In other words, "It's my money. I can do with it as I like."

Admittedly, that attitude may not be palatable to labor unions, but I like the feel of it theologically. You see, I don't want what I deserve. I'm not like those workers who began at dawn. I've not kept all the laws and observed all the ordinances. Have you? Before you say, "Yes," remember that there are over six hundred laws in the Old Testament. I find it tough just managing the Ten Commandments. Six hundred are absolutely overwhelming.

I have coveted. Maybe you've never looked at someone else's sports car or summer home and thought, *I wish it were mine.* Most of us have. I have borne false witness. Even little white lies count, you know. "Son, grab the phone, and tell them I'm not home." "Why, you haven't aged at all." My parents would have contended that I did not always honor them properly. Adultery and murder? No. "Thou shalt not steal?" Well, I have borrowed a few sermon ideas and illustrations without asking permission first.

The point is, in one way or another most of us show up about quitting time. Very few are sinless Law abiders. Very few are spiritually spotless. Thus, I don't want justice. I want mercy. I don't want fairness. I want grace. I don't want to play by the books. I want an Employer with a soft heart who doles out wages even to those of us who showed up around sundown.

And that's what this parable promises: a God who gives us not what we deserve but what we need. And that is the meaning of good news!
(Michael B. Brown)

SEPTEMBER 29, 1996

ಶಿ

Eighteenth Sunday After Pentecost

Worship Theme: It is not religious activity but faith that leads to new life in God's kingdom.

Readings: Exodus 17:1-7; Philippians 2:1-13; Matthew 21:23-32

Call to Worship (Psalm 78:1-4, 12-16):

Leader: Give ear, O my people, to my teaching; incline your ears to the words of my mouth.

People: I will open my mouth in a parable; I will utter dark sayings from of old,

Leader: things that we have heard and known, that our ancestors have told us.

People: We will not hide them from their children; we will tell to the coming generation the glorious deeds of the LORD, and his might, and the wonders that he has done.

Leader: In the sight of their ancestors he worked marvels in the land of Egypt, in the fields of Zoan.

People: He divided the sea and let them pass through it, and made the waters stand like a heap.

Leader: In the daytime he led them with a cloud, and all night long with a fiery light. He split rocks open in the wilderness, and gave them drink abundantly as from the deep.

People: He made streams come out of the rock, and caused waters to flow down like rivers.

Pastoral Prayer:

Lord, we sometimes feel like the Pharisees, who lined the road to destruction with their boasts of religious prowess. They seemed so sure of themselves and their rules, Lord; they were so positive that heaven was reserved for folks like themselves—for fellow travelers who looked like them, talked like them, acted like them. What a stunning announcement it must have been to them to hear Jesus say that all their religious activity didn't give them a head start on paradise. And how much more remarkable it must have been, Lord, when they learned that you might welcome some of those public sinners into your kingdom.

Don't let us be guilty of the same self-righteous blindness, Lord. Don't let us become so consumed with good things that we forget the most important thing: loving and serving you. And help us remember that you love those public sinners every bit as much as you love those of us with more private sins. As Jesus reached out to them, so help us to extend hands of grace as well. For we ask it in the name of the One who offered grace to all. Amen.

SERMON BRIEFS

OUT OF WATER

EXODUS 17:1-7

The wandering about in the wilderness did not suit the Israelites. At times, the whole deliverance project seemed aimless. And the people would grow unhappy and say so. I think it was educator Roy Blitzer who once observed, "The only person who likes change is a wet baby."

The people certainly did not take into account that change was inevitable; most people resist change. The Israelites had had quite enough of hardship and loss of dignity, and they would complain bitterly to Moses. Moses, in turn, would complain to God. Some-times, the people would complain to God, and God would complain to Moses! I wouldn't have blamed God in the least if more than once he pulled out some angel hair and thought, *Why in heaven's name did I even think to bring these people out of Egypt?*

There seems an almost endless ritual of complaint and gift giving. The manna got dull and boring after years of eating nothing but that. Hear the complaint? "This manna stuff is awful! We should have stayed behind. If we hadn't followed Moses, we could be sitting at home to a nice bowl of leek and onion soup. Instead, we get these health food pancakes. Now the water supply is dwindling. Hey! Moses! Why have you brought us way out into the desert from Egypt? Did you do it in order to kill us and our children and cattle with thirst?" They were, to use a phrase I heard some time ago, dying of thirst at the edge of the river, experiencing more spiritual dryness than physical.

After all, they were being led by God. Had God not provided them with food? Had God not given them protection from their enemies? God knew their needs and would have provided if asked prayerfully. The Lord had done so before and would do as much again, but the people were too stiff-necked, too stubborn to see it. So they complained, and God gave in to their groaning because of the promise made with Abraham.

To whom do we turn when we feel spiritually dry? "Everyone who thirsts, come to the waters. Come to me and drink, and be thirsty no more," Jesus calls out to us. It's a wonderful thing, this fountain of living water, because when we drink deep from it, living water wells up within us and we can share it with those who thirst for life in Christ. There is no need for us to complain once we have tasted this water, for our spiritual wells cannot run dry.

The good news is that we are sustained. We are nurtured *despite* our complaining and fretting and worrying. All we have to do is trust in the Lord who provides. (Eric Killinger)

WHEN THE CHEERING STOPS

PHILIPPIANS 2:1-13

Have you heard the expression "home team advantage"? Ask professional sports players whether or not the cheers and affirmation of fans, friends, and family make a difference. They will tell you about the home team advantage. The annals of sports have plenty of examples of winning teams who lost, partly because they were not playing in home territory.

What does that have to say to us about Christians living in a less-than-affirming environment? How is our faith, our commitment to God, affected by whether or not we are affirmed in our discipleship?

I. Commitment to God Must Come from Within

Paul uplifts Christ's encouragement and God's love as reasons to be faithful (vv. 1-5). Luke's Gospel tells us that there were throngs who lined the road to Jerusalem when Jesus rode in as the Messiah (Luke 19:36-38). Where were those crowds on the Friday of the Crucifixion, and what were they shouting then? Jesus' commitment to God was not determined by the whim of the crowd. Jesus' commitment came from *within*.

Consider these voices:

"I can be a disciple as long as it is comfortable."

"I can be a disciple under somewhat demanding conditions as long as I am rewarded."

"It is difficult to follow Christ when people think you are different or weird."

What voices do we hear today? How can we make room to hear God's voice, and what influence do we allow God to have in our lives?

II. Commitment to God Demands Complete Obedience

Paul quotes a hymn about Christ in verse 8 and reminds us, he "became obedient to the point of death—even death on a cross." How obedient are we? What limitations do we set on our discipleship?

One good test of integrity in belief and actions is consistency. How consistent are we as followers of Christ? Consider these personalities and test their consistency:

The Go Along: the one who cheers when the crowd cheers and hurls insults when the crowd turns.

The Judge: the critic and cynic who focuses on failure and on whatever is negative in any given situation.

The Discounter: the apathetic and undependable churchgoer who thinks, *My participation doesn't matter.*

The Controller: the individual who takes vocal positions on issues, often for personal gain and self-esteem rather than in service to Christ.

III. We Must "Work Out Our Own Salvation with Fear and Trembling"

This passage challenges us to be in touch with the power that God has placed within us: "For it is God who is at work in you, enabling you both to will and to work for his good pleasure" (v. 13).

It matters what we do and say. We make a difference in this world. The difference that we make can be enormous when we allow the power of God to work through us.

While sitting in a hospital waiting room, I overheard a woman who was talking about her church. Her voice was loud, her tone was critical, and her audience was clinging to her every word. I did not know the woman. I never did hear the name or denomination of her church. It did not matter; what she said had that familiar ring of famous quotations and complaints often heard by pastors and church leaders:

"We never did it *that* way before!"

"Pastor, I'm so glad you preached that sermon today. There are folks who need to hear it (of course, I'm not one of them)."

"I remember how Pastor ———— used to do things."

What if that woman's comments were someone's *only* impression of the church of Jesus Christ?

For the sake of the gospel, even when the cheering stops, we must be about the work of Christ. This is the true test of discipleship: obedience to God and fidelity to Christ's church. How we live. Whom we love and forgive. What we believe. Such a life, anchored in God, is not hindered by the passing storms of life. (Gary G. Kindley)

BETTER LATE THAN NEVER

MATTHEW 21:23-32

Have you ever known big talkers? You know the type: whatever accomplishment you've just enjoyed, theirs was better; whatever operation you just had, theirs was much worse; whatever your summer vacation was like, theirs was even better! But you will notice with big talkers that when it comes time to get something done, they are usually nowhere to be found.

The New Testament leaves no doubt that discipleship is a matter of actions, not simply words. In our text, Jesus is confronting the religious establishment, a group that made its living on words. The men want to entangle Jesus in a debate that will compromise him, but Jesus makes it plain that he isn't interested in meaningless talk—he is concerned with meaningful action.

I. God Does Not Honor Those Who Talk Religion but Fail to Respond to God's Call

The members of the religious establishment had reason to defend the status quo. It was their source of support; so long as they didn't antagonize the Roman rulers, they pretty much were allowed to run the show in the religious realm. An itinerant preacher like Jesus—particularly one the people were beginning to think might be the Messiah—well, such a person complicated their lives and threatened the status quo. That was why, as the week in Jerusalem went on, the religious leaders became more and more desperate to eliminate him from the scene.

They hoped to get him involved in theological debate, but Jesus would have none of it. Why talk about the things of God with those who refused to respond to the call of God? He turned the tables on them by posing a question about John the Baptist. They were on the spot; clearly, they had rejected John, but his memory as a prophet was still quite popular with the people. Any answer would get them in trouble—so they passed.

That led Jesus into a parable about two men: one didn't talk the talk but walked the walk; the other talked the talk but didn't walk the walk. Guess which one Jesus honored? The one who acted, not the one who merely talked about it.

The religious leaders opted for argument rather than acceptance. They were more concerned with self-image than with self-surrender; more concerned about status than about sacrifice. And Jesus had no use for them.

II. God Honors Those Who Respond to the Divine Call

If the parable hadn't been telling enough, Jesus must have infuriated the religious types with his application. The prostitutes and tax collectors—the most reviled of all professions in that culture—

would arrive in the kingdom of heaven before the religious leaders because when they heard God's call, they responded in faith and repentance, unlike their religious brethren.

There's a wonderful truth here for all of us: it does not matter what you have done, where you have been, who you were before trusting Christ. If you will give your life to him—walk the walk, not just talk the talk—God has a special place reserved for you in his kingdom.

Likewise, there is a word of warning to those of us who may assume our religion will be satisfactory. All the religious words and ceremony in the world will not replace authentic faith and repentance. God wants actions, not mere words. (Michael Duduit)

OCTOBER

ૹ

Preparing to Serve

The Symbol of the Trumpet

Paraphrase Assignment:

Psalm 47:5-6: "God has gone up with a shout,/ the LORD with the sound of a trumpet. / Sing praises to God, sing praises;/ sing praises to our King, sing praises."

Prayer Assignment:

Begin a list of those events in your life that you have had a yearning to know Christ, face-to-face. Do you want to see Christ only when you have a toothache, or are there lingering evidences in your life when you long to see and know him in the spiritual consummation that begins the eternal union with Christ? Write your feelings as you might write a love letter. Let what you have written be your prayer throughout the month of October. This may be a suitable prayer for the congregation to read together as you examine the church's hope.

Journal-in-Worship Assignment:

Consider the following three passages in what they promise about Christ's return. Remember Advent is just weeks away. Apply the joy of the Second Coming to your own life. Try to move through the written paragraphs remembering this: as your hunger for the trumpet goes, so goes the reality of your faith. Advent is an unreasonable celebration to the person who has no hunger for the Second Coming. Those who get emotional about Bethlehem really only demonstrate their true faith in getting excited over the New Jerusalem.

Matthew 24:31. This trumpet passage includes the all-encompassing summons to the church that is estranged from the coming Savior. Christ has called you and me to preach redemption so that the "elect" will understand that they are chosen to celebrate the trumpet call as well. Write a prayer of submission accepting his call to missionize those who need to receive him.

1 Corinthians 15:52*b*. With Advent approaching, think of all those who will not celebrate this Christmas but did last year. What does this "trumpet" passage have to say about the mending of earth's griefs? How shall we celebrate a "trumpet" eschatology? Write a paragraph on how you anticipate reunion with some special loved one now in heaven. Record your last earthly moments of seeing the person as you write how you anticipate seeing him or her again.

Revelation 1:10-11*a*. In this passage, the apostle makes his homesickness for heaven apparent. He was in the Spirit when he heard the trumpetlike voice. Would we hear more trumpets if we were more in the Spirit? Put yourself in John's place. Write a paragraph imagining how you would feel if you were involved in these very Bible studies and you were suddenly transported by a loud trumpet and vivid pictures of the Second Coming. (Calvin Miller)

OCTOBER 6, 1996

❧

Nineteenth Sunday After Pentecost

Worship Theme: God's discipline allows us to share in his holiness.

Readings: Exodus 20:1-4, 7-9, 12-20; Philippians 3:4*b*-14; Matthew 21:33-46

Call to Worship (Psalm 19:7-9):

Leader: The law of the LORD is perfect, reviving the soul;

People: the decrees of the LORD are sure, making wise the simple;

Leader: the precepts of the LORD are right, rejoicing the heart;

People: the commandment of the LORD is clear, enlightening the eyes;

Leader: the fear of the LORD is pure, enduring forever;

People: the ordinances of the LORD are true and righteous altogether.

Pastoral Prayer:

Our Creator and Redeemer, we thank you for the precious life that you have given us. We thank you for the gift of your Word, both its precepts and its promises, for in it we know you enable us to find your truth. We thank you also for the gift of your presence with us through your Holy Spirit as you guide us in your ways and bring to fulfillment your work in our lives. Thank you for the Law, which teaches us how inadequate our lives are compared to your infinite holiness; and thank you for your grace through our Lord Jesus Christ, whose sacrifice on our behalf has allowed us, in him, to enter into your very presence. For it is in his name alone we are able to pray. Amen.

SERMON BRIEFS

STOP AND LISTEN

EXODUS 20:1-4, 7-9, 12-20

It is to laugh. My father is being dragged—kicking and scream-ing—into the information age. The kicking and screaming part is over learning how to use his new computer. He was quite happy working an old, out-of-date computer, but now he's coming to grips with a faster and better machine. He watches in awe as my brother and I work more or less nimbly in Windows and resolve conflicts without breaking into a sweat. But Dad is slow to catch on to anything newfangled.

Soon, I am to instruct him in the art of using his new toy, and I can well imagine the conversation. "You, son, can show me how to use it. But all these bells and whistles terrify me, and I am not ready to make the jump into future relationship with this ma-chine."

As we hear these stories of a people's initiation to relationship with God, do you get the feeling that they (and we) are undergoing a certain amount of intense preparation? We should. God is checking out Israel from stem to stern, restructuring and fine-tuning their lives to see if this people really can fit into the designs and rhythm of life the Lord has in mind.

The people needed conditioning, toughening up. Let them suffer enough so they won't turn away from the Lord once problems were resolved. They needed to learn thankfulness and order. They needed a framework for living in the land flowing with milk and honey, all outlined for them in these Ten Commandments.

There is a trouble spot, though. After the tablets are engraved with the ten words, after all the thunder and lightning, after the blaring of the trumpet, the people are frightened out of their wits. "You speak to us, Moses, and we'll listen. But don't let God speak to us, or we shall surely die!" The people run the risk of not hearing.

Rabbi Adin Steinsaltz observes, "The mighty voice on Sinai did not stop." He mentions that later writings repeat this same idea, that the voice of God did not stop. In fact, it is still giving the Law forever and ever. "The thing that has changed," laments Steinsaltz, "is that we are no longer listening."

Were the Israelites afraid the power of heaven might come crashing down on them? Had the writer of Hebrews been around, they might have seen that God's discipline was for their own good and ours, so they and we may share in the Lord's holiness. We are reminded: "Now, discipline always seems painful rather than pleasant at the time, but later it yields the peaceful fruit of righteousness to those who have been trained by it" (Heb. 12:11).

Therefore, we are to endure for the sake of discipline, as the Israelites had to learn to do. Athletes undergo rigorous training to discipline themselves to play the game well. Olympic athletes don't reach such levels of achievement just because of luck. Hours of practice go into every movement. There are painful muscles, bruised joints, and instruction from the coach to do better. But the athletes persevere, enduring the hardship and discipline of the coach.

God chooses us to participate in an extraordinary life relationship with the holy. Let us do so with intensity and fearlessness of spirit. Above all, let us listen and not be afraid, for the Lord is only preparing us for the kingdom of God. (Eric Killinger)

WHEN LOSS IS GAIN

PHILIPPIANS 3:4*b*-14

It is difficult to communicate to persons with twentieth-century understanding that establishing a relationship with Jesus Christ is the most important thing that can happen to them in their lives. The empirical mind-set of many twentieth-century people looks for facts that can be measured, seen, and touched.

Cynics or skeptics, when considering such a proposition, may ask, "How can you have a relationship with Someone who is dead and gone?" (Or if they have enough faith to believe in the Resurrection, if not dead, at least gone.)

Others may query, "Wealth is power and influence in today's world, so how can the mystical idea of a Savior be more important than the security of money, possessions, and power?"

Contrast this with what the apostle Paul said: "Look at what I have, yet it is nothing compared to knowing Jesus Christ" (v. 7, paraphrase). Consider these two ideas reflected in Paul's writings:

I. We Are Saved Only by Grace

We can say that with our lips and write that in our doctrine, but are we living as if we believe it? Read again what Paul says in today's text: *"I regard everything as loss because of the surpassing value of knowing Christ Jesus my Lord.* For his sake I have suffered the loss of all things, and I regard them as rubbish, in order that I may gain Christ and be found in him, *not having a righteousness of my own that comes from the law, but one that comes through faith in Christ,* the righteousness from God based on faith" (vv. 8-9, emphasis added).

We are not saved by the church we attend, the money we tithe, or the persons we have invited to worship. We are saved *only* by grace through faith in Christ!

God's grace is not "cheap grace," as Dietrich Bonhoeffer so well describes in his book *The Cost of Discipleship*. Our response to God's grace is a life of Christian service. Good works, however noble, are still only a response to what God has done.

When on some final day we are called before our Maker, it will not be our good works that save us. What ultimately will save us will be God's mercy. It is all grace!

II. Jesus Christ Is the Ultimate Truth

Knowing the God revealed through Christ brings meaning, purpose, and fulfillment to our lives. When we know *whose* we are, we have a new perspective on *who* we are and how special and sacred is life (vv. 10-14).

A man was preparing to shave one morning when he noticed blood streaming down his cheek. He looked at the razor in his hand that had not yet touched his face, looked back in the mirror at his bleeding face, and was stunned.

He made an appointment that same day with a dermatologist. The dermatologist removed a lesion from his face and said, rather matter-of-factly, "It's probably cancer," and walked out of the room.

The man's whole life flashed before his eyes. Consider how you might respond to such news! He was fortunate. There was no spreading malignancy, and he was cured by that one surgical procedure.

What do we do when we are faced with the reality of death or dread disease? Hope that our resources will buy a cure? Search for a solution through dubious alternative medicine?

The first thing that many people do is pray to God because we turn to the one relationship that ultimately matters. Many foxhole conversions and deathbed affirmations of faith have been made because of this truth. It is within the soul to seek out the One who is greater than ourselves, the God who makes sense of the chaos and brings purpose to our existence.

When is loss gain? When we surrender our control and our search for security in tangible things, and we discover that trusting in God and God's design is ultimately more satisfying. (Gary G. Kindley)

BEING FRUITFUL

MATTHEW 21:33-46

On a recent trip to Washington D.C., I visited the Vietnam Veterans Memorial. It was brought to my attention that hairline cracks have developed in the marbled stone wall that bears the names of the soldiers who died in the war. It seems the stone slabs were cut too thin, and they were damaged by the dramatic temperature changes of the winter of 1994. Some experts predict the monument will have to be completely replaced. In a way, though, a broken memorial is a fitting monument to Vietnam. The cracks are hauntingly reminiscent of the shattered lives that the war left behind.

In this text, Jesus quotes to the chief priests and elders from Psalm 118, describing how a stone that builders rejected becomes the Lord's cornerstone. Jesus uses this verse to signify his own tragic rejection and to foretell the coming of God's kingdom. Jesus warns that the kingdom of God will be taken away and given to a people who produce fruit. Jesus makes it clear that the people of God are to have fruit. But what is fruit, and how does one produce it?

I. What Is Fruit?

The Gospel writer Matthew uses fruit as a symbol for the works of the people of God. Jesus preaches that one should produce fruit in keeping with repentance (3:8); the tree that bears bad fruit should be cut down (3:10); every good tree bears good fruit and every bad tree produces bad fruit (7:17); and the tree is known by its fruit (12:33).

II. How Do We Produce Fruit?

Ultimately, God is the source of fruit in a Christian's life, but we can do some things to increase the harvest. Fruit is really the by-product of a healthy plant. Likewise, fruit for the Christian is a by-product of right living through God's grace. God will produce fruit in our lives if we honor him in the garden of the soul. We can do this by remembering to:

Seed the garden. Before a plant can grow and produce fruit, a seed must be planted. This planting of seed refers not only to the initial beginning of one's journey with Christ. God wants to plant orchards in new fields of our lives.

In each of us, there are new gifts waiting to be discovered. Are there times in your life when you have consciously made an effort to cultivate a new talent for the purpose of giving it to others? What new area of your life have you committed to God in the last six months? What have you done for God lately?

Weed the garden. Every gardener spends time weeding the garden. The weeds of bad habits can sprout and quickly creep up the wall of our lives. In his autobiography, Benjamin Franklin tells of his efforts to eliminate the bad habits that plagued him. Franklin concentrated on twelve bad habits in his life and charted his progress, focusing on a different habit each week in a twelve-week cycle. He returned to this cycle at different times in his life, attempting to keep his garden weed free.

Feed the garden. We all need to spend time with God if we are to produce fruit. We are fed through activities such as corporate worship, Bible study, and quiet time with God in reflection and meditation. If we work at keeping our garden in order, the tremendous resources God has given us can produce abundantly more than we ever dreamed. (Scott Salsman)

OCTOBER 13, 1996

৯

Twentieth Sunday After Pentecost

Worship Theme: Christians are called to encourage and support one another.

Readings: Exodus 32:1-14; Philippians 4:1-9; Matthew 22:1-14

Call to Worship (Psalm 106:1-3):

Leader: Praise the LORD! O give thanks to the LORD, for he is good;

People: for his steadfast love endures forever.

Leader: Who can utter the mighty doings of the LORD, or declare all his praise?

People: For his steadfast love endures forever.

Leader: Happy are those who observe justice, who do righteousness at all times.

People: For his steadfast love endures forever.

Pastoral Prayer:

Gracious God, in these quiet moments, we gather our thoughts to give you thanksgiving and praise, as well as to intercede for others who are in need. We first give you thanks, Lord, because we are richly blessed. There is the blessing of warm clothing on cool days, and the blessing of snug and dry homes. There is the blessing of technological achievements: of miracle drugs and medical equipment, telephones and computers and much more—all of these blessings coming from you through the hands of individuals here on earth. Yet in spite of our great blessings, Lord, we know there are many needs. We know many still suffer. We know many lack the basics of life: warm clothing, adequate shelter, nutritious food, decent education. Our world is filled with such people in need, and too often, the thought staggers our imaginations and freezes us from action. Help us to be more compassionate and loving, willing to share of our possessions to help others. Help us to act with the love and charity of Christ, in whose name we pray. Amen. (Steven R. Fleming)

SERMON BRIEFS

MOSES, THE ADVOCATE

EXODUS 32:1-14

In John's Gospel, Christians read about Jesus sending the Advocate when he departed from his disciples. In truth, though Jesus is understood by the community of faith as the premier advocate, there have also been advocates for the Hebrew community of faith—primarily Abraham and Moses.

Our text contains a remarkable drama of a leader's intervention on behalf of a sinful people. The drama begins with the first act.

I. A Leader Delayed

We all know the story of Moses going up to Mount Sinai and receiving the tablets of stone "written with the finger of God." In the meantime, the Israelites become impatient with Moses' absence and go to Aaron saying, "We do not know what has become of him" (v. 1). These people, who seem to think that they are now leaderless because Moses is out of their sight, are not different from other anxious people about which the Bible speaks.

Matthew, alluding to a comparable assembly, says of Jesus, "When he saw the crowds, he had compassion for them, because they were harassed and helpless, like sheep without a shepherd" (Matt. 9:36). Sheep without a shepherd are in danger from wolves as well as the self-inflicted chaos that may put them into danger. It is this anxious state in which the children of Israel find themselves.

II. A People's Sin

Aaron bounds to action and encourages the people to "take off the gold rings that are on the ears of your wives, your sons, and your daughters, and bring them to me" (v. 2). With the gold, which may have been part of the booty from the Egyptians, Aaron fashions an image of a golden calf. This act is in direct violation of God's command, "You shall not make for yourself an idol" (Exod. 20:4). This is an uncertain moment for the Hebrews. The people persuade Aaron to act in a way that puts them in grave danger.

Idolatry is a constant temptation for all who call on the name of the Lord. The amount of biblical material warning against this violation of God's law should convince all of us about the danger of the temptation to worship other gods. That was one of the issues with which Satan tempted Jesus in the wilderness.

Even for us modern, sophisticated twentieth-century Christians, the temptation to place something above or beside God is always before us. The temptation to read the newspaper or to attend a youth soccer game or to watch television in the privacy of our homes on any given Sunday morning remains strong. This temptation flies in the face of the Christian obligation to gather as a community of faith and worship God. Idolatry is ever with us.

III. An Advocate Intercedes

To Moses' credit, however, as the Lord's anger rises against Israel, Moses becomes their advocate. Even though his sojourn with them had been a difficult one at best, he prevails upon God not to follow his initial intention; namely, "I have seen this people, how stiff-necked they are. Now let me alone, so that my wrath may burn hot against them and I may consume them; and of you I will make a great nation" (vv. 9-10). Even though God promises not to cut Moses off from making him a great nation, Moses will not forsake his people. This willingness to intercede for them illustrates a great leader.

Moses, in this transaction with God, becomes a true advocate for the people of Israel. By not forsaking his people, Moses shows his leadership ability—this in spite of having every human reason to do so. His compassion is amazing and, in the end, redemptive.

All Christians are called to be leaders. In Christ and in Moses, we have models of leadership to follow. These leadership guides show us to what length and breadth godly leaders are willing to go on behalf of their people. (David Neil Mosser)

HERE WE STAND

PHILIPPIANS 4:1-9

Let us for a moment ignore the chapter divisions in this book. It is, after all, a letter. Verse 1 of chapter 4 is as surely connected to chapter 3 as it is to the rest of chapter 4. It appears that Paul's "therefore" in verse 1 begins a specific application to the "joy and crown" referred to in chapter 3.

Paul called for the Philippians, especially Euodia and Syntyche, "to be of the same mind"—to be controlled by the truth in one's whole being. With this mind, the Philippians could stand as soldiers holding their position in the face of the enemy. Paul emphasized that such a stance could be theirs only in the Lord. This is especially pertinent since God calls us "to will and to do"—a phrase used three times in chapter 4. What does it mean to have the "mind of Christ"?

I. We Recognize the Real Enemy

The challenge is no different for Christians today. As soldiers of Christ, we must hold our positions in the face of the enemy. The true enemy of Christians, as Luther said, is our ancient foe, the devil, who doth seek to work us woe. Each of us, with our feet of clay, needs to be of one mind in Christ to withstand the allurements of the world.

Sometimes Christians think that other Christians are their chief enemies. That was the case in a quarrel between Euodia and Syntyche. Rather than mocking the leadership of the two women, Paul praised them as fellow workers (v. 3). His appeal to them was on the basis of their being in the Lord. He called on them to humble themselves by taking on the mind of Christ and to promote unity. He called on an unidentified yokefellow to assist the two women in their reconciliation.

II. We Rejoice in One Another

Paul's mention of their names being in the book of life refers to Luke 10:20. Because their names were written together in the book of life, Euodia and Syntyche were out of Christian character in their argument. As good Christians, they should be of the same mind; they should "rejoice in the Lord always" (v. 4). Rejoicing was to replace petty strife. This rejoicing is done as we have the mind of Christ in us.

Paul called them to forbearance. Paul called for them to meet halfway, to emphasize grace over insistence on who was right and who was wrong (v. 5).

Being of the "same mind" and having the "mind of Christ" are worthy goals that require a lot of effort on the part of Christians. The "mind of Christ" calls for us to be humble before God, to be servants rather than masters, and to extend grace rather than insist on justice. When we are striving toward this, the resulting fellowship is both beautiful to observe and too powerful to resist.

III. We Resist the World's Power

Paul encouraged the Philippians to stand fast against the problems they faced. In addition to the rift between their leaders, they were worried about Paul's imprisonment, about people who insisted that individuals become Jews before becoming Christians, about the immoral lifestyle so widely accepted in the Roman Empire, and about the increasing persecution of Christians. Paul's advice was, "Don't worry! Pray!"

Finally, Paul called for the Philippians to think (v. 8) and do (v. 9). We are to think on things that show the world that Christ lives in us. And as the mind of Christ becomes our minds, we are to live according to the ways of Christ. The thought is akin to that of James 1:22.

Where do Christians stand? The general answer to such a question: here we stand, arm in arm, linked together with the same mind—the mind of Christ. (Al Fasol)

CRIME AND PUNISHMENT

MATTHEW 22:1-14

American revivalism has historically been characterized by hell-fire-and-brimstone preachers. One of the most popular of these preachers was an ex-professional baseball player for the Chicago White Stockings, turned evangelist, named Billy Sunday.

Sunday was known for his dramatic "Gatlin' gun" preaching style. He challenged the men in his congregations to be "man enough to trust Jesus." On occasion he would chase the devil around the church, running wildly through the aisles, and slide home into the pulpit, "into the arms of Jesus."

Although his theatrics received criticism in his day and since then, Sunday did take sin seriously. The evangelist was known for hanging a huge banner over the stage of his evangelism crusades: "Get Right with God." For Billy Sunday, being a Christian required living a Christian lifestyle.

Matthew the evangelist could be called a hellfire-and-brimstone preacher. Matthew's Gospel provides vivid imagery of the threat of judgment to motivate disciples to do good works. The theme of judgment is found in at least sixty sections of the Gospel. Matthew warns of being burned in fire (3:10; 7:19), an unquenchable fire (3:12), a fiery furnace (13:42, 50), eternal fire (18:8-9; 25:41), or a fiery Gehenna (5:22; 18:9; see 5:29); being delivered to the tormentors until the last penny is paid (18:34); being dismembered (24:51); entering the way that leads to perdition (7:13); and being consigned to eternal punishment (25:46).

One of the places that speaks of judgment is found in Jesus' parable to the chief priests concerning the wedding banquet (Matt. 22:1-14). There is a problem about the punishment of a wedding guest. A man is bound hand and foot and thrown into outer darkness, where there are weeping and gnashing of teeth—usually symbolic of eternal damnation—simply for showing up at a wedding improperly dressed (v. 13)!

Images of judgment and punishment are controversial in today's society. Two years ago, a teenage American boy was convicted of spray painting cars in Singapore. The story drew international attention in response to his sentence, a severe form of physical punishment known as caning. Some applauded the sentence as appropriate, and others deplored it as excessive. The debate over the issue concerned the appropriate amount of punishment for the crime.

I. What Does Jesus Mean by Clothes?

How are we to make sense of Jesus' parable where the wedding guest is sentenced to what seems to be eternal damnation when he has committed no crime? To make sense out of this story, it is vital to understand the type of biblical literature that we are dealing with—allegory. An allegory is a story in which people, things, and events are used as metaphors to carry symbolic meaning.

Today, we may have a problem with what seems to be an unfair judgment of a man failing to have proper attire when he has just been called in off the street corner. In the New Testament, however, clothing is often used as a metaphor, frequently as an apocalyptic image for moral worthiness (Rev. 3:4-5, 18; 6:11; 7:13-14; 22:14-15). On at least one occasion (Rev. 19:8), clothing is used to represent the righteous deeds of the saints.

II. We Are to Be Clothed in Obedience

Throughout Matthew's Gospel there is an emphasis that grace does not cancel the reality of judgment. The vivid imagery in this story is used to shock the chief scribes. God requires his people to be clothed in good deeds. God requires a changed life that results in fruit (21:43).

At a recent wedding in which I officiated, two of the groomsmen showed up with their cummerbunds on backward. They had never worn tuxes before and weren't sure where and how everything was supposed to fit. One day all of us will be called to a wedding party. On that day will we be appropriately attired by our good works?

When we stand before St. Peter's pearly gates, the sign in the window might read, "No shoes, no shirt, no service." This allegorical parable reminds us that the true picture of God must include wrath as well as grace. (Scott Salsman)

OCTOBER 20, 1996

❧

Twenty-first Sunday After Pentecost

Worship Theme: Above all other obligations, our primary loyalty is to God.

Readings: Exodus 33:12-23; 1 Thessalonians 1:1-10; Matthew 22:15-22

Call to Worship (Psalm 99:1-3, 9):

Leader: The LORD is king; let the peoples tremble!

People: For the LORD our God is holy.

Leader: He sits enthroned upon the cherubim; let the earth quake!

People: For the LORD our God is holy.

Leader: The LORD is great in Zion; he is exalted over all the peoples.

People: For the LORD our God is holy.

Leader: Let them praise your great and awesome name. Holy is he!

People: For the LORD our God is holy. . . .

Leader: Extol the LORD our God, and worship at his holy mountain.

People: For the LORD our God is holy.

Pastoral Prayer:

Holy and righteous God, we live in a nation that speaks your name but too often ignores your will. We are eager to claim your blessing, even of deeds you will not bless. Help us to be wise and discerning, understanding that not all who say, "Lord, Lord," will enter into the kingdom of heaven—or even understand the nature of that kingdom. We are in a time when political debate is heated, with elections only days away. Help us to remember that government is ordained by you and should be operated in such a way that you will be honored, but remind us often that human government and your kingdom are not the same thing. Help us to be ever mindful that our first loyalty is not to the things of Caesar but to the things of your kingdom. Make us good citizens, but even more make us faithful disciples of Jesus Christ, in whose name we pray. Amen.

SERMON BRIEFS

THE REQUESTS HE MAKES

EXODUS 33:12-23

Exodus 32–33 recalls the biblical story of Israel's disobedience and the role Moses plays as mediator and advocate. Last week's Exodus passage, the story of the golden calf, sets the stage for this week's lesson—Moses' further negotiations with Yahweh.

Moses' requests of Yahweh reflect the legitimate concerns of one who seeks to faithfully follow God.

I. The Faithful Follower Seeks God's Promise

Much like those with whom Paul will later contend, the Jews want signs as the Greeks seek wisdom, Moses seems to say: I need proof. Moses wants Yahweh to be even more specific, becoming almost pressing with his questions to Yahweh. Moses says, "Show me your ways" (v. 13).

As usual, Moses wants divine assurance. Earlier in their first meeting, Moses craves God's divine name, but the answer is solely the mysterious response: "I AM WHO I AM." He says further, "Thus you shall say to the Israelites, 'I AM has sent me to you' " (Exod. 3:14). God's response to Moses' request is that they will be given rest. That is, soon Israel will rest in the promised land of milk and honey. To know God's ways is to know God's promise.

II. The Faithful Follower Seeks God's Presence

Moses keeps pressing, however. He asks that Yahweh "go with them," by saying, in effect, unless you go with us, then how can we be a distinct people and how will people know I (Moses) have found favor in the Lord's sight?

Yahweh's answer is affirmative in yet another promise: "I will do the very thing that you have asked; for you have found favor in my sight, and I know you by name" (v. 18). Thus, from the text, it appears that Moses does indeed receive divine assurance.

III. The Faithful Follower Seeks God's Person

But Moses presses on. He wants to see God's glory. Much to the reader's surprise, God grants still another request and tells Moses how the Lord will be made manifest to Moses. When the Lord passes by Moses, the glory of the Lord will be shown to Moses, and Moses will see the Lord's back, though not face-to-face as was earlier alluded to in Exodus 33:11: "The LORD used to speak to Moses face to face, as one speaks to a friend." In Moses' persistence is his success as he receives the divine blessing of relationship with the Lord.

Any accomplished musician will tell us that the secret of being able to master a complex piece of music is no secret but is contained in the adage to practice, practice, practice. Perseverance is a character quality difficult to develop. Many people want to do things well; few pay the personal price to master a skill or develop an art.

One of the most amazing qualities of faithful people is the ability to stick with a task until it is complete. I often wonder if one of the reasons faith seems so difficult for many of us is that we want it to be present in our lives without cost. Faith worth having, however, means being put under God's authority. This is contrary to our nature but necessary for our salvation. We do not work for salvation, but neither do we expect to be handed a relationship with God that is thoroughly one-sided. Any covenant worth having is a covenant between two partners.

The story of Moses gives great guidance in what a person who truly desires God can become by God's great grace. Perhaps Moses was a spiritual relative of the woman about whom Jesus spoke when he said, "In that city there was a widow who kept coming to him and saying, 'Grant me justice against my opponent' " (Luke 18:3). Good faith on people's part is faith that keeps coming and coming. (David Neil Mosser)

THANKS FOR THE MEMORIES

1 THESSALONIANS 1:1-10

Many people are reluctant to give and receive gratitude. Perhaps saying thanks seems like an admission that another's assistance was needed. This acknowledgment reminds us of our interdependence when we would rather take pride in our independence.

Paul had no trouble giving thanks. He thanked God for Jesus (Rom. 7), and he thanked God for memories of the Philippians (Phil. 1:3). The record is not as clear as to how Paul received thanks, but if he received it as well as he gave it, he would be an excellent role model for us.

A high point in Paul's expression of gratitude came in the opening verses of 1 Thessalonians. Following his usual greeting, Paul enthusiastically wrote, "We always give thanks to God for all of you" (v. 2). The word picture is one of deep and joyful thanks. What moved Paul to such a superlative expression—and what should cause us to give thanks as well?

I. We Can Be Thankful for the Faithfulness of God's People

In verse 3, Paul specified three reasons for his gratitude: "work of faith and labor of love and steadfastness of hope in our Lord Jesus Christ." This is a favorite collection of words for Paul—faith, love, and hope. The accolades were appropriate. The Thessalonians had the benefit of Paul's presence for a short time, perhaps as little as three weeks. Paul fled the city after threats were made on his life, and he worried about the welfare of the Christians left behind. The report he received of the Thessalonians' work of faith, labor of love, and steadfastness of hope gave reason for his expression of gratitude.

II. We Can Be Thankful for the Proclamation of God's Word

In verses 5-10, Paul wrote that the power of God was at work in Thessalonica through preaching. He made three particular points about this preaching:

The preaching of the gospel came in power (v. 5a). The verb Paul used indicates some vital force was in operation. It was used to describe the coming of various natural phenomena—earthquake, thunder, or lightning. Paul's point was that the preaching of the gopsel was accompanied by this kind of power because God was in the preaching.

The gospel came in the Holy Spirit (v. 5b). This thought complements what Paul had just said about power.

The preaching of the gospel came "with full conviction" (v. 5c). This completes the thought. Conviction is the result of the Holy Spirit's working in believers. They had the Spirit's assurance as they preached.

Paul virtually broke into rhapsody as he described what happened as a result of this preaching of the gospel (vv. 6-10). First, they became followers (read it, Christians) after receiving this gospel in affliction to be sure, but also in the joy of the Holy Spirit (v. 6). Second, they became role models for Christians throughout the surrounding territory (v. 7). Paul knew that because their faithfulness had been literally broadcast everywhere (v. 8). Third, Paul knew that their testimony was built not only on their radical new lives as Christians but also by their patient hope in the return of Christ (vv. 9-10).

In many nations of the world and in many communities in our own country, the same kind of affliction awaits those who would share the gospel. Rather than seeing them as hopeless situations, we should view them as potential Thessalonicas; that is, places in which people need to and sometimes will make a radical change in their lives and then will share with us the steadfast hope as we await the return of Christ. (Al Fasol)

DEATH AND TAXES

MATTHEW 22:15-22

There is a story about an Internal Revenue Service agent who made a phone call to the county-seat town's best-known pastor: "Mr. Bob Smith put down on his tax return that he made a contribution of $3,000 to your church last year. Is that true?" After a brief pause on the other end of the line, the pastor quietly responded, "If he didn't, he will." The familiar adage goes that the two things one cannot escape are death and taxes. Today, we are going to look at what, to some, is the more frightening of the two—taxes.

In this text, Jesus is confronted with a question concerning the head tax paid to the Romans. The Pharisees use false flattery in an attempt to disarm Jesus so that they then can entrap and humiliate him with a tricky yes or no question.

In Jesus' day, questioning the tax system was dangerous business. The establishment of this tax had provoked a revolt of the Jews in Galilee in the year A.D. 6. The Jews had become enraged concerning the placing of God's land at the service of pagans.

Jesus sets his own trap for the Pharisees by asking to see the coin used to pay the tax. By doing this, Jesus reminds the Pharisees that they already acknowledge Caesar's authority by having his money in their possession. They possess a Roman coin, bearing the image of the emperor and conveying Roman ideology.

I. We Have a Legitimate Obligation to the State

Jesus simply and profoundly declares that Caesar is owed what bears his image and name—money. Jesus is not drawn into a debate between church and state. He acknowledges that being a servant of God does not exempt you from being a tax-paying servant of the state. Jesus emphasizes, however, that the higher duty is to be rendered to God.

II. We Have a Greater Obligation to God

God, Caesar's Lord, is to be rendered the things that are God's. God is owed what bears his image and name—our very lives.

There is a lovely estate in Georgia, the beautiful grounds of which were being expertly tended by a caretaker. Every tree was trimmed, the grass was mowed, and stately beds of flowers were in bloom. Yet not one soul was around to observe any of the beauty except for the caretaker himself. A visitor surprised the man after stopping to see the striking sight and asked, "When was the owner last here?"

"Oh, ten or twelve years ago, I guess," said the caretaker.

"Then from whom do you get your instructions?"

"From the agent who lives in Atlanta," the caretaker replied.

"Does *he* ever come around to inspect the place?"

"No, can't say that he does," answered the caretaker.

"And yet you keep it trim as if he were going to come tomorrow?"

And with that the gardener interrupted the curious visitor: "As if he were going to be here today!"

God calls us to be good stewards of all with which we have been entrusted. One day the Master will come back to check on things— you can count on it. Will he find you and me ready?

Waiting patiently at the cash register, Uncle Sam stands ready to receive a seemingly ever-increasing portion of the money we spend. It's as inevitable as death. The next time you see tax figured into your bill, while you sign the ticket for the credit transaction, remember the words of the penniless itinerant preacher. Render to Caesar what is Caesar's and to God what is God's. (Scott Salsman)

OCTOBER 27, 1996

ૠ

Twenty-second Sunday After Pentecost

Worship Theme: We are called to demonstrate love for God and one another.

Readings: Deuteronomy 34:1-12; 1 Thessalonians 2:1-8; Matthew 22:34-46

Call to Worship (Psalm 90:1-4):

Leader: Lord, you have been our dwelling place in all generations. Before the mountains were brought forth, or ever you had formed the earth and the world,

People: from everlasting to everlasting you are God.

Leader: You turn us back to dust, and say, "Turn back, you mortals." For a thousand years in your sight are like yesterday when it is past, or like a watch in the night.

People: From everlasting to everlasting you are God.

Pastoral Prayer:

We are consumed by the idea of love, O Lord, but we seem to know so little of love as you intended it. You created love as a precious jewel, but we too often treat it as a casual and cheap trinket. You intended love to be faithful and persevering, but we too often treat love as a fleeting, impersonal emotion. You have told us that love involves sacrifice, but we have used it as a tool for manipulation and self-serving. In Jesus, you demonstrated the ultimate act of love, but so many of us treat that incredible event as if it meant nothing. Forgive us, Lord, for selfish, thoughtless actions that treat your awesome love with apathy and indifference. Work within us to create a new and higher perspective; help us to love you more deeply and demonstrate that love in our actions toward others. In the name of the One who loves us no matter what. Amen.

SERMON BRIEFS

THE CALL TO MINISTRY: PAIN OR PROMISE?

DEUTERONOMY 34:1-12

A common misunderstanding of baptism is that baptism is the end of a Christian's search for God. To walk the "sawdust trail" and surrender to God's call during a tent revival or an emotional moment is about as far as some persons get in their faith journey. If one equates the call to ministry with the rite or sacrament of baptism, however, then baptism becomes a beginning—and not an end—for ministry.

Deuteronomy 34 is a synopsis of Moses' ministry. The book's final words describe the end of Moses' prophetic ministry given to Yahweh and Israel. Moses' call to ministry may prove instructive for us as we follow our own call, understanding it in the light of baptism as Christians who identify ourselves as disciples of Jesus Christ.

Like Moses, we see from the perspective of our relationship with God.

I. We Live in Utter Dependence on God

Through the many experiences of his life—from his miraculous rescue as an infant, to his call at the burning bush, to the divine leadership of the exodus from Egypt—Moses had learned to place his absolute trust in God.

The baptismal ritual helps Christians confess the source of life. Baptism helps us establish life around the principle that we are human creatures and God is the absolute ruler of life—the Sovereign of creation. Baptism reminds us that every time we participate in the sacrament's liturgy, we do so as absolutely and completely dependent children of God—no matter our chronological age. This is both a confession and an affirmation of faith.

Jesus knew his own baptism was necessary, saying to John that it was "to fulfill all righteousness" (Matt. 3:15). The word *ministry* is derived from the Latin root *ministerium,* which means "the service of a greater by a lesser." Surely, this is what we acknowledge at baptism, as it surely was what Moses acknowledged with his life. We serve a God who not only gives us life but also takes it for divine purposes. Moses' life testifies to this fact.

II. We Look Back with Thanksgiving

When Moses was on Mount Nebo, he undoubtedly reflected on his call to Yahweh's service. From the perspective of Midian, we know that Moses was skeptical about Yahweh's confidence in calling him. However, like any human activity, the call is best measured from twenty-twenty hindsight provided by the panorama from Mount Nebo: "And the LORD showed him the whole land" (v. 1). Here is a clear measurement of Moses' success.

Moses' call to ministry can prove instructive for our own baptismal calls to the service of our Lord. Most of us would hold as commonplace the notion that God calls unlikely persons into the service of divinity—after all, most of us are unlikely candidates for nearly everything we undertake. God used Moses—a hothead and a murderer—to do his work.

Moses could look back on a life in which God had allowed him to be used in remarkable ways. How has God used you to minister to others? Will you be able to look back at the end of your life and see "the whole land" of your faithful service?

III. We Look Forward in Faith

Rarely do we have a second chance at opportunities for service to God. There are always forks in the road; the taking of one fork precludes the opportunity the other fork might have afforded. We will never pass this way again, nor will we repeat the moments before us. It is equally certain that no one has ever ventured alone into tomorrow; we will get there along with everyone else. We are unlikely persons to be called by God, and God calls each of us to tasks faced by no other disciple. Moses had his unique tasks; so do we. And we move forward in faith into the future only God knows.

We, like Moses, have our stock set of excuses and questions for resisting God's call: Why? Why me? Why now? Why this? Why not someone else? Whatever the method by which we came to Christ, it does not matter! "Just do it," as our young people would say.

And if you are truly blessed, perhaps you, too, can look out from your own Mount Nebo before you die. (David Neil Mosser)

THE ANATOMY OF A SERVANT

1 THESSALONIANS 2:1-8

First Thessalonians 1 is a portrait of an ideal church; chapter 2 provides a picture of an ideal servant: Paul. In chapter 2, Paul outlines his follow-up program, which formed the basis of the Thessalonian converts' loyalty to the Lord and growth in Christ. Our texts suggests four aspects of the anatomy of a servant.

I. A Suffering Servant (v. 2)

Paul and Silas had been beaten, imprisoned, and literally escorted out of Philippi prior to coming to Thessalonica. Suffering did not make Paul bitter; it made him better. He was better equipped to proclaim the gospel.

Too much of modern Christianity focuses on the glory of servanthood instead of the gory reality of suffering as a Christian. For Paul, a crossless religion results in a crownless reality. Paul reminds believers that if they suffer with Christ, they will reign with Christ.

II. A Courageous Servant (v. 2)

Paul experienced a variety of physical afflictions and verbal insults throughout his ministerial career. He felt the pain of the rod across his back; the discomfort of his limbs in stocks; the pangs of his stomach from hunger; the brokenness of his heart because of friends who abandoned him and enemies who verbally accosted him.

However, Paul was emboldened by God and could not be silenced by threat or attack. Like the prophet Jeremiah of old, he had fire in his bones (Jer. 20:9) and could not hold his peace. Like Simon Peter of his generation, he had the "can't help it's" and was energized to relate the things he had seen and heard.

III. An Authentic Servant (vv. 3, 5-6)

Aware of the prevalence of religious racketeers, roaming peddlers, and swindling sorcerers, Paul reminds the Thessalonian Christians of his authentic ministry in their midst. His ministry was emblematic of the ministry of the Holy Spirit. In fact, he introduces the marks of a genuine ministry with the words "for our exhortation"

(v. 3 KJV). The Greek word for "exhortation" is the word used for the Holy Spirit—*paraklesis*. Paul sees his ministry as an extension of the Holy Spirit. Consequently, unlike the contemporary false prophets of his day, his message was one of truth and not deceit, impurity, insincerity, adulteration, or flattery. Paul did not seek human approval. His message reverberated with "to God be the glory."

IV. A Nurturing Servant (vv. 7-8)

Paul has been misconstrued as being a male chauvinist. In verse 7, he depicts himself in the light of possessing a feminine quality. He pictures his ministry among the Thessalonian Christians in terms of a mother nursing her children through breast-feeding. This is an intriguing image and one of the most beautiful portraits of Christian nurture in the New Testament.

Paul had been nurtured by God through Ananias, Barnabas, and others. He shares with these believers the "sincere milk" of the gospel that had been imparted to him. He also bares his heart and enters into Christian fellowship with them.

What do I have to do? One has to be willing to suffer for Christ's sake. What do I have to say? One has to be courageous in proclaiming Christ's message in the face of opposition. Tell me what does it cost if I carry the cross? One has to be authentic in handling and communicating the word of Christ and self-giving in nurturing the people of Christ. (Robert Smith, Jr.)

LOVING GOD AND NEIGHBOR

MATTHEW 22:34-46

What a relief to hear a scientist distill his lengthy research to the most important component! Jurors appreciate gifted lawyers capable of succinctly bringing an involved case to the crucial decision point. An expert in the Old Testament law, who probably had his own carefully constructed thesis, challenged Jesus to state "the greatest commandment." Jesus provides the bottom line of our spiritual life: "Love the Lord your God . . . love your neighbor." This is the marrow of authentic Christian living. Life for now and all eternity hangs on loving God and neighbor.

I. How Do You Spell Love?

My four-year-old daughter yelled from the back door, "Daddy, how do you spell love?" I stopped my yard work and gave her the four letters. Later at a birthday celebration, her handmade card was printed with "I Love You." How do you spell love? We really spell it as we live it and express love in relationships. In that way, love may be the most misspelled word in the vocabulary of our lives.

Jesus spelled love with unreserved commitment: "Love the Lord your God with all your heart, and with all your soul, and with all your mind" (v. 37). Helmut Thielicke said, "We always put God off with installment payments and only give him piece by piece a bit of something from us, but never ourselves." Real love trusts the whole person to God, surrenders the will to God's way, and allows the mind to be guided by the mind of Christ.

Jesus rejected popular usages of love, erotic and friendship, and focused on *agape* to describe an authentic relationship with God and others. *Agape* love sacrifices self for the best interest of others. *Agape* love deliberately chooses the highest good. Lesser love fluctuates with emotions.

II. How Do You Practice Love?

Agape love acts. Jesus placed the second commandment on par with the first: "Love your neighbor as yourself." In 1991, racial bias prompted 60 percent of the nation's hate crimes, and religious bias accounted for about half of the remaining incidents. "Whoever says, 'I am in the light,' while hating a brother or sister, is still in the darkness" (1 John 2:9). The parable of the good Samaritan (Luke 10:30-37) radically expands the limits of our love.

III. How Can You Love?

Jesus' response silenced the Pharisees. They found it easier to talk about love than to practice it. While they regrouped for a rebuttal, Jesus threw them a question: "What do you think of the Christ?" (v. 42). Craig Blomberg observes, "This is the topic they really should be talking about." The possibility of *agape* love hangs on Jesus: "We love because he first loved us" (1 John 4:19). As Son of David, he understands our difficulty with love. As Lord, he sacrificed himself to free us from sin and provide the power to love. All of life hangs on love because Love hung on the cross. What do you think about Jesus? What will you do with Jesus?

You may only want to debate with Jesus about love. He says "Follow me," and start loving God and neighbor. (Bill Whittaker)

NOVEMBER

❧

Preparing to Serve

The Symbol of the Treasure

Paraphrase Assignment:
Philippians 4:19: "My God will fully satisfy every need of yours according to his riches in glory in Christ Jesus."

Prayer Assignment:
As the Thanksgiving season draws near, make your prayer agenda a celebration of the various treasures you have because you own Christ. In the passages noted below, there are some suggested types of treasure that we possess because we have him. Write a prayer of thanksgiving for your material blessings. It may actually be one that you use at your church's Thanksgiving service or your church's annual fall dinner. Then write similar prayers of thanksgiving celebrating the faithfulness of God when things aren't going well (Hab. 3:17-19). Write another thanking God for the treasure that is yours because you bought the field (Matt. 13:44). Best of all write a prayer of thanksgiving for God's grace and the great treasure of God's love you hold within the clay vessel that is yourself.

Journal-in-Worship Assignment:
Read Psalms 1 and 100. Then write a psalm of thanksgiving of your own. It need not be high sounding. But it should rehearse the joy you have found in all God's abundance. Flavor this homemade psalm with the issues of thanksgiving found in all of the following passages.

Matthew 13:44. In this parable, we can easily celebrate the symbol of the treasure that we must certainly apply to all of the great things we have come to find in Christ. At what moment did you come to treasure grace as a "treasure hidden in a field"? At what moment did you commit to buying that field? Describe on paper those experiences and savor the moment all over again.

Luke 12:15. Let us celebrate the treasure of material and spiritual reality in this verse. People sometimes treasure only those things that are soon to pass away. Our wealth is never in what we own. Write a paragraph enumerating your specific areas of "grace wealth." Describe what unseen values matter most to you.

Habakkuk 3:17-19. If loving God could be done only by those who knew the unfailing stream of material blessings, those millions of Christians who are our starving brothers and sisters in other lands could never celebrate the treasure of their God. What about those times when we are not in the chips? What is the basis of our praise and worship in those times? Describe, on paper, some specific moments when you felt the pain of Habakkuk's experience. Write about the moment when you felt that God didn't come through for you. What brought you back to some special time of praise and thanksgiving, even though you saw no specific improvement in your circumstances?

2 Corinthians 4:17. The real treasure we hold is not to be measured in a checkbook balance, CDs, stocks and bonds, or real estate holdings. The real treasure is the diamond of grace we carry within the frail bodies that are ours. Write a paragraph describing how you would make this treasure real to those who, as Paul says, still live without inwardness—without the Spirit (1 Cor. 2:14). (Calvin Miller)

NOVEMBER 3, 1996

৯৯

Twenty-third Sunday After Pentecost

Worship Theme: Jesus Christ calls us to genuine discipleship.

Readings: Joshua 3:7-17; 1 Thessalonians 2:9-13; Matthew 23:1-12

Call to Worship (Psalm 107:1-2):

Leader: O give thanks to the LORD, for he is good;

***People:* for his steadfast love endures forever.**

Leader: Let the redeemed of the LORD say so,

***People:* those he redeemed from trouble.**

Pastoral Prayer:

We thank you, O Lord, for your gracious blessing. We thank you for the gift of life and health, for family and friends, for work to do and the capacity to serve. Most of all, we thank you for the salvation you have made available through Jesus Christ, and for the presence of your Holy Spirit in our lives. Yet we know, Lord, that there are people all around us who lack the blessings we enjoy. To those who are hungry, make us generous givers; to those who are in pain, make us gentle encouragers; to those who lack knowledge, make us supportive teachers; to those who do not yet know the new life in Christ Jesus, make us faithful witnesses. Help us to be doers of the Word and not hearers only. Amen.

SERMON BRIEFS

LIVING THE COVENANT

JOSHUA 3:7-17

Moses is dead, and Joshua has been commissioned by the Lord. Israel is making plans to enter the land promised by Yahweh. Joshua sends spies to Jericho, and they find shelter from, of all people, Rahab, a prostitute of the city.

In any event, Israel makes provisions for battle to possess the land Yahweh has promised to generation after generation of Israelites. Israel is camped by the Jordan and awaits further instruction from Yahweh via the new leader Joshua.

I. The Importance of the Land

For us moderns, it is easy to overlook the anticipation that the Israelites were feeling. For generations, they had anticipated the fulfillment of promise the land represented. As early as Genesis 12:5, our Scripture tells us "Abram took his wife Sarai . . . and all the possessions that they had gathered . . . and they set forth to go to the land of Canaan." Isaac, Jacob, and Joseph also formed their identities around this land of promise.

For these ancestors, the land represented what the metaphor "heaven" represents for Christians. It was a destination where God could be celebrated in life's fullness. For hungry, nomadic people, the promise of "a land flowing with milk and honey" symbolized everything for which they had ever hoped.

The most disappointing words heard by Moses surely must have been the Lord saying, "This is the land of which I swore to Abraham, to Isaac, and to Jacob, saying, 'I will give it to your descendants'; I have let you see it with your eyes, but you shall not cross over there" (Deut. 34:4). Joshua and the people would inhabit what Moses had worked a lifetime to attain.

II. The Promise and the Assurance

Our text today helps us anticipate and participate vicariously with the Hebrew children of promise in the attainment of the dream. The Lord tells Joshua many things that will encourage the people: "I will

353

begin to exalt you . . . I will be with you as I was with Moses. You . . . shall command the priests [to] stand still in the Jordan" (vv. 7-8).

Joshua said, "By this you shall know that among you is the living God who without fail will drive out from before you" the enemies of the people of God (v. 10). And the ark of the Lord does pass before them into the Jordan. This scene reminds the biblically alert of another water crossing at the beginning of the wilderness wanderings. Now, like then, the Lord will be with them. The living God will act *without fail!*

III. The Promise to the New Israel

Pastors regularly have the privilege of standing with people at the church's altar as they make sacred marriage covenants. Anyone who has stood where pastors stand can see in people's eyes and by their actions how seriously they take the covenant they make "in the presence of God and these witnesses." Each time we, as members of the church, hear the story of Israel and their battles to remain faithful in the wilderness, we, too, are reminded of our own battles in our own wilderness. Though we must translate Israel's wilderness wanderings into our own cultural and social milieu, we know how difficult the battles with principalities and powers are.

But we also do well to remember that, through the testimony of Scripture, we have a God who wants more for us than we can ever imagine. This is divine assurance, and it comes to us on the cross of Jesus and in Christ's resurrection.

For those who have placed their faith in Jesus, these age-old words from Deuteronomy still ring true: "The LORD our God made a covenant with us at Horeb. Not with our ancestors did the LORD make this covenant, but with us, who are all of us here alive today" (Deut. 5:2-3). Thanks be to God. Amen. (David Neil Mosser)

MARKS OF MINISTRY

1 THESSALONIANS 2:9-13

Paul explained how the gospel came to Thessalonica (vv. 1-2); now he narrates how he ministered to the Thessalonian believers, thereby exemplifying significant marks of ministry. Christians who effectively serve Christ in ministry will be identified by these marks. These characteristics suggest how a ministry can develop and be maintained and how people can be influenced for Christ's sake.

I. Diligent Industry (v. 9)

According to rabbinic tradition, in order for a rabbi to teach, he had to have a job. Paul worked as a tentmaker to support himself so he would not be a financial burden to the Thessalonian congregation. In his second letter to the Thessalonian believers, he harshly criticized those who stopped working and focused completely on the day of the Lord's coming. His judgment was that if Christians did not work, they were not to be supported and fed by the hardworking members of their congregation (2 Thess. 3:10).

Paul could have claimed his rights as an apostle and required the Thessalonian church to financially support him (1 Thess. 2:7); instead, he sacrificially labored with his hands so that he could minister to the church in freedom. Ministers should use the gospel for their rightful needs and benefits. They should also be used by the Lord and the gospel in order to benefit the church and the world.

II. Exemplary Conduct (vv. 10, 12)

The old cliché, "Do as I say and not as I do," does not work in parenting or in ministry. Paul's ministry among the Thessalonian believers is backed up by a holy lifestyle. Both the work and the worker are holy. Paul calls these believers to the court of human justice to assess his behavior while he served them. He even appeals to the highest court in the universe, the supreme court of heaven, and requests the Almighty God to testify on his behalf.

He is confident there will be a consensus that he has lived an exemplary Christian life among these believers. As a result of his credibility, he challenges the Thessalonian believers to imitate him and to live lives worthy of God, who called them into his kingdom (v. 12).

III. Fatherly Firmness (v. 11)

Paul said to the Thessalonians, "You have become very dear to us" (v. 8). The Greek word for "dear" or "beloved" is *agapetoi,* which represents the unconditional love of God. One characteristic of God's love is recognized in the feminine trait of a mother nursing or breast-feeding her children (v. 7). This is love in the mode of nurturing. Another characteristic of God's love is discerned in the masculine trait of a father advising and admonishing his children (v. 11). This is love in the form of instruction.

There is a caring spirit in the apostle Paul. This warm-spirited demeanor is especially seen in Paul through the windows of the images of a nurturing mother and an advising father. As a father, Paul involves himself with these believers and helps them move toward maturity in Christ. As a father, Paul watches over his Thessalonian family and makes sacrifices for their welfare.

Christians must imitate the posture of Paul through his threefold ministry as a father (v. 11 KJV): (1) "exhort" or give godly instruction to fellow believers who are seeking counsel; (2) "comfort" or console fellow Christians who are hurting from life's disasters; and (3) "charge" or urge fellow saints to become all they can be in Christ.

IV. Incessant Gratitude (v. 13)

These verses are an expansion of the condensed thought of 1 Thessalonians 1:2-3. Paul and his companions are holding a service of thanksgiving as they reflect on their growing ministry to these believers: "We also constantly give thanks to God for this." They thanked God for the manner in which the Thessalonians received the proclaimed word. The word "received" appears twice in verse 13 (KJV). The Thessalonians doubly received the word. In the Greek text, there are two different words for "received." The first denotes a taking of the word; the second indicates a welcoming of the word. It is possible to appropriate the word and fail to appreciate the word.

Christians embrace biblical principles that will afford them blessings; and yet they may not appreciate God's Word for its essence—for what it is. Christians must learn to appropriate what comes out of God's hand as well as to appreciate God's hand for mere fellowship. In this way God will not simply be endured; God will be enjoyed.

Jesus discussed the badge of discipleship: "By this shall all men know that ye are my disciples, if ye have love one to another" (John 13:35 KJV). Paul wears this badge of discipleship as he ministers to the Thessalonians. The marks of ministry are seen through the Pauline lens of diligent industry, exemplary conduct, fatherly firmness, and incessant gratitude. Are these characteristics of your ministry? (Robert Smith, Jr.)

LIVING OUT OF CHARACTER

MATTHEW 23:1-12

My son John, a college student with a theater minor, had a part in Steinbeck's *Of Mice and Men*. His friends attended a performance and had trouble controlling their laughter each time John spoke. Afterward they told him, "That was so much out of character for you. You are rarely serious." Some of the most effective stage presentations come from actors who share the experience of the character they portray.

The word *hypocrite* transliterates a Greek word for playacting. Greek and Roman actors spoke in a large mask with mechanical devices for augmenting the force of the voice. The actor was a hypocrite—one who played the part. Jesus leveled his strongest judgment against spiritual hypocrites—God's people living out of character. Because hypocrisy takes so many casualties in the Kingdom, Jesus issues this strong warning.

Max Lucado calls this "the crackdown of Christ on midway religion."

I. Playing the Part

The irreligious have no problem living out of character. Jesus described individuals who "sit on Moses' seat" and handle the Word of God: "They do not practice what they teach" (vv. 2-3).

The Bible outsells all other books each year. One survey of customers at secular bookstores noted the Bible influenced them more than any other book. Yet the gap widens between reverence for the Bible and life governed by its principles.

Is your religion for show or for real? Do you serve God to be seen by others? I still remember from my youth a businessman who left our church for one that needed him much less, but "it was better for business."

Playing the part may get you the best seat in the house or have you on center stage, but "all who exalt themselves will be humbled" (v. 12).

II. Living the Life

Jesus calls us to live the life of genuine discipleship instead of playing the part. "But you . . ." (vv. 8-12) contrasts with the hypocritical character pictured in verses 2-7.

Anthony Munoz, Cincinnati Bengals defensive lineman and three-time NFL offensive player of the year, rejected an interview and feature story for *Playboy* magazine. "It was a decision between me and the Lord. When you get into what the Bible says you find out what God wants you to do," he said.

"You have one teacher, the Christ" (vv. 8, 10), and his life and word provide the standard for living the life.

"You are all brethren," Jesus says, reminding us of the "fellowship of kindred minds." Hypocrites look out for themselves. Christians care for each other, admonish each other, and learn from each other.

Jesus calls us to servanthood: "The greatest among you will be your servant" (v. 11). Robert E. Lee exemplified the servant who denied self for the sake of others. On what was probably his last trip to northern Virginia, a young mother brought her baby to Lee to be blessed. With the infant in his arms he slowly said, "Teach him he must deny himself."

If we just play the part, everything ends when the curtain falls. When we live the life of Christ, the action continues. (Bill Whittaker)

NOVEMBER 10, 1996

❧

Twenty-fourth Sunday After Pentecost

Worship Theme: Faith requires a choice.

Readings: Joshua 24:1-3a, 14-25; 1 Thessalonians 4:13-18; Matthew 25:1-13

Call to Worship (Psalm 78:1-4):

Leader: Give ear, O my people, to my teaching;

People: **incline your ears to the words of my mouth.**

Leader: I will open my mouth in a parable; I will utter dark sayings from of old,

People: **things that we have heard and known, that our ancestors have told us.**

Leader: We will not hide them from their children; we will tell to the coming generation

People: **the glorious deeds of the LORD, and his might, and the wonders that he has done.**

Pastoral Prayer:

Eternal God, maker of heaven and earth, sustainer of life and conqueror of death, we praise you with all that is in us. We thank you for your wonderful provision for us, far beyond all that we deserve or even comprehend. We thank you for your power, displayed in the wonders of nature and in the smile of a tiny child. We thank you for your love, demonstrated most clearly on the cross of Jesus, who gave himself for our redemption. We thank you also, Lord, for your gift of faith, which enables us to know your grace in our own lives. Help us, Lord, in all our words and actions to honor your name. Help us to respond to you in faith, even as you have shown your love to us in Christ, in whose name we pray. Amen.

SERMON BRIEFS

CHOOSING FAITH

JOSHUA 24:1-3*a*, 14-25

If the truth be told, all life involves choice. M. Scott Peck's best-selling book is titled *The Road Less Traveled*. We know too well why it is less traveled. The choices and discipline are too severe for most folks; therefore, there are few on the road.

Our text from Joshua is the story of covenant renewal at Shechem. It involves the opportunity and celebration of choice. We might even say that every act of covenant is both a choice and a celebration.

I. The Choice of Faith Must Be Made Again and Again

Joshua gathers the people, reminding them about who they are: "Long ago your ancestors—Terah and his sons Abraham and Na-hor—lived beyond the Euphrates and served other gods" (v. 2).

These Hebrew people have made a previous choice for Yahweh. Now it is time to renew their pledge of faith and allegiance to this God who was able to do many things for them. Joshua then recounts part of the story of salvation.

II. Faith Must Be Acted on Again and Again

As Joshua finishes recounting Yahweh's gracious dealings with Israel, he puts the choice, or *re-choice,* to Israel: "Now therefore revere the LORD, and serve him in sincerity and in faithfulness; put away the gods that your ancestors served beyond the River and in Egypt, and serve the LORD" (v. 14).

This choice is one that we still make today, just as Joshua asked his people to make long ago. Do we worship our professed God? Or are we idolaters who worship whatever "divinity" of the moment strikes our fancy?

III. Faith Requires Taking a Stand

Joshua, as good leaders often do, lets the people know exactly where he stands, saying, "But as for me and my household, we will serve the LORD" (v. 15). Joshua's decision influences beyond himself. He makes the profession for himself and also for "my household."

Our important decisions—especially our professions of faith—go beyond our individuality; they affect our families and others. This turns the modern "what's in it for me" question slightly askew when we realize that those we love are affected by the ultimate, and even the smallest, decisions and professions we make.

The last part of the text (vv. 19-24) is a dialogue between Joshua, speaking as a prophet of the Lord, and the people, represented by one voice saying, "Far be it from us that we should forsake the LORD to serve other gods" (v. 16).

Joshua wants them to realize the gravity of their decisions. A decision for covenant relationship with Yahweh means, to Joshua's way of thinking, there is no going back. This image—going back to Egypt—is a powerful one, symbolizing that there is always a tension between the promise of Yahweh for a future and the safety of a past that was familiar—though often painful.

Faith decisions are just that—decisions of faith. And this bothers those of us with modern sensibilities because we want our understanding of God and the world to be infallible. Faith, however, is never a guarantee of anything except a relationship with God. But for the one whose life has been transformed by such faith, that is more than enough. (David Neil Mosser)

AFTER DEATH, WHAT?

1 THESSALONIANS 4:13-18

In a letter to his wife opened after his death, Samuel Shoemaker, rector of the Calvary Episcopal Church, Pittsburgh, Pennsylvania, wrote the following credo:

> As I sit in the study . . . I look back with many thanks. It has been a great run. I wouldn't have missed it for anything. Much could and should have been better, and I have by no means, done what I should have done with all that I have been given. But the over-all experience of being alive has been a thrilling experience. I believe that death is a doorway to more of it: clearer, cleaner, better, with more of the secret opened than locked. I do not feel much confidence in myself as regards all this, for very few have ever "deserved" eternal life. But with Christ's atonement and him gone on before, I have neither doubt nor fear. . . . I believe that I shall see him and know him, and that eternity will be an endless opportunity to consort with the great souls

and the lesser ones who will have entered into the freedom of the heavenly city. (*Faith at Work,* January-February, 1964)

Two months after writing this letter, Shoemaker died (October 31, 1963).

How will it all end? What will occur after death? The former question cannot be answered until one has faced up to the end of life. The latter question is addressed by Paul in 1 Thessalonians 4:13-18. Paul contends that the end of it all is not death. The end of it all is God's triumphant return through Christ, which will signal the beginning of the beginning.

I. Death in Christ Brings Restoration (vv. 13-17)

Paul's fundamental thesis of his theology is the Resurrection—not the Crucifixion. Without the Resurrection every sacrificial work performed in Christ's name would be in vain. The Thessalonian church did not know how to handle the matter of Christ's return in light of believers who died before his return. The Thessalonian believers expected the Lord to return within their lifetimes. They grieved over fellow saints and saved loved ones who died before the day of the Lord. The question on their minds was whether the believers who died prior to the Parousia would be left behind at the return of Christ. Paul corrects their erroneous thought, relieves their anxiety and assures them that those who had been saved and died before the day of the Lord would also share in the glory of eternal life.

"Sleep in Jesus" (v. 14 KJV) literally means "to put to sleep through Jesus." The Greek word we translate as "cemetery" means "a sleeping place." It is the place where bodies sleep, awaiting the resurrection. Death separates loved ones. When Christ returns, there will be a reunion. The living saints will not precede the resurrection of the dead saints; but all saints will come together to meet Christ.

The dead saints will receive a wake-up call, the living saints will receive a "formation notice," and all saints, both living and dead, will receive new bodies (Phil. 3:20-21; 1 John 3:1-3). The saints will be snatched away speedily and moved to a new place of rest and repose.

II. Death in Christ Brings Consolation (v. 18)

Christians are expected to be sorrowful when loved ones die. However, their grief is not a hopeless grief. Their grief is *good* grief. They go through the normal stages of grief, walk through the valley of loneliness, and shed tears of sorrow for their saved brothers and sisters—but not without hope. Their hope is built on nothing less than Jesus' blood and righteousness. The dead in Christ shall rise!

No Christian knows how life will end. We don't know about tomorrow. We know who holds tomorrow, and we know God holds our hands. God's tomorrow will be better than our today. (Robert Smith, Jr.)

READY OR NOT, HE'S COMING!

MATTHEW 25:1-13

Our family moved from the United States to the Philippines for a mission assignment. Part of the culture shock was adjusting to the Asian sense of time. The event was more important than the announced time for it to occur. Consequently we spent a good amount of time waiting. We would arrive before the time of a wedding, but it was not unusual for it to start an hour or more later. You feel that some Eastern sense of time in the wedding Jesus described in Matthew 25.

The bridesmaids waited and waited and waited some more for the arrival of the groom. All ten knew he was coming, and all of them dozed off with apparent confidence. With the announcement of the groom's coming, five bridesmaids discovered they had no oil for the lamps. They could not walk in the street processional from the bride's house to the home of the bridegroom. "While they went to buy it, the bridegroom came, and those who were ready went with him into the wedding banquet; and the door was shut" (v. 10). Ready or not, Jesus is coming!

I. Be Ready at Any Time

"Watch therefore, for you know neither the day nor the hour in which the Son of Man is coming" (v. 12 NKJV). Twenty-three New Testament books speak of Christ's return. The Scripture emphasizes the certainty of his coming at any time. Speculators abound. Full-page ads in *USA Today* announced his imminent return. Thousands of pastors received a booklet citing eighty-eight reasons why Jesus would return on Halloween night a few years ago. He didn't. But he is coming. Be ready!

II. Now Is the Time to Get Ready

Five of the bridesmaids made a wise decision. They prepared before the bridegroom arrived. "Those who were ready went with him into the wedding banquet." When the bell rings for the fight to begin, it is too late for the boxer to find his gloves. When the expectant mother tells her husband, "It's time," he better be ready.

All ten maidens looked alike in outward appearance. Each of them had the opportunity to be in the wedding. All of them knew the place and the people involved. When the crucial moment arrived, only five were ready. The foolish ones could have been prepared but were not. Time ran out, "and the door was shut."

A sixty-five-year-old construction worker responded to an evangelistic appeal at the close of worship and submitted his life to Christ. I later discovered he had often attended church with Robert Schuller at the Crystal Cathedral. Many opportunities to trust Christ were lost. An accident brought him near death. Emotionally, he approached the time when "the door was shut." He told me, "Life can be snuffed out in a moment. We all need to be ready."

III. All Things Are Ready, Are You?

The radiant bride became excited with the approaching arrival of the groom. Everything was ready while five bridesmaids scattered to find oil. They returned to find the door shut and heard the sad word, "I do not know you" (v. 12).

People are not ready for the Kingdom unless they know the Lord. "Everyone who believes in him may not perish but may have eternal life" (John 3:16). Jesus is the way into the kingdom of heaven. Are you ready to go?

Lee Atwater managed the successful 1988 campaign for George Bush. Two years later Atwater collapsed during a speech. Physicians located a brain tumor, and when it spread to the other side of his brain, "the master of political hardball sat there and cried. Now, he realized, was a time for coming to terms with the less virtuous acts of my life" (Associated Press, November 14, 1993). We may go before Christ comes. Be ready for either eventuality. (Bill Whittaker)

NOVEMBER 17, 1996

۞

Twenty-fifth Sunday After Pentecost

Worship Theme: God has given us talents and abilities to use in his service.

Readings: Judges 4:1-7; 1 Thessalonians 5:1-11; Matthew 25:14-30

Call to Worship (Psalm 123:1-2):

> *Leader:* To you I lift up my eyes, O you who are enthroned in the heavens!
>
> **People: As the eyes of the servants look to the hand of their master,**
>
> *Leader:* as the eyes of a maid to the hand of her mistress,
>
> **People: so our eyes look to the LORD our God, until he has mercy upon us.**

Pastoral Prayer:

Redeemer God, we pray this day for all who are lost, all who are forlorn and friendless. In a world that puts so much emphasis on love and intimacy, all around us are people starving for love, for friendship, for a caring person. Help us to be more loving—to use the gifts you have given us to serve those in need. We hold up before you the down-and-out persons of this world—from the starving masses in Africa and Asia to the deserted mother in a North American city; from the unemployed and underemployed to the person with severe physical and emotional disabilities. We pray for those caught up in the terrible web of alcohol, drugs, or meaningless living. Help all of these persons in your special way to find hope and joy in spite of their circumstances. We especially pray for missionary efforts around the world. May we all be drawn to a better understanding of the commitment we must have as disciples and churches to "go and make disciples of all nations." Help us to share the good news with all the world. Amen. (Steven R. Fleming)

SERMON BRIEFS

A CRY FOR HELP

JUDGES 4:1-7

Two young men were walking along discussing life and its problems. One man said, "Some folks say that the events of life are completely random and there is no purpose to life in the universe."

The other replied, "I don't believe that at all. There's too much evidence of a higher will working in my life. I mean, look at my social life, my schoolwork, my family life. *Somebody* is out to get me!"

We know how that young man felt. We've all been there. From time to time it seems like everything falls apart and the whole world is out to get us. We feel like the country song that says, "Every time I make my mark, someone paints the wall." In the midst of those situations or days like that, we have an answer. When we cry out to God, God answers.

I. Sometimes We Are Unwilling to Call on God

Some people never learn. The Israelites, at least in this situation, just didn't seem to learn. Scripture tells us the Israelites brought their disaster on themselves. They had sinned in the eyes of God, and their sin caught up with them. That's the case with all sin. The effects of sin always catch up with us.

A little boy with a paper sack over his head prayed, "Lord, I'll tell you what I did today, but I won't tell you who I am."

We are like that little boy. We would gladly confess what we have done or what we didn't do if we didn't have to let God know who it was. The Israelites were the same. It just took them twenty years to realize it. It took twenty years for them to call out to God.

Like the Israelites, we look up one day and wonder how we got into this predicament. We feel like God has sold us out or abandoned us. We wonder how we got into the mess we are in. What do we do in those situations?

The answer is really second nature. Most of us do it without even thinking. There is a scene in the children's classic *Winnie-the-Pooh* where Pooh sees Eeyore floating down the river. The conversation between the two goes something like this:

Pooh:"Did you fall into the river, Eeyore?"

Eeyore:"Silly of me, wasn't it?"

Pooh:"Is the river uncomfortable this morning?"

Eeyore:"Well yes, the dampness you know."

Pooh:"You really ought to be more careful!"

Eeyore:"Thanks for the advice."

Pooh:"I think you're sinking."

Eeyore:"Pooh, if it's not too much trouble, would you mind rescuing me?"

The best thing we can do in all situations is pray, but especially when our sinful nature catches up with us. When our sin catches up with us, we should call on God to rescue us.

II. When We Call, God Answers

The Israelites finally called on God for help, and God responded. God's answer to the Israelites was to send the judge, Deborah. God's answer for today is not a judge but God's own Son.

Jesus may not pull us out of all situations in the way we might wish, but he does promise to be with us and guide us through them all. Just as he promised the disciples, "I am with you always" (Matt. 28:20), he promises us, too. We can be assured that God will hear and answer our prayers, just as God heard the prayers of Israel and sent Deborah. (Billy D. Strayhorn)

HURRY UP AND WAIT

1 THESSALONIANS 5:1-11

"Hurry up and wait." We understand that phrase well. We push ourselves at breakneck speeds only to discover that we have rushed for no reason, for we must still wait. For example, more often than not we make a mad dash to the doctor's office, making sure we arrive precisely on time, only to discover that we must wait an extra hour to see the doctor.

I'll never forget an experience of running from one end of the Atlanta airport to the other to catch a place. The doors were just closing as I arrived. I rushed to my seat only to hear the pilot say, "I'm sorry, there has been a delay. We will not depart for another hour."

We are often caught in the paradox of excitement coupled with the call for patience. Even the gospel makes such a demand of us. In today's text, Paul is reminding his audience of the certainty of Christ's return. It will come "like a thief in the night" (v. 2). As Luke 12:39-40 states, "It will come at an hour you do not expect."

When it comes, there is no time for decision, no time for preparation. Paul compares the Parousia to a woman in labor. When it's time, there is no stopping the process. As Christians who live with the promise of that day, we must live expectantly and wait patiently.

I. We Must Live Expectantly (vv. 4-10)

Paul refers to the times in the history of Israel when the people engaged in the pursuits of peace with no suspicion of danger. Yet their peace was shattered as devastation overtook them. The people of Noah's day and the inhabitants of Sodom are just two examples. People who remain unprepared morally and spiritually will be judged in the day of Christ's return.

In contrast, the "children of light" are to live in an attitude of great expectation. Christians not only expect it to happen; we want it to happen. We embrace the day; we do not shun it. It will be a day of joy, of peace, of victory. It will mark the completion of the walk of faith. Paul reminds his audience that all the saints of the Lord, those who are alive and those who are dead, will be caught up in the wonder and splendor of that day (v. 10). We live with the expectation of what that day will bring.

II. We Must Wait Patiently (v. 11)

As we wait for that day, we must do so with patience. Patience is not a call to idleness or to waste away the hours; it is a call to occupy ourselves with God's work, diligently and carefully, until he comes.

A deacon once told me (in reference to the Lord's return), "Let us be prayed up and paid up!" Translation: Let us live our lives ready to receive him at any moment, while serving him with every moment.

In my home I have a small rechargeable flashlight. It plugs into an electrical outlet, waiting for use. I sometimes forget that I even own it until I need it. It is always ready to serve; it stays charged up.

Paul asks that Christians, as we wait, engage in two activities. We are to encourage each other and build up each other. The call to encourage is the call to comfort and affirm each other. The instruction to build up is the call to push each other toward spiritual maturity. As Christians, we are to use our time waiting in a productive way as we help others prepare for the coming of our Lord and share with them the excitement of that day.

Christ is coming again. We pray that he will hurry, and we labor as we wait. (John R. Roebuck)

DON'T BURY YOUR TALENT

MATTHEW 25:14-30

The text contains a parable of warning and promise. It is a reminder that the use of our talents demonstrates our faithfulness to God. The Father distributes gifts and opportunities for service to his followers as the basis for us to use and improve throughout our lives.

When the discussion in a small group turned to evangelism, one person gave a big sigh of relief and stated, "Well, that's just not my gift." With that statement he buried his God-given talent to share Christ's love with his world. How many of us have buried the gifts God offers us in search of that "special" gift?

Myron Augsburger calls this parable one of "responsibility" and "risk." We need some risk takers for Jesus who offer themselves to him and allow him to help them. Don't bury your talent!

I. Don't Bury Your Talent: It Is from God

Our gifts, abilities, or talents are distributed by God. Talents may be simple or complex, visible or behind the scenes. They take a variety of forms including speaking, playing a tuba solo, making pies, teaching, singing, healing, offering hospitality, counseling, administering and others, but they must be done in the spirit of humility and love.

II. Don't Bury Your Talent: It Is to Be Used

The Master gives the talents; the servants use the talents. Wade Burton in *Amusing Grace* tells about a salesman who appeared to be a born loser. The man was a lousy dresser, could not spell, and used atrocious grammar. However, he was a terrific salesman for an appliance maker. The overall company sales were down, and the chairman of the board posted the following message: "Attention all sales personnel: We will have an important meeting March 1 at 10:00 a.m. and the subject will be 'How to sell our product.' Be there!" When the salesman received his telegram announcing the meeting, he responded to the chairman with a note. It read, "I ain't got time to come to no meetin'. I just sold 2,000 appliances to customer #13 and I gotta get goin' to ketch #14, where I 'spect to sale at least 4,000 more. . . ." A short time later a second memorandum was sent to all sales people: "Forgit the meetin' called fer March 1. Get out there and ketch all the customers you can and 'spect to make big sales! (The Boss)."

What God expects of us is that we quit talking, speculating, and thinking about the talents he has given to us and do something with them! It may be risky, and occasionally, we may feel foolish as we seek to develop our talents; but God will bless and bring new opportunities of service.

Don't bury your opportunities!

III. Don't Bury Your Talents: It Is Eternal

This parable reveals the eternal consequences of our decision to bury or not to bury our talents.

William McCumber observes that the faithfulness reward is twofold. First, there is an increase in responsibility. Second, there is joy.

Joy comes through satisfaction that a good deed has been accomplished for Jesus and others. It is not an ecstatic, wild-eyed, spontaneous expression; rather, it is a deep settled peace in the heart.

The darker side of the picture is the punishment reserved for the wicked. McCumber reminds us that wickedness is not merely a matter of gross misconduct. It is also a matter of indolence in the face of the Kingdom—service opportunities. "Hell," says McCumber, "is also for those who do nothing!" Unfaithfulness results in a lack of joy, loss of opportunities for Kingdom building, and horror beyond understanding.

Don't bury your talent. Invest your talent for eternity! (Derl G. Keefer)

NOVEMBER 24, 1996

ॐ

Christel the King

Worship Theme: God calls us to love a hurting world in Christ's name.

Readings: Ezekiel 34:11-16, 20-24; Ephesians 1:15-23; Matthew 25:31-46

Call to Worship (Psalm 100):

Leader: Make a joyful noise to the LORD, all the earth.

People: Worship the LORD with gladness; come into his presence with singing.

Leader: Know that the LORD is God. It is he that made us, and we are his;

People: we are his people, and the sheep of his pasture.

Leader: Enter his gates with thanksgiving, and his courts with praise.

People: Give thanks to him, bless his name.

Leader: For the LORD is good; his steadfast love endures forever,

People: and his faithfulness to all generations.

Pastoral Prayer:

O God our Father, who has taught us to make all requests with thanksgiving, help us to remember with gratitude all the love and mercy of the past week. We are grateful for this special season of the year and particularly for this day; may it be a day of rest and gladness, a day of prayer and peace. May every evil thought be arrested, every faithless fear stilled, and give to all who worship this day a sense of your living presence. We thank you, Lord, for every good gift, for the loving care with which you have watched over us all our days. We thank you for all who have helped us by their example, their words, and their prayers, and for all who have been kind to us in our times of joy and sorrow. Above all, we thank you for your greatest gift, your Son Jesus Christ, who though he was rich became poor for our sakes; who humbled himself that we might be exalted; who was wounded for our transgressions and even now makes intercession for us. Open our eyes that we behold the wondrous things you are doing among us, and open our lips that we may show forth your glory, for the sake of Jesus Christ our Lord. Amen. (John Bishop)

SERMON BRIEFS

THE SEARCH IS ON

EZEKIEL 34:11-16, 20-24

A pastor overheard a little girl ask her mother, "Mommy, does God believe in us?"

The more I've thought about it, the more serious that question has become. *Does* God believe in us? God created us. God sustains us. But does God believe in us?

God believes in us and wants to help us find our way to him.

I. We Must Admit We Are Lost Before We Can Be Found

The Texas educational bureaucracy recently received and approved a new set of textbooks. A group of concerned parents conducted their own review. They found 231 errors, including the following: Napoleon winning the battle of Waterloo, President Truman dropping the atom bomb on Korea, and General Douglas MacArthur leading the anti-Communist campaign in the 1950s (it was actually Senator Joe McCarthy). When called to account for these errors, the bureaucrats studied the texts again and found more errors than the parents first found. Then the parents found more. Now the tally stands at 5,200 mistakes.

How did the publishers react to this mess? One publisher's spokesperson argued that "except for the errors," everyone agreed that these were the finest textbooks they had ever seen. "Except for the errors"?

"Except for the error," that teenage girl wouldn't be pregnant and contemplating an abortion. "Except for the error," that man's wife wouldn't be leaving him because he had an affair. "Except for the error," the young man and that young women wouldn't have AIDS.

"Except for the errors." Except for his drinking problem, he is a pretty good guy. Except for her drug problem, she is a pretty good mother. Except for his sticky fingers, he was a pretty good banker. Except for her gossiping, she is a pretty good friend.

Who are we kidding, except ourselves? We make excuses. We let ourselves off the hook. And when we do, we become lost.

II. God Seeks and Saves the Lost: Even Us

The good news is that the search is on. Like a shepherd, God seeks us. Sometimes we run. Sometimes we hide, but God always seeks us. For we are lost and the lost must be found.

Sitting on a table near the sanctuary was the Lost and Found box. It was just a cardboard box with "Lost and Found" written in bold letters. But in the box was a little girl's doll. The doll looked as if she was resting comfortably, waiting for her little girl to claim her. Her arms were extended, and it looked as if she were saying, "Please come get me. I'm lost and I need to be found. Please hunt for me and take me home."

That's a parable for today. Sometimes we think that God has forgotten us or left us sitting on the pew in church when, in reality, we have lost our way. The good news is that Christ searches for us.

III. Only Christ Can Bring Us Home

We don't have to go in search of our salvation. God came to us in Christ. God loves us so much that Christ sought us out. And if we will but stretch out our arms to God through Christ, then we will become the lost who have been found. God will rescue us. And once we are found, God will lead us to good pastures. God promises to be our shepherd.

Does God believe in us? Of course God believes in us. God believes in us so much that he sent his only Son to die on the cross for our sake and to be the Good Shepherd. (Billy D. Strayhorn)

NOT YET FINISHED

EPHESIANS 1:15-23

Most of us tend to shy away from religious bumper stickers. They are usually long on tackiness and short on theology. There is one, however, that has proven to have lasting appeal. No doubt you have seen it many times. It reads, "Be patient with me. God isn't finished with me yet." That attitude is reflected in the words of Paul to the Christians at Ephesus.

Paul writes with thankfulness in his heart. He has learned the lesson of thankful praying. He knows of the joy of praising God for God's marvelous grace. He begins this text by offering praise for the church at Ephesus. They have demonstrated their "faith in the Lord Jesus and their love toward all the saints" (v. 15). He continues to offer prayers of thanksgiving to God for their good work. Paul then points to the future, knowing that there is more to be done, more growth to come, and more grace that will be needed.

In the verses that follow, Paul shares with his readers a glimpse of his prayer list. Knowing that "God is not finished with them yet," he prays that they will have the wisdom to know God better, and that their eyes will be opened in appreciation of God's grace.

I. The Wisdom to Know God Better (v. 17)

It is Paul's desire that the Christians of the Ephesian church progress to maturity. Reflecting the attitude of James who writes, "If any of you is lacking in wisdom, ask God, who gives to all generously and ungrudgingly" (1:5), Paul prays that these Christians might have more wisdom so that they will develop a deeper relationship with God. Paul wants them to grow up. Growth is the result of the right environment, diet, and exercise. Spiritual growth occurs as believers place themselves in an environment of wisdom, created by the Spirit of God.

Each generation of believers should challenge all the notions concerning the identity of God. Christians should be involved in a self-discovery of God: asking new questions, discovering new ways of seeing and relating to God. Our knowledge of God must increase. We, too, must seek the wisdom to know God better.

II. Eyes Opened in Appreciation (vv. 18-19)

With apologies to Robert Fulghum, I did not learn everything I need to know in kindergarten. I learned some lessons much earlier. One lesson that I was taught at a very early age was the lesson of thanksgiving. I was taught to say "thank you" when people did nice things for me. In turn, my wife and I are trying to instill that lesson in our children.

Paul desired that the Ephesians appreciate God's continual grace in their lives. Paul had offered his prayers of thanksgiving, and now he prays that these Christians will also have their eyes opened in appreciation.

Many of our day-to-day blessings go unappreciated. We do not remember to be thankful for some things until we no longer have them. Spend a warm week without air-conditioning in your car. Try living without a telephone. Imagine living without running water in your home. It is easy to neglect our thankfulness for simple blessings that are ours to enjoy each day.

The blessings of God in our lives are so constant and boundless that we almost forget to acknowledge them. Paul prays that the Ephesians will have an awareness of God's grace displayed in three ways. Paul challenges them to appreciate the *hope* that is in Christ Jesus, the *glorious riches* of salvation, and the *power* made possible by a "Spirit-filled" life. By having their eyes opened in appreciation of these things, all uncertainty of the future is dispelled, and daily struggles with temptation and anxiety are defeated.

God is not finished with us yet. Let us pray for the wisdom to know God better as we appreciate divine grace in our lives. (Jon R. Roebuck)

EXTENDING LOVE

MATTHEW 25:31-46

In this text, Jesus delivers a message on the topic of judgment. He states that the people who extend a heart of love to a hurting world will receive a righteous assessment. God's judgment is in accordance with our reaction to humanity's need. God's estimation of us depends not on how scholarly or famous we become but on the help we choose to give others.

Missionary Albert Schweitzer, known for his life of sacrificial service, appeared on a late night talk show. The talk show host told him, "I'd like to be an Albert Schweitzer if I could commute."

Many want the fame without the work of love. As we love, we give back to the world God's holy love and compassion.

I. Extending Love Means Going Back to the Basics

I enjoy a good game of racquetball. The exercise and competition make my heart pump rapidly with excitement. Often I find myself beginning to trail my opponent so I have to analyze the reason. Usually, it happens because I have not focused on the basic principles of racquetball. I must then begin a routine of talking to myself with these words, "Center the ball and patience." I repeat them often to draw myself back into the basic game plan and intensity.

Too often the Christian becomes distracted from the basic game plan of God. The game plan of God's priorities as Jesus outlines them includes caring for the needy by giving the basics of food to the hungry, water to the thirsty, and clothing to the poor.

The Christian's game plan includes inspiring hope to the hopeless. Hal Lindsey said, "Man can live about forty days without food, about three days without water, about eight minutes without air . . . but only for one second without hope."

The basic game plan of hope brings us to looking for the good in people and not dwelling on their failures. It asks what can be done instead of grumbling about what cannot be accomplished. It views problems as challenges and opportunities. It moves ahead when it would be easier to stop. Extend that hope in love!

II. Extending Love Means It Comes from the Heart

William Barclay stated that those Jesus cites in the text did not even realize they were being helpful to the world around them. They helped because they could not stop themselves. Christ's love in the heart compelled them to compassionate action. It was the natural, instinctive, uncalculated reaction of a loving heart. It was honest generosity.

Francis Clark said, "To feel sorry for the needy is not the mark of a Christian—to help them is." Earl Allen pointed out, "The fragrance of what you give away stays with you."

If you claim to have a religious experience, it must be verified in the action of extending love. Who can you be generous to in the name of the Lord of love?

III. Extending Love Means It Goes to People and God

Myron Augsburger tells of taking his wife to Basel, Switzerland. While there they visited St. Martin's Church. Both of them were impressed by the sculpture on the front wall of the church depicting Martin of Tours, a Roman soldier converted to Christianity.

The inspiration for the sculpture originated from a story that occurred on a bitterly cold winter's day. Martin was entering a city and was approached by a beggar pleading for alms. Having no money, Martin removed his coat, cut it in two, and gave half to the beggar. That night he had a vision that he had died and gone to heaven. There he saw Jesus, and on the back of Christ was half of a Roman soldier's coat. An angel asked the King of heaven and earth, "Master, why are you wearing that battered old coat?" Jesus answered, "My servant Martin gave it to me."

We are called to action in our extension of love. Will you respond? (Derl G. Keefer)

DECEMBER

Preparing to Serve

The Symbol of the Star

Paraphrase Assignment:

Matthew 2:2*a*: "Where is the child who has been born king of the Jews? For we observed his star."

Prayer Assignment:

Make your prayer agenda throughout this Advent a prayer that you will celebrate the Incarnation. Write out a promise-prayer with which you will begin each day. The prayer should be a call to remembrance of how poor and dark the world was before Jesus came. Promise the Father that through both the secular hassle of shopping and the religious hassle of a church program gone mad, you will celebrate the meaning of the season. Perhaps this prayer could be one that you lead the whole church to pray and it could even be printed on every single Advent calendar, both the church altar cycle and, above all, the home altar dates. Let your prayer life address the need for keeping Christ central in your life and the life of the church.

Journal-in-Worship Assignment:

Write out three statements that will guide your remembrance of what the star means. Let each of these three prayers be celebrations of the prophecies of Numbers and Isaiah. You can celebrate in those passages Christmas past. Then move on to Matthew 2:9-10 and celebrate in that statement Christmas present. Finally, in the joy of what we shall become when the star symbol completes its utter reality in the rising of the morning, you can write a celebration of Christmas yet to come.

Numbers 24:17. Celebrate the first words of this wonderful passage with a paragraph of anticipation: "I see him, but not now!" This verse speaks of the expectancy of our face-to-face experience with Christ. "The star out of Jacob" was the same kind of anticipation that we all feel as we await the season of his coming again. Be sure that your journaling anticipates all the eagerness this verse expresses.

Isaiah 60:3. The Magi may have been the very first Gentiles to "come to the light" of Christ's shining. Because of the missionary dimensions of this expectant scripture, try to write on one piece of paper the greatest missionary hymn of your acquaintance along with the most celebrative and incarnational of the Christmas carols. Write an exultant synthesis of these two glorious ideas.

Matthew 2:9-10. The star symbol in the second chapter of Matthew is a powerful metaphor of how God is sent to guide all nations to himself. The Magi followed the light to a fuller understanding of God's self-revelation in Christ. Reach back into your past and draw from it a guiding light experience at the end of which was hidden a better understanding of King Jesus and his requirement of your personal adoration.

2 Peter 1:19. Advent is a time of celebrating our future hope. God has given us illumination enough for the present time, but he is waiting to give us the fullness of his face-to-face encounter. As you conclude this year's preaching and anticipate that time when the morning star arises, write what you believe should be the final benediction over your ministry as you are, at last, received into God's presence. Contrast your final movement from the dingy illumination of your current understanding to that glorious world where Christ says, "Come, you that are blessed by my Father, inherit the kingdom" (Matt. 25:34). (Calvin Miller)

DECEMBER 1, 1996

૨૨

First Sunday of Advent

Worship Theme: God has prepared us for effective Christian service.

Readings: Isaiah 64:1-9; 1 Corinthians 1:3-9; Mark 13:24-37

Call to Worship (Psalm 80:1*a*; 2*b*-3):

Leader: Give ear, O Shepherd of Israel, you who lead Joseph like a flock! . . .

People: **Stir up your might, and come to save us!**

Leader: Restore us, O God;

People: **let your face shine, that we may be saved.**

Pastoral Prayer:

We gather here, O God, as your little ones, people who do not deserve your grace or attention but have been overwhelmed by your unmerited favor. We are not a great church; much of what we do and are lies in the ceremony of this hour, in this building where our memories of the community are stored, in the rituals of recognition and fellowship that keep us alive from year to year. Some of us are tired. Some are afraid. Some are even skeptical. But we gather today in love and repentance to confess our sins and feel your forgiveness in our hearts as we enter this Advent season. Even as the people of God, we need to experience our brokenness before your wholeness, our finiteness before your unlimited power.

Come, Spirit of the living God, and fall fresh on us. Come, O Christ, whose very coming is judgment on those in whose midst you arrive, and chasten and prepare us for the Father's presence. Grant that every man and woman and child among us may begin this day a time of serious self-appraisal so that by Christmas we shall be appropriately humbled and ready to receive and acknowledge your lordship in every part of our lives, in every shred of our beings. Let the star that shone over Bethlehem when Christ was born shine once more in our troubled skies, and give hope to millions who dwell in darkness, doubt, and sin, for you are indeed a God of grace and kindness. We beseech you in the name of our Savior. Amen. (John Killinger)

SERMON BRIEFS

COME ON DOWN!

ISAIAH 64:1-9

Like the announcer on the popular television game show "The Price Is Right," Isaiah prays, "Hey, God, come on down!" Is that what we really want, for God to come down from heaven? Not likely. We want God safe in the heavens and away from everyday life until we really need him. But these prophets won't leave well enough alone. Isaiah had to pray this prayer:

> O that you would tear open the heavens and come down,
>   so that the mountains would quake at your presence—
> as when fire kindles brushwood and the fire causes water to boil—
> to make your name known to your adversaries, so that the nations
>   might tremble at your presence! (vv. 1-2)

I. We Want God to "Come On Down"

That's fine for the prophets but that's not really what we want. We want the safety of God in the Bette Midler song "At a Distance." We prefer God at a distance and not in our midst.

That's how we feel. But then that's what this passage is all about, isn't it? We are the people of this passage.

But deep in our hearts we really do want God to come on down so God will know what life is like. It might be frightening, but we still want to see the glory of God. And so with the prophet we call out, "Hey, God, come on down!"

II. God Has Already Come

God came down. That's what this season is all about: the day God came down to be one of us.

Gramps found his grandson jumping up and down in his playpen, crying at the top of his voice. When Johnnie saw Gramps, he reached out his chubby little hands and said, "Out, Gramps, out."

Gramps reached down to lift his grandson out of his predicament, but as he did, Johnnie's mom stepped up and said, "No, Johnnie, you are being punished. You have to stay in your playpen."

Gramps didn't know what to do. His grandson's tears reached deep into his heart. Mom's firmness couldn't be taken lightly. But love found a way. Gramps could not take his grandson out of the playpen; instead he climbed in with the little boy.

That is exactly what Jesus did for us at Christmas. Christ Jesus left heaven for earth and climbed in with us. God came down. The Word was made flesh. God in Christ moved in next door.

God did tear open the heavens, not in the mighty way we expected, but when the angelic chorus burst forth in song at the birth, all heaven broke loose. We said we didn't want it, but we were wrong.

God came down and walked as one of us. The world trembles in awe and wonder at the miracle of that birth. God came down and wasn't angry. God came down and, through an infant, said "I love you." (Billy D. Strayhorn)

PARTY FAVORS

1 CORINTHIANS 1:3-9

My son is rapidly turning into a socialite. As a first grader, he has reached the age of having his own *schedule.* No longer does his world revolve around the world of his parents; he now has his own world of ball games, school activities, and birthday parties. Last year, for example, he attended eleven birthday parties. Parties are always fun for him. He loves the invitation, and he loves the party favors that he brings home when the cake and ice cream are long gone. Party favors remind him of the joy of the party.

The salvific call of God is a call to a celebration. It is a call to an everlasting party thrown in honor of his Son. Paul states it this way: "God is faithful; by him you were called into the fellowship of his Son, Jesus Christ our Lord" (v. 9). As Paul offers words of introduction in his first letter to the Corinthian church, he reminds his readers of the party favors given to those who have responded to the invitation of fellowship. Blessings of God come to those who respond in faith to Christ Jesus. To the faithful, God enriches, God equips, and God sustains.

I. We Are Enriched by God (vv. 5-6)

The Corinthian church was spiritually rich. Paul writes of two ways in which God had blessed the church. The people were enriched in their speech and in their knowledge. These first-century Christians not only had an ability to proclaim the truth of God to others; they also had an understanding of that truth.

In Acts 8, Luke tells the story of an Ethiopian eunuch traveling from Jerusalem to Gaza. Philip, led by the Spirit of God, joins the chariot and talks with this man. The Ethiopian is reading from the book of Isaiah. Philip asks, "Do you understand what you are reading?" He responds, "How can I, unless someone guides me?" (vv. 30-31). He holds truth in his hands but has no understanding of its meaning.

Truth without knowledge can be worthless. For example, I can watch a green plant grow from a seed to a fruit-bearing plant. It happens constantly and consistently in this world of ours. Yet why or how it knows to grow is a complete mystery to me. I can proclaim the mystery of growth, yet not understand it.

God has enriched (gifted) each believer not only with the power of proclamation but also with a knowledge of his will and purpose. Every Christian can be used of God to proclaim the good news of God because every Christian has a personal knowledge of God. Because of God's enrichment, we proclaim what we know.

II. We Are Equipped by God (v. 7)

Paul offers a word of encouragement, reminding the Christians of Corinth that God has well equipped them for ministry. "You are not lacking in any spiritual gift," writes Paul. When individuals respond to Christ in faith, through the power of the Holy Spirit, they receive all the spiritual gifts needed to do the work of ministry assigned to them by God.

I'll always remember my first "real" summer job. I was sixteen, and for forty hours a week I bagged groceries and stocked shelves in a local supermarket. On the first morning of work, I received the tools of the trade: a white apron, a price stamper, a box cutter, and a lecture on how to bag groceries. I was equipped for success at my new job.

There is an old expression: "Where God guides, God provides." That's good theology. As we are called into the fellowship of Christ's kingdom, we are equipped by God to do ministry in the lives of others. We do not lack anything; we have all we need to love with compassion and witness with sincerity. God blesses us with divine gifts of grace. We are equipped.

III. We Are Sustained by God (v. 8)

The relationship with humankind, established by God through Christ Jesus, is always a permanent relationship. Through Christ, we belong to the forever family of God. We will never be abandoned or forsaken. We are kept strong until the end of our earthly lives when we will be made complete in Christ Jesus.

God sustains us in a number of ways. We are fed by his Word, encouraged by his Spirit, and forgiven through his Son. God's sustaining grace is constantly given to us so that we can enjoy continual fellowship in the Kingdom. Paul offered the same words of assurance to the church at Philippi: "I am confident of this, that the one who began a good work among you will bring it to completion by the day of Jesus Christ" (Phil. 1:6).

Party favors remind the partygoer of the joy of the party. As a constant reminder of the joy of knowing Jesus, God enriches our lives, equips us for ministry, and sustains us by his infinite grace. (John R. Roebuck)

THE TRUTH ABOUT THE END

MARK 13:24-37

Everything has a genesis—a beginning, a starting point. But just as everything has a beginning, it also has an ending. Life began somewhere in the murky past. We know little of its history except for the broad strokes that the Bible paints for us. Scientists of various disciplines attempt to fill in the finer lines, but still it seems out of focus. The one thought we know is that "in the beginning God created the heavens and the earth" (Gen. 1:1 NKJV).

One day the world will have to deal with *the end.* Our text deals specifically with the truth concerning the end. What is that truth as described in this passage?

I. God Has a Plan for Every One of Us

God's plan includes:

Purpose. Individuals should be working toward an action, an aim, or a design that God desires for their lives.
Leadership. Individuals should be following God's leadership, not leading God!
Achievement. Being successful means reaching the goals God has for people.
Nurture. Being educated and trained by God in the rigors of the Christian life is basic to the plan.

Walt Kallestad describes two people who took a journey through a forest. One had a destination, a compass, and a map. The other was out for a pleasant stroll through the forest. As day began to wane, the shadows lengthened, and both began thinking about getting home.

The individual who did not bring a map or a compass thought that if he went from tree to tree, he could find his way out of the forest. So the traveler wandered until darkness overtook him.

The second traveler also realized that darkness was descending. He pulled the map and compass out of his pocket and aligned the instruments and began walking until he was out of the forest.

Effective Christians follow God's destination for their lives by reading the map (Bible) and following the compass (prayer.) There's another truth here:

II. The World Is Going Somewhere

The world's viewpoint is dominated by the philosophy that history goes in a circle. The biblical viewpoint is that the world, including humankind, is headed to a consummation. God is in control of the universe. It is wonderful to know that the hand that controls the universe handles our cares, too!

In *The Birth of the New Testament,* C. D. F. Moule writes, "New Testament thought on the last things, at its best, always concentrates on what God has already done for man in Christ. It does not say, How long will it be before the last whistle blows full-time? Rather it says, Where ought I to be to receive the next pass? What really matters is that the kick-off has already taken place, the game is on and we have a captain to lead us on to victory."

The third truth here is a call to action:

III. Christians Are Challenged to Watch

Christians must not become so enthralled with this world's priorities that we lose sight that this world is not our home. Jesus is coming back to gather his people home. The question is, Are you ready? Be prepared! Watch! (Derl G. Keefer)

DECEMBER 8, 1996

ès

Second Sunday of Advent

Worship Theme: The Incarnation has opened the door for us to experience God.

Readings: Isaiah 40:1-11; 2 Peter 3:8-15*a*; Mark 1:1-8

Call to Worship (Psalm 85:8-9, 12-13):

Leader: Let me hear what God the LORD will speak, for he will speak peace to his people,

People: **to his faithful, to those who turn to him in their hearts.**

Leader: Surely his salvation is at hand for those who fear him,

People: **that his glory may dwell in our land. . . .**

Leader: The LORD will give what is good,

People: **and our land will yield its increase.**

Leader: Righteousness will go before him,

People: **and will make a path for his steps.**

Pastoral Prayer:

Today, O God, as the world lurches once more toward Bethlehem like some great beast dreaming of transformation, hear our prayers for the many peoples of the earth: for the children of every land, whose lives will be forever affected by what they are taught and how they are cared for; for the poor, who can never rest until they know there will be food and shelter for them and their families; for those entrusted with the good news of Christ, who face such awesome difficulties in the achievement of their mission; and for the leaders of nations, whose honesty and skillfulness mean so much in determining the future welfare of millions. We pray especially for our president and his cabinet as they seek to lead our nation toward the fulfillment of its great duty in a world of suffering and want; grant that your Spirit may so preside in their hearts that their efforts will coincide with your holy will. Our wills are ours, O God, to make them yours. Grant that the child of Bethlehem may lead us, that we may find new centeredness for our own lives this Christmas, that we may not lose our sensitivity through busyness or crowdedness, that we may surrender to love and faith and find joy in denying ourselves for the sake of others. Let the mysteries and memories of this season that affect us in such deep ways bring us caroling to your throne, overwhelmed by the knowledge that we are yours and you are ours, through Jesus Christ our Lord. Amen. (John Killinger)

SERMON BRIEFS

A VOICE IN THE WILDERNESS

ISAIAH 40:1-11

Speak tenderly? Not John! Isaiah might have expected it, but the John who quotes this passage, the John of tradition, the John who dressed in camel's hair and ate a weird diet, did anything but speak tenderly. Here in this tender season of preparation, John seems harsh and discordant. But here the voice of the prophet is less confrontational and more comforting, helping to prepare our hearts and the way of the Lord.

I. God's Coming in Christ Brings Comfort

This is the season of comfort. God does comfort us.

Dr. Barry Bailey, pastor of First United Methodist Church in Fort Worth, Texas, was asked to hold the funeral for rock guitarist Stevie Ray Vaughan. Part of the tragedy was that life for Stevie Ray Vaughan had just turned good. He had been clean and sober for the last couple of years, and his career was on the rise. He had just finished an album with his brother.

Bailey says the most moving part of the service was when Stevie Wonder, Bonnie Raitt, and Jackson Browne asked if they could sing a special song at the conclusion. It was impromptu and a cappella. They chose to sing "Amazing Grace."

Imagine, there was Stevie Wonder, a man born blind, singing, "I once was lost, but now am found; was blind, but now I see." Those are words of faith, hope, grace, and resurrection. They sang of and found comfort and hope through the gift of God's presence. Why? Because God brings comfort to God's people.

II. God's Coming in Christ Reveals Glory

God's comfort comes as God is revealed in Christ.

One day while going through the radio stations, I heard Garth Brooks's song, "I've Got Friends in Low Places." I'd heard it before, but it suddenly dawned on me that those words could have been Jesus' words. That's what the Incarnation is all about. Jesus does have friends in low places. That's what got him in trouble. He hung out with outcasts, winebibbers, people who were blind or deaf, people who had leprosy; sinners of every shape and color. Jesus does have friends in low places: *us.*

And it is in the very nature of who Jesus calls friends that the glory of God is revealed. There is comfort because the Word became flesh. God stepped down and became one of us.

III. God's Coming in Christ Demonstrates Power

In that stepping down, God revealed true power. Advent and Christmas are about God's heart being wrapped in swaddling clothes and the frailty of human flesh to show us God's might. We find God's might revealed not in earth-shaking thunder, not in mountains being leveled, but in a baby born in Bethlehem and in arms outstretched in love. We see God's might as God seeks us out and shows divine love. We see God's might in God's power and desire to forgive.

One evening while putting her daughter to bed, a mother asked what it was like to be four years old. The little girl responded, "It's special." Mom smiled and asked her why.

The little girl looked at her mother in disbelief, doubting her mother's sincerity, than smiled and said, "Because I know my mommy loves me."

The voice in the wilderness reminds us that God became one of us. God's might and glory are revealed in a humble birth, a blood-stained cross, and an empty tomb, signs of God's great love for us. Life becomes special and we find comfort. (Billy D. Strayhorn)

ARE YOU READY FOR CHRISTMAS?

2 PETER 3:8-15a

Are you ready for Christmas? That's the question you'll probably be asked a hundred times during this season. I think it's a good question. We Christians can take it in its purest sense: "Are you ready for the coming of Christ?"

After all, Christ's coming *is* at the center of our celebration. And Christ's coming is the determining factor in how we live our lives—not only his first coming, but his second coming. That's Peter's message to his church: "Are you ready for the coming of Christ?"

Peter makes at least three observations about Christ's coming that will ready us for this Advent season.

I. God's Watch Keeps a Different Time

God doesn't operate according to Timexes, Casios, or Swiss-made chronometers. God made time and stands outside it. That's why a thousand years is as one day and one day is as a thousand years.

"How long 'til Christmas?" ask the little voices beginning about this time of the year. "I wish Christmas would hurry up and get here!" As a child, I remember it seemed like a thousand years between Thanksgiving and Christmas!

God works according to his watch, not ours. When Jesus arrived in a stable, the timing even caught many of those looking for a Messiah off guard.

If he'd arrived when Sennacherib had surrounded Jerusalem seven hundred years earlier, God's timing might be more easily understood. If he'd arrived when Nebuchadnezzar besieged the city, while the people were crying for a deliverer, God's timing might be more easily understood. But God's watch runs on a different time. Jesus' advent occurred at the precise time God decided because God's watch keeps the best time of all.

His second coming will be according to that same timing. Not when we expect or when we deem appropriate, but when God's watch sounds the hour, Jesus will come again.

II. God's Tendency Is Patience

While many of us long for a hurried-up Christmas, we all know that, officially at least, Christmas doesn't come until December 25. Our tendency is impatience. Whether it's government bureaucracy or church committees, the checkout lane or the interstate, we are an impatient people.

But God is a God of patience. While many of us might like to see Christ's second coming today, God waits, providing an opportunity for more people to respond to his love. Even in Jesus' life, God displayed patience. He allowed Jesus to be born as a baby, waiting thirty years for him to become the man we came to know as the Christ. God's tendency is patience.

III. God's Surprise Entrance Calls for Readiness

Peter warns that the second coming will be a surprise. Like a thief in the night, Christ will come as an unexpected and, in many cases, uninvited Savior.

Just like his birth, Jesus' next coming will catch many by surprise. While in minor tones we call, "O come, O come, Emmanuel," when he comes, his arrival will still be unexpected. For that reason, Peter says, as we anxiously await his arrival, our lives ought to be holy, godly, spotless specimens of purity. The ethics of Christianity are based on this eschatological surprise. Peter says we ought to live today as if it were our last because it might be! Every day is a constant recommitment to holy living because today just might be *the* Day.

During this season when someone asks you, "Are you ready for Christmas?" take the question in its fullest sense: "Are you ready for the coming of Christ?" (H. Blake Harwell)

AN ADVENT CAROL

MARK 1:1-8

"Old Marley was as dead as a doornail. . . ." You remember that Charles Dickens begins *A Christmas Carol* in this way. And why?

Because, as a recent video version intones, if that fact if not distinctly understood, "nothing wonderful can come of this story I am going to relate."

Dickens gives us what we need to know at the very beginning so that we will understand—even better than Scrooge—what's really going on here. Because we do, we can appreciate just how wonderful are the things that do happen.

Think of today's text in much the same way. Mark is telling us what we need to know, what we must understand, and distinctly—that Jesus is the Son of God—so that we can really understand, even better than the disciples and John the fire-breathing baptizer, what wonderful things are happening in the story.

I. Old Words, New Words

Part of the wonder of the story of Jesus is how the ancient message is made new. When the people went streaming into the desert to hear John, it wasn't for the novelty of the message that they went. They had heard the words before.

Rather, they went for the power of old words made new. John's presence and preaching made the ancient message fresh. Jesus, of course, will go that one better and make the ancient message flesh.

John's message of expectation was powerful, and precisely because of its familiarity, Jesus' incarnation was more powerful still. Because, in him, expectation gives way to realization.

II. Old Place, New Place

The wilderness, of all places, is where the gospel of Jesus Christ begins. That new message is rooted in the old message that God's delivering of his people always begins is the wilderness.

God's *speaking* is heard in the wilderness. Remember how Moses heard the call? God's *saving* is experienced in the wilderness. Remember how the children of Israel escaped Pharaoh in the wilderness? God's *molding* is accomplished in the wilderness. Remember how the saved children were disciplined and shaped in the wilderness before reaching the Promised Land?

The wilderness is where the redemption of enslaved Israel took root and flourished. As God now begins to save all his children, this old venue is the new context for salvation. And whether the wilderness is literal or metaphorical, the truth remains: God's call can be heard in the wilderness. God's salvation can be experienced in the wilderness. God's people are to be formed in the wilderness.

III. Old Message, New Message

The sermon is an old one—preached by John and by prophets before him. Preached by Jesus, too, and by all who followed him. Repent and believe! But as old as the message is, it is ever new, for each time it is preached, according to John's testimony, there comes one after to baptize with the Holy Spirit.

Jesus himself attends the preaching of the old word and brings it to reality in new ways. And so, as the old hymn says, does the "old, old story" become the "new, new song."

Mark tells us what we need to know right from the beginning so that wondrous things can come from our telling and retelling of the story. Reading the title is, then, like having read the story's last page. The beginning, then, is the end, and the end just the beginning. (Thomas R. Steagald)

DECEMBER 15, 1996

❦

Third Sunday of Advent

Worship Theme: The best preparation for Christmas is a life yielded to Christ.

Readings: Isaiah 61:1-4, 8-11; 1 Thessalonians 5:16-24; John 1:6-8, 19-28

Call to Worship (Luke 1:47-50):

Leader: My soul magnifies the Lord and my spirit rejoices in God my Savior,

People: for he has looked with favor on the lowliness of his servant.

Leader: Surely from now on all generations will call me blessed; for the Mighty One has done great things for me, and holy is his name.

People: His mercy is for those who fear him from generation to generation.

Pastoral Prayer:

At the manger, O God, all things are transformed: the haughty are made humble, the powerful become weak, the weak find strength to endure, the rich learn that they are really poor, the poor discover that they have an Advocate from heaven. Our dreams are no longer for self but for others; our desire is no longer for security but for risk and insecurity; our worship is no longer for things of the world but for you, Almighty Creator, Lover, Redeemer, Bright and Morning Star, and Hope of all the ages. In the light of the stable, O God, teach us to see the world as you see it, where disabled persons and persons with leprosy and persons with AIDS are more important than kings and governors and legislators; where it matters more that children go to bed hungry than that spaceships reach distant planets; more that there are men and women who cannot read than that there are men and women too busy to read; more that there are elderly people frightened of going to the grocery store than that there are beautiful shopping malls all around us.

You have given us so much, O God, and we have given you so little. What can we give you this Christmastime? Help us to give you our hearts, like little children, in joyful, loving trust so that they become filled with radiance beyond our own making; and then help us to live our lives for others, bearing their burdens, being sensitive to their feelings, healing their wounds, being their friends and advocates, until they know you are in the world, reconciling all things unto yourself and making every day Christmas Day, till Christ himself shall be Lord of lords and King of kings. Amen. (John Killinger)

SERMON BRIEFS

THE GOOD NEWS OF CHRISTMAS

ISAIAH 61:1-4, 8-11

In the comic strip *Garfield* by Jim Davis, Odie is asleep on the floor. Garfield walks up, lifts Odie's ear, and whispers, "Christmas is coming," then walks off. Odie is still asleep, but now there is a smile on his face and his tail is wagging ninety to nothing.

Christmas is coming and the excitement builds. The prophet speaks the words Jesus will read in his hometown and then proclaim, "Today this scripture has been fulfilled in your hearing" (Luke 4:21). In the very life of Jesus, these words become flesh and blood. The birth of Christ brings the good news of joy, unity, and salvation for all.

I. Christmas Is Good News Because It Brings Joy

Christmas is more than just lights and trees and presents. It is more than just a warm feeling. Christmas is that sense of renewal and liberation that comes from knowing great joy. Filled with the Spirit of God, the prophet promised that joy through the proclamation of the good news, through the binding of the brokenhearted, through liberty for captives and release for prisoners.

After ripping into a Christmas present, a three-year-old girl picked up the toy and said, "Ooohhh, I've wanted one of these ever since I was a little girl."

The marvelous thing about the joy of Christmas is that we didn't know we wanted it until it came. And the minute we first beheld God's glory wrapped in swaddling clothes, we knew it was what we had always wanted; what we had always needed. It fills us with joy.

II. Christmas Is Good News Because It Brings Unity

Through the gift and proclamation of this good news of comfort, liberty, and release, we find unity in Christ. The differences that exist between us no longer seems important when we stand at the foot of the manger, knowing that the innocent Christ child will one day grow to be the innocent Savior who loves us so much he willingly dies for us. That love removes all differences and makes us truly one in Christ.

One of the greatest instances of Christian unity I've ever witnessed was in Israel in 1992. On a tour of the Holy Land, our group was made up of United Methodists, Presbyterians, Disciples of Christ, and Roman Catholics. On Russian and Greek Orthodox Christmas Eve, our Epiphany, we stopped at the Church of the Nativity in Bethlehem. Attached to the church is an ancient monastery. We visited the room where the Roman Catholic priest Jerome lived and translated the Old and New Testaments from the Hebrew and Greek into the Latin Vulgate, making the Bible accessible to ordinary people.

There, we paused to sing Christmas carols. While we were singing, a group of Korean and German Christians joined us. In mixed languages, in mixed national and denominational affiliations, we sang and celebrated the birth of the Savior of us all.

III. Christmas Is Good News Because It Brings Salvation

A cartoon shows two lightning bugs. One asks the other: "Do you think this is *all* there is, or do you believe in an afterglow?"

That's a pertinent question. We live in the afterglow of both Christmas and Easter. We can't have one without the other. Easter without the Incarnation becomes a supernatural myth. Christmas without the Cross, the Resurrection, and the empty tomb is just a sentimental story that has no purpose or meaning. But the afterglow of both events gives life direction, purpose, and meaning. The One whose birth we celebrate also died and was raised from the dead to bring us salvation.

Living in the afterglow is living in the light of Christ and being the light for others by proclaiming God's good news. (Billy D. Strayhorn)

PEACE? AT CHRISTMAS?

1 THESSALONIANS 5:16-24

Eight-year-old Johnny was sitting in church watching as the third Advent candle was lit. As the flame sputtered and then grew to life, Johnny tugged on his mother's dress and asked loudly, "Why are they lighting another candle, Mommy?" His mother leaned down and, as quietly as possible, explained, "We're getting ready for Jesus to get here." Quickly, Johnny shot back, "Well, I sure wish he'd hurry up!"

The Thessalonians also wanted to "hurry up" the coming of Jesus. In fact, his second coming is the major subject of both letters to this church. The Thessalonians were consumed by this future event. Many questions and doubts arose in their minds. Living in the in-between time is not the easiest place to live. So Paul writes them to explain how they should live until Jesus comes.

In his closing prayer, Paul mentions "the God of peace" who will make us faultless "at the coming of our Lord Jesus Christ" (v. 23). In this often hurried-up season we celebrate the first coming of Jesus, the one called the Prince of Peace.

Peace. Something seldom found in our world. Whether the conflict is in the Middle East or in the heart of a struggling teenager, in Europe between two "religious" factions or in the worried mind of a fixed-income senior adult, peace is a rare commodity.

For the Thessalonians, peace was also rare. There was anxiety about those who died (4:13). There was concern about the coming of the Lord, its timing and its nature (4:16). But Paul reassures them all with this letter: "Be at peace among yourself" (5:13). Then, he shows us all the way to peace while we wait for Jesus' arrival.

I. We Experience Peace by Living Peacefully

In verses 16-18, Paul lists three characteristics of peace-filled people. "Rejoice always, pray without ceasing, give thanks in all circumstances," sounds remarkably like his counsel to his other Macedonian congregation, the Philippians (Phil. 4:4-6). But in Philippians, he includes the results of doing these three things: "The peace of God, which surpasses all understanding, will guard your hearts and your minds in Christ Jesus" (v. 7). Peace at Christmas is possible if we heed Paul's words.

If we're going to have peace in the church and in our personal lives this season, the "big three" are essential.

II. We Experience Peace by Yielding to God's Spirit

The second way to peace in our hearts and in the church involves the Spirit (vv. 19-22). God's Spirit must be given free rein in our hearts and in the church. His word must be proclaimed, and his people must "test everything."

In celebrating the coming of the Prince of Peace, our personal lives may be anything but peaceful. Christmas can be a time for flaring department store tempers, churning checkout lane stomachs, and parking-spot brawls at the mall! "Test everything," Paul says.

We Christians must reevaluate how agitated and tumultuous we've allowed our celebration to become. While the rest of the world hurries and worries, God calls on us to hold fast to the good of this season and discard the bad.

Is your Christmas a time of peace? If not, examine your life. Then, as Paul commands, "hold fast to what is good" and avoid the evil, chaotic temptation to be swept away in the commercialization of Christmas.

You think it's too late? Has your celebration of the coming of our Lord already been anything but peaceful? Paul's final words are hopefilled: "The one who calls you is faithful, and he will do this" (v. 24). Only the God of peace can ensure that the Prince of Peace finds his way into our hearts this season. (H. Blake Harwell)

PLAYING GAMES

JOHN 1:6-8, 19-28

The whole passage reads like three TV game shows, with John the Baptist being questioned by a panel of celebrity judges, all trying to find out who he is, what he is doing, and what it all means. Some of the questions prove better than others.

I. "To Tell the Truth"

On the show "To Tell the Truth," a panel of near-famous questioners would face a panel of three contestants with all three claiming to be the same individual. "My name is . . ." whatever—all three said the same name, and then there would be some clues given about this person and the occupation. The challenge was to see whether the near-famous could determine, by asking questions, which of the three was the real one. The three played it close to the vest, trying not to reveal too much. It was funny to the extent that the questioners got befuddled and confused.

This passage is funny in the same way. Celebrity questioners—priests and Levites sent from the Pharisees—are asking questions in turn and trying to figure out who John really is. "Are you Elijah? A prophet? An impostor?" John plays it close, of course, saying more of who he is not than who he is. And they are so confused, comically so.

At the end of the game show, the announcer would say, "Will the real ——— please stand up!" One would, and confusion would give way to clarity. One can only imagine that the Pharisees wished, if secretly, someone would stand and clear things up concerning John.

II. "What's My Line"

A variation on "To Tell the Truth" was "What's My Line." It was up to the panelists, through questions, to determine the occupation of one contestant, who did his or her best to confuse the celebrities. The studio and TV audience would know what the panelists didn't—that is, the contestant's "line"—and the show was funny to the extent that the celebrities were off target and unable to see what, to us, was so obvious. If the contestant could keep them that way, he or she would win the money.

The text for today is funny in the same way. We already know who John is—a witness sent to testify to the Light, one who has come to proclaim the advent of the Savior. A prophet, in other words, after the fashion of Elijah, if not precisely Elijah himself.

And the questioners in our text are very confused: unable to see what we already know; unable to see what seems to us so obvious. They know something of what John is doing, but they do not know what it means or, more precisely, what his real job is. And they are off target.

Why are you baptizing? Who are you? What do you say about yourself? And you get the sense that John has the money in the bag.

III. "Jeopardy!"

The last game show is still on, the one where Alex Trebek gives the answer, and the contestants supply the question. If they get the question right, they win the prize.

John has given his questioners the "final Jeopardy" answer, but it would seem they have gotten the question wrong. When John says, "Among you stands one whom you do not know . . .", their answer seems to be, "Where is the Messiah?" Why, in Bethany, of course. Across the Jordan where John was baptizing. But that's the wrong question.

The real question is not, "Where is he, that we might see him?" It is, "Who is he, that we might follow him?" One has to feel sorry that these unfortunate contestants seem to have missed the grand prize. (Thomas R. Steagald)

DECEMBER 22, 1996

és.

Fourth Sunday of Advent

Worship Theme: Christmas provides hope to a hopeless world.

Readings: 2 Samuel 7:1-11, 16; Romans 16:25-27; Luke 1:26-38

Call to Worship (Psalm 89:1-2):

Leader: I will sing of your steadfast love, O LORD, forever;

People: with my mouth I will proclaim your faithfulness to all generations.

Leader: I declare that your steadfast love is established forever;

People: your faithfulness is as firm as the heavens.

Pastoral Prayer:

Into the darkness of the human night, O God, you have injected a song of peace and hope and love. Now, after all these centuries, we gather here amidst holly, wreaths, and candles to pray for the continuance of that song. Our world, as always, is in deep trouble. Nations are at war with one another, and classes and races still struggle for supremacy. The generations and the races and the sexes are in conflict over what is due them. Even as individuals we are caught up in competition and strife and desire for what *we* can get out of life. Turn up the volume of the angels' song, O God, and let us hear it for this one day at least. Reduce our fever for getting ahead. Control our lust for the things that do not matter. Remind us of one another and of the poor who surround us like grains of sand on a beach. Give us a vision of your new age, where all war is over, all competition is laid to rest, all envy and jealousy put behind us, all prejudice ended, all hatred swallowed up in love and forgiveness, and all energy devoted to worshiping you and enjoying what you have made.

Give safety to all who travel in this busy week, that the joy of reunions may be unhampered. Show mercy on all who have done what was evil or wrongheaded or simply confused, and guard from seduction all who face temptations beyond their power of resistance. Let the light that shone over the birthplace of that most special Child shine now for us, that our hearts may be filled with gladness and goodness, and that we may be purified of our old selves and born anew in the power of the manger, to walk in the holiness of your love and your will forever and ever, world without end. Amen. (John Killinger)

SERMON BRIEFS

CHRISTMAS HOPE

2 SAMUEL 7:1-11, 16

David was a man of action. He had defeated Goliath and had outlived King Saul, succeeding him on the throne. David defeated all Israel's enemies, made Jerusalem his capital, and built a palace lined with cedar. He developed a bad conscience because God was still being worshiped in a tent.

David told the prophet Nathan that he wanted to build God a temple. The Lord said no—instead, he would establish the house of David. There is a play on words here: instead of building God a house, God would establish David's house (dynasty) forever.

I. Our God Is a God of Grace

Consider what the Lord did for David:

"I took you from . . . following the sheep to be prince over my people Israel" (v. 8).
God enabled him to defeat all his enemies.
The Lord gave him a great name—still honored after many centuries (v. 9).
Despite David's sin, the Lord was gracious to him. He was not rejected.

Think how much we owe to God's grace this Christmas. He has blessed us beyond anything we could deserve. He has forgiven us and given us another chance. He sent his Son and his Holy Spirit to pay our debt and to guide us.

Celebrate the graciousness of God.

II. Our God Is a God of Hope

This passage has been a seedbed of hope for both Jews and Christians. King David's descendants ruled from his throne for four hundred years. After the destruction of Jerusalem in 587 B.C., this passage became the source of messianic hope—that God's anointed would establish his rule on earth.

Christians saw that hope fulfilled in Jesus.

We celebrate the fulfillment of this divine promise at Christmas. Jesus was born to establish the kingdom of God on earth. David's descendant rules still, "and he shall reign forever and ever—hallelujah!" Christ is our hope, the anchor of our faith.

Ours is a universal faith, not limited to one place such as a Temple in Jerusalem. Christ is present every place in the church of God the Holy Spirit. The church is a living temple. Our bodies are the temple of the Holy Spirit.

Avoid a "cathedral psychology" this Christmas—giving the devotion due God to a building. We worship not a place but a person. We are to serve the One worthy of all honor and glory. (Alton H. McEachern)

WHAT A MIGHTY GOD WE SERVE

ROMANS 16:25-27

Paul ended his Epistle to the Romans where every sermon and every Christian writing should end: in thanksgiving to God for what God has done. In this doxology, Paul acknowledged several truths about the work of God.

I. The Power Behind God's Work

Paul wrote of God who is able (v. 25). The idea of God's adequacy is a common theme in the New Testament. Paul told the Ephesians that God was able to do greater things than we can ask for or envision

(Eph. 3:20). Jude declared that God was able to keep us from falling or stumbling (Jude 24). Paul reminded the Corinthians that our adequacy was not in ourselves but in God (2 Cor. 3:5). To the Philippians, Paul gave the assurance that the God who began his good work in them had the power to complete that good work (Phil. 1:6). Behind the glorious gospel that Paul proclaimed to the Romans was a God who was able.

One of the most famous sermons in American history was Jonathan Edwards's sermon "Sinners in the Hands of an Angry God." He suggested, "It is a fearful thing to fall into the hands of the living God." On the same theme, John Donne, one of the noblest of all English preachers, wrote, "It is a fearful thing to fall into the hands of the living God: but to fall out of the hands of the living God, is a horror beyond our expression, beyond our imagination."

Without God, we are nothing. With God, we have adequate provisions for life, for he is able.

II. The Purpose of God's Work

Paul's mind worked so quickly that at times his words could not keep up with it. That appears to be the case in this doxology. The key idea in these phrases cascading from the pen of the Apostle is found in the "mystery," which "is now disclosed." Paul explained in his Ephesian letter that this mystery was God's plan to include Gentiles as fellow members of the family of God (Eph. 3:1-11). This is the universalism of the New Testament—not the declaration that everyone *will* be saved but the declaration that everyone *can* be saved. From the time of Abraham's call (Gen. 12:3), God's purpose has been to include all humankind in his eternal family. However, each person must respond by faith to the offer of grace.

Alexander Maclaren expressed this truth concisely in his statement: "One thief was saved upon the cross that none might despair; and only one that none might presume."

III. The Product from God's Work

What happened when this gospel was proclaimed to the world? Paul explained in the final phrase in verse 26. When the gospel was proclaimed, people responded in faith and obedience.

With the gospel, the first disciples turned the world right side up. With the gospel, Paul conquered the Roman Empire. With the gospel, Martin Luther ushered in the Reformation. With the gospel, John Wesley captured England for Christ. With the gospel, Billy Graham has brought light to the world.

If we are faithful to do what we can do, then God will be faithful to do what we cannot do.

When a simple Christian woman shared the gospel with a young boy dying in the hospital, he was touched by the simplicity of the message. "Say it again," he whispered to the woman. She repeated her earlier litany, "God made you. God loves you. God sent his Son to save you. God wants you to come home with him." Johnny looked into her face and said, "Tell God, 'Thank you.'" When Paul concluded his Roman Epistle with a repetition of the mighty acts of God, he responded in the same way: "Tell God, 'Thank you.'" (Brian Harbour)

ANGEL ETIQUETTE

LUKE 1:26-38

The writer of the Gospel of Luke has a fondness for angels. They instruct, announce, guide, and protect. The appearance of these visitors, these *aggelos* or "messengers," produces a standard response from the human community: fear, doubt, and an awe-ful wonder. The normal manners of conversation and community are always turned upside down in these holy/human encounters. One of the church's tasks in this celestial season is to review the handbook for angel etiquette: Holy Scripture.

I. Proper Greetings

Luke's Gospel describes Mary's response to her visitation as "perplexed" (v. 29). Small wonder. All the normal rules for conversation are broken in the first thirty seconds. The carefully preserved distinctions between strangers and all of the gender roles have been reversed in the words, "Greetings, favored one! The Lord is with you!" No wonder Mary "pondered what sort of greeting this might be" (v. 29). There was no socially approved pattern for this response.

She was in the middle of a conversion conversation, a dialogue that no one could dictate or predict.

II. Calendar Sins

If Gabriel's first sentence broke the conventions of human speech, then the next announcement threatened the conventions of human behavior. At the very least, Mary would be guilty of calendar sins, a pregnancy prior to the proper time and season. More unnerving than the disregard of human timetables for newly engaged couples was the angel's declaration that God's time was now to be measured in human life cycles. Immortality putting on mortality broke all the conventions of time. A human birth would mark the cosmic calendar. Centuries would have a birthdate to count on, if and when Mary agreed.

III. Only the Impossible Required

One sign of good manners is the observation of limits. A well-mannered person does not insist on the impossible, at least not with perfect strangers. In a Gospel filled with concern for the poor and the marginalized, those who represent the unable, the basic rule of moderation is broken.

The power of this good news is that *God* is able. An older woman and a young girl will soon be comparing notes over their pregnancies. The only human etiquette required here is a radical "Yes!" to a holy possible end. This is the creed behind the creeds: God is able.

IV. No Time to Think Twice

Angels seem to operate with a kind of wild patience. All the human/holy encounters in this Gospel are over in a flash, or at least that's the impression that the Gospel writer leaves. Perhaps that flashpoint quality is not universal, but it seems as if Mary has little time to make a forever choice. Perhaps the minutes not only seem like hours in the presence of a member of an angelic host but actually are hours. Perhaps the visitation lasted centuries, at least on Mary's part, but the handbook, the Scriptures, seems to indicate that encounters of this kind are the heartbeat kind. It's over before she knows it or at least can explain it.

What Mary does, she does quickly. She agrees to a lifelong relationship to the holy, and the length of that life is in eternal terms. What she does is magnificent: a free-willed human being beginning a brand-new text of holy/human manners. (Heather Murray Elkins)

DECEMBER 29, 1996

First Sunday After Christmas

Worship Theme: We can enter the new year with confidence in God's saving grace.

Readings: Isaiah 61:10–62:3; Galatians 4:4-7; Luke 2:22-40

Call to Worship (Psalm 148:1-5a):

Leader: Praise the LORD! Praise the LORD from the heavens; praise him in the heights!

***People:* Praise him, all his angels; praise him, all his host!**

Leader: Praise him, sun and moon; praise him, all you shining stars! Praise him, you highest heavens, and you waters above the heavens!

***People:* Let them praise the name of the LORD.**

Pastoral Prayer:

An old year is passing from the scene, Almighty God, and a new year is rushing toward us filled with promise and opportunity, but also laced with temptation and challenge. Help us make it a good and gracious year with your help and presence, O Lord. Show us day by day how to serve you more effectively, how to love you more completely, how to walk with you more fully. Some enter the new year in pain; grant them peace and comfort, we pray. Some enter the new year with great questions on their hearts; grant them wisdom and courage, we pray. Anoint us with your Spirit and with power, that the coming year might be transformed because we have been transformed by your love and by your grace. Amen.

SERMON BRIEFS

GOD'S SILENCE AND OUR SALVATION

ISAIAH 61:10–62:3

Have you been able to hear the voice of God in all the din of Christmas preparation and celebration? This is such a busy season that we can easily lose sight of its central purpose. Perhaps you encountered the Lord in Christmas worship and great music such as Handel's *Messiah*.

The prophet Isaiah was concerned about the silence of God. There was a time when God did not appear to be answering prayers on behalf of his people. Isaiah refused to keep silent until the Lord saved Jerusalem: "For Zion's sake I will not keep silent" (62:1).

I. A Hymn of Praise and Thanksgiving (61:10-11)

When in doubt, pray and worship. Look for something for which to be grateful. Focus not on what you have lost but on what you have left. Isaiah celebrated "the garments of salvation" and "the robe of righteousness."

As God renews the earth in springtime, so he will revive his people—righteousness and praise will " spring up." The new year at hand provides us a fresh opportunity to praise and serve the Lord. Approach it in a spirit of gratitude.

II. Vindication and a New Name (62:2)

The prophet prays that God will vindicate his people, Zion, in a highly visible way. The nations (Gentiles) shall see it and know that Yahweh is God.

He promises that God will give Jerusalem a new name (character) much as God changed the names and nature of Abram and Jacob. They will have a change of character. John Wesley defended his movement by pointing out that people were being changed: "The habitual drunkard is now temperate." The strongest argument for Christianity is transformed people.

410

III. We Are the Lord's Crown (62:3)

The Babylonian god Marduk was pictured as wearing the walls of a city as a crown or tiara. Here Isaiah portrays Jerusalem as "a crown of beauty in the hand of the LORD." This means that we are precious to the Lord. We have worth and God values us. Jesus bore the cross and wears the church like a crown of triumph.

Even when God seems silent, we can praise and worship him. In due course God will vindicate us and change our character into the likeness of his dear Son. Never forget, you are precious in the Lord's sight. In the stressful time of Christmas past, let us worship the Lord and enter the new year unafraid. (Alton H. McEachern)

BEYOND LEGALISM

GALATIANS 4:4-7

Legalism was the enemy of grace in the New Testament, and it was Paul's target in the letter to the Galatians. Paul's gospel of grace indicated that everything necessary for our salvation had already been done. All we have to do is to accept it by faith. For many, the offer of grace was too risky. They wanted something more tangible so they added some requirements. When anything is added to faith, the result is not grace but legalism.

Legalism has returned in our day with a vengeance. Requirements to be saved, requirements to remain saved, and requirements to demonstrate we are saved are being suggested by many. Understanding the biblical concept of grace will help us move beyond legalism.

In our text, Paul compared legalism to the gospel of grace at two points.

I. What the Law Couldn't Do, God Did (4:4-5a)

The redemption provided by Jesus (v. 5a) stands in contrast to the bondage experienced under the law (v. 3). The word *redeem* means "to purchase a slave with a view to his freedom." The law provided not freedom but bondage. What the law couldn't do, God did in Jesus Christ.

How was Jesus able to provide this redemption? Paul explained in verse 4. Jesus was God's Son and at the same time was "born of a woman." To speak of Jesus as the Son of God implied a unique relationship between him and God. It is a reference to his divinity. To speak of Jesus as being "born of a woman" implied a relationship with us as human beings. It is a reference to his humanity.

This dual relationship enables Jesus to redeem us. If Jesus was less than God or different from us, he would not be able to save us. Because he was both man and God, he is able with one hand to gather all humanity under his care and with the other to usher us into the presence of God. As one of the ancient fathers put it, "he became what we are so that we may become what He is."

II. What the Law Couldn't Give, God Gave (4:5b-7)

The resources provided by Jesus (v. 7) stand in contrast to the limitations experienced under the law (v. 2). The word *heir* refers to "a person who will receive an inheritance." An inheritance is not earned or necessarily deserved. It is a gift to be received. The benefits of the law are determined by our abilities; the benefits of grace are determined by God's abundance.

How do we become heirs of God? Paul explained in verse 5b. Through Jesus Christ, we have been adopted into God's forever family. This adoption is not the common property of all people by creation. Instead, it is a gift given to those who identify with Jesus Christ. This adoption is not determined by our merit. Instead, it is a gift of grace.

At the turn of the century, Billy accompanied his daddy into town on Saturday to pick up the necessary supplies at the dry goods store. He stood patiently at the door as his father gathered the supplies. As his dad paid the bill, the proprietor of the store spoke to Billy, "Son, I am impressed with your patience as your dad did the shopping. As a reward, why don't you reach your hand into this candy jar and get a handful of candy." Billy didn't move. After a minute, the proprietor reached his hand into the jar and gave Billy more candy than he could hold in both hands. As they boarded the wagon to head back home, Billy's father expressed surprise at his son's hesitancy. "I've never known you to be bashful," the father said. Billy explained, "I wasn't being bashful, Dad. I just knew that his hands were bigger than my hands!"

When we follow the pathway of legalism, we will have only what we can hold in our own hands. By contrast, when we follow the pattern of grace, we will have what God can hold in his hands. And God's hands are bigger than our hands! (Brian Harbour)

A SOUL-MAKING SEASON

LUKE 2:22-40

In the writings of Augustine, an early church doctor of souls, time is conceived as consisting through a threefold extension of the human soul: (1) time past is time present in memory; (2) time present is time present in attention; (3) time future is time present in expectation. For Augustine, the soul is formed through the dynamics between memory, attention, and expectation that constitute the time of the soul.

In this Gospel passage, there are two "soulful" models, Simeon and Anna, who teach us how to remember, attend, and expect the presence of Christ.

I. We Live in Memory

Anna of Asher, widowed and childless, is the only woman in the Gospel called "a prophet." She, like Simeon, is looking for the One who would redeem Jerusalem. This looking forward is rooted in a backward vision, a memory of the promises of God. Part of Anna's memory would have been of the blood flowing in the streets of Jerusalem when the city and its Temple were conquered by Rome. Anna would have seen hundreds of youths and men die trying to prevent the military standards of Rome, the golden eagles, from being placed inside the Temple walls. To finally see the One who would redeem his people from this oppression as well as from their sins would have been a soul-making vision.

Anna, of the tribe of Asher (meaning "happy"), has no children of her own to remember. Her memory of the God who redeemed the slaves in Egypt becomes the prophecy of a child who will be called Redeemer. From the past will come the future, and Anna blesses God for this fulfilling of the mystery.

II. We Live in Attention

Jewish law required two witnesses to establish the truth of an event, and Luke's Gospel skillfully weaves this "twoness" of truth into a prophetic narrative of Simeon and Anna. Here are two who have spent years in attention to the daily revelations of God and Israel's particular task of prayer and praise. Simeon's prayer, the *Nunc Dimittis* (named after the first two words in the Latin translation), has remained at the center of the church's worshiping life for nearly two thousand years.

Its inspired speech is often set in an anthem or used as the benediction. This is a powerful expression of life and liturgy lived "in attention" to God instead of "in tension" or "inattention." This is also a poignant request of a faithful watcher of God to be allowed to be released from a lifelong watch.

A congregation that used this prayer many times as the concluding benediction of worship also experienced this prayer in another setting. When a minister or church member would reach the end of a hospital visit with someone who was gravely ill, dying, this prayer became a benediction to the parting. It spoke to the reality of death and the promise of another gathering. Here is a means to both bless and express faith with the sound of good-bye, God be with you. Above all, Simeon's prayer is a soul-making witness to the living God.

III. We Live in Expectation

What is the best that can be expected over time? This beginning of the story of Jesus has signs of its end clearly marked for the Christian who hears and believes. In memory, in attention, in expectation, the Christian church recites its faith: "Christ has died. Christ is risen. Christ will come again." But the Word precedes these and turns this season into a soul-making time, "Christ is born."

In memory, attention, and expectation, the community of Christ continues to pray, fast, prophesy, and praise God while experiencing the Holy Spirit and watching for the presence of the One who is "set for the fall and rising of many." This is the season of soul-making: the hallowing of human time with the radical interruption of the Incarnation. Like Augustine, our very souls depend on this fulfilling of time. (Heather Murray Elkins)

Hymn Suggestions*

₰

Jan. 7:
    "Jesus Shall Reign" (Isa.)
    "For the Healing of the Nations" (Isa., Acts)
    "We Meet You, O Christ" (Acts)

Jan. 14:
    "Holy God, We Praise Thy Name" (Isa.)
    "Just As I Am, Without One Plea" (John)

Jan. 21:
    "The Church's One Foundation" (1 Cor.)
    "Softly and Tenderly Jesus Is Calling" (Matt.)
    "Blest Be the Tie That Binds" (1 Cor.)

Jan. 28:
    "O Master, Let Me Walk With Thee" (Mic.)
    "Thine Be the Glory" (1 Cor.)

Feb. 4:
    "O For a Thousand Tongues to Sing" (Isa.)
    "Spirit of God, Descend upon My Heart" (1 Cor.)

Feb. 11:
    "Come, Thou Fount of Every Blessing" (Deut.)
    "For the Fruits of This Creation" (1 Cor.)
    "O Master, Let Me Walk With Thee" (Deut. Ps.)

Feb. 18:
    "Guide Me, O Thou Great Jehovah" (Exod.)
    "O Morning Star, How Fair and Bright" (2 Pet., Matt.)

Feb. 25:
    "God, Who Stretched the Spangled Heavens" (Gen.)

*Based on *The Music and Worship Planner, 1995–1996,* Abingdon Press.

"Amazing Grace" (Ps., Rom.)
"Lord, Dismiss Us with Thy Blessing" (Rom.)

Mar. 3:
"Sing Praise to God Who Reigns Above" (Gen., Ps.)
"O God, Our Help in Ages Past" (Ps.)
"Faith of Our Fathers" (Rom.)

Mar. 10:
"Joyful, Joyful, We Adore Thee" (Ps. John)
"O Love That Wilt Not Let Me Go" (Rom.)
"Guide Me, O Thou Great Jehovah" (Exod., John)

Mar. 17:
"Previous Lord, Take My Hand" (1 Sam., Ps.)
"O Zion, Haste" (Eph.)

Mar. 24:
"Trust and Obey" (Rom., John)
"Now the Green Blade Riseth" (Ezek., John)

Mar. 31:
"All Glory, Laud, and Honor" (Psalms Gospel)
"At the Name of Jesus" (Phil.)
"Rejoice, Ye Pure in Heart" (Phil.)

Apr. 5: [Good Friday]
"Hallelujah! What a Savior" (Isa.)
"O Sacred Head, Now Wounded" (John)
"Were You There" (John)

Apr. 7:
"Christ the Lord Is Risen Today" (John, Matt.)
"Crown Him with Many Crowns" (John)

Apr. 14:
"The Day of Resurrection" (1 Pet., John)
"O Sons and Daughters, Let Us Sing" (John)
"Thine Be the Glory" (Acts, John)

Apr. 21:
"We Know That Christ Is Raised" (Acts)
"Just As I Am, Without One Plea" (1 Pet.)
"Amazing Grace" (1 Pet.)

Apr. 28:
"Sweet, Sweet Spirit" (Acts)
"The King of Love My Shepherd Is" (Ps., John)

May 5:
"God of Grace and God of Glory" (Acts)
"The Church's One Foundation" (1 Pet., John)

May 12:
"For the Beauty of the Earth" (Acts)
"I Sing the Almighty Power of God" (Acts, John)

May 19:
"My Hope Is Built" (Eph.)
"All Hail the Power of Jesus' Name" (Eph., Luke)
"Thine Be the Glory" (Acts, Ps.)

May 26:
"O Worship the King" (Acts, Ps.)
"Many and Great, O God" (Ps.)

June 2:
"All Things Bright and Beautiful" (Gen.)
"How Great Thou Art" (Ps.)

June 9:
"The God of Abraham Praise" (Gen.)
"Faith of Our Fathers" (Rom.)
"O For a Thousand Tongues to Sing" (Ps. Matt.)

June 16:
"Praise to the Lord, the Almighty" (Ps.)
"The God of Abraham Praise" (Gen.)
"Blessed Assurance" (Rom.)

June 23:
"We Know That Christ Is Raised" (Rom.)
"O Master, Let Me Walk with Thee" (Gen., Ps.)
"Take Up Thy Cross" (Matt.)

June 30:
"Faith of Our Fathers" (Gen.)
"Breathe on Me, Breathe of God" (Rom.)
"Where Cross the Crowded Ways of Life" (Matt.)

July 7:
"Lord, I Want to Be a Christian" (Rom.)
"Jesus Loves Me" (Matt.)

July 14:
"Alas! and Did My Savior Bleed" (Rom.)
"Come, Ye Thankful People, Come" (Matt.)

July 21:
"The God of Abraham Praise" (Gen.)
"The Church's One Foundation" (Rom.)

July 28:
"Holy God, We Praise Thy Name" (Rom.)
"Seek Ye First" (Matt.)

Aug. 4:
"Standing on the Promises" (Rom.)
"If Thou But Suffer God to Guide Thee" (Rom.)

Aug. 11:
"By Gracious Powers" (Gen.)
"At the Name of Jesus" (Rom.)
"Dear Lord and Father of Mankind" (Matt.)

Aug. 18:
"In Christ There Is No East or West" (Ps., Rom.)
"My Faith Looks Up to Thee" (Matt.)

Aug. 25:
   "Guide Me, O Thou Great Jehovah" (Exod.)
   "Take My Life, and Let It Be" (Rom.)
   "Jesus, the Very Thought of Thee" (Matt.)

Sept. 1:
   "All Creatures of our God and King" (Ps.)
   "Go Down Moses" (Exod.)

Sept. 8:
   "I Come with Joy" (Matt.)
   "How Great Thou Art" (Ps.)

Sept. 15:
   "Come, Ye Faithful, Raise the Strain" (Exod.)
   "Lord, Speak to Me" (Rom.)

Sept. 22:
   "Lift Every Voice and Sing" (Ps.)
   "Glorious Things of Thee Are Spoken" (Exod., Matt.)

Sept. 29:
   "How Sweet the Name of Jesus Sounds" (Exod., Phil.)
   "What Wondrous Love Is This" (Phil.)

Oct. 6:
   "Christ Is Made the Sure Foundation" (Phil., Matt.)
   "Jesus Calls Us" (Exod., Phil.)
   "When I Survey the Wondrous Cross" (Phil.)

Oct. 13:
   "Rejoice, Ye Pure in Heart" (Phil.)
   "There's a Wideness in God's Mercy" (Exod., Matt.)

Oct. 20:
   "Sing Praise to God Who Reigns Above" (Exod., Matt.)
   "Rock of Ages, Cleft for Me" (Exod.)
   "How Firm a Foundation" (Exod., 1 Thess.)

Oct. 27:

"O God, Our Help in Ages Past" (Ps.)
"Praise, My Soul, the King of Heaven" (Ps., 1 Thess.)
"Lord, I Want to Be a Christian" (Matt.)

Nov. 3:

"A Mighty Fortress Is Our God" (Matt.)
"He Leadeth Me: O Blessed Thought" (Josh.)
"All Who Love and Serve Your City" (1 Thess., Matt.)

Nov. 10:

"Rejoice, the Lord Is King" (1 Thess.)
"Near to the Heart of God" (Josh.)
"Wake, Awake, for Night Is Flying" (Matt.)

Nov. 17:

"God, Who Stretched the Spangled Heavens" (Matt.)
"Ah, Holy Jesus" (1 Thess.)

Nov. 24:

"Savior, Like a Shepherd Lead Us" (Ezek., Ps., Matt.)
"For All the Saints" (Eph.)

Dec. 1:

"Come, Thou Long-Expected Jesus" (Mark)
"All My Hope Is Firmly Grounded" (Isa.)

Dec. 8:

"O Come, O Come, Emmanuel" (Ps., Mark)
"Hail to the Lord's Anointed" (Isa.)

Dec. 15:

"Holy, Holy, Holy! Lord God Almighty" (Isa.)
"Hark! the Herald Angels Sing" (John)

Dec. 22:

"Lo, How a Rose E'er Blooming" (Luke)
"It Came upon the Midnight Clear" (2 Sam., Rom., Luke)

Dec. 29:
"Once in royal David's City" (Gal.)
"Away in a Manger" (Luke)
"What Child Is This" (Luke)

BENEDICTIONS

ॐ

Advent

O God of new beginnings, make us a people of new beginnings. Let the works of our hands reflect the works of your hand. Let us mirror the light that illumined the deep and brightened a cold, dark stable.

Await with the farmer the fall of the rain, the warmth of the sun, the life of the soil. Await with God, and even the desert shall blossom. And as the wilderness becomes oasis, stretching its fields around the world, a highway shall appear, and you shall walk the holy way.

Christmas

God has sent the Spirit of the Child dancing into our hearts. The time has come for our birth. Leap within the world's womb! Go forth into an expectant world. Do not take with you a cry of pain, believing that you are thrust into the midst of strangers. Take with you a cry of recognition, knowing that you have entered the company of sisters and brothers.

In the dwelling-place of God we are christened with a new name. The mouth of God breathes into us the name that is above every name. We rise from our resting-place and step into a busy world, where God would have us dwell. May our presence in that world be a healing one, that the world may be a glorious crown in the hand of its Creator, the Name-giver.

Season After Epiphany

May God touch you with the Holy Spirit and with power; may you go forth from this place to do good and heal all who are oppressed by evil, for God is with you.

We have found the Messiah. As witnesses to the God who walks the earth, we proclaim the promise of the spirit. In Christ's name, let us go from this place, carrying that promise to those with whom we walk, living that promise among those with whom we dwell.

423

Lent

Do not live by bread alone, but by the will of God. May God give the angels charge over you; may their hands bear you up and keep you from falling.

May God, the Help of the helpless, grant you the strength that passes all expectation. May Christ, the Hope of the hopeless, grant you the peace that passes all understanding. May the Spirit, the Comfort of the comfortless, grant you the assurance that passes all doubt.

Easter

Do not be afraid. Jesus has risen. You have seen the empty place where he lay. Go and tell the world that Jesus is alive. Even now he is going before you into your streets and your homes, your offices and your markets, your prisons, and your hospitals. Look, and you will see him.

O Christ, thanks to you, we have known God, and we have seen God. Grant that the God whom we have known and seen in you will now be revealed through us.

Season After Pentecost

Receive now the Holy Spirit. You are sent out by the Son, as the Son was sent by God. Do not travel alone, but go two by two and three by three. And do not go with empty hands, but carry the peace of God wherever the Spirit leads.

Go forth to greet the world at work, as here the Lord has greeted us in worship. Go forth in the name of God the Creator, whose strength empowers us; in the name of Christ the Redeemer, whose love transforms us; and in the name of the Holy Spirit, whose presence guides us.

Martin Luther King, Jr., Day

God of the prophets, through whom you comfort the troubled and trouble the comfortable, let us feel the troubling presence of your prophets in our midst. Give us the vision to recognize them, the courage to hear them and the will to heed them, through Jesus Christ our Lord.

National Observance

The God who made this world and everything in it, who gives to all people their life and breath, sends you into a world caressed by divine love. Remember that this God is not far from each of us; in this God all persons live and move and have their being. May we be so humbled by God's love of us that we shall love one another.

TEXT GUIDE

THE REVISED COMMON LECTIONARY (1996), CYCLE A*

Sunday	First Lesson	Second Lesson	Gospel Lesson	Psalm
1/7/96	Isa. 42:1-9	Acts 10:34-43	Matt. 3:13-17	Ps. 29
1/14/96	Isa. 49:1-7	1 Cor. 1:1-9	John 1:29-42	Ps. 40:1-11
1/21/96	Isa. 9:1-4	1 Cor. 1:10-18	Matt. 4:12-23	Ps. 27:1, 4-9
1/28/96	Mic. 6:1-8	1 Cor. 1:18-31	Matt. 5:1-12	Ps. 15
2/4/96	Isa. 58:1-9a, (9b-12)	1 Cor. 2:1-12, (13-16)	Matt. 5:13-20	Ps. 112:1-9, (10)
2/11/96	Deut. 30:15-20	1 Cor. 3:1-9	Matt. 5:21-37	Ps. 119:1-8
2/18/96	Exod. 24:12-18	2 Pet. 1:16-21	Matt. 17:1-9	Ps. 99
2/25/96	Gen. 2:15-17; 3:1-7	Rom. 5:12-19	Matt. 4:1-11	Ps. 32
3/3/96	Gen. 12:1-4a	Rom. 4:1-5, 13-17	John 3:1-17	Ps. 121
3/10/96	Exod. 17:1-7	Rom. 5:1-11	John 4:5-42	Ps. 95
3/17/96	1 Sam. 16:1-13	Eph. 5:8-14	John 9:1-41	Ps. 23
3/24/96	Ezek. 37:1-14	Rom. 8:6-11	John 11:1-45	Ps. 130
3/31/96	Isa. 50:4-9a	Phil. 2:5-11	Matt. 26:14–27:66	Ps. 118:1-2, 19-29
4/7/96	Jer. 31:1-6	Col. 3:1-4	John 20:1-18	Ps. 118:1-2, 14-24
4/14/96	Acts 2:14a, 22-32	1 Pet. 1:3-9	John 20:19-31	Ps. 16

*This guide represents one possible selection of lessons and psalms from the lectionary. For a complete listing see *The Revised Common Lectionary.*

Sunday	First Lesson	Second Lesson	Gospel Lesson	Psalm
4/21/96	Acts 2:14a, 36-41	1 Pet. 1:17-23	Luke 24:13-35	Ps. 116:1-4, 12-19
4/28/96	Acts 2:42-47	1 Pet. 2:19-25	John 10:1-10	Ps. 23
5/5/96	Acts 7:55-60	1 Pet. 2:2-10	John 14:1-14	Ps. 31:1-5, 15-16
5/12/96	Acts 17:22-31	1 Pet. 3:13-22	John 14:15-21	Ps. 66:8-20
5/19/96	Acts 1:6-14	1 Pet. 4:12-14; 5:6-11	John 17:1-11	Ps. 68:1-10, 32-35
5/26/96	Num. 11:24-30	Acts 2:1-21	John 20:19-23	Ps. 104:24-34, 35b
6/2/96	Gen. 1:1–2:4a	2 Cor. 13:11-13	Matt. 28:16-20	Ps. 8
6/9/96	Gen. 12:1-9	Rom. 4:13-25	Matt. 9:9-13, 18-26	Ps. 33:1-12
6/16/96	Gen. 18:1-15; (21:1-7)	Rom. 5:1-8	Matt. 9:35–10:8, (9-23)	Ps. 116:1-2, 12-19
6/23/96	Gen. 21:8-21	Rom. 6:1b-11	Matt. 10:24-39	Ps. 86:1-10, 16-17
6/30/96	Gen. 22:1-14	Rom. 6:12-23	Matt. 10:40-42	Ps. 13:5-6
7/7/96	Gen. 24:34-38, 42-49, 58-67	Rom. 7:15-25a	Matt. 11:16-19, 25-30	Ps. 45:10-17
7/14/96	Gen. 25:19-34	Rom. 8:1-11	Matt. 13:1-9, 18-23	Ps. 119:105-112
7/21/96	Gen. 28:10-19a	Rom. 8:12-25	Matt. 13:24-30, 36-43	Ps. 139:1-12, 23-24
7/28/96	Gen. 29:15-28	Rom. 8:26-39	Matt. 13:31-33, 44-52	Ps. 105:1-11, 45b
8/4/96	Gen. 32:22-31	Rom. 9:1-5	Matt. 14:13-21	Ps. 17:1-7, 15
8/11/96	Gen. 37:1-4, 12-28	Rom. 10:5-15	Matt. 14:22-33	Ps. 105:1-6, 16-22, 45b
8/18/96	Gen. 45:1-15	Rom. 11:1-2a, 29-32	Matt. 15:(10-20), 21-28	Ps. 133
8/25/96	Exod. 1:8–2:10	Rom. 12:1-8	Matt. 16:13-20	Ps. 124
9/1/96	Exod. 3:1-15	Rom. 12:9-21	Matt. 16:21-28	Ps. 105:106, 23-26, 45c
9/8/96	Exod. 12:1-14	Rom. 13:8-14	Matt. 18:15-20	Ps. 149

9/15/96	Exod. 14:19-31	Rom. 14:1-12	Matt. 18:21-35	Ps. 114
9/22/96	Exod. 16:2-15	Phil. 1:21-30	Matt. 20:1-16	Ps. 105:1-6, 37-45
9/29/96	Exod. 17:1-7	Phil. 2:1-13	Matt. 21:23-32	Ps. 78:1-4, 12-16
10/6/96	Exod. 20:1-4, 7-9, 12-20	Phil. 3:4b-14	Matt. 21:33-46	Ps. 19
10/13/96	Exod. 32:1-14	Phil. 4:1-9	Matt. 22:1-14	Ps. 106:1-6, 19-23
10/20/96	Exod. 33:12-23	1 Thess. 1:1-10	Matt. 22:15-22	Ps. 99
10/27/96	Deut. 34:1-12	1 Thess. 2:1-8	Matt. 22:34-46	Ps. 90:1-6, 13-17
11/3/96	Josh. 3:7-17	1 Thess. 2:9-13	Matt. 23:1-12	Ps. 107:1-7, 33-37
11/10/96	Josh. 24:1-3a, 14-25	1 Thess. 4:13-18	Matt. 25:1-13	Ps. 78:1-7
11/17/96	Judg. 4:1-7	1 Thess. 5:1-11	Matt. 25:14-30	Ps. 123
11/24/96	Ezek. 34:11-16, 20-24	Eph. 1:15-23	Matt. 25:31-46	Ps. 100
12/1/96	Isa. 64:1-9	1 Cor. 1:3-9	Mark 13:24-37	Ps. 80:1-7, 17-19
12/8/96	Isa. 40:1-11	2 Pet. 3:8-15a	Mark 1:1-8	Ps. 85:1-2, 8-13
12/15/96	Isa. 61:1-4, 8-11	1 Thess. 5:16-24	John 1:6-8, 19-28	Luke 1:47-55
12/22/96	2 Sam. 7:1-11, 16	Rom. 16:25-27	Luke 1:26-38	Ps. 89:1-4, 19-26
12/29/96	Isa. 61:10–62:3	Gal. 4:4-7	Luke 2:22-40	Ps. 148

CONTRIBUTORS

❧

Don M. Aycock
Editor, Special Projects
SBC Brotherhood Commission
1548 Poplar Avenue
Memphis, TN 38104

Greg Barr
Baptist Minister
811 Springdale
Louisville, KY 40280

Barbara Bate
Board of Discipleship
United Methodist Church
P.O. Box 840
Nashville, TN 37202

Barry Beames
Pastor
First Baptist Church
523 N. Polk Street
Jefferson, TX 75657

Rick Brand
Pastor
First Presbyterian Church
P.O. Box 726
Henderson, NC 27536

Linda Bridges
Professor of New Testament
Baptist Theological
　　Seminary at Richmond
P.O. Box 9157
Richmond, VA 23227

Michael Brown
Pastor
Central United Methodist
　　Church
27 Church Street
Asheville, NC 28801

Douglas Bunch
Pastor
Trinity Southern Baptist
　　Church
309 East Shelby Street
Falmouth, KY 41040

Joseph Byrd
Pastor
Stewart Road Church of God
14539 Lincoln Road
Monroe, MI 48161

Gary L. Carver
Pastor
First Baptist Church
401 Gateway Avenue
Chattanooga, TN 37402

Earl C. Davis
Trinity Baptist Church
7680 Walnut Knoll Lane,
　　Suite 3
Cordova, TN

Penelope Duckworth
Chaplain
Stanford Canterbury
Foundation
1719 Fabian Drive
San Jose, CA 95124

Michael Duduit
Editor, *Preaching* Magazine
P.O. Box 7728
Louisville, KY 40257-0728

Heather Murray Elkins
The Divinity School
Drew University
Madison, NJ 07940

Paul R. Escamilla
Pastor
First United Methodist
Church
203 Terry Lane
Heath, TX 75087

Al Fasol
Professor of Preaching
Southwestern Baptist
Seminary
P.O. Box 22216
Fort Worth, TX 76112

Steven R. Fleming
Pastor
First United Presbyterian
Church
65 Washington Road
Westminster, MD 21157

Travis Franklin
Pastor
First United Methodist
Church
200 Church Street
Azle, TX 76020

Mike Graves
Assistant Professor of
Preaching
Midwestern Baptist
Seminary
5001 North Oak Street
Trafficway
Kansas City, MO 64118

Bill Groover
Pastor
Bethany Baptist Church
2319 Taylorsville Road
Louisville, KY 40205

Brian L. Harbour
Pastor
First Baptist Church
P.O. Box 832427
Richardson, TX 75083

H. Blake Harwell
Pastor
First Baptist Church
P.O. Box 226
Adel, GA 31620

C. Thomas Hilton
Presbyterian Minister
9404 Constitution Drive
Cincinnati, OH 45215

Derl G. Keefer
Pastor
Three Rivers Church
of the Nazarene
15770 Coon Hollow
Road
Three Rivers, MI 49093

James L. Killen, Jr.
Pastor
Williams Memorial United
    Methodist Church
4000 Moores Lane
Texarkana, TX 75503

Eric Killinger
Presbyterian Minister
1239 Lake Forest Circle
Birmingham, AL 35244

John Killinger
Distinguished Professor of
    Religion and Culture
Samford University
800 Lakeshore Drive
Birmingham, AL 35229

Gary G. Kindley
Pastor
St. John's United Methodist
    Church
311 E. University Avenue
Georgetown, TX 78626

Robert R. Kopp
Pastor
Logans Ferry Presbyterian
    Church
730 Church Street
New Kensington, PA 15068

Alton H. McEachern
Pastor
Cornerstone United
    Methodist Church
50 Rockland Way
Sharpsburg, GA 30277

J. Lawrence McCleskey
Pastor
Myers Park United
    Methodist Church
2335 Richardson Drive
Charlotte, NC 28211

N. Allen Moseley
Pastor
First Baptist Church
414 Cleveland Street
Durham, NC 27701

David N. Mosser
Pastor
First United Methodist
    Church
410 E. University
Georgetown, TX 78626-6899

Jerry E. Oswalt
Academic Dean and
    Professor of Preaching
Florida Baptist Theological
    College
1306 College Drive
Graceville, FL 32440

Harold C. Perdue *(deceased)*
Development Officer
Texas Methodist Foundation
1203 St. Williams Avenue
Round Rock, TX 78681

Kathleen Peterson
Pastor
Palos United Methodist
    Church
P.O. Box 398
Palos Heights, IL 60463

Jon Roebuck
Pastor
First Baptist Church
P.O. Box 347
Gatlinburg, TN 37738

Scott Salsman
Baptist Minister
525 Primrose, #1
Louisville, KY 40206

Robert Smith
Assistant Professor of
Preaching
Southern Baptist Seminary
2825 Lexington Road
Louisville, KY 40280

Thomas R. Steagald
Pastor
First United Methodist
Church
511 Robert Street
Marion, NC 28752

Billy D. Strayhorn
Pastor
First United Methodist
Church
P.O. Box 150
Groesbeck, TX 76642

Craig M. Watts
Pastor
First Christian Church
7700 US 42
Louisville, KY 40241

Bill D. Whittaker
President
Clear Creek Bible College
300 Clear Creek Road
Pineville, KY 40977

INDEX

ào

OLD TESTAMENT

NEW TESTAMENT

Mark

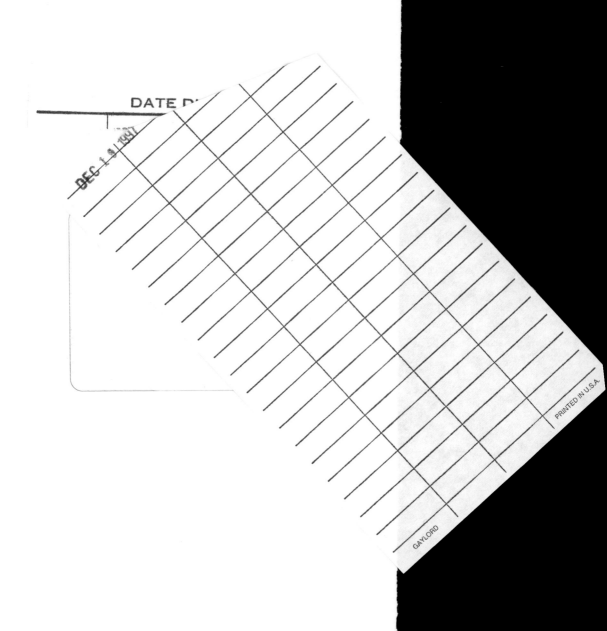